T0174152

Privacy, Due Process and the Computational Turn

Privacy, Due Process and the Computational Turn: The philosophy of law meets the philosophy of technology engages with the rapidly developing computational aspects of our world, including data mining, behavioural advertising, government, profiling for intelligence, customer relationship management, smart search engines, personalised news feeds and so on, in order to consider their implications for the assumptions on which our legal framework has been built. The contributions to this volume focus on the issue of privacy, which is often equated with data privacy and data security, location privacy, anonymity, pseudonymity, unobservability and unlinkability. Here, however, the extent to which predictive and other types of data analytics operate in ways that may or may not violate privacy is rigorously taken up, both technologically and legally, in order to open up new possibilities for considering, and contesting, how we are increasingly being correlated and categorised.

Mireille Hildebrandt holds the Chair of Smart Environments, Data Protection and the Rule of Law at the Institute for Computer and Information Sciences (ICIS) at Radboud University Nijmegen, and is Associate Professor of Jurisprudence at the Erasmus School of Law, Erasmus University Rotterdam. She is a senior researcher at the Centre for Law, Science, Technology and Society (LSTS), Vrije Universiteit Brussel.

Katja de Vries is based in the interdisciplinary Center for Law, Science, Technology and Society (LSTS) at the Vrije Universiteit Brussel (VUB).

Privacy, Due Process and the Computational Turn

The philosophy of law meets the philosophy of technology

Edited by
Mireille Hildebrandt and
Katja de Vries

Routledge
Taylor & Francis Group

a GlassHouse Book

First published 2013
by Routledge
2 Park Square, Milton Park, Abingdon, Oxon OX14 4RN

Simultaneously published in the USA and Canada
by Routledge
711 Third Avenue, New York, NY 10017

A Glasshouse Book

Routledge is an imprint of the Taylor & Francis Group, an informa business

© 2013 Mireille Hildebrandt and Katja de Vries

The right of Mireille Hildebrandt and Katja de Vries
as authors of this work, and the individual chapter contributors for their
chapters, has been asserted by them in accordance with sections 77 and
78 of the Copyright, Designs and Patents Act 1988.

British Library Cataloguing in Publication Data
A catalogue record for this book is available from the British Library

Library of Congress Cataloging in Publication Data
A catalog record for this book has been requested

ISBN 978-0-415-64481-5 (hbk)
ISBN 978-0-203-42764-4 (ebk)

Typeset in Garamond by
Cenveo Publisher Services

Contents

Acknowledgements

This volume developed from the Philosophers' Reading Panel on Privacy and Due Process after the Computational Turn, organised by the present editors, together with Solon Barocas from New York University. The Reading Panel – a real treat for those keen on trenchant but careful and responsive reflection – took place on 26 January 2011. It was the second of its kind: the first took place in January 2009 and resulted in the first volume in the series of the Philosophy of Law Meets the Philosophy of Technology, entitled *Law, Human Agency and Autonomic Computing*, also published by Routledge, in 2011. We especially thank Antoinette Rouvroy, who co-edited the first volume and contributed with a captivating chapter in the present volume. We would like to extend our gratitude and appreciation for all who participated in the Reading Panel, providing a first draft of their papers well in advance to enable a high level of discussion, and for working with us on the chapters of this volume: Finn Brunton, Elena Esposito, Ian Kerr, Lorenzo Magnani, Helen Nissenbaum, Martijn van Otterlo and Antoinette Rouvroy. We are indebted to Bert-Jaap Koops, whose cutting-edge questions during the discussion prompted our invitation to contribute to the volume, though he is neither a philosopher nor a data scientist.

We would like to credit Solon Barocas for his enthusiastic initiatives and interventions in the process of organising the Reading Panel. He proposed to invite a data scientist to keep us, the philosophers of law and technology, down to earth – or, in this case – close to the intricate operations of machine learning. His acuity in understanding the inner workings and unprecedented implications of profiling technologies has been of enormous value for this project. His contributions have been awesome, to use one of his own favourite phrases.

The Philosophers' Reading Panel formed a part of the larger annual international Conference on Computing, Privacy and Data Protection 2011 (CPDP11) in Brussels. We thank the organisers of the larger Conference, LSTS, CRID, TILT, INRA and Fraunhofer Institute,[1] and express our special thanks to Paul de Hert, Serge Gutwirth, Rocco Bellanova and Rosamunde van Brakel of LSTS for enabling the synergy of a reading panel that practises 'slow thinking', with the main programme of the larger Conference, which entails a hectic succession of highly informative presentations on the intersection of law and computer science with regard to privacy and data protection. Grietje Gorus and Katrijn de Marez provided professional logistical support for all participants.

The Reading Panel was also part and parcel of the five-year research project on 'Law and Autonomic Computing: Mutual Transformations' that was funded by the Vrije Universiteit Brussel, of which Mireille Hildebrandt was co-author and co-ordinator, together with Serge Gutwirth (director of LSTS), Paul de Hert (initiator of the CPDP Conferences) and Laurent de Sutter (researcher at LSTS).

We admire the professional patience and stamina of Routledge's editorial assistant, Melanie Fortmann-Brown, who helped us through the editing process from its very beginning and, last but not least, we are once again immensely grateful to Colin Perrin for his trust, enthusiasm and support in getting this second volume published by Routledge.

Note

1 The Center for Law, Science, Technology and Society (LSTS), Vrije Universiteit Brussels. Centre de Recherche d'Informatique et Droit (CRID), Université de Namur. The Tilburg Institute for Law, Technology and Society (TILT), University of Tilburg. Institut national de recherche en informatique et en automatique (INRIA), Paris. Fraunhofer Gesellschaft.

Notes on Contributors

Finn Brunton is an Assistant Professor of Information at the School of Information at the University of Michigan. He was trained in the history of science, receiving a PhD from the Centre for Modern Thought at the University of Aberdeen. Subsequently he worked extensively on issues of privacy and security online as a postdoctoral researcher with Helen Nissenbaum at NYU. He now focuses on technological adaptation and misuse, writing on topics including digital anonymity and currency, the history of experimental and obsolete media, and Wikileaks; his first book, Spam: A Shadow History of the Internet (MIT Press) will be out in March 2013.

Katja de Vries is a PhD student at the Centre for Law, Science, Technology, and Society (Vrije Universiteit Brussel). Her PhD research is focused on the collisions and interactions between legal and technological modes of thinking. More in particular she studies probablistic understandings of rationality and equality, and the differences and continuities between their functioning within advanced data technologies and within the legal semantics of privacy, data protection and antidiscrimination law. De vries publishes on a wide range of topics such as technology-mediated identity construction; Foucault's technologies of the self; Ambient Intelligence; the continuity between cybernetics and current algorithmic personalization technologies; the case law, practices and political debates with regard to online searches and data retention; the role of proportionality in privacy law; enlightened ways of relating to digital spaces like Second Life; legal semiotics and Latour's empirical-philosophical way of studying the mode of enunciation of law. She is a member of the European "Living in Surveillance Societies"-network. De Varies studied at Sciences Po in Paris, obtained three masters degrees with distinction at Leiden University (Civil Law, Cognitive Psychology and Philosophy) and graduated at Oxford University (Magister Juris).

Elena Esposito teaches Sociology of Communication at the University of Modena-Reggio Emilia in the Facoltà di Scienze della Comunicazione e dell'Economia. She graduated in Philosophy in Italy with Umberto Eco and obtained her PhD in Sociology in Germany with Niklas Luhmann. She has published many works on the theory of social systems, media theory and sociology of financial markets, including: *The Future of Futures. The Time of Money in Financing and Society* (Elgar, 2011); *Die Fiktion der wahrscheinlichen Realität* (Suhrkamp, 2007); *Die Verbindlichkeit des Vorübergehenden. Paradoxien der Mode* (Suhrkamp, 2004); and *Soziales Vergessen. Formen und Medien des Gedächtnisses der Gesellschaft* (Suhrkamp, 2002).

Mireille Hildebrandt holds the Chair of Smart Environments, Data Protection and the Rule of Law at the Institute of Computing and Information Sciences, Radboud University Nijmegen. She is Associate Professor of Jurisprudence at the Erasmus School of Law, Rotterdam and senior researcher at the centre for Law, Science, Technology and Society studies at Vrije Universiteit Brussels. She is editor in chief of the *Netherlands Journal of Legal Philosophy* and co-editor of several books, notably with Serge Gutwirth, *Profiling the European Citizen* (Springer, 2008) and with Antoinette Rouvroy, *Law, Human Agency and Autonomic Computing* (Routledge, 2011). She publishes widely on the nexus of law, philosophy and smart environments. Her Berkeley Press website is available at http://works.bepress.com/mireille_hildebrandt/.

Ian Kerr holds the Canada Research Chair in Ethics, Law & Technology at the University of Ottawa, Faculty of Law, with cross-appointments in Medicine, Philosophy and Information Studies. Dr Kerr's research lies at the intersection of ethics, law and technology and is currently focused on two broad themes: (i) privacy and surveillance; and (ii) the 'human–machine merger'. Building on his Oxford University Press book, *Lessons from the Identity Trail*, his ongoing privacy work focuses on the interplay between emerging public and private sector surveillance technologies, civil liberties and human rights. Dr Kerr's recent research on the human–machine merger examines some of the potential legal and ethical implications of emerging technologies – such as roboticised implantable devices – in the health sector and beyond.

Bert-Jaap Koops is Professor of Regulation & Technology at the Tilburg Institute for Law, Technology, and Society (TILT), the Netherlands. His main research interests are law & technology, in particular criminal-law issues such as cybercrime, investigation powers and privacy, and DNA forensics. He is also interested in other topics of technology regulation, such as data protection, identity, digital constitutional rights, 'code as law', human enhancement, and regulation of bio- and nanotechnologies. From 2004–2009, he co-ordinated a VIDI research program on law, technology, and shifting power relations. He co-edited six books in English on ICT regulation, including Emerging Electronic Highways (1996), Starting Points for ICT Regulation (2006), Constitutional Rights and New Technologies (2008), and Dimensions of Technology Regulation (2010).

Lorenzo Magnani, philosopher and cognitive scientist, is a professor at the University of Pavia, Italy, and the director of its Computational Philosophy Laboratory. He is visiting professor at the Sun Yat-sen University, Canton (Guangzhou), China. He has taught at the Georgia Institute of Technology and at The City University of New York and currently directs international research programmes in the EU, USA and China. His book *Abduction, Reason, and Science* (New York, 2001) has become a well-respected work in the field of human cognition. His book *Morality in a Technological World* (Cambridge, 2007) develops a philosophical and cognitive theory of the relationships between ethics and technology in a naturalistic perspective. The book *Abductive Cognition. The Epistemological and Eco-Cognitive Dimensions of Hypothetical reasoning* has been published by Springer, Berlin/Heidelberg/New York (2009). His latest book, *Understanding Violence. The Intertwining of Morality, Religion, and Violence: A Philosophical Stance*, has also been published by Springer in 2011. In 1998 he started the series of International Conferences on Model-Based Reasoning (MBR). Since 2011 he has been the editor of the book series *Studies in Applied Philosophy, Epistemology and Rational Ethics* (SAPERE) (Springer, Heidelberg/Berlin).

Helen Nissenbaum is Professor of Media, Culture and Communication, and Computer Science, at New York University, where she is also director of the Information Law Institute. Her areas of expertise span social, ethical and political implications of information technology and digital media. Nissenbaum's research publications have appeared in journals of philosophy, politics, law, media studies, information studies and computer science. She has written and edited four books, including *Privacy in Context: Technology, Policy, and the Integrity of Social Life*, which was published in 2010 by Stanford University Press. The National Science Foundation, Intel, Air Force Office of Scientific Research, U.S. Department of Homeland Security, and the U.S. Department of Health and Human Services Office of the National Coordinator have supported her work on privacy, trust online and security, as well as several studies of values embodied in computer system design, including search engines, digital games, facial recognition technology and health information systems. Nissenbaum holds a PhD in philosophy from Stanford University and a BA (Hons) from the University of the Witwatersrand. Before joining the faculty at NYU, she served as Associate Director of the Center for Human Values at Princeton University.

Antoinette Rouvroy is FNRS (National Fund for Scientific Research) research associate and researcher at the Research Centre in Information, Law and Society (CRIDS) of the University of Namur, Belgium. She is particularly interested in the mechanisms of mutual production between sciences and technologies and cultural, political, economic and legal frameworks. In *Human Genes and Neoliberal Governance: A Foucauldian Critique* (Abingdon/New York, Routledge-Cavendish, 2008), she looked at the knowledge power relations in the post-genomic era. Her current interdisciplinary research interests revolve around the ethical, legal and political challenges raised by the new information, communication and surveillance technologies (biometrics, RFIDs, ubiquitous computing, ambient intelligence, persuasive technologies etc) and their convergence. She focuses her research on the types of normativity carried and reinforced by the new usages of statistics (data mining, profiling in the big data era), the impacts of these new usages on knowledge, power and subjects, and the modes of critique, resistance and recalcitrance in such data-rich environments.

Martijn van Otterlo obtained his PhD from the University of Twente (Netherlands, 2008), with a dissertation on expressive knowledge representation frameworks (such as first-order logic) in the field of reinforcement learning, that is, learning (sequential) decision-making under uncertainty from evaluative feedback. During his PhD period he spent nine months in Freiburg (Germany) as a Marie Curie Fellow. He then moved to the Katholieke Universiteit Leuven (Belgium) and started working on various machine learning topics. In 2009 he published a book about relational reinforcement learning with IOS Press and, in 2012, together with Marco Wiering from the University of Groningen, he published a book on reinforcement learning, with Springer. In September 2011 he started at the Radboud University Nijmegen (Netherlands), where he teaches courses in cognitive artificial intelligence, human–robot interaction and reinforcement learning. His current research interests are learning and reasoning in visual perception, reinforcement learning in cognitive systems and the implications of adaptive algorithms on privacy and society. He has served as committee member and reviewer for dozens of international journals and conferences on machine learning and artificial intelligence.

Preface

How do we co-exist with the 'perceptions' of machines that anticipate, profile, cluster or classify? Such machines 'learn' on the basis of feedback. Teachers know that the process of learning is accompanied by an uncertainty and an opacity as to what, precisely, the student has learned. This uncertainty and opacity are also present when machines are trained on labelled or unlabelled examples. The models or patterns learnt by the machine can appear as enigmatic as the riddles told by the Great Sphinx of Giza to Oedipus.

It seems that the accuracy claimed for data mining technologies does not stem from a pre-existing correspondence to a given reality, but thrives on the productive nature of knowledge. This reminds one of the famous Thomas Theorem: 'If men define a situation as real, it is real in its consequences.' In this volume, we encounter the follow-up for the era of profiling and data analytics: 'If profiling machines define a situation as real, it is real in its consequences.' Although the inferred correlations do not stand for causes or reasons, they do produce meaning when marketing, management, financial institutions, the police, medical researchers, policy-makers and credit rating companies apply them.

In his thought-provoking article in *Wired Magazine* of 2008, Chris Anderson claims 'the end of theory', arguing that 'the data deluge makes the scientific method obsolete'. In a 2008 report, the Informal High Level Advisory Group on the Future of European Home Affairs Policy (also known as 'The Future Group') speaks of a 'digital *tsunami*' that provides a fantastic resource for data mining. Data deluges and digital *tsunamis* are interesting metaphors for the turbulent masses of machine-readable data that are flooding our systems of knowledge production. It is clear that, in order to make sense of all these data, we need computing techniques capable of differentiating noise from information, detecting the difference that makes a difference. The science of mining knowledge from big data has been coined data science, to which *The Economist* devoted a special issue in February 2011, highlighting the broad scope of computational techniques for data analytics and the unprecedented impact this has on the state of knowledge in the information society. Risk assessment, credit-scoring, marketing, anti-money laundering data mining techniques, criminal profiling, customer relationship management, predictive medicine, e-learning and financial markets all thrive on data mining techniques that enable a novel abductive type of knowledge construction based on a type of computation not within the reach of the human mind. In a diversity of scientific and professional fields, a computational turn is unfolding that challenges 'traditional' scientific methodologies and long standing professional practices. Anderson's point is twofold: first, the knowledge that is generated establishes correlations between different types of data without any claim as to the causal meaning of these correlations; second, this knowledge is not discovered by testing a hypothesis against empirical data, but basically entails the production of hypotheses inferred from a population of machine-readable data. In so far as this knowledge is predictive, its value is not truth in the traditional sense of causal explanation or theoretical understanding, but rather its performance as an accurate prediction machine.

This edited volume first of all aims to confront philosophers of law with the implications of emerging technologies, such as smart environments, that thrive on knowledge discovery in databases. Second, it aims to inquire into the implications of the relevant knowledge claims from the perspective of philosophy of technology (including information ethics), rather than taking the more abstract perspective of philosophy of science. However, as the editors of this volume, we hoped the contributions would reach out *beyond* the fields of philosophies of law and technology towards both the developers of the discussed computational techniques and the policy-makers who are faced with their regulation. To realise this aim the volume also offers an accessible yet state-of-the-art introduction about the technological constitution of profiling. We encouraged the authors to go beyond abstract and general philosophical observations, and to write their contributions in direct engagement with the matters of concern for practitioners. This approach has generated a wide range of perspectives which are refreshingly novel. They may not solve the riddle of the Sphinx, but they should provide the *clair-obscur* that puts the computational turn in the limelight, providing a first attempt to assess its implications for some of the core fundamental rights of constitutional democracy.

Mireille Hildebrandt
Katja de Vries

Privacy, due process and the computational turn at a glance

Pointers for the hurried reader

Katja de Vries and Mireille Hildebrandt

> '*Dear Average Reader, I am a member of the Information Temperance League. My local branch has been examining your use of information. Are you aware that, during your lifetime to date, you have consumed enough information to fill this hall up to here?*' The middle-aged woman dressed in country tweeds, who is addressing the average reader, stretches her arm dramatically to shoulder height. '*We want to know what you intend to do about it.*' The average reader has carefully watched the woman's arm move upwards, and now slowly gazes up even further – towards the ceiling. '*So little time, so much to read,*' says the average reader.
>
> A variation (by de Vries and Hildebrandt) on the famous anecdote about Churchill's alcohol usage[1]

In the age of big data (boyd and Crawford 2012; Bollier 2010) and information overload (Bozdag and Timmermans 2011) the average reader has 'so little time, so much to read'. To deal with this information overload, the average reader increasingly relies on the algorithmic filtering of information. However, the benefits of neat algorithmic pre-selection will often come at a cost: not only a loss of nuance but also the creation of 'echo chambers' or 'filter bubbles', filtering out any information that does not align with our preconceived or inferred preferences, interests and ideas (Pariser 2011; Sunstein 2007). While the existence of such echo chambers is not undisputed (Bakshy 2012; Manjoo 2012), it is clear that when information is sorted out or summarised this requires rather a large amount of epistemic trust to whoever or whatever is in charge of the selection. In a recent interview (Funnell 2012), Ted Striphas points out how our current 'algorithmic culture' is characterised by:

> ... a tremendous amount of deference being afforded to engineers, mathematicians, computer scientists. [...] [I]ncreasingly [...] their work is having a significant hand in defining our realities. When we go to search for something on Google, that tells us what we need to know, it gives us our bearings in the world [...]. And you know that's a tremendous responsibility to fall on the shoulders of any one group, and to reduce that to a

mathematical formula, however complex, [...] doesn't really do justice to the full richness of culture, ultimately.

As editors of this book it pains us to reduce the nuances of its contributions. And yet we must admit that we know the predicament of the 'average hurried reader' all too well. This Introduction provides a quick overview of the contents of this volume. In contrast to Chapter 1, which provides an in-depth analysis of the issues at stake in this volume, this chapter does not engage in analysis or critique. It is intended as a helping hand for the hurried reader and a springboard from where to plunge into the depths of the various contributions. If the reader finds that the profile of the 'average hurried reader' does not apply and prefers to make up her own mind about the 'core message' of the various chapters, this chapter can be safely skipped. As a final disclaimer: while we did not have the luxury of sharing the responsibility of summarising the contents of this volume with a helpful algorithm (how nice it would have been to 'hide' behind a semblance of 'algorithmic objectivity'!)[2], we did benefit from the input provided by the contributors in the course of writing, composing and editing this volume.

Privacy, Due Process and the Computational Turn: The philosophy of law meets the philosophy of technology engages with the rapidly developing computational aspects of our world – including data mining, behavioural advertising, iGovernment, profiling for intelligence, customer relationship management, smart search engines, personalised news feeds and so on – in order to consider their implications for privacy and due process. The contributions to this volume do not so much explore privacy and due process from the perspective of detailed research into positive law, but rather understand them as public goods that inform the legal, moral and political framework of constitutional democracy.

The book is organised by a tripartite structure. The first part (Chapter 2) is entitled *Data Science* (Davenport and Patil 2012) and introduces the machine learning techniques on which the computational turn thrives. The second part (Chapters 3–6) is called *Anticipating Machines* and takes a more philosophical stance towards these techniques. The final part (Chapters 7–9), *Resistance and Solutions*, is mainly focused on proposing possible answers to the challenges posed by the computational turn. While the boundaries between these three parts are not always very strict, they are an indirect reflection of the original aim behind the workshop (The Philosophers' Reading Panel at the Computers, Privacy & Data Protection Conference, Brussels 2011) which formed the basis for this book. The volume aims to offer (1) an accessible yet state-of-the-art introduction to the techniques fuelling the computational turn and tackle some of the challenges posed by this turn, (2) reflections from the perspective of philosophy of technology and information ethics, and (3) reflections from the perspective of legal philosophy. Yet, probably none of the authors would feel exhaustively characterised by a simple label like 'data scientist', 'philosopher of technology', 'philosopher of law' or 'information ethicist'. The computational turn is complex and multifaceted, eluding a simple characterisation, and so are the chapters engaging with it. The three parts of this volume together reflect the original triple aim, although the boundaries between them should be taken with a pinch of salt. After all, *all* the contributions reach out beyond the fields of 'pure' philosophy of law, philosophy of technology or information ethics, and engage with the concerns of those who develop or regulate the computational technologies under discussion, or those who suffer the consequences. This approach has generated a wide range of perspectives, some of which are refreshingly novel.

Chapter 1 by de Vries introduces the various concepts, phenomena and solutions at stake in the volume. First, she presents an overview of the various usages of the notions 'computational turn', 'privacy' and 'due process'. Second, she provides a personal reading of the various contributions gathered in this volume by looking at how they address issues related to the ecology (how to coexist with the perceptions of machines?) and pragmatism (can the formula 'whatever works best', when preferring one algorithm over another, be complicated by asking 'for *whom*?' and 'on which task'?) of the computational turn. The chapter opens with a parable about three robotic dogs, thus presenting the issues of ecology and pragmatism in a playful manner. At the end of the chapter, the parable is revisited. Armed with recommendations and ideas derived from the chapters collected in this volume it offers four practical lessons for the era of the computational turn: (1) when a machine has to make sense of the world based on *general instructions regarding how to recognise similarity and patterns*, rather than *explicit, top-down definitions describing a particular class*, the perception of the machine gains a degree of autonomy; (2) machines can be instructed in *many* ways to 'learn' or generalise, and there is no silver bullet that works in all situations; (3) it is difficult to tell which machine categorisation is correct and which is incorrect; (4) whether a solution is good or not is not a matter of objective fact, but implies political choices.

In Chapter 2, van Otterlo presents a machine learning view on profiling. He provides an accessible yet fine grained introduction to the data techniques discussed in this volume. Profiling in general is inferring patterns of behaviour from large amounts of data on the users of electronic systems. Profiling is, when viewed computationally, essentially a form of machine learning; a particular branch of artificial intelligence in which automated algorithms are used to 'learn' from data. Machine learning – and data mining – consists of representations, tools and methodological systems that together can be used to sift through data, databases, web pages, texts and customer records to find correlations, interesting patterns and rules. These can then be used to predict characteristics of people that they have not explicitly disclosed about themselves. Van Otterlo positions the concept of profiling in the active machine learning area of activity recognition. One particular focus is the use of probabilistic graphical models for the representation and learning of full probability distributions of the data, thus enabling (probabilistic) predictions about particular properties of particular individuals. In addition, van Otterlo explains important deductive, inductive and abductive patterns of reasoning and highlights some recent directions of research concerning caveats of statistical models, transparency, feedback and adaptive behaviour.

In Chapter 3, Magnani argues, building on his 2007 book *Morality in a Technological World*, that knowledge has to become a duty in our current technological world. It is evident that the new ethical importance acquired by many 'external things' (both natural and artificial) has been mainly caused by modern technological achievements. According to Magnani, this has two consequences: first, we need appropriately to project values to *people* that we tend to attribute to *things*; second, he delineates a new role of knowledge (both scientific and ethical). Magnani suggests that in our technological world a more massive and skilful exploitation of knowledge is needed. Within the scope of the intellectual framework sketched above, he proposes that enhancing free will, freedom, responsibility and ownership of our destinies is one of the main targets for improving human dignity in our technological era, and that to achieve this the respect of knowledge is essential. However, knowledge as a duty also has various limitations. He warns against the problem of identity and cyberprivacy, and contends that when too much knowledge about people is incorporated in external artificial things, human beings' 'visibility' can become excessive and dangerous. People have to be protected from being seen but also from 'feeling' visible to avoid, for example, ostracism and stigmatisation, to be protected from insult, to avoid becoming more conformist and conventional, and to avoid the possibility of being oppressed. The chapter concludes by examining how privacy also entails the protection against interference with the self-realisation of the individual.

In Chapter 4, Kerr examines two related issues: first, he looks at the path of law after the computational turn; second, he argues that current data scientists might find inspiration in the predictive stance or 'bad man' theory of law. Famously proposed in *The Path of Law* (1897), Holmes's legal pragmatism conceptualises law as a field of prediction which tells the 'bad man' how to avoid legal damages and stay out of jail. Kerr juxtaposes the predictive stance in law with probabilistic and predictive techniques currently under research and development in international and domestic law enforcement. He argues that today's predictive technologies threaten due process by enabling a dangerous new philosophy of pre-emption, which could cause a fundamental jurisprudential shift from our current *ex post facto* systems of penalties and punishments to *ex ante* preventative measures. Unlike Holmes's predictive approach, which was meant to shed light on the nature of law by shifting law's standpoint to the perspective of everyday citizens who are subject to the law, pre-emptive approaches enabled by the computational turn would obfuscate citizens' legal standpoint. This brings Kerr to his second argument, namely that Holmes's 'bad man' theory can also be a useful heuristic device outside the law to understand and evaluate predictive technologies at large. Kerr then explains how 'the prophecy of what the courts will do in fact' is directly related to the right to due process in its broad sense, which he defines as citizens' 'ability to observe, understand, participate in and respond to important decisions or actions that implicate them'.

In Chapter 5, Esposito analyses web intelligence – that is intelligence produced by the network of the World Wide Web. Such *intelligence without consciousness* is interesting because it is different from our own and does not try to reproduce the structures and procedures of our own intelligence. The network functions without a central project or control: the very fast increase in data produces structures to manage and select these same data. These structures *produce* meanings, but they depend neither on the intention nor on the consciousness of anyone; they result a posteriori from the very functioning of the net. The result is a kind of 'explanation' that does not refer to causes but to correlations, works on the surface, proceeds from the past to the future and has a perfect memory. Esposito then introduces a challenging similarity with the procedures of a divinatory rationality. In pre-modern societies, the mystery of the oracle was the guarantee of the rationality of the procedure: it was convincing and reliable precisely because humans lack the ability to understand fully the logic of the world. Today again we are faced with something that human rationality cannot fully grasp: the functioning of the web. However, in our contemporary society, assumedly constituted by autonomous subjects, this may be scary rather than reassuring, and may threaten to spread a general unintelligibility and an increasing loss of control. Esposito suggests, however, that the structure of divinatory rationality provides a way of coping with the problems of privacy and those of the protection of an open future. By further increasing the availability of the data and the inferred predictions the relevance and validity of such predictions will become fragile and confirm that the present futures not only predict but also influence the future present.

In Chapter 6, Rouvroy inquires whether the state of knowledge, power and subjects after the computational still allow for critical thinking. She sketches how the epistemic universe emerging after the computational turn, despite its pretences to 'objectivity', is turning away from the ambitions of modern rationality anchored in empirical experiment and deductive, causal logic. She suggests how the epistemic universe is governed by a mode of government which no longer presupposes that its subjects are rational, moral, intentional agents and no longer relies on socially tested categorisations. How, despite its promises of individualisation and of better taking into consideration individual merits, needs, abilities and preferences through pervasive profiling, the emerging epistemic universe fails to address individuals' reflexive capabilities, nor their inscription within collective structures, but merely addresses their algorithmically produced 'profiles'. She then argues that what makes critique so difficult to practise vis-à-vis the computational turn is the vanishing of the transversal dimension of 'test', 'trial', 'examination', 'assessment' or 'épreuve', or even 'experience'. This dimension, Rouvroy contends, is essential in the scientific, the judicial and even the existential domains. Rouvroy's chapter presents a defence of all those things that usually appear as the weaknesses of the legal framework, compared with regulation by algorithms. Over and against the speed of automated regulation she applauds the ineffectiveness, inefficiency and the delays that are part of the legal sphere, since they create a temporal space and a (judicial) scene where meaning regains autonomy vis-à-vis the pure factuality of 'data behaviourism', thus leaving intact the 'potency' of the human subject.

In Chapter 7, Brunton and Nissenbaum start off with the observation that computer-enabled data collection, aggregation and mining has dramatically changed the nature of contemporary surveillance. What to do when opting-out is not feasible and when one cannot rely on law, technology or the scruples of the data gatherers? Brunton and Nissenbaum propose an alternative strategy of informational self-defence, a method that acts as informational resistance, disobedience, protest or even covert sabotage – a form of redress in the absence of any other protection and defence, and one which disproportionately aids the weak against the strong. They call this method *obfuscation* and argue for the political and ethical philosophy it expresses and embodies. Linking contemporary and historical cases, Brunton and Nissenbaum develop a descriptive account of obfuscation that is able to capture key commonalities in systems ranging from radar chaff to the circulating exchanges of supermarket loyalty cards and BitTorrent systems protecting their users from legal action. The tactical modes of obfuscation range from the production of misleading, false or ambiguous data with the intention of confusing an adversary to simply adding to the time or cost of separating bad data from good. In evaluating its ethical and political legitimacy, the authors distinguish among the different motivations and power arrangements of key actors and between obfuscation practices that constitute legitimate assertions of autonomy and justifiable refusal and those that become problematic instances of economic free ridership or the destructive contamination of collective data.

In Chapter 8, Koops argues that a focus on decision transparency is needed to enhance the protection of individuals after the computational turn, in which decisions are taken on the basis of large-scale, complex and multi-purpose processes of matching and mining enormous amounts of data. After briefly analysing the limitations of the Data Protection Directive and of the current plans for revision, it provides a theoretical and practical perspective on effecting decision transparency. The first, theoretical, part applies the conceptual framework of David Heald on transparency relations to explain data processing relationships. This implies a dual strategy: diminishing transparency of data subjects, through shielding and obfuscating data, and enhancing transparency of data controllers, through introducing mechanisms for outcome (and not only process) transparency, retrospective transparency in (near) real time for individual cases and, most importantly, effective (and not only nominal) transparency. This requires receptors who are capable of understanding transparency information and who are able to use it. The second part of the chapter discusses ways in which the theoretical approach could be effectuated in practice. It describes existing models of transparency in legal, social and technical regulatory measures and discusses how these models could enhance transparency of data controllers in illustrative cases of commerce, government service provisioning and law enforcement.

In Chapter 9, Hildebrandt argues that machine learning makes us transparent in a rather counterintuitive manner: we become entirely translucent in the sense that the profiling software looks straight through us to 'what we are like' instead of making transparent 'what or who we are'. There is a fascinating indifference with regard to individual persons in machine learning, profiling or the 'statistical governance of the real', that invites further inquiry. The chapter introduces the Deleuzian concepts of de-realisation and virtualisation to elucidate what it is that profilers construct when they create large 'populations' of anonymous profiles (here termed dividuals) that can be applied to large populations of individual human beings. To investigate whether the proliferation of dividuals enhances our freedom (virtualisation) or forces us to comply with our past behaviour patterns (de-realisation), Hildebrandt investigates the construction of data models and critiques the aura of objectivity that is often claimed for them. She then brings in the concept of double contingency, which highlights the double and mutual anticipation that is constitutive for self, mind and society. The concept refers to the fundamental uncertainty that rules human communication, creating the possibility for new meaning amidst inevitable but productive misunderstandings. To explain how machine learning techniques disrupt this constitutive uncertainty, Hildebrandt aligns with Stiegler's notion of tertiary retention and the need to reinvent what he terms 'introjection' in the digital age. This relates to the kind of profile transparency needed to renegotiate a novel double contingency. She argues for a transparency that is aware of the subtle but crucial play of light and shadow, taking the example of the Renaissance painter's technique of the *clair-obscur*.

Notes

1 On one occasion during an election campaign Churchill was speaking in a church hall in rural England. The hall was decorated in the well accepted colour scheme of that era – mission brown up to shoulder height, then cream up to and including the ceiling. When he finished his speech Churchill called for questions. The first came from a middle-aged woman dressed in country tweeds. "Mr Churchill, I am a member of the Temperance League," she said, "My local branch has been examining your use of alcohol. Are you aware Prime Minister that, during your lifetime to date you have consumed enough alcohol to fill this hall up to here" stretching her arm dramatically to indicate the mission brown zone on the wall. "We want to know what you intend to do about it." Churchill looked at the woman, followed her arm to the top of the mission brown zone, and then slowly allowed his gaze to

move up through the cream zone to the ceiling. "So little time, so much to do" he said. For the original anecdote see http://en.wikiquote.org/wiki/Talk:Winston_Churchill (accessed 30 October 2012).

2 A nice example of a claim to algorithmic 'objectivity' and 'neutrality' is the way Google describes the functioning of its autocomplete algorithm: 'Predicted queries are algorithmically determined based on a number of purely algorithmic factors (including popularity of search terms) without human intervention' (http://support.google.com/websearch/). This claim to algorithmic objectivity and neutrality has been contested in a series of legal cases regarding pejorative or racist suggestions (eg Foucart 2011).

References

Bakshy, E. (2012) 'Rethinking Information Diversity in Networks', *Facebook Data Team*, 17 January, available at http://www.facebook.com/notes/facebook-data-team/rethinking-information-diversity-in-networks/10150503499618859 (accessed 29 October 2012).

Bollier, D. (2010) *The Promise and Peril of Big Data*, Washington, DC: Aspen Institute.

boyd, d. and Crawford, K. (2012) 'Critical Questions For Big Data. Provocations for a cultural, technological, and scholarly phenomenon', *Information, Communication & Society*, 15(5): 662–79.

Bozdag, E. and Timmermans, J. (2011) 'Values in the Filter Bubble: Ethics of personalization algorithms in cloud computing', in *Proceedings of the Workshop on Values in Design – Building Bridges between HCI, RE and Ethics {at 13th IFIP TC13 Conference on Human-Computer Interaction (Interact)}*, 6 September, Lisbon: 7–15.

Davenport, T. H. and Patil, D. J. (2012) 'Data Scientist: The sexiest job of the 21st century', *Harvard Business Review*, 90(10): 70–76.

Foucart, S. (2011) '"Juif" – Une requête très française', *Le Monde*, 14 February.

Funnell, A. (2012) 'Transcript of the Radio Broadcast of 25 March 2012 of "The Algorithm. Antony Funnell in conversation with Ted Striphas, John MacCormick, Nick Meaney, Michael Kearns and Andreas Calianos"', *Future Tense*, available at http://www.abc.net.au/radionational/programs/futuretense/the-algorithm/3901466#transcript (accessed 29 October 2012).

Holmes, O. W. Jr (1897) 'The Path of Law', *Harvard Law Review*, 10: 457–78.

Magnani, L. (2007) *Morality in a Technological World. Knowledge as duty*, Cambridge: Cambridge University Press.

Manjoo, F. (2012) 'The End of the Echo Chamber. A study of 250 million Facebook users reveals the Web isn't as polarized as we thought', *Slate* available at http://www.slate.com/articles/technology/technology/2012/01/online_echo_chambers_a_study_of_250_million_facebook_users_reveals_the_web_isn_t_as_polarized_as_we_thought_.html (accessed 29 October 2012).

Pariser, E. (2011) *The Filter Bubble: What the internet is hiding from you*, London: Viking.

Sunstein, C. R. (2007) *Republic.com 2.0*, Princeton: Princeton University Press.

Privacy, due process and the computational turn

A parable and a first analysis

Katja de Vries*

The parable of the three robotic dogs

Once upon a time, in a land far, far away, there were three families who each owned a robotic dog. The robotic dogs were a great source of entertainment for their owners: the family members enjoyed playing with them the same way as one would with a real dog. Next to their roles as loyal canine companions, the dogs were also supposed to patrol around the house of the families and protect them from 'suspect types',[1] such as potential burglars, child molesters and any other unwelcome intruders. The eyes of these robotic dogs registered all the passers-by and stored their image and gait. Whenever a dog spotted a 'suspect type' around the family house it would bark, set off the alarm system, contact all family members and call the police. If the 'suspect type' continued to approach the house, the dog could set off tear gas. The instruction manual opened with:

> Congratulations! You have made a great choice. No real dog could ever provide the same level of security as your new robotic pet. No burglar can distract your robotic dog with a simple piece of sausage. The robotic dog will never waggle its tail at an unwelcome guest, because you instruct it *exactly* about who should be kept away from your family. Robo-dog has an extremely user-friendly interface: just talk to the dog as you would to a child.[2] And which real dog would be able to call the police if they spot a suspicious type? Precisely. But your robotic dog will.

The manual offered different ways of instructing the dog about who qualifies as a 'suspect type'. Each family picked a different strategy. The first family had very strict ideas about who could be trusted and who not, so they decided to pre-program the dog with a set of fixed rules reflecting their ideas. The family compiled a long and complex set of rules such as: 'Somebody is suspect *if* possessing the characteristics "adult" *and* "passing by more than three times within a time span of one hour", *or* the characteristics "bearded" *and* "climbing" *and* is *not* a "family member", *or* the characteristics [...] *or* [...] etc.' They instructed the dog to proceed with the alarm routine if it detected the presence of a set of characteristics described by their rules. On the eve of the dog's first patrol the mother had looked sternly into the eyes of the dog and said: 'You rule the street, but we rule you, understood?' From that day onwards all the family members called the dog by the name 'Ruler'.[3]

The second family said: 'We personally think it is quite easy to distinguish suspect types from trustworthy ones, but we have difficulty articulating what the common denominators are that give them away.' So instead of giving their dog a precise definition of what to look for they would point out passers-by who looked trustworthy to them and those they considered untrustworthy. Thus, in contrast to the first family they did not provide their metallic pet with any explicit rules, but merely with examples of passers-by they had labelled as either 'trustworthy' or 'suspect'. The dog was told to compare every new passer-by to the examples it was given and to classify the passer-by in the same category as the example that was the most *similar* to it. Because 'similarity' is quite an equivocal concept (just think of how opinions can differ on which siblings in a family are most alike) the family gave a formalised definition of similarity. The family explained to the dog that 'similarity' should be understood as 'closest in terms of Euclidian distance'. They also told the dog which characteristics to take into account, how to represent these characteristics as points in Euclidian space and how to calculate the distance between those points. Observing how the dog assigned each passer-by to the class of the *closest* labelled example, the family named the dog 'Closer'.

The third family thought it would be silly to impose their own stereotypes onto the dog. 'Is it not precisely the problem that intruders make use of our prejudiced expectations? The good thing about this robotic dog is that it is not burdened by such prejudices and maybe we can learn something from its naive perspective', they pondered. Thus, the family told the dog, whom they had named 'Cluster': 'Now go outside and after a month you can tell us what categories of people you think there are. Let us begin with four different categories, ok, Cluster?' Although the third family had not provided the dog with any explicit definition of 'suspect' behaviour (such as family 1) or given it any examples of what it should look for (such as family 2), it had instructed the dog with a very precise definition of similarity in terms of Euclidian distance and told it to come up with four classes.

Later that week Ruler, the robotic dog of the first family, called the police after noticing the characteristics 'beard', 'adult' and 'climbing' when a roofer came to replace a few missing tiles on the roof. The family had to come over to the police station and explain the misunderstanding. The family realised that making a list of rules defining 'suspect types' was not that easy after all. The second family, who had tried to teach their dog Closer to recognise 'suspect types' by providing it with examples, also had some mixed feelings about the result. If Closer barked at people whom the owners did not consider suspect, they could correct the dog so that it could adjust its 'model'.[4] However, the mere fact that Closer barked at a passer-by made this particular person seem more suspect.[5] A person who might have looked harmless to the owners before now gained an aura of potential danger. So, in practice the owners did not correct their dog very often. As time went by they began to rely increasingly on the judgment of Closer.

Cluster, the dog of the third family, strolled around for a month in the surroundings of the family home and then came up with a very elaborate categorisation of people involving, among other things, the colour of their socks, the rhythm of their walking pace and the presence of jewellery on their fingers. 'Isn't that exciting?', the father said. 'Without any explicit instruction Cluster came up with this categorisation that eludes me but probably is a very truthful one, because we have not influenced our robotic pet with our prejudices and ingrained ideas.' (The father did not give much thought to how he had biased the family dog by defining similarity in terms of proximity, by providing it with a long list of characteristics that possibly could be of interest and by telling it that it had to classify people in four categories.) The mother added: 'It seems to me that what Cluster describes as "category three" is the type of person we should be suspicious of.' Soon the whole family became convinced that Cluster had unearthed a very profound categorisation. When the dog barked and signalled that a 'category three' person was passing by, the whole family shivered. Sometimes they had difficulty recognising these 'category three' people themselves but they had great trust in the judgment of their robotic dog.

One day the three families decided to organise a garden party. They had invited all their neighbours but none had showed up. People were fed up with these metallic surveillance machines. The three families who owned the robotic dogs belonged to the ruling elite of the community and the robotic dogs had merely accentuated already existing social differences. People were annoyed with these devices that recorded everything they saw and moreover had the capacity to contact the police independently of their owners. The three families cared little about these feelings of their neighbours. Now that they were the only guests at their own party, they had plenty of opportunity to observe and discuss the behaviour of their robotic dogs. To their surprise, they noticed that there was hardly any overlap between the passers-by at which Ruler, Closer and Cluster would bark.

What is the moral of this parable? Normally, a parable is directly followed by the lessons that can be drawn from it. However, because the moral of this parable is based on the various ideas, analyses and recommendations presented in this volume, I will first present some more conventional introductory observations regarding the contents of this book. In the last section of this introductory chapter, I will finally return to the 'parable of the three robotic dogs' and suggest some lessons it could teach us about the computational turn, due process and privacy.

Family resemblance concepts and kaleidoscopic patterns

The 'computational turn', 'due process' and 'privacy': all the contributions presented in this volume engage with these three notions; notions that are of utmost importance for every contemporary information society intending to function in accordance with constitutional and fundamental human rights. However, as much as the three notions are important, they are also complex, multifaceted and sometimes even evanescent. Solove's observation that '[privacy] seems to be about everything, and therefore it appears to be nothing' (2006: 479), could easily be extended to 'due process' and the 'computational turn'. To make things worse, the notions consist of a multiplicity of concepts that share some traits but only share a minimal, if any, common core. For example, a privacy interference can refer to concepts of privacy as disparate as 'surveillance' (eg wiretapping by the police), 'decisional privacy' (eg a state does not allow a woman to decide for herself whether to have an abortion or not) and 'exposure' (eg a newspaper that publishes candid pictures of a naked celebrity) (Solove 2006). Nevertheless, this does not make the notions 'computational turn', 'due process' and 'privacy' incoherent or useless. Like members of a family, the different uses of these notions form 'a complicated network of similarities overlapping and criss-crossing' (Wittgenstein 1997: §66 as quoted in: Solove 2006: 485). The importance of these notions in contemporary debates might partly be explained precisely by their multifaceted and contested natures. An invocation such as: 'Let us not forget the requirements of due process!' will hardly provide a straightforward instruction. More likely it will act as an invitation to discuss what those requirements are. Instead of simplifying the meaning of the 'computational turn', 'due process' and 'privacy', the contributions in this volume bear witness to their multifaceted nature and their capacity to oblige us to think, debate and rethink our epistemology (how to compute valid, reliable and valuable knowledge?) and political constitution (which power balance should we preserve in our society, and how can we articulate those requirements in terms of due process and privacy?). Taking the provocative, obliging and multifaceted character of the notions 'computational turn', 'privacy' and 'due process' seriously has resulted in this volume, offering a polyphony (Bakhtin 1984: 6) of perspectives and analyses on the relations between these three notions: 'A plurality of independent and [...] fully valid voices [...] with equal rights and each with its own world'. This polyphony is further enhanced by the diverging disciplinary backgrounds of the contributors: a specialist in machine learning, philosophers and sociologists of technology, and legal philosophers. Nevertheless, there are some shared characteristics as well. One aspect that all the contributions have in common is their engaged outlook. Epistemological questions are never treated in a strictly analytical manner, as is sometimes done within philosophy of science (Harizanov et al 2007; Harman and Kulkarni 2007;

Thagard 1990), but are always related to the power relations between different actors, to the choices which policy-makers, engineers and citizens face in the present computational era and to the way these choices affect the constitutions of our societies. Another shared characteristic is the appetite for unconventional and novel approaches: for example, data minimisation, a classical and venerated pillar of data protection, is (at least partly) rejected by all authors in favour of other solutions. To give an impression of some of the solutions[6] proposed by the authors, see the following tentative listing:

- 'effective outcome transparency instead of the current focus on nominal procedural transparency (Koops)
- obfuscation tactics, which make the process of profiling more time consuming, costly, complex and difficult (Finton and Nissenbaum)
- a duty to acquire knowledge of the profiling artefacts (Magnani)
- explicitation of the profiling process by using experiment databases (van Otterlo)
- taking into account that profiling algorithms should not only be made on behalf of the state or companies, but also of the citizen who is subjected to them (Kerr)
- increasing the amount of available data and profiles to make it more difficult to get univocal indications (Esposito)
- re-introducing actual persons, objects and situations in profiling practices which operate mostly on the infra- and supra-individual level (Rouvroy)
- developing profiles transparency in the front-end, the interface and back-end of the computational decision systems that have a significant impact on our lives (Hildebrandt).

A third trait shared by all contributions is that they are not simply concerned with data collection, storage, processing or retrieval as such, but with the computational operations through which additional knowledge is squeezed out of these data. These computational operations are known under a variety of names such as machine learning,[7] data mining,[8] profiling[9] and knowledge discovery in databases.[10]

Next to these three commonalities many others can be discovered. Like the constitutive parts of a kaleidoscope, the different texts collected in this book 'are related to one another in many different ways' (Wittgenstein 1997: §65 as quoted in Solove 2006: 485). An introduction to such a book can never capture all the patterns of convergence and divergence between the different texts that precede it. The role of the present introduction is twofold. First, this introductory chapter offers a concise overview of some of the different uses of the notions 'the computational turn', 'privacy' and 'due process'. This overview is not an exhaustive taxonomy but a basic tool that might help the reader to connect the different themes addressed by the authors in this volume. Second, this introductory chapter contains a personal reading of how the analyses and proposals made by the various authors relate to each other. This interpretation is organised around two questions. The first one concerns both the epistemology and ecology of the computational turn: what are these various 'android epistemologies'[11] (Ford et al 2006; Bynum and Moor 1998: 8), which increasingly organise our human world, and how do we coexist with them? Profiling machines act both as epistemological extensions and epistemological companions for their users. In principle, there is nothing strange about the use of extensions or companionship to change or supplement our perception. For example, humans are quite experienced in using *animals* as both companions and epistemological extensions.[12] A blind person knows how to trust, train and treat his or her guide dog. The police know how to act together with their sniffer dogs. But how to coexist with the algorithmic predictions of a machine regarding questions such as whether someone will commit a crime, pay back a mortgage or be a good customer? The second question asks after the kind of pragmatism that governs the choice for one particular algorithm over another. The choice of one algorithm over another will often seem to be guided by a neutral pragmatism: an algorithm that generates better models is the one that should be preferred. For example, facial recognition software that has more correct identifications than its competitor is the one that should be preferred. It seems straightforward: *whatever works best*. However, what works best is not always easy to establish. Two questions that complicate the all too simple *whatever works best* formula are, first, 'For *whom?*' and, second, 'On *which* task?' Additionally, one could ask what it means to 'work best' if privacy and due process are also brought into the equation. I use the different contributions of this volume to propose a pragmatism 2.0.

However, before I can address the questions of ecology, epistemology and pragmatism, I will first take a closer look at the three aforementioned notions – the computational turn, privacy and due process – and their different uses that recur throughout the chapters of this book.

Three uses of the computational turn

While most uses of the notion 'computational turn' seem to have *something* to do with the growing importance of making sense of large data sets through advanced computational techniques, they diverge with respect to the precise *when*, *where*, *who* and *what* of this turn. Some of this divergence can be clarified by distinguishing three different uses of the notion: the 'computational turn' as a societal phenomenon, as a methodological shift and as a philosophical approach.

The first usage of the computational turn, as a societal phenomenon, is as an umbrella term to describe the recent avalanche of governmentalities (Berns and Rouvroy 2010), which act through machine learning and data mining techniques. These computational governmentalities blossom in both the private and public sector. The applications of such techniques can be found, for example, in the risk assessment of airline passengers, credit-scoring, smart cameras in health care, targeted marketing, anti-money laundering, criminal profiling, customer relationship management and interventions on financial markets.

The second way in which the computational turn is understood is methodological. In particular in the humanities (Berry 2012, 2011), social sciences (Varenne 2011) and the arts (Morel 2007) the term is used to describe the recent increase in the use of technologies such as digital databases, algorithmically facilitated search and analysis and computer simulations.

Next to the societal and methodological computational turn, a related but slightly broader use of the notion can be found in philosophy (Ess and Hagengruber 2011; Cavalier 2000; Bynum and Moor 1998). The computational turn in philosophy, better known as *computationalism*, is the equation of *cognition* with computation. Dennett (1998: 217) identifies three dogmas of this approach:

1. Thinking is information processing.
2. Information processing is computation (which is symbol manipulation).
3. The semantics of these symbols connects thinking to the external world.

In contrast to the methodological computational turn in the humanities, social sciences and arts, the computational turn in philosophy relates not merely to a change in the tools of research but also to the objects of study and the models through which they are understood (Bynum and Moor 1998: 1):

> [C]omputing is changing the way philosophers understand foundational concepts in philosophy, such as mind, consciousness, experience, reasoning, knowledge, truth, ethics and creativity. This trend in philosophical inquiry that incorporates computing in terms of a subject matter, a method, or a model has been gaining momentum steadily.

There have been various waves of computationalism in philosophy. In the 17th century there was a surge of computationalism *avant la lettre*, most notably expressed by Hobbes and Leibniz. Hobbes (1998/1651: 27–28) equates reasoning with computation ('reckoning'):

> In sum, in what matter soever there is place for addition and subtraction, there also is place for reason; and where these have no place, there reason has nothing at all to do. [...] For REASON, in this sense, is nothing but reckoning (that is, adding and subtracting) [...].

The model which seems to underlie both the computationalism of Hobbes and Leibniz is that of *mechanical* calculation, which, when properly applied, leads to *one* correct solution. Leibniz, who was anything but an armchair philosopher and actually invented an ingenious digital mechanical calculator named the 'Step Reckoner', dreamed of digital computing as the key to the establishment of a universal language (Dyson 2012):

> There would be no more need for disputation between two philosophers than between two accountants. For it would suffice to take their pencils in their hands, to sit down to their slates, and say to each other (with a friend to witness, if they liked): *calculemus* – let us calculate.
>
> (Leibniz 1890: 200, translated from Scheutz 2002: 5;
> Leibniz 1999/1688)

The first 20th century wave of computationalism began in the 1960s and was heralded by philosophers such as Putnam (eg 1975) and Fodor (eg 1987). This computationalism largely follows the 17th century understanding of computation as the syntactic, formal manipulation of symbols: 'the *semantics* of symbols, or more generally, *intentionality* plays no role in cognitive processing' (Scheutz 2002: 13). Searle (1980) famously attacked this stance in his *Chinese Room* thought experiment by arguing that successfully manipulating symbols does not imply necessarily that one also *understands* their meaning. The second wave of computationalism in the 1990s, mainly inspired by cognitive science, goes beyond computation as the formal, syntactic and disembodied manipulation of symbols and stresses the semantic and embodied concreteness of cognitive computation (Magnani 2009; Scheutz 2002: 13). Although the conceptual boundaries between the two waves are not always very strict, it is clear that in the last decade there has been a growing realisation that computation should not be understood as isolated and abstract, but that it has to work in a certain environment and on a particular task. In particular, the field of machine learning has shown that problems may have *multiple* solutions and that there is no one universal *Calculemus!*, which works anywhere and anytime. When computation produces semantics (eg a spam filter trying to compute a way successfully to distinguish 'spam' from 'ham' emails), there are many roads that lead to Rome. Breiman (2001) calls the multiplicity of good models in statistical modelling the 'Rashomon effect'.[13] I return to this effect later in this chapter.

Looking at 20th century philosophical writings that equate cognition and computation, it is clear that the term the 'computational turn' is a not only a more recent invention (first used in the 1990s: Cavalier 2000) than 'computationalism', but also continues to be the lesser known term.[14] Nevertheless, the way in which the notion the 'computational turn' plays on a parallelism with the 'linguistic turn' in philosophy (Cavalier 2000) provides a solid reason for preferring it over 'computationalism'. Parallel to the influential adage of the 'linguistic turn' in 20th century philosophy (Rorty 1967) that *everything is language*, the computational turn follows the axiom that *everything is computation*.[15] In essence, the linguistic turn suggests that there is no *direct* experience of, for example, 'that suspicious, but attractive young woman' or 'that beautiful and important poem' without the mediation through all kind of discourses regarding, for example, gender, taste, importance. The computational turn takes this a step further and suggests that the mediating perceptions of gender, importance, beauty, attractiveness, age etc result from computations. There are at least two important consequences for philosophy that follow from this computational turn. In the first place, it erases any fundamental difference between the perception by humans and machines.[16] After all, computations can be performed by machines as well as by humans. I can perceive gender but so can the smart camera; I can discern importance but the Google search engine beats me in ranking skills. Learning algorithms enable machines to invent new ways of making *sense* of things.[17] The second point of importance (cf Thagard 1990) has to do with the way in which such learning algorithms create and attribute meaning. Because such algorithms are built by humans, with the purpose of supporting human perception and decision-making, their epistemology is closely related to a human way of reasoning and making sense. By way of contrast, the models generated by learning algorithms will often go *beyond* human understanding. The success of the Google search engine is precisely that it goes beyond human capacities while at the same time being attuned to human needs, logic and interests. This opens up a field which can be called 'android epistemology'[18] (Ford et al 2006; Bynum and Moor 1998: 8).

Privacy and due process: a search for the public goods that inform the legal rights

The right to due process (Coudert et al 2008; Citron 2007; Steinbock 2005) and the right to privacy (Nissenbaum 2009; Solove 2006; Solove et al 2006; Gutwirth 2002) are not simply moral imperatives or philosophical concepts but fully fledged legal rights that can be derived from a variety of provisions. For example, in the United States due process is mainly to be found in two provisions of the Bill of Rights, namely the Fifth and Fourteenth Amendments to the US Constitution. Both provisions contain a due process clause prohibiting that any person should be deprived of life, liberty or property without 'due process of law'. In criminal cases, the Fourth (Steinbock 2005) and Eighth Amendments are also invoked to safeguard values that are related to due process. The Fourth Amendment grants a protection against unreasonable searches and seizures, while the Eighth Amendment prohibits the infliction of disproportional, cruel and unusual punishments. In contrast to this *smorgasbord* of legal sources, due process in the European Convention on Human Rights (ECHR) is identified with one single provision, namely the right to a fair trial such as described in Article 6 ECHR. This right encompasses, for example, the right to a public hearing before an independent and impartial tribunal within a reasonable period of time, the right to an adversarial process and, in the case of criminal proceedings, the presumption of innocence, the right to be informed of a charge in a language you understand and adequate time and facilities to prepare a defence. The protection of privacy in the ECHR is regulated in Article 8, which states: 'Everyone has the right to respect for his private and family life, his home and his correspondence.' Moreover, the Charter of Fundamental Rights of the European Union (CFREU) also distinguishes a right to data protection (Article 8 CFREU), which states that, next to the protection of private and family life, personal data must be processed in a fair and legitimate way (Article 7 CFREU). The right to privacy is often equated with the right to data protection, although many authors point out that this latter right concerns both more and less than privacy (Gutwirth and de Hert 2008; de Hert and Gutwirth 2006). For instance, the purpose specification and limitation principles stand out as obviously less and more than privacy, reminiscent of the criminal law principle of *détournement de pouvoir* (abuse of power). In the USA, the legislation regarding privacy is mainly found in tort law (Warren and Brandeis 1890), particularly in cases of disclosure of confidential information and in constitutional law, particularly when privacy is understood as a right to self-determination and freedom from decisional interference.[19]

The prime focus of the contributions in this volume, however, is not an exegesis of the manifold legal articulations of due process and privacy. Instead, the texts explore the kind of constitutional set-up that these rights aim to safeguard. A tentative[20] hypothesis, which might help to understand the role of the right to privacy (Nissenbaum 2009; Solove 2006; Solove et al 2006; Gutwirth 2002) and the right to due process (Coudert et al 2008; Citron 2007; Steinbock 2005) in the various contributions to this volume, is that both privacy and due process have to be understood as expressions of the aspiration of modern constitutional democracies to empower the individual citizen against all too intrusive, unbridled, arbitrary and Kafkaesque actions by the state or other powerful actors.[21] Both the right to privacy and the right to due process can be seen as tools to safeguard a certain level of symmetry in the power relations within society, where no actor may be simply smothered by the brute and arbitrary force of another actor. The right to due process provides some positive safeguards (presumption of innocence, opportunity to be heard, independent and impartial tribunal etc) to guarantee the possibility to diminish power asymmetries during all legal proceedings, whereas the right to privacy is a shield against illegitimate interference by others (Gellert et al 2012) that is not restricted to one particular area of life.

The idea that a society is more fair, just or productive when one avoids flagrant power asymmetries has reoccurred in many guises throughout history.[22] In modern constitutional democracies, both the right to due process and privacy are tools to realise this political ideal,[23] to diminish power inequalities and structure society in such a way that no actor can exercise the kind of violence, physical determination or power that obliterates any *possibility* of resistance or counter-manipulation whatsoever. Due process and privacy are conceptual–legal tools through which alleged power asymmetries can be put to the test. Whether invoking privacy or due process is successful also depends on the societal norms and values that determine the meaning of the legal right. For example, at present I would be very surprised if any European court would rule that killing someone in the seclusion of one's bedroom is protected by the right to privacy[24] or would honour the request of the murder suspect to have another additional 1000 days of court time to expand on childhood experiences leading up to the act of violence. The right to privacy and the right to due process do not prohibit power asymmetries as such but allow one to put the appropriateness of a power asymmetry to the test.

However, existing legal provisions regarding due process or privacy do not always offer effective means to put the logic and effects of profiling techniques to the test. The main problem here is the lack of knowledge and transparency of these profiling techniques. If one is unaware of being subjected to profiling techniques, it is unlikely that one would use the possibility to invoke privacy or due process to protect one's decisional freedom, contest decisions based on profiling techniques or to make the responsible government agencies or other large organisations accountable for the harmful impact of profiling-based decisions on the life of individual citizens. Awareness that a possible infringement has occurred is an indispensible prerequisite to invoke the right to privacy or the right to due process. Thus, some basic awareness of the profiling techniques and transparency as to the grounds for being treated in a certain way are indispensable to make the existing legal provisions effective tools in fighting power asymmetries related to machine learning. Acknowledging that narrow interpretations of due process and privacy will fail to provide effective protection against power asymmetries that are related to machine learning, the authors in this volume explore alternative ways (both legal and extra-legal) to realise the political ideals embedded in these two rights, as discussed below.

The epistemology and ecology of the computational turn: how to coexist with the perceptions of machines?

Epistemology: perception by humans/ perception by machines

To perceive is to make sense. Thus, to perceive is more than simply to record data. To put it differently, to perceive is to see something *as* something. Much philosophical ink has been spilled on the insight that the world appears to its inhabitants in many diverging ways. Perception is never the *direct* perception of a thing in itself but is always mediated through something: the antennae of an insect, the fingers of a blind man, the eyes and glasses of a reader, the sniffing nose of the dog, the echolocational sense of a bat etc. You and I will never have a first person experience of how the world appears to a bat, and the bat will never know what it is to be you or me (Nagel 1974).

Perception, then, is not limited to humans, or even to living beings.[25] Today some machines, following the instructions of so-called 'learning algorithms', are capable of perception as well. The days when computers were passive receptacles and processors of data are long gone. Learning algorithms enable machines to make *sense* of all kind of data: faces, handwritten digits, objects, movements, financial transactions, web pages, passenger records of travellers, emails etc all can become subjected to machine classification. When a machine learning algorithm creates a model according to which it attributes meaning (for example: 'the face is male', 'the digit is a 1', 'the object is a car', 'the movement is abnormal', 'the financial transaction is suspicious', 'the web page ranks high in terms of relevance', 'the passenger needs to be inspected at the border', 'the email is spam'), this attribution will not always coincide with the way you or I would perceive the same data. Sometimes one attempts to teach a machine to mimic human perception, by giving it labelled examples ('Look, here are 5000 examples of what we humans perceive as the digit 3') or by correcting what is perceived as an incorrect categorisation by human standards ('That is not the digit 2, but the digit 3!').

However, teaching (and learning) through examples is not an exact science. The rule induced by the learner might be quite different from the one intended by the teacher. A toddler, whose parents have spent several days pointing out instances of dogs, can suddenly surprise by pointing to a visiting neighbour and triumphantly saying: 'Dog!' What is the rule inferred by the child? And by which standards do we judge if the child is mistaken? Maybe the child was very perceptive and noticed a dog-like feature of the neighbour that was overlooked by the parents? Finding standards to judge the correctness of a solution in so-called 'unsupervised machine learning' is even more difficult. Here, the learning process is not guided by labelled examples or feedback and the tasks are less specific. We ask questions such as: 'If we want to organize data set X in eight groups, what is the best way to do this?' or 'Which three attributes correlate most intensely in data set Y?' Unsupervised learning algorithms function by following one or several general algorithmic principles according to which the data structure should be inferred: for example, constructing clusters in such a way that the Euclidean distance *within* the clusters is minimised and the Euclidian distance *between* the clusters is maximised, the maximalisation of margins between clusters, the optimisation of probabilities, identification of features that have a correlation exceeding a certain value etc.

Especially when large and complex data sets are involved, the function of machine learning is not to mimic but to go *beyond* human perception. When an unsupervised learning algorithm discovers certain patterns in a data set consisting of many millions of rows or 'records' (every record representing, for instance, one transaction or one individual) and thousands of columns or 'tuples' (every column containing all the different scores on a certain attribute, for example, time of transaction or age of the individual) there is no 'human solution' against which the proposed machine solution can be checked. The unenhanced human mind and eye are not well adapted to see any wood for the trees in a data set of such size and complexity. The only way to evaluate the proposed data structure is indirect: one could either cross-validate it against a new set of data to see if the same structure emerges, compare it with structures inferred from the same data set by other machine learning algorithms or judge it with general standards of aesthetics (Guyon et al 2011) or efficiency.

The problem with such indirect standards is that it is easy to end up in a philosophical swamp when deciding which standard to use. For example, is the best description always the most parsimonious? Or does Occam's razor sometimes simplify the complexities too much? For example Vapnik (1995), who invented one of today's most influential machine learning algorithms (so-called 'support vector machines'), argues that Occam's razor is often not an appropriate standard to measure the value of algorithmically generated models. He argues that complex data sets might be best described by complex, not parsimonious, models: 'At the end of the 1990s it became clear that *the Occam's Razor principle of induction is too restrictive: Experiments with SVMs, boosting, and neural nets provided counter-examples.* [...] In the beginning of the 2000s it also became clear that *in creating a philosophy of science for a complex world the machine learning problem will play the same role that physics played in creating the philosophy of science for a simple world*' (Vapnik 2006: 484, original emphasis). Vapnik's criticism of Occam's razor is just one example of how difficult it is to find appropriate standards to judge the quality of a machine perception.

Ecology: how to coexist with the perceptions of machines?

As Esposito agues in her contribution, it is a fallacy to assume that learning machines, because they have been built by humans to further human purposes, function analogously to human consciousness or in accordance with a rationality that is transparent to human understanding. On the contrary, she proposes that one should stress the difference between human consciousness and artificial intelligence. This raises the question of ecology (Stengers 2010, 2005): how to coexist with the perception of machines? Following Esposito a first step would be to accept that, in the same way as we recognise 'the black box of the individual psyche' of another person or animal, the epistemology of a profiling machine also has its own alterity and opacity. Because of this alterity and opacity a profiling machine is not a mere epistemological extension but also an epistemological companion.[26] Such an approach would bear some similarity with pre-modern cultures of divination in that it does not attempt to study underlying structures but stays on the surface in interpreting indications and signs. Whether it is children, sniffer dogs or machines that are trained on labelled examples,[27] there is always a certain opacity as to what, precisely, the learner has learned. Moreover, as became clear in the previous section, the algorithms according to which machines build their models of understanding vary widely and unequivocal standards to judge which algorithm is better are not always available. As a result, machine X might end up profiling the world quite differently from machine Y. Yet the ideology surrounding profiling is still very much one of objectivity. According to Leibniz's adage 'Let's calculate' (Leibniz 1890: 200, translated from Scheutz 2002: 5; Leibniz 1999/1688), there is the belief that an optimal, universally rational solution could be reached. To break the spell of this ideological fallacy Esposito proposes that, instead of minimising data, privacy could benefit more from an increase in data and profiles that would make it impossible to obtain 'univocal indications'.

This strategy seems to coincide largely with what Brunton and Nissenbaum call obfuscation: tactics that will confuse the process of profiling or simply add to the time or cost of separating bad data from good. While Esposito's proposal to increase data is a long-term vision for a more privacy friendly society in general, Brunton and Nissenbaum propose active tactics for concrete situations in our present life that might benefit from civil disobedience. Their chapter is a good example of extra-legal interim methods to preserve the ideals of privacy and due process. Brunton and Nissenbaum's tactics include polluting the data in such a way that more time is needed to separate 'the wheat from the chaff'; cooperative obfuscation such as loyalty card swapping where data of different individuals become mixed up; making a selective part of the data inaccessible which can, for example, result in the anonymisation of data; and permanent distortion of the data, for example by mixing genuine requests with dummy requests. Because all of these tactics are extra-legal, a large part of Brunton and Nissenbaum's chapter is devoted to finding the ethical conditions that would make such subversive acts permissible. These conditions are closely related with power asymmetries and the preservation of the ideals of due process and privacy.

Increasing the amount of data and obfuscation are 'tactics of the surface'. In contrast to such tactics, other authors have more 'enlightened' proposals, relying on knowledge and transparency. Clearly, tactics of the surface and of depth can easily supplement each other. When a blind person uses the eyes of a guide dog as a stand-in for his or her lacking visual perception, or when the nose of a sniffer dog acts as a prosthesis for the limited olfactory capacities of the police, the users of these epistemological extensions do not need to know precisely what goes on in the mind of their dog. However, some additional knowledge of dog psychology does not hurt either. Magnani argues that knowledge of the technological artefacts in our age is to be considered an ethical duty. In the 18th century it was enough for Kant to say that there was 'no need of science or philosophy for knowing what man has to do in order to be honest and good, and indeed to be wise and virtuous' (Kant 1964/1785: 72).

By contrast, Magnani suggests that 'ethics and decision-making should always be accompanied by suitable knowledge related to the situations at hand.' In order to coexist with profiling machines in a fruitful ecology, we better acquaint ourselves with them, distinguishing the 'dogs' from the 'wolves'. The ethical imperatives of Magnani resonate with van Otterlo's hopes that novel techniques will make it possible to make 'the whole process of learning from data *transparent* and *reusable*' by explicating '*everything* [...] (data, hypotheses, algorithms, parameters and results) in formal languages' (original emphasis). A relevant development van Otterlo refers to are the so-called experiment databases,[28] which 'store, in addition to data itself, the used *algorithms, settings and parameters* and *results* of experiments in ML [machine learning]. The main goal is to be able to *compare* algorithms more carefully, and to not repeat experiments that have been done over and over again'. Hildebrandt also stresses the importance of transparency. Yet she argues that *merely* creating transparency about the functioning at the 'back-end' of computational decision systems is not enough. According to Hildebrandt, only a triple approach will be effective in alleviating the negative effects of machine profiling on due process: what is needed is, first, profile transparency in the front-end of computational decision systems; second, user-friendly interfaces; and, finally, a back-end that is subjected to public oversight.

Koops proposes the enhancement of so-called 'downwards transparency': the profiled individual should get more insight in the decisions that are taken by the profilers. His proposed solution is 'an alternative approach, one that focuses less on data minimisation, user control and procedural accountability, but instead directs its arrows at the outcome of computation-based decision-making: the decision itself' (Koops). This is, like Hildebrandt's proposals, something of a middle way between the tactics of surface and the tactics of depth: while promoting the enlightened ideal of transparency he wants to shift the focus away from the procedure, to the outcome of profiling-based decisions. Instead of adhering to the solutions currently dominating data protection legislation, he proposes to start from the desire to 'rebalance the relationship between data-processing organisations and individuals' (Koops).

The tools to realise this ideal are, according to Koops, transparency legislation, social sousveillance movements such as Wikileaks, embedding privacy and due process enhancing values in technology. The criticism on the nominal, ineffective and abstract nature of existing legislation is shared by Rouvroy. Before one can even speak of an ecology, the inhabitants of that ecology should be able notice each other. The use of rights of access and contestation are of course very limited if one does not even know that one is profiled and, consequently, does not know what to contest. Thus, the main problem of our coexistence with profiling machines is, according to Rouvroy, that they act on an infra- and supra-individual level, never addressing the subject. The new inhabitants of our ecosystem are not just opaque black boxes that we should get to know, as Magnani argues, but we often do not even know *that* they are there. What is absent from our experience is not the profiling machines as such but the categorisations and meanings according to which they organise the world. This is in fact where the linguistic turn of the 1970s and the computational turn meet. What the linguistic turn sought to make clear is that all human perception is structured through language.

However, it is also precisely by challenging these categories that we can exercise critique. For example, using the words 'he' and 'she' structures the way I see people. Yet this awareness of gender biases in language also allows me to challenge this structure, for example, by structurally using 'she' and not 'he' as a generic pronoun, or inventing new combinations: s/he. In contrast, in our present post-computational turn era it could easily happen that I am subjected to profiles, categories and semiotic structures ('suspect type', 'profitable customer' etc) of which I am not aware. This lack of knowledge and transparency not only makes the current legal privacy and due process provisions toothless as discussed above, but also makes it very difficult to challenge or critique those structures with the tools of the linguistic turn of the 1970s.

Pragmatism 2.0: complicating the equation of what 'works best'

The choice of one algorithm over another will often seem to be guided by neutral pragmatism: an algorithm that generates better models is the one that should be preferred. For example, facial recognition software that has more correct identifications than its competitor seems to be the one that should be preferred. It seems simple: *whatever works best*. However, even if we leave aside the situation of a draw between various models,[29] what works best is not always easy to establish.

A first question is: best – *on which task*? To evaluate the quality of an algorithm standardised databases[30] are often used as a benchmark. The performance of an algorithm on such a database allows for the comparison of algorithms. However, doing well on a standardised database does not necessarily say something about the real life performance[31] of an algorithm (Introna and Wood 2004). While comparing supervised learning algorithms (the target variable is known and there is a set of labelled data to test how well the model is able to categorise) already poses a number of problems, making a comparison between unsupervised learning algorithms (the target is not known and there is no set with the 'right answers' with which the discovered patterns could be compared) even more complicated. In supervised learning, there is at least a human standard and the possibility of human feedback. For example, a smart camera that learns to distinguish female faces from male ones is first trained on examples labelled by humans, and can be corrected by a human observer if the categorisation is wrong. In unsupervised learning, the machine is instructed to discover an underlying structure. Often it is thought that there is a single 'right', or even 'natural', clustering to be discovered, while in fact '[d]epending on the use to which a clustering is to be put, the same clustering can either be helpful or useless'. (Guyon et al 2011: 2). Moreover, as Ramsay (2003: 173) notes, when one is not looking for a 'right' classification but for an 'interesting' pattern, many of the traditional statistical measures of evaluation are of little use: 'Empirical validation and hypothesis testing simply make no sense in a discourse where the object is not to be right (in the sense that a biologist is ever "right"), but to be interesting (in the sense that a great philosopher is "interesting")'.

A second question which complicates matters is: 'works best' – for *whom?* This point has been eloquently elaborated by Kerr in this volume. He opposes the contemporary predictive profiling techniques with the predictive stance of the 19th century legal pragmatism of Oliver Wendell Holmes. The pragmatist understanding of law is that it is the art of making predictions about what the courts will do: law gives 'the bad man' the opportunity carefully to consider which actions to take, given the likely outcomes. This legal predictive stance in a way anticipates the risk society. Law, after it has been bathed in Holmes's '"cynical acid" [...], cleansing it of any and all moral stain' (Kerr), is simply the business of legal risk avoidance. For Holmes 'legal prediction is intimately and inextricably connected to the standpoint of those on whose behalf the predictions are made. ... [It] requires lawyers to adopt the perspective of their clients in order to promote their future interests, regardless of their moral stance' (Kerr). In contrast, current techniques are often merely 'designed to promote corporate and state interests such as profit, prosperity, security and safety, often at the expense of any given citizen' (Kerr). In a constitutional democracy, which claims to cherish values such as due process and privacy, pragmatism should not merely be about the best score on a standardised database or about the biggest profit, but should also reckon with other values and perspectives. If privacy and due process would *also* be taken into the equation as factors to reckon with, and if the profiled citizens would be considered *as much* stakeholders in today's profiling techniques as the businesses and governments that pay for their creation, the outcome of what it means to 'work best' might be altered. Holmes's exhortation that '*point of view matters*' and that 'predictions should be understood with reference to the standpoint of everyday people, from their point of view and their sense of purpose' can be a fruitful additional guideline in developing learning algorithms.

Complicating the banal formula 'whatever works best' with the questions 'on which task?' and 'from whose perspective?' could result in a pragmatism 2.0.[32] The irony is that this pragmatism would come closer to the original sense of pragmatism. When the American pragmatists, such as Peirce,[33] James and Dewey, coined the notion pragmatism they definitely did not have a utilitarian platitude in mind. Pragmatism, according to James, points to that '[w]hat really exists is not things made but things in the making' (1920: 263). In this sense, pragmatism invites us to think that reality is not simply given, but always under construction, and how our concepts are not simply representations of a static reality but tools with which we can construct the world. With its explosion of profiling algorithms, the computational turn might actually, surprisingly enough, contribute to this pragmatist and constructivist outlook. Contrary to the classical idea of universally valid computation, in which we must all agree that $1+1=2$, profiling algorithms can show that there can be a multiplicity of computations without a single best solution. 'Pragmatism is an art of consequences, an art of "paying attention" that is opposed to the philosophy of the omelette justifying the cracked eggs' (Pignarre and Stengers 2011: 17).

The knowledge generated by profiles is not static universal knowledge, but it is knowledge that is always in the process of being made. The kind of profiling that would follow the imperatives of this old–new pragmatism 2.0, would 'foreground [...] performance [*how* things work, *italics mine*] rather than treating it as some forgettable background to knowledge' (Pickering 2010: 381). Such a practice would have the openness to consider the suggestions made in this volume to allow due process and privacy to enter the equation as additional standards of evaluation. Moreover, the genuine constructivist outlook of a pragmatism 2.0 would offer novel opportunities and possibilities of knowledge when applied to the construction of profiling algorithms. Instead of forcing learning algorithms to converge to a single best solution, they could be like the contributions in this book: '*A plurality of independent and {...} fully valid voices {...} with equal rights and each with its own world*' (Bakhtin 1984: 6, original emphasis). Each algorithm could be a contribution to a 'polyphonic truth' (Bakhtin 1984).

The moral of the 'parable of the three robotic dogs'

This chapter opened with a parable about three robotic dogs that have to protect their owners from 'suspect types'. The first dog, Ruler, is programmed in an explicit way: it is equipped with a precise model of what constitutes a 'suspect type'. The second and the third dogs, Closer and Cluster, are programmed differently, according to so-called machine learning principles that require the machine to build its own model[34] based on former experiences. This implies that a machine is merely equipped with some general principles about how to discover structures and patterns in data. In other words: it is instructed with principles that it can follow to recognise 'similarity', but not with a model of how to recognise a 'suspect type'. Closer, the second dog, is presented with examples of people categorised by its owner as 'suspect types'. Based on these examples, Closer constructs a model of a how to recognise a 'suspect type'. It applies the principles of similarity to classify new instances it is presented with. This is called supervised learning. Cluster, the third dog, is not provided with any labelled examples. It is only told to group all the people it encounters into four categories, according to their similarity.

Such discovery of data structures without predefined class labels (for example, 'suspect type' and 'non-suspect type') is called unsupervised learning.

Based on the contributions presented by the various authors in this volume, it seems that there are at least four lessons that can be learned from the parable.

The first lesson is that when a machine has to make sense of the world based on *general instructions regarding how to recognise similarity and patterns* (Closer and Cluster) rather than *explicit, top-down definitions describing a particular class* (Ruler), the perception of the machine gains a degree of autonomy. In the first family, the dog is a mere executor of explicit instructions. In the second and third families, the dogs are not only executors of instructions, but also the creators of categorisations. When a machine makes sense of the world based on general instructions regarding similarity rather than explicit class definitions, its categorisations are not a direct result of the commands given by its instructor. It becomes possible to compare and juxtapose the machine observations with those made by its instructor and/or users. As such, a learning machine is not merely an executor but also a companion. Although teaching is *never* a one-way, top-down process (even the first family has to reconsider its instructions after Ruler identifies the roofer as a 'suspect type'), the potential influence of the learner on its teacher tends to increase when the machine is provided only with 'general' instructions on similarity.

The second lesson, better known as the *no free lunch* theorem[35] (Wolpert 1996), is that machines can be instructed in *many* ways to 'learn' or generalise and that there is no silver bullet that works in all situations. Some 'general' principles of similarity and inference, according to which a machine can infer a model or discover a data structure, might be more popular[36] than others but there is no algorithmic panacea that can build a perfect model from no matter which data set. An algorithm that generates good results in one situation will fail to do so in another. In the parable of the three robotic dogs, each dog follows a different set of instructions and consequently often barks at different passers-by.

The third lesson is that it is difficult to tell which machine categorisation is correct and which is incorrect. The three robotic dogs all bark at different passers-by. During the garden party each family probably thought that its own dog was superior to the others in identifying 'suspect types'. Moreover, it seems impossible to find principles of generalisation and inference on which everyone agrees and which always give good results. Who is to say that the most parsimonious model describes the data best? Who is to say that people who live close to each other or have a similar score on a particular test are also similar in other respects? How is it possible to know whether a person who was identified as 'suspect' by the dog *truly* had bad intentions or not? The identification by the dog interferes in the course of events, making it impossible to tell what would have happened otherwise. At best the owners can compare the dogs' assessments of passers-by with their own assessments.

However, in the parable, the assessments of the owners were also *shaped* by those of their barking dogs. Someone who might have seemed innocent if the dog had not barked can suddenly appear suspect after the dog has barked. Yet, the assumption that there is an objective, neutral truth to be approximated is not very frequently challenged when discussing the value of a learning algorithm:

> We're always learning from experience by seeing some examples and then applying them to situations that we've never seen before. [...] How do we make generalizations from fragmentary bits of evidence? A dog of mine was once hit by a car, and it never went down the same street again – but it never stopped chasing cars on other streets.
>
> (Minsky 1988: 203, as quoted by van Otterlo 2009: 10–11)

The dog in this example is presented as a 'silly' dog, because it made the wrong inference (avoiding the street where it was hit by a car) instead of the right one (stop chasing cars). However, who is to say that the inference of the dog ('this is a dangerous street') was incorrect and the inference by Minsky ('chasing cars will often result in accidents') is better? Which solutions are good, better or best is an *empirical* question that cannot be given a universal or abstract answer. A constructivist, pragmatist approach to learning algorithms would abandon the search for a single best solution and allow for a 'polyphonic truth' (Bakhtin 1984). Allowing for a polyphonic truth does not imply that any solution is equally good. It would, however, imply the need to debate as to why one solution is better than the other and the acknowledgement that this debate does *not* have to converge on a single solution.

This brings me to the fourth lesson that can be drawn from the 'parable of the three robotic dogs': whether a solution is good or not is not an objective but a political question. What a good solution is will differ depending on the values it cherishes. The parable opens, as a fairy tale, with 'once upon a time' and 'in a land far, far away'. The reader does not learn anything about whether the presence of the three robotic dogs changes power relationships in the community, or about the political ideals and aspirations of the society in which these dogs act. It is only at the end of the parable that it becomes clear that the presence of the robotic dogs has had a negative effect on the surrounding community and that the presence of the dog acerbates existing social structures and power differences. Constructing machine learning algorithms is all too often seen as a universal, apolitical practice. When the quality of an algorithm is assessed, based on how well it performs on a standardised data set, the benchmark of quality is as time- and placeless as the 'once upon a time' and the 'in a land far, far away' that opens the parable.

What would happen if the community in the parable were exposed to the proposals in this volume? If the profiled neighbours and the owners of the dogs were to gain more knowledge about how these robotic dogs function this could help them to act morally (cf Magnani). This knowledge could consist in expliciting the profiling process (cf van Otterlo). Next to these general tactics of knowledge and transparency the neighbourhood could also benefit from so-called outcome transparency in concrete cases (cf Koops): the owners could be forced to explicitate in retrospect why their dog barked at a particular person. The community could also take recourse to tactics of the surface. By introducing more robotic dogs, each with its own particular outlook, the status of an alarmed dog would be devaluated (cf Esposito). Another tactic of the surface is obfuscation (cf Brunton and Nissenbaum). For example, if it became clear that some of the robotic dogs relied strongly on the gait of the passers-by, the profiling logic would be obstructed if everyone adopted an artificial limp. Another way to adjust the functioning of the robotic dogs would be not merely to take the wishes and needs of the dog owners into account, but also those of the passers-by (cf Kerr). Such an adjustment could very well be combined with an approach where not only the owners are addressed (it is only the owners and the police who are informed of the presence of a 'suspect type'; the 'suspect' is not informed or is simply attacked without much further ado), but also the profiled passer-by (cf Rouvroy). One could, for example, imagine that the robotic dogs would send out a message to the phone of a passer-by informing it of its suspicions and allowing it to come up with counter-arguments. All of these tactics could contribute to create a more desirable power balance within the community. They could help to create a happier ending to the parable: a garden party where neighbours enjoy each other's company and engage in productive dialogues about how to shape their community.

Notes

* The author would like to thank Sebastian Abrahamsson, Solon Barocas, Mireille Hildebrandt and Martijn van Otterlo for their salient comments and feedback on this chapter.
1 I would like to thank Solon Barocas (New York University) for bringing to my mind the complexities surrounding the target class 'suspect types.' Does the fact that the robotic dogs are on the look-out for a rather elusive category like 'suspect types', steer the narrative in a particular direction? What if the target class had been, for example, 'convicted felons', 'nervous tics' or 'red cars'? I would like to suggest that in this regard it might be useful to dintinguish between the use of machine recognition to spot characteristics that function as *indices* of an assumed underlying characteristic (eg a nervous tic, a beard and a particular gait as *indices* of possible criminal intent and suspiciousness) or to spot characteristics *for their own sake* (eg spotting the number of cars in a street because this is precisely what one wants to know: *how many cars pass through the street*). Personally, I would like to argue that *all* machine recognition is based on an 'index' or 'proxy' logic (something stands for something else), although is some cases the presence of an index-rule (ie a rule that associates a certain index X, eg 'a nervous tic', to an increased likelihood of a Y, eg 'suspiciousness') is more apparent than in others.

2 The goal of this parable is to provide a metaphoric narrative that makes it easier for the reader to grasp some of the complex issues surrounding the relationship between the computational turn, due process and privacy. In the fairytale world of this parable, robotic dogs are effortlessly programmed by means of natural language and no drop of sweat is spilled on the tedious process of programming. It should be underlined that this is not a realistic depiction of any existing practice.

3 I am much indebted to Martijn van Otterlo's creative suggestion to name the three robotic dogs Ruler, Closer and Cluster instead of simply referring to them as dogs 1, 2 and 3.

4 To a certain extent the word 'model' is misplaced, because Closer does not build a model (ie does not abstract any generic rule, explicit generalisation or pattern from the training data) but simply classifies every new passer-by in the same category (either 'suspect' or 'trustworthy') as the nearest labelled example provided by his owners. Closer operates according to the k-nearest neighbour algorithm (with k=1), which is an example of so-called 'memory-based learning', 'instance-based learning' or 'lazy learning'. The learning is 'lazy' because it sticks to the training data and does not abstract any model from them. Closer compares a new, unlabelled passer-by with the nearest of all labelled examples, and *not* with a model abstracted from them. Or, to put it differently: training data and model coincide. The 'laziness' of the k-nearest neighbour algorithm (ie that it does not abstract a model from the training data) makes it somewhat special in comparison with other supervised learning algorithms, for example neural networks, support vector machines and linear regression, that do create a model based on the training data.

5 The phenomenon that human users tend to abandon their own judgment in favour of suggestions provided by a computer is called 'automation bias' (Citron 2007; Skitka et al 2000).

6 This list is merely an appetiser, presenting some of the solutions that can be found is this volume. It does not exhaustively list all the solutions proposed in this volume; neither does it capture their subtleties and complexities.

7 'Machine learning is the systematic study of algorithms and systems that improve their knowledge or performance with experience' (Flach 2012: 3).

8 'Data mining is the application of specific algorithms for extracting patterns from data' (Fayyad et al 1996: 39).

9 'A simple working definition of profiling could be: the process of "discovering" correlations between data in data bases that can be used to identify and represent a human or non-human subject (individual or group), and/or the application of profiles (sets of correlated data) to individuate and represent a subject or to identify a subject as a member of a group or category' (Hildebrandt 2008: 41).

10 'KDD [Knowledge Discovery from Databases] refers to the overall process of discovering useful knowledge from data, and data mining refers to a particular step in this process. [...] KDD places a special emphasis on finding understandable patterns that can be interpreted as useful or interesting knowledge' (Fayyad et al 1996: 39–40).

11 The term 'android epistemology' (Ford et al 2006; Bynum and Moor 1998: 8) points to the hybrid status of the perceptions generated by 'profiling machines' (Elmer 2004). On the one hand, profiling machines are extended sense organs of their human users, created according to human standards of reasoning, and with the purpose of strengthening or changing the way the user makes sense of

the world. As such they resemble other epistemological tools that shape perception, such as glasses, the cane of a blind man, the alphabet or a dictionary. On the other hand. profiling machines have a certain level of autonomy from, and opacity towards, their makers/users. The interpretations that they generate can sometimes surprise or startle, precisely because they can differ from the ones held by their users. In this sense, profiling machines are more of a *companion* to their users (in the same way as a dog can be a companion to its owner) than an extension. The adjective 'android' expresses simultaneously the familiarity (as extended sense organs) and alterity (as companions) of the way profiling machines perceive the world.

12 The term 'epistemological extension' does not imply that there ever was 'pure', 'natural' or 'uncontaminated' human perception. I argue that that it suffices to say that human perception is mediated through sense organs and that the type and number of sense organs are not fixed givens. Merleau-Ponty has forcefully described how instruments that are foreign to the human body at first can become fully incorporated by it: 'To get used to a hat, a car or a stick is to be transplanted into them, or conversely, to incorporate them into the bulk of our own body. Habit expresses our power of dilating our being-in-the-world, or changing our existence by appropriating fresh instruments' (Merleau-Ponty 2002: 166).

13 '*Rashomon* is a wonderful Japanese movie in which four people, from different vantage points, witness an incident in which one person dies and another is supposedly raped. When they come to testify in court, they all report the same facts, but their stories of what happened are very different. What I call the Rashomon effect is that there is often a multitude of different descriptions [equations $f(x)$] in a class of functions giving about the same minimum error rate' (Breiman 2001: 206).

14 As a frivolous wink to the 'methodological computational turn': on 26 October 2012 'computationalism' generated 52,400 hits on Google Search, while the 'computational turn' only brought up 6520 results. It should be noted that such a simple comparison of Google Search results, or even a slightly more sophisticated plot showing the increase and decrease of the usage of these words with the Ngram Viewer for Google Books, lack academic rigour and are not representative of the methods of the digital humanities. For a better impression of academic inquiries into methods after the computational turn, see for example www.digital methods.net (accessed 30 October 2012).

15 The adage that *everything is language* does not say that all that exists can be reduced to discourse; neither does it deny the existence of a vibrant material world. It merely shows that a bare, non-discursive reality in itself is *meaningless*. Similarly, the turn taking place under the banner of *everything is computation* advances the idea that *meaning* is always born from computation.

16 A similar observation can be made about the cybernetic precursors of today's learning machines: 'cybernetics [...] threaten[s] the modern boundary between mind and matter [...] Cybernetics thus stages for us a non-modern ontology in which people and things are not so different after all' (Pickering 2010: 18). As an aside, it could be noted that revisiting the work of classical cyberneticians, such as Norbert Wiener (1894–1964), William Ross Ashby (1903–1972) and Stafford Beer (1926–2002), can be very helpful in understanding contemporary machine learning (de Vries 2009). Many of today's machine learning algorithms and

architectures are direct descendants of cybernetic pattern recognising models from the 1950s, such as the 'Perceptron' (Rosenblatt 1957) and the 'Pandemonium' (Selfridge 1959). The difference between classical cybernetics and contemporary machine learning is that the former was not merely involved in the engineering of informational devices, but also encompassed a broader vision of the workings of society and nature. This can be illustrated, for example, by opposing cybernetic *teaching machines* (Pickering 2010: 329ff) developed in the 1960s and 1970s by Gordon Pask (1928–1996) that trained human learners by monitoring their performance and adapting the training task to *optimise the learning progress*, to contemporary *learning machines* that are used to *find structures and make sense* out of labelled or unlabelled training data. Classical cybernetics studied how adaptive, rational *behaviour* could emerge from the negative feedback loops of any kind of system (organic, societal, artificial etc). In contrast, contemporary machine learning is narrower in scope: it is mainly concerned with how negative feedback loops in *machines* (that is, artificial systems) can create adaptive, rational *meanings*.

17 An alternative argument could be that algorithms do *not* make sense of data themselves but merely allow the *researcher* to make new sense. Whether a model (or 'pattern') generated by an algorithm already can be considered to be an (algorithmic) 'interpretation' *before* the researcher interprets the model, depends on one's understanding of the word 'interpretation'.

18 Note 11.

19 For example, *Griswold v. Connecticut*, 381 U.S. 479 (1965) and *Roe v. Wade*, 410 U.S. 113, 153 (1973). These landmark cases concerned the right to self-determination and reproductive privacy. The right to privacy can be derived from a wide range of provisions in the Bill of Rights: the freedom of association clause in the First Amendment, the Third Amendment protection of the privacy of the home, the Fourth Amendment protection against unreasonable searches and seizures, the Fifth Amendment protection against self-incrimination and the due process clause of the Fourteenth Amendment.

20 Both due process and privacy have so many uses that my tentative hypothesis can never cover all of them. Privacy has been described as a private interest, a public good, a recent invention, a cross-cultural phenomenon, as a right, a liberty, a value, an expectation, a practice, referring to the right to withdraw, to be left alone, to the control over information about oneself, to contextual integrity, informational self-determination, personal autonomy, a relational good, a condition for public autonomy in the public sphere etc. Computer scientists tend to equate privacy with data privacy and data security, location privacy, anonymity, pseudonymity, unobservability and unlinkability. Due process is often related to fair trial and equality of arms but is articulated in a broad variety of ways.

21 Thus, conceptually, due process and privacy can sometimes overlap. This was the case in *Whalen v. Roe*, 429 U.S. 589 (1977), where the right to privacy was derived from the due process clause of the Fourteenth Amendment. However, in later decisions, the court has preferred to derive the right to privacy from other provisions, such as the Fourth and Fifth Amendments.

22 "'Amongst us, nobody should be the best; but if somebody is, let him be somewhere else, with other people" [Heraclitus, fragment 121]. For why should nobody be the best? Because with that, the contest would dry up and the permanent basis of life in the Hellenic state would be endangered. [...] That is the kernel of the

Hellenic idea of competition: it loathes a monopoly of predominance and fears the dangers of this [...]' (Nietzsche 2006: 98), As Nietzsche argues the aversion of a 'monopoly of predominance' pre-dates modernity.

23 The political dimension of fundamental rights is explored by Vincent (2010). When fundamental rights are conceptualised as belonging to a regime of moral universality their political dimension is often neglected. However, this is not to say that fundamental rights are merely *political* tools. As *legal* rights they are subjected to legal requirements and obligations that are independent of politics. See Gutwirth et al 2008.

24 Even though some would argue that this is exactly what happened in *Roe v. Wade*, 410 U.S. 113, 153 (1973), when the decision regarding abortion was protected by bodily privacy. That which is protected by privacy is very contextual and changes over time. For instance, from the contemporary perspective it is quite baffling that in 1868 a husband would not be prosecuted for whipping his wife because the judge deemed it inappropriate that the state would interfere in the private sphere (*State v. Rhodes*, 61 N.C. 453). See also the salient commentary of Gutwirth and de Hert (2005) on a judgment of the European Court of Human Rights (ECHR) regarding sadomasochistic practices and the limits to the right to privacy: *K A and A D v Belgium* (applications nos 42758/98 and 45558/99) 17 February 2005.

25 In his *Monadology*, Leibniz argues that everything that exists does so insofar as it perceives. According to Leibniz, perception is not limited to humans or even to living beings. The tree, the rock, the clock and the dog: they all perceive. This should not be understood as some animism or anthropomorphism. Perception is the way in which a body relates to the world and should be 'carefully distinguished from awareness or consciousness' (Leibniz 2004: §14). Contrary to Descartes, Leibniz does not distinguish two substances (corporeal substance and mental substance) but only one substance: the monad. Every monad is characterised by its unique way of perceiving the world. Deleuze rearticulates Leibniz's philosophy of perception by relating it to Uexküll's biosemiotics and Fechner's psychophysics: 'The tiniest of all animals has glimmers that cause it to recognize its food, its enemies, and sometimes its partner. If life implies a soul, it is because proteins already attest to an activity of perception, discrimination, and distinction [...]. If life has a soul, it is because it perceives, distinguishes or discriminates, and because a whole world of animal psychology is first of all a psychology of perception. In most cases, the soul gets along quite well with very few clear or distinguished perceptions: the soul of the tick has three, including a perception of light, an olfactory perception of its prey, and a tactile perception of the best place to burrow, while everything else in the great expanse of Nature, which the tick nevertheless conveys, is only a numbness, a dust of tiny, dark, and scattered perceptions. [..] Whence the possibility for an admittedly summary classification of monads as functions of their perceptive qualities: there are almost naked monads, remembering monads, and reflexive or reasonable monads. Fechner, another of the great disciples of Leibniz, and the founder of a psychophysics inseparable from the spiritual mechanisms of the monadic soul, does not hesitate to develop classifications endlessly, from vertigo or dizziness to luminous life' (Deleuze 1993: 92).

26 Note 11. The standard reference for coexisting with a 'companion species' is Haraway (2008). The search for a fruitful way of coexistence between algorithms

and humans is nicely illustrated by the following observation of Andreas Calianos, an investment strategist: '[A]t the end of the day the value that's produced, ideally, cannot be ascribed simply to either the algorithm or the human. We're working together in concert to come up with something better than either one could do separately' (Funnell 2012).

27 For the distinction between unlabelled and labelled data, see Chapter 2 by van Otterlo. In the 'parable of the three robotic dogs', with which this introductory chapter opens, the second robotic dog is presented with so-called 'labelled data'. The family points to passers-by and *labels* them either as 'suspect types' or 'non-suspect types'. The dog has to infer a model from these labelled examples to categorise future, unlabelled, instances. This is called supervised learning. The robotic dog of the third family is not presented with such labelled examples, but is asked to discern four categories in the passers-by it observes. Discovery of structures in a data set in which the categories are not predefined is called unsupervised learning.

28 Machine learning experiments try to evaluate the performance of a model or learning algorithm on a particular data set. They 'bear some similarity to experiments in physics in that *machine learning experiments pose questions about models that we try to answer by means of measurements on data*' (Flach 2012: 343–44, original emphasis). Gathering many experiments in one database would ideally help to create 'a clear overview of algorithms and their performance on various datasets' (Vanschoren 2008–2012).

29 See the Rashomon effect (n 14).

30 See for example http://mlcomp.org/. Under the heading of 'Frequently asked questions', the first question is: 'What is the problem with machine learning these days?', followed by the answer: 'Anyone who has worked with machine learning knows that it's a zoo. There are a dazzling array of methods published at conferences each year, leaving the practitioner, who just wants to choose the best method for his/her task, baffled.' The site tries to address this problem by offering a service to compare different machine learning algorithms: 'MLcomp is a free website for *objectively comparing* machine learning programs across various datasets for multiple problem domains: (1) Do a comprehensive evaluation of your new algorithm: Upload your program and run it on existing datasets. Compare the results with those obtained by other programs. (2) Find the best algorithm (program) for your dataset. Upload your dataset and run existing programs on it to see which one works best' (Liang and Abernethy 2010, original emphasis).

31 Introna and Wood (2004) offer an interesting critique of the 'facial recognition vendor test', which is an important tool in assessing the quality of facial recognition systems.

32 In fact, the proposed pragmatism 2.0 is not very new: it is closely related to the meaning in which the American pragmatists, such as William James, used it. It differs, however, from the blunt understanding of pragmatism as 'whatever works best'. As long ago as 1888 Nietzsche critiqued the naivety of such utilitarian pragmatism because it does not take into account the limitations of any perspective on what is useful. Something that seems to be very fruitful today might turn out to be catastrophic from the perspective of tomorrow: 'The value of an action must be judged by its consequences, say the utilitarians: to judge it by its origins implies an impossibility, namely that of *knowing* its origins. But does one know

its consequences? For five steps ahead, perhaps. Who can say what an action will stimulate, excite, provoke? [...] The Utilitarians are naive. And in any case we must first *know what* is useful: here too they look only five steps ahead' (Nietzsche 1999: volume 13, notebook 14 [185]; Nietzsche 1968: 164 [aphorism 291]).

33 The importance of Peirce's pragmatism in understanding of contemporary machine intelligence is explored in more detail by Magnani (2009). He argues that *abductive* reasoning is pivotal both to contemporary machine intelligence and to Peirce's pragmatism.

34 See n 4 for an explanation why in the case of Closer (dog 2) the word 'model' is problematic.

35 Wolpert's *no free lunch* theorems are a series of mathematically quite complicated theorems which can be very roughly be paraphrased as expressing 'that there are no learning algorithms that are always optimal. For every learning algorithm, there exist problems for which it performs worse than others' (van Otterlo 2009: 81).

36 For an example of an influential list of the top 10 most influential data mining algorithms, see Wu et al (2008).

References

Bakhtin, M. M. (1984) *Problems of Dostoevsky's Poetics*, Minneapolis: University of Minnesota Press.

Berns, T. and Rouvroy, A. (2010) 'Le nouveau pouvoir statistique', *Multitudes*, 40: 88–103.

Berry, D. M. (2011) 'The Computational Turn: Thinking About the Digital Humanities'. *Culture Machine*, 12, available at http://www.culturemachine.net (accessed 30 October 2012).

Berry, D. M. (ed.) (2012) *Understanding Digital Humanities: The computational turn and new technology*, London: Palgrave Macmillan.

Breiman, L. (2001) 'Statistical Modeling: The Two Cultures', *Statistical Science*, 16(3): 199–231.

Bynum, T. W. and Moor, J. H. (1998) 'How computers are changing philosophy', in Bynum, T. W. and Moor, J. H. (eds) *The Digital Phoenix: How computers are changing philosophy.* Oxford: Blackwell: 1–14.

Cavalier, R. (2000) 'From the Chair', *APA Newsletter on Philosophy and Computers*, 0(1): 1.

Citron, D. K. (2007) 'Technological Due Process', *Washington University Law Review*, 85: 1249–313.

Coudert, F., de Vries, K. and Kowalewski, J. (2008) 'Legal implications of forensic profiling: of good old dataprotection legislation and novel legal safeguards for due processing', in Geradts, Z. and Sommer, P. (eds) *Forensic Profiling. Deliverable 6.7c of the FIDIS (The Future of Identity in the Information Society) Consortium*, EU Sixth Framework Programme: 38–67, available at http://www.fidis.net (accessed 30 October 2012).

Deleuze, G. (1993) *The Fold: Leibniz and the baroque*, London: Athlone.

Dennett, D. C. (1998) 'The Logical Geography of Computational Approaches: a view from the east pole', *Brainchildren: Essays on designing minds*, Cambridge, MA: MIT Press: 215–34.

Dyson, G. (2012) *Turing's Cathedral. The origins of the digital universe*, New York: Random House.

Elmer, G. (2004) *Profiling Machines: Mapping the personal information economy*, Cambridge, MA: MIT Press.

Ess, C. and Hagengruber, R. (eds) (2011) *The Computational Turn: Past, presents, futures? Proceedings of the First International Conference of the 'International Association for Computing and Philosophy' (IACAP): Celebrating 25 years of Computing and Philosophy (CAP) conferences.* Aarhus, 4–6 July 2011, Münster: MV-Wissenschaft.

Fayyad, U., Piatetsky-Shapiro, G. and Smyth, P. (1996) 'From Data Mining to Knowledge Discovery in Databases', *AI Magazine*, 17(3): 37–54.

Flach, P. (2012) *Machine Learning. The art and science of algorithms that make sense of data*, Cambridge: Cambridge University Press.

Fodor, J. A. (1987) *Psychosemantics: The problem of meaning in the philosophy of mind*, Cambridge, MA: MIT Press.

Ford, K. M., Glymour, C. and Hayes, P. J. (eds) (2006) *Thinking about Android Epistemology*, Cambridge, MA: MIT Press.

Funnell, A. (2012) 'Transcript of the Radio Broadcast of 25 March 2012 of "The Algorithm. Antony Funnell in conversation with Ted Striphas, John MacCormick, Nick Meaney, Michael Kearns and Andreas Calianos"', *Future Tense* available at http://www.abc.net.au/radionational/programs/futuretense/the-algorithm/3901466#transcript (accessed 30 October 2012).

Gellert, R., de Vries, K., de Hert, P. and Gutwirth, S. (2012) 'A Comparative Analysis of Anti-Discrimination and Data Protection Legislations', in B. Custers, T. Zarsky, B. Schermer and T. Calders (eds) *Discrimination and Privacy in the Information Society*, Berlin: Springer: 61–89.

Gutwirth, S. (2002) *Privacy and the Information Age*, Oxford: Rowman & Littlefield.

Gutwirth, S. and de Hert, P. (2005) 'De seks is hard maar seks (dura sex sed sex). Het arrest K.A. en A.D. tegen België', *Panopticon*, (3): 1–14.

Gutwirth, S. and de Hert, P. (2008) 'Regulating profiling in a democratic constitutional state', in Hildebrandt, M. and Gutwirth, S. (eds) *Profiling the European Citizen. Cross-disciplinary perspectives*, Dordrecht: Springer: 288–309.

Gutwirth, S., de Hert, P. and de Sutter, L. (2008) 'The trouble with technology regulation from a legal perspective. Why Lessig's "optimal mix" will not work', in Brownsword, R. and Yeung, K. (eds) *Regulating Technologies. Legal futures, regulatory frames and technological fixes*, Oxford: Hart Publishers: 193–218.

Guyon, I., von Luxburg, U. and Williamson, R. C. (2011) 'Clustering: Science or art?', available at http://users.cecs.anu.edu.au/~williams/papers/P185.pdf (accessed 30 October 2012).

Haraway, D. J. (2008) *When Species Meet*, Minneapolis: Minnesota University Press.

Harizanov, V., Goethe, N. and Friend, M. (eds) (2007) *Introduction to the Philosophy and Mathematics of Algorithmic Learning Theory*, Dordrecht: Springer.

Harman, G. and Kulkarni, S. (2007) *Reliable Reasoning. Induction and statistical learning theory*, Cambridge, MA: MIT Press.

Hert, P. de and Gutwirth, S. (2006) 'Privacy, data protection and law enforcement. opacity of the individual and transparency of power', in Claes, E., Duff, A. and Gutwirth, S. (eds) *Privacy and the Criminal Law*, Antwerp/Oxford: Intersentia: 61–104.

Hildebrandt, M. (2008) 'Defining profiling: a new type of knowledge?', in Hildebrandt M, and Gutwirth S, (eds) *Profiling and the Identity of the European Citizen*, Dordrecht: Springer: 39–50.

Hobbes, T. (1998/1651) *Leviathan*, Oxford: Oxford University Press.

Introna, L. D. and Wood, D. (2004) 'Picturing Algorithmic Surveillance: The politics of facial recognition systems', *Surveillance Society*, 2(2/3): 177–98.

James, W. (1920) *A Pluralistic Universe: Hibbert lectures at Manchester College on the present situation in philosophy*, London: Longmans, Green & Co.

Kant, I. (1964/1785) *Groundwork of the Metaphysics of Morals*, 3rd edn, New York: Harper & Row.

Leibniz, G. W. (1890) *Die philosophischen Schriften von G.W. Leibniz*, vol 7, Berlin: Weidmannsche Buchhandlung.

Leibniz, G. W. (1999/1688) 'De arte characteristica ad perficiendas scientias ratione nitentes', in Schepers, H, Schneiders, W. and Kabitz, W. (eds) *Gottfried Wilhelm Leibniz. Sämtliche Schriften und Briefe. Reihe 6: Philosophische Schriften. Band 4: 1677–Juni 1690*, Münster: Akademie Verlag: 909–915.

Leibniz, G. W. (2004) *The Principles of Philosophy known as Monadology*, available at http://www.earlymoderntexts.com/ (accessed 30 October 2012).

Liang, P. and Abernethy, J. (2010) *MLcomp*, available at http://mlcomp.org/ (accessed 30 October 2012).

Magnani, L. (2009) *Abductive Cognition. The epistemological and eco-cognitive dimensions of hypothetical reasoning*, Berlin: Springer.

Merleau-Ponty, M. (2002) *Phenomenology of Perception*, London: Routledge.

Minsky, M. (1988) *Society of Mind*, New York: Simon & Schuster.

Morel, P. (2007) 'Catalogue of the Exhibition "Architecture au-delà des formes, le tournant computationnel" ["Architecture beyond form – the computational turn"]', Février–Avril 2007, Maison de l'Architecture et de la Ville, Marseille.

Nagel, T. (1974) 'What is it Like to be a Bat?', *Philosophical Review*, 83(4): 435–50.

Nietzsche, F. W. (1968) *The Will to Power*, New York: Vintage Books.

Nietzsche, F. W. (1999) *Sämtliche Werke: Kritische Studienausgabe in 15 Einzelbänden*, München: Deutscher Taschenbuch Verlag.

Nietzsche, F. W. (2006) 'Homer's contest (1872)', in Ansell-Pearson, K. and Large, D. (eds) *The Nietzsche reader*, Malden, MA: Blackwell: 95–100.

Nissenbaum, H. F. (2009) *Privacy in Context: Technology, policy, and the integrity of social life*, Stanford, CA: Stanford Law Books.

Pickering, A. (2010) *The Cybernetic Brain: Sketches of another future*, Chicago, IL: University of Chicago Press.

Pignarre, P. and Stengers, I. (2011) *Capitalist Sorcery: Breaking the spell*, Basingstoke: Palgrave Macmillan.

Putnam, H. (1975) 'Minds and Machines', *Philosophical papers, volume II. Mind, language, and reality*, Cambridge: Cambridge University Press: 362–85.

Ramsay, S. (2003) 'Toward an Algorithmic Criticism', *Literary and Linguistic Computing*, 18(2): 167–74.

Rorty, R. (ed.) (1967) *The Linguistic Turn: Recent essays in philosophical method*, Chicago, IL: University of Chicago Press.

Rosenblatt, F. (1957) *The Perceptron, a perceiving and recognizing automaton (Report No 85-460-1)*. Cornell: Cornell Aeronautical Laboratory.

Scheutz, M. (2002) 'Computationalism—the next generation', in Scheutz, M. (ed.) *Computationalism: New directions*, Cambridge, MA: MIT Press: 1–21.

Searle, J. (1980) 'Minds, Brains and Programs', *Behavioral and Brain Sciences*, 3(3): 417–57.

Selfridge, O. G. (1959) 'Pandemonium: a paradigm for learning', in Blake, D. V. and Uttley, A. M. (eds) *Proceedings of the Symposium on Mechanisation of Thought Processes*, London: HM Stationery Office: 511–29.

Skitka, L. J. Mosier, K. L., Burdick, M. and Rosenblatt, B. (2000) 'Automation Bias and Errors: Are crews better than individuals?', *International Journal of Aviation Psychology*, 10: 85–97.

Solove, D. J. (2006) 'A Taxonomy of Privacy', *University of Pennsylvania Law Review*, 154(3): 477–560.

Solove, D. J., Rotenberg, M. and Schwartz, P. M. (eds) (2006) *Information Privacy Law*, New York: Aspen.

Steinbock, D. (2005) 'Data Matching, Data Mining, and Due Process', *Georgia Law Review*, 40(1): 1–84.

Stengers, I. (2005) 'Introductory Notes on an Ecology of Practices', *Cultural Studies Review*, 11(1): 183–96.

Stengers, I. (2010) 'Including non-humans in political theory: opening Pandora's Box', in B. Braun and S. J. Whatmore (eds) *Political Matter: Technoscience, democracy, and public life*, Minneapolis: University of Minnesota Press: 3–33.

Thagard, P. (1990) 'Philosophy and Machine Learning', *Canadian Journal of Philosophy*, 20(2): 261–76.

van Otterlo, M. (2009) *The Logic of Adaptive Behavior: Knowledge representation and algorithms for the Markov decision process framework in first-order domains*, Amsterdam: IOS Press.

Vanschoren, J. (2008–2012) *The Open Experiment Database. Machine learning. Open*, Leuven University and Leiden University, available at http://expdb.cs.kuleuven.be/expdb/ (accessed 30 October 2012).

Vapnik, V. N. (1995) *The Nature of Statistical Learning Theory*, New York: Springer.

Vapnik, V. N. (2006) *Estimation of Dependences based on Empirical Data. Reprint of 1982 edition. Empirical inference science. Afterword of 2006*, New York: Springer.

Varenne, F. (2011) *Modéliser le social – Méthodes fondatrices et évolutions récentes*, Paris: Dunod.

Vincent, A. (2010) *The Politics of Human Rights*, Oxford: Oxford University Press.

Vries, K. de (2009) 'Real time adaptivity from cybernetics to intelligent environments: rewriting the history of ubiquitous computing', in Schneider, M., Kröner, A., Encinas Alvarado, J. C., Higuera, A. G., Augusto, J.C., Cook, D. A. (eds) *Intelligent Environments 2009. Proceedings of the 5th International Conference on Intelligent Environments, from Ambient Intelligence and Smart Environments*, IOS Press: 517–23.

Warren, S. D. and Brandeis, L. D. (1890) 'The Right to Privacy', *Harvard Law Review*, 4(5): 193–220.

Wittgenstein, L. (1997) *Philosophical Investigations*, Oxford: Blackwell.

Wolpert, D. H. (1996) 'The Lack of a priori Distinction between Learning Algorithms', *Neural Computation*, 8(7): 1341–90.

Wu, X., Kumar, V., Quinlan, J. R., Ghosh, J., Yang, Q., Motoda, H. (2008) 'Top 10 Algorithms in Data Mining', *Knowledge and Information Systems*, 14(1): 1–37.

Part I

Data science

2

A machine learning view on profiling

*Martijn van Otterlo**

Introduction

> To the right and to the left as in mirrors, to the right and to the left through the glass walls I see others like myself, other rooms like my own, other clothes like my own, movements like mine, duplicated thousands of times. This invigorates me; I see myself as a part of an enormous, vigorous, united body; and what precise beauty!
>
> (Zamyatin 1924/1993: 31–34)

Our current information age is shifting the concept of *privacy* day by day. Privacy may eventually be a futile notion, drowned in an ocean of *big data* (Bollier and Firestone 2010).[1] The main eroding forces on privacy include the amount of information that is available, the data hunger of public and private institutions, the (perceived) threat of terrorist attacks and the corresponding business opportunities of companies, as well as the rise of *smart algorithms* (Nilsson 2010) automatically to gather, store, analyse, and utilise enormous amounts of data.[2]

When it comes to big data and privacy, we can find examples in every newspaper on an almost daily basis, ranging from medical records, chip cards for public transport, smart energy meters and biometric data in passports. Many systems are tacitly introduced into our societies and generate huge amounts of private information about individuals. When people talk about negative aspects of privacy they often employ terms such as 'Big Brother' and 'Orwellian', to connect to the idea of an all-seeing eye overseeing every bit of information we (have to) reveal about ourselves. Sometimes we are aware of this modern electronic version of Bentham's panopticon and consciously think about the fact that we are being watched continuously, and sometimes act accordingly. Mostly, however, privacy is seen as attached only to the information we reveal, or have to give up, about ourselves to governments, companies and other parties. Our concerns are often solely about what personal information, that is, information attached to a specific identity, is out there, who can see it, who owns it, and how that information is used to control, track, monitor or even manipulate us. Many studies concerning the legal aspects of such information have been conducted, and counter-measures exist in the form of *privacy preserving* algorithms.

Attaching data and information to specific individuals is related to *identification* and *control*, and it is here where the connection to Orwell's *1984* and its 'telescreens' is appropriate. However, in the context of big data, the concept of *profiling* makes it possible to go beyond the individual level (that is, identity; cf de Vries 2010) and track, monitor, measure and manipulate various groups of individuals. Profiling amounts to building (statistical) models from large amounts of data from many individuals, after which the profiles themselves can be exploited to derive novel information about particular individuals. For example, even though I may not know the writer Murakami, a quick look at my book purchases on the internet may reveal that it is very likely that I will appreciate his writing. This aspect of privacy comes much closer to the dystopian novel *We* by Zamyatin (see the opening quote in this chapter) than to Orwell's book. Indeed, one can imagine walking through one of the streets Zamyatin describes, filled with glass houses, and observing many citizens at the same time, seeing correlated behavioural patterns; in other words, building profiles. Extending the metaphor, even if I – as an individual – replace all the glass in my own house with wood (that is, protect my data) it would still be possible to build profiles of all my neighbours and derive information about me for exploitation, manipulation or control by third parties.

Profiling is enabled by progress in faster computers, the availability of data, the internet and, especially, smart *algorithms* to process, understand and employ the data. These algorithms stem from the field of *artificial intelligence* (AI), and include *machine learning* (ML) and *data mining* (DM). Many people do have experience with some of these techniques, for example when Amazon or online music stores make recommendations based on previous purchases or click-data from different users. Online stores can use their customer data to 'guess' that you may like a particular product you have never seen before. Privacy as in *who-can-see-what-information* has always been an issue and described for decades, eg concerning the *database society* (Warner and Stone 1970), yet the broader possibilities and implications of smart algorithms and profiling have not yet been well studied, especially not from the viewpoint of privacy (but see Hildebrandt and Gutwirth 2008c). In order to facilitate such studies into so-called *ambient law* (Hildebrandt and Koops 2010) and encourage a debate on the implications[3] of profiling, we highlight aspects of data science and smart algorithms, with a light emphasis on *probabilistic* approaches.

Elements of profiling in data sciences

First, however, we must consider several important notions.

Data and behaviours

In order to understand ML approaches to profiling, we need to distinguish data and behaviour, on the one hand, and persons and profiles, on the other. Nowadays there are many data available and they come from various sources. Put very simply, governments want plenty of data for security and control, companies want to make money and scientists want interesting data. Furthermore, people like to share information on social networks, list sites and blogs. Computers, and especially the internet, enable the generation and storage of massive amounts of data *in electronic form* which makes size and location relatively meaningless. In contrast, decades ago scientists, companies and governments were relying on manual labour[4] and annotation to obtain useful data. A notorious example is the East German security agency *Stasi*, with a large part of the population physically gathering physical information about citizens.[5] Companies such as Google and Facebook have greatly expanded their automated data gathering efforts.[6] Many data come from people leaving electronic traces when they perform ordinary daily activities, that is, services provided by companies, or travelling on public transport. Companies harvest data mainly because they can use them for targeted advertisements[7] and governments are much concerned with surveillance.[8] Increasingly, many data are supplied and maintained by people themselves, in the form of personal pages on social networks, life blogging and making lists, Flickr photo accounts, general blogs, chat rooms and Skyping and many more methods.

With *data* we consider all pieces of information in electronic databases, on the internet and so on. However, in the context of profiling, we talk more specifically about *user data* and *user behaviour*. User data are any set of information pieces that can be attributed to the *same entity*, eg network account details or some facts filled in on a web page. User behaviour is defined similarly, but now the pieces of information are *actions*, for example the path walked in front of a surveillance camera or click behaviour on a web page. Often it is not necessary to distinguish between actions and facts and we can combine all information into one *record*. De Vries (2010) calls these pieces informational *shibboleths* and we discuss aspects close to her so-called *algorithmically constructed* shibboleths below. Various data pieces can become useful together if they can be attributed to the same (virtual) entity.

Persons and profiles

An important dichotomy is that between data at an *individual level* and those at an *aggregated level*. The first deals with personal data (of any kind) of a specific individual, consisting of individual pieces of information. The second level is the profiling level, comprised of (statistical) models that model correlations between pieces of information appearing in the individuals' data, causal patterns and general rules that apply to a subset of the individuals; for example, those people *who have bought X and Y are more likely to buy product Z if they have already looked at product W*. Profiles provide means to *infer* knowledge about an individual who is not actually observed.[9]

The crucial difference is that the information at the individual level is actually *observed*, that is, it is factual knowledge. Knowledge at the profiling level is not usually available to the individual user and is often not observed. Instead, the profile is *applied to* the individual user to infer additional facts, preferences or assumed intentions (eg to buy certain product). Thus, we aim mostly at what Hildebrandt (2008) calls *non-distributive* profiles, eg a checklist for psychopaths in which the profile lists properties that will not hold for all people who will most *likely* belong to that profile. An interesting fact is that, in order to apply a profile to an individual, one generally does not need to identify the individual with a real person; some observed facts may be enough to predict what is needed (see Neudecker 2010 for interesting examples). By the same token, identification can be useful to *link* information belonging to the same individual.

Hiding personal information will often not work, as the service's provider (eg Facebook) owns all data anyway and there are many ways in which additional personal information may be revealed by other users, applications and so on. In one famous case in 2006, the internet provider AOL released *anonymised* data of 20 million search keywords of over 650,000 users. However, users often provide much information about themselves in their search queries. The *New York Times* successfully discovered the identity of several searchers and exposed user number 4417749 as Thelma Arnold, a 62-year-old Georgian widow.[10] In some cases, privacy preserving techniques can be useful, although they are no safeguard against profiling.

Automated profiling: activity recognition

Profiling[11] is the formation of general models on the basis of data from a number of individual users. The *automated way* version of this amounts to *machine learning* and *data mining*. In addition to information available about people in databases and on the internet, a large number of additional *sensors* are available for increased data gathering and behaviour monitoring. These sensors include RFID tags, video cameras (eg CCTV), GPS signals and mobile phones. A common feature of these devices is that they are widely available in our daily life, as opposed to specialised or expensive sensors such as ultrasonic sensors or brain scanners. A subfield of AI particularly interested in learning profiles from such rich (sensor) data is *activity recognition* (Yang 2009; Turaga et al 2008; Cao 2006). Here we view activity recognition as the main research area subsuming profiling. Its aims are to *interpret the sensor readings of humans (or moving things) and tell us in high-level, human understandable terms what is going on*.

In recent years there has been a growing interest in privacy aspects of such automated procedures for profiling and activity recognition.[12] 'Profiling is a matter of pattern recognition, which is comparable to categorisation, generalisation and stereotyping. To understand what is new about profiling we must differentiate between classification (*ex ante* categorisation) and clustering (*ex post* categorisation)' (Hildebrandt and Gutwirth 2008a). Classification is a classical ML setting in which some function is learned from data. The *ex post categorisation* approaches are more aimed at finding corresponding (behavioural) patterns among users, finding interesting new knowledge and clusters of people who share certain features. In the latter, the feedback (or guidance) is less related to *what* we want to learn (eg a classification), but more related to *why* we want to learn it (eg what are the interesting characteristics of people who are likely to buy my product).

Automated learning has been extensively applied to learn models of users and their behaviour and we can only scratch the surface of what is going on. Applications of behaviour modelling, recognition and prediction can be found in video surveillance, robot control, social networks, physical movement tracking, online shopping, computer games and many more (Turaga et al 2008).

Well known profiling applications are webshops and search engines. Most people will have seen the recommendations of books or music or web advertisements based on search behaviour. People are often quite surprised how accurate they can be and the occasional blunder may be rationalised afterwards. Many systems are web based (Torre 2009; Perkowitz et al 2004) and especially social networks are a gold mine for ML. Using information in photo collections, Singla et al (2008) learn *rules* to classify persons on the photos into *spouse, friend* etc. Commonsense background knowledge, eg *parents are older than their children* and *spouses have opposite genders* can be utilised to help learning efforts.

Many approaches are based on *video* as input, encouraged by the increasing number of cameras in public and private spaces and advances in *computer vision* technology (Le et al 2010). In addition to monitoring CCTV cameras in underground stations an interesting example can be found in care of the elderly. The *GerHome* project uses a replica of a home for the elderly, full of cameras and other sensors, and aims at learning from inhabitants' behaviours. For example, usually when people move from the kitchen to the living room, they will sit on a chair, but if Mr X is staying in between – not in a standing position – then it is likely that something is wrong. In a technically related application, Damen and Hogg (2009) learn typical patterns of *bicycle theft*.

Other kinds of approach that will become increasingly important are based on *location-based sensors* such as GPS. Applications such as Google Maps can already make use of location to recommend a good pizza place in the immediate vicinity. These features can also be used to learn typical behavioural patterns. Liao et al (2005) learned to extract and label a person's activities and significant places from GPS traces. Behaviour profiles were learned from complex relations between readings, activities and significant places and certain areas on the map could be labelled as being related to work, sleep, leisure, visiting, picking-up car etc.

Automated computational methods for profiling

Machine learning is a *branch of AI that seeks to develop computer systems that improve their performance automatically with experience*, taking inspiration from computer science, statistics, optimisation and psychology. The terms *pattern recognition, machine learning, data mining* and *optimisation* are often used interchangeably. We use the general term *machine learning* and take it to stand for any methodology and set of techniques that finds novel patterns and knowledge in data, and generates *models* (eg profiles) that can be used for effective predictions about the data. A classic textbook is Mitchell (1997) and a more recent book with the same scope is Alpaydin (2004). The more recent *relational* setting is surveyed by de Raedt (2008). Current approaches are firmly grounded in *statistics* and *probabilistic models*, more generally called *probabilistic graphical models* (Koller and Friedman 2009). *Data mining* as a separate technique is treated in Witten and Frank (2005). *Reinforcement learning*, and (pro)active settings are extensively discussed elsewhere (Wiering and van Otterlo 2012; van Otterlo 2009). In this next section, we discuss some *representational* and *algorithmic* aspects of ML, illustrated by some specific techniques.

Representational aspects

'You can only learn what you can represent': every piece of information employed by a computer, or generated by it as a pattern or a model, should be *represented* in a formal *language* (see Sowa 1999 for an introduction). In ML, we distinguish between an *example language* and a *hypothesis language*. The first is used to represent the observations of the data and the second is used to represent hypotheses about the data or, more generally, models (profiles).

An *example language* consists of a set of *features*. Data about a single person are a set of features with their *values*. Examples are that the person with ID = 246876 is *vegetarian, married*, is sitting on chair number 23D and that he (another feature) is Dutch. The feature *vegetarian* is called *Boolean* because it can have only one of the values *true* or *false*. A set of feature—value pairs represents a *record* in a database or, equivalently, as a row or column in a spreadsheet program and is called an *example* in ML. This type of representation is called *propositional*, or *attribute value* and a *data set* corresponds to a complete table in a database.

Whereas the example language describes individuals, and usually consists of *observed* data, the *hypothesis language* describes general patterns that hold for a group of individuals. We consider a profile as a construction in the hypothesis language, that is, *a model*. A large variety of languages exist and we treat some of them in more detail below. A generic, simple hypothesis language is the example language itself, extended with simple *logical connectives*. For example, we could have the following expression in the hypothesis language: (A): (*vegetarian=yes* AND *gender=female* AND *nationality=Dutch*). This expression models all female Dutch vegetarians.

More complex models could, for example, state (B): *people from the Middle East 'usually' do not eat pork*. This type of model requires more sophisticated expressions, incorporating *probabilistic* information. In such models, merely assuming that individual X is married and from the Middle East might allow us to infer with some confidence that he will not eat pork – even though this is *not* factual knowledge (that is, we have no explicit record stating that fact). In general, a profile enables us to make (probabilistic) *predictions* about an individual, backed by knowledge about the distribution in the population. Profiles can consist of *rules* or *correlations* between features, but they can also divide the group of individuals up into a number of subgroups in which the members share certain properties or they can be complex functions that compute a value or class label based on certain features.

The relation between models and examples is intuitively that *a model holds for an example*, eg model A holds for all female Dutch vegetarians. In technical terms, this is called a *coverage relation*; it also means that the model is *more general* than a specific example (eg it holds for other examples too). In the same way, models can be compared in terms of *how general* they are. For example, if we drop *vegetarian=yes* from model A we get a more general model. Rules A and B above can be seen as *local* models, because presumably they will be part of larger models. In addition to generality, the *model complexity* is important; models can be complex (complicated interactions between features) or simple and, in general, models are preferably only *as complex as needed* to model the data.

An additional representational aspect of ML is *background knowledge*. This type of knowledge includes 'everything' that is (effectively) available about a certain domain. This includes commonsense knowledge in the form of rules. This type of knowledge can be used to answer more complex queries about a domain or to build more complex models. For example, a very simple piece of knowledge expressing the set of countries belonging to the Middle East (eg Egypt, Lebanon etc) can help to build models in which the more general concept Middle East (that is, a new feature) can be used to group sets of observed features expressing only countries. Such forms of background knowledge form the basis of so-called *ontologies*, which relate pieces of knowledge to each other. For some models, the use of background knowledge is less supported (eg in neural networks) but, for others, for example *relational* learning techniques, it is natural (de Raedt 2008). Lately, interest in *probabilistic* ontologies has been increasing (Poole et al 2009).

So far, we have dealt with *propositional* knowledge representations and models. However, for many domains it is desirable to have more powerful representations that can deal with explicit *relations between individuals*. This is useful for modelling social network relations, but also for example for pedigrees concerning blood types. In the latter, the blood type of one person is probabilistically dependent on the blood type of his or her parents. This constitutes a *relation* between features of one individual and those of others. *Relational representations* of knowledge can make these aspects explicit. Hypothesis languages for these systems are based on *first-order logic* in which one can state things such as $\forall x \exists y$: parent (y, x), meaning *for all persons x, there is a person y who is the parent of x*, or *everybody has a parent*. These representations also enable new things such as *collective classification*, in which one can classify people in a social network *in the context of how his or her friends are classified*.

These representations are beyond the scope of this chapter and we refer to de Raedt (2008) for pointers to the literature. They are important to mention for three reasons:, first, they are becoming widespread in AI; second, many ML systems use them (eg the examples on the photo categorisation and the bike theft we mentioned earlier); and, third, and most importantly, many of them are based on the exact same graphical models we discuss later in this chapter.

Models

One way to distinguish the many models appearing in ML is by looking at *what* they model. Here we return to the difference between the *ex ante* and *ex post* categorisation (see earlier in this chapter). Many ML models are based on *ex ante* categorisation, for example classification and regression techniques. They are focused on mapping examples (eg individuals) onto an a priori defined set of *class labels*. Examples include *neural networks, support vector machines* and *decision trees*. These models are often called *discriminative* models and they are used to learn a desired input–output mapping; for example to map people into distinct categories (see Anrig et al (2008) and the ML textbooks cited above). In contrast, as Hildebrandt (2008) describes, for profiling other settings are more relevant: the *ex post* category. In ML terms, these include clustering techniques, but more generally models that *capture the data* in some way and which highlight interesting patterns or correlation in those data. These include (association) rules and especially probabilistic models, such as Bayesian networks, which can represent causal and probabilistic patterns in the data. These models generally fall into the category of *descriptive* or *generative* models.

An important thing about models is that they usually have *qualitative* and *quantitative* parts. The qualitative part may express some (causal) relations between features, for example that a person's *length* feature depends on the *gender* feature. The quantitative aspect expresses *how strong* this dependency is. Most models have some form of *weights, parameters* or *probabilities* and these quantities provide the flexibility of the (qualitative) model class.

Rules and patterns

A simple form of models consists of *local patterns*, or *association rules*. In this case, the hypothesis language gives rise to *rules* of the form: IF feature(1) =value(1) AND feature(2)=value(2) AND ...feature(n)=value(n) THEN feature(n+1)=value(n+1). This rule says that if some features (1 to n) have specific values, then we can *infer* that another feature (n+1) has some specific value. In probabilistic models, we would say that feature (n+1) has value (n+1) with a probability *p*. Many rule learning and data mining approaches are based on this type of local model. A similar device is the *frequent itemset* often employed in data mining. A frequent itemset is a set of features with their value that occurs 'often enough'. For example, in shopping scenarios, it might be useful to know that people who buy *chips* will often also buy *beer* and *wine*. Frequent itemsets are dependent on a threshold (eg what exactly is 'frequent'?) and can provide useful information about *common* patterns in examples. Both rules and itemsets are *local* models, often used within larger (classification) models or they provide the components of joint models such as Bayesian networks.

Probabilistic graphical models: Bayesian networks

Since profiling deals with uncertain data, unreliable sources and uncertainty in what it can predict about users and their behaviour, models that can explicitly deal with *probabilistic* aspects are desired. For example, a webshop might have plenty of knowledge about its customers, although most of it is not very certain and therefore the webshop can only make predictions about *how likely* it is for someone to buy a product. One of the core models in ML is the class of the *probabilistic graphical models* (Koller and Friedman 2009), which includes *Bayesian networks*.

For profiling purposes, we are not so much interested in learning a specific classification function; a more general model of the data themselves is desired. The problem, however, is that a set of features gives rise to an enormous number of different combinations of these features because of all the possible dependencies among them. Estimating distinct probabilities for all these possibilities, so-called *joint probabilities*, is almost impossible because it leads to huge models and long computations. To illustrate this, take the following (Boolean) features about an automobile engine:[13]

*p*1: The starter motor is ok
*p*2: The starter motor cranks the engine when the starter switch is turned on
*p*3: The fuel system is ok
*p*4: The car starts when the starter switch is turned on

These four statements are obviously related. We can assume that *p*4 is dependent on the other three and if we knew that it was false, it would tell us something about the other three. Now, the number of different feature–value combinations is $2^4 = 16$, because we can have two different values for each feature (eg if we take not-$p1$ to stand for $p1 = false$, then the combinations are $p1,p2,p3,p4$ or not-$p1,p2,p3,p4$ or not-$p1$,not-$p2,p3,p4$ etc). A full probability model would have to represent (and learn) these 16 values. If we expand the number of features to only 20, we already arrive at more than a million (2^{20}) different combinations and this number grows very quickly.[14] In some small domains, such as this one, a domain expert might be able to specify all numbers, from which (using probability theory) one could compute probabilities for situations such as 'the car starts and we only know that the fuel system is ok for sure'. If, instead, we assumed that all features are *independent*, we would only have to remember the four probabilities $P(p1)$, $P(p2)$, $P(p3)$ and $P(p3)$, from which we could calculate the probability of eg not-$p1,p2,p3,p4$ as $(1 - P(p1)) \times P(p2) \times P(p3) \times P(p4)$. A natural assumption is that, in most common domains, the features will neither be completely independent nor completely dependent on all other features and we can assume the number of relevant probabilities to represent falls in between 4 and 16 in our domain. *Bayesian networks* are capable of making these dependencies (and independencies) explicit.

A *Bayesian network* consists of *nodes*, which represent the features in our domain and *arrows*, which represent *direct influences among features* but also indicate certain probabilistic *independencies* among them. The only restriction is that there can be no cycles in the model (that is, no endless loops of arrows). The Bayesian network for our automobile domain is depicted in Figure 1 (left). For example, the probability of $p4$ (car starts) does not depend on the probability of $p1$ (starter motor ok) *if* we already know (or we are given) $p2$ (car cranks) and $p3$ (fuel ok). In the model we can see this because there is no direct link between $p1$ and $p4$. Furthermore, if we know $p1$ then we do not possess more information about $p4$ if we already know $p2$ and $p3$. Technically, the probability of $p4$ is *conditionally independent* of $p1$, *given $p4$'s parents*,[15] $p2$ and $p3$.

Now, instead of the full joint distribution of 16 probabilities, the network only contains 8 probabilities and they are kept in local probability distributions

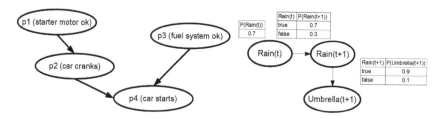

Figure 1 (left) Bayesian network, (right) dynamic Bayesian network (with CPTs)

at each node, called *conditional probability tables* (CPT). For example, since the probability of $p4$ depends on the features $p2$ and $p3$, the CPT in $p4$ consists of the values (where $P(X|Y)$ stands for *the probability of X given that we know that Y holds*) $P(p4|p2,p3)$, $P(p4|\text{not-}p2,p3)$, $P(p4|p2,\text{not-}p3)$ and $P(p4|\text{not-}p2,\text{not-}p3)$. For the node $p2$ we only need two values (the different states of $p1$) and for the nodes $p1$ and $p3$ we need only one value each (the *unconditional* probability of being true, also called the *prior*). Using probability theory, we can compute all 16 joint probabilities from just these 8 values. How these CPTs come about in the presence of data is discussed in the next sections. Coming back to the previous discussion; for Bayesian networks, the *topology* of the network (nodes and connections) is the *qualitative* part, and the CPTs form the *quantitative* part. Bayesian networks are expressive enough to model *any* probability distribution over a given set of variables. Another main reason for their widespread use is that efficient algorithms for inference and learning exist.

Bayesian networks represent the base model for the case where all features can – in principle – be observed and support for various inference mechanisms. With the right algorithms, networks of considerable size (more than hundreds of nodes) can be used. Several extensions exist, for example in the form of *Markov networks*, where the influences are modelled through *undirected* arrows, allowing cycles. Some extensions add a *temporal* dimension. Many domains have features that are measured at different points in time, eg we can have a feature visited(t) denoting that a user has visited our web page at time t. Now, presumably, a visit at a next time (visited(t+1)) will depend on visited(t). Figure 1 (right) shows an example of a *dynamic Bayesian network* in which the probability of rain is dependent on yesterday's weather, and the probability of bringing an umbrella today will depend only on today's weather. A third extension are *unobserved* features in the model. For example, *hidden Markov models* are well known in *speech recognition*, where the observed features are the *phonemes* (that is, sounds in the speech signal) and the unobserved features are the words that are spoken. Such networks model the probability distribution over a sequence of phonemes, *conditioned on* the word (which is not observed, but can only be inferred).

Distances, kernels and prototypes

Here we briefly discuss *instance-based* and *distance-based* methods. Instead of building an explicit model of the probability distribution of the data, as before, we can look at the *similarity* between examples. The simplest way to do this is to consider each set of features (an example) as a *vector* in n dimensions, where n is the number of features. Now, one can compute the standard *Euclidean distance* between two vectors, in the same way one would compute a distance between points in a 3D space (that is, between feature vectors (X, Y, Z)). Distances are used in any *clustering* technique and render the data themselves the model.

Figure 2 A clustering of music artists

For example, the *Music Map*[16] in Figure 2 shows the band *Epica* centred among bands that are similar in terms of their music. Based on this clustering, I can find out about bands I might possibly also like, even though I may not know them. Instance-based learning (or, memory-based) learning uses the complete data set and assigns a new example to the closest (or the *n* closest) example(s) that is (are) already in the data set. In terms of profiling, one could find the closest individual in the data set and most properties of that closest one will also apply to the new individual. Cluster *centres*, or *prototypes*, can be seen as typical representatives of some kind. Nowadays, more sophisticated approaches under the name of *kernels* exist (Schölkopf and Smola 2002). Kernels generalise distances and can be used to compare complex data structures such as graphs, web pages, images and many more.

Algorithmic aspects

Representation is about which phenomena one can model; algorithms are all about how models come about. *Inductive methods* are the most typical ML setting, in which a data set of examples is used to learn a model, that is, to generate new knowledge. In addition, we discuss the related notions of *deduction* and *abduction*. Let us assume we have a data set *D* of examples (each consisting of features and their values) and a model class *M* of all possible models (profiles):

- *Deduction* assumes the existence of a specific model *m* (from *M*) and computes statements (or their probability) that are entailed by *m*. These statements are about the general characteristics of the data *D* modelled by *m*. In addition, one can infer statements about a particular example *d*. Deduction is about *employing* profiles to derive information.

- *Induction* takes a data set D and finds a specific model m in M which *best fits the data*. Induction is the core mechanism for *profiling* and is about *obtaining* models from data.
- *Abduction* takes a specific example e (from E) and a specific model m (from M) and computes an *explanation* (eg a set of *assumed* facts) that would allow us to infer the example from the theory (with some certainty). Abduction supports *diagnostic reasoning* about individuals.

Deduction and inference

Deductive inference assumes a model is present and amounts to *reasoning from causes to consequences*. These models are like theories about a domain supporting these inferences. From *if A then B* and *A* one can *infer* that *B*. Deduction can generate 'new' knowledge that is entailed by the model but that is maybe not immediately present. For example, mathematical theorems are often a consequence of basic mathematics, but it takes deductive inference to make that explicit.

Let us take a look at probabilistic inference in the Bayesian network in Figure 1 (right). If we know that it rains at time t, we can infer that the probability that it will rain at time t+1 is 0.7 and based on that we can compute that the probability I will bring my umbrella is 0.66. This is the sum of bringing it when it rains at time t+1 (0.7*0.9) plus bringing it when it does not rain at time t+1 (0.3*0.1). Bayesian networks are typically used to compute a *posterior probability* of some features, *given* that one knows about the values of some other features. Similarly, if we know that it rains at time t+1 then we can infer that the probability of raining at time t is now 0.845, which is 0.49 (the probability that both are true, which is 0.7*0.7) divided by the probability that it rains at time t+1 (which is 0.7*0.7 + 0.3*0.3). This is called the *conditional* probability of raining at time t, based on the information that it does rain on time t+1. Inference needs a *query* (eg a question) and a model, and it will determine whether the query is entailed by the model (possibly with a probability attached). Note that in this example, by coincidence, the probabilities for raining at time t+1 (0.7) and not raining on time t+1 (0.3) sum up to one; however, these probabilities are independently based on whether it rained at time t and therefore 0.3 could have been 0.2, for example.

Since *exact* inference for large networks or theories can take a long time to compute, many efficient *approximations* exist that can guarantee a *good enough* answer in less time. Typically they do this by *sampling*. Instead of computing the probabilities using exact rules, they 'try out' a number of values for features (in a smart way) and see what the probability of the feature you are interested in is in that sample set. This is typically *extrapolation* and consequently more samples lead to more accurate answers.

An example of inference using a simple probabilistic model of relations in a social network was described by van den Broeck et al (2010). The goal of the system is to find the best selection of people to whom to send direct mail. Rules are very simple and state that, first, *if I send an advertisement to person X he will buy my product with some probability*, and, second, *if person X buys my product and person X and Y are friends, then Y will buy my product too with a certain probability*. Sending mail costs money, but selling products will raise profits. The system is capable of making probabilistic inferences on what would happen (for thousands of people in the network) if a certain selection of people were sent a mailing. Thus, the query was about which people would (probably) buy the product, *given* that I send a mailing to certain people.

Induction, learning and mining

Learning (and mining) is essentially a *search process*. Given a space of models (generated by a choice for hypothesis language and background knowledge) the goal of learning is to find the 'best' model for a given data set. A *general-to-specific ordering* on the space of models can help to search, starting from simple models followed by more complex models. A crucial component is a *scoring function* that tells us how well a model fits the data. For example for Bayesian networks, this comes down to comparing the distribution specified by the model with that of the data. In order to make sure the model can *generalise* new data, usually the data are split into a *training set* and a *test set*. The first is used to find a model and then the second (which is not used for learning the model) is used to *validate* how good the model actually is on data it has never seen before.

Learning can focus on the *parameters* (the quantitative part) of a *known* model structure or on the model structure itself (the qualitative part). We will discuss both in turn. First of all, learning the parameters is basically a matter of counting on 'sample statistics'. This means that, eg for $p4$'s CPT in our automobile example, to estimate $P(p4|p2,p3)$ we can count in the data in how many examples $p4$ is true when $p2$ and $p3$ are both true. The network structure gives us the knowledge of which probabilities we actually have to compute from the data. For temporal models and especially models with hidden features algorithms exist, but things become more complicated, since some of the features are not really observed and we have to guess whether they were true or not.

Learning the qualitative part of models, that is, which feature interactions exist, is more complex and roughly follows these steps:

1. *Start.* First an initial model is chosen. Based on a generality order, we would like to start with the simplest one, which for Bayesian networks is a topology with no arcs (so, just the nodes). Here, this amounts to assuming all features are independent. For rule learners, or pattern miners, one might start with rules with an empty condition, or the pattern *true* (which applies to any example).

2. *Find out how good the model is.* Based on a scoring function, we can *score* the current model. For Bayesian networks, we can estimate (read: do parameter learning) how well it models the distribution in the data and, for rules or patterns, we can calculate to how many examples they apply.

3. *Improve the model.* We can alter a model to find an improved model. The model class determines what we can do. In Bayesian networks, we can add an arc between two features or delete one that is already there. For rules we can add or delete conditions. Since there are several ways to modify the model, we can try them all (or a selection) and compute their score. The best modification is chosen and we continue from this model with the previous step and so on.

Given any space of models, the search for the right model is much influenced by a *search bias* (how do we search?, do we keep multiple candidate models?), by a *language bias* (which models do we 'visit'?, which modifications are allowed?, can we add hidden features?) and the *scoring function*. The last one relies on the (deductive) inferences we can make with our model. For Bayesian networks, there are many applications in which the network was successfully learned from data (see Koller and Friedman 2009 for pointers).

Abduction, assumptions and explanations

Abduction (Josephson and Josephson 1994) is something akin to the opposite of deduction, in that it *reasons from consequences to causes*. If we assume that *if A then B* and we observe *B* then we could *assume that A*. But if we also assume that *if C then B* then also *C* could be an *explanation* for the observation *B*. Abductive inference is *unsound*, which means that we do not know for sure whether *A* or *C* are true, but we can only *assume* that they are. Both *A* and *C* are *hypotheses* that we could assume to explain the observation *B*. Each of these two could be considered new knowledge the moment we accept them as being true (that is, assume them). The problem remains: how to choose between them? In some cases, we could choose the 'simplest' one, in the same way as we can compare models using a generality order.

In probabilistic models, choosing the best one can be stated as finding the hypothesis with the highest probability of having *caused* the observation. For example, in speech recognition we are looking for the *word* with the highest probability of having caused a certain speech signal. Or, in activity recognition, we are looking for that *activity* for which the probability of causing the observed user behaviour is the highest. In our automobile application, one possible hypothesis for not-$p4$ (car does not start) is that not-$p3$ (fuel system down). But another possibility is that not-$p1$ (starter motor broken), and there are several other possibilities (eg they could be both broken). Finding the *most likely values* of $p1$, $p2$ and $p3$ given that not-$p4$, is called the *maximum a posteriori* (MAP) hypothesis.

Summary

As we have seen, deduction is about deriving knowledge that is (probabilistically) entailed by the model and both inductive and abductive techniques can deliver new knowledge; the former in the form of rules (or patterns) and the latter in the form of facts (features). For many ML applications it is natural, and it makes sense, to integrate the three styles of reasoning to make the best out of the data. As an example of such a successful combination is the *robot scientist*, a physical robot capable of fully automatically doing real scientific experiments, by combining the deductive, abductive and inductive methods (King et al 2009). The domain is *bioinformatics* and the goal is to find out the function of yeast genes. The system is given knowledge about biological theories and, based on that, it applies abduction to come up with hypotheses to be tested. Deductive consequences of these can help in selecting them, based on the predicted costs of conducting them. Based on actual physical experiments (conducted by the robot Adam himself) and their outcomes, Adam learns new rules by applying inductive learning techniques and has even made some new discoveries.

Computer says 'no'

Using computers for profiling and controlling people in what they can or cannot do based on those profiles has the potential to create circumstances in which the computer simply says 'no'.[17] Below we highlight some caveats and recent relevant directions in ML.

Caveats of statistical models

'A man who travels a lot was concerned about the possibility of a bomb on board his plane. He determined the probability of this, found it to be low but not low enough for him, so now he always travels with a bomb in his suitcase. He reasons that the probability of two bombs being on board would be infinitesimal' (Paulos 1988: 21). Humans are notoriously bad[18] with numbers and statistics but there is no guarantee that if we use computers for profiling, things are settled. Since ML is basically statistics with knowledge representation, most of the general issues with statistics carry over to ML. This includes *sample size* (do I have enough data to make predictions?), *data set distribution* (does my target population have the 'same' characteristics as the population I have trained my model on?) and *completeness of the model* (do storks really bring babies or is there an unmodelled factor explaining a possible correlation between births and stork populations?).

In ML, owing to the rich set of hypothesis languages and models, important additional aspects are the search and language biases, the scoring function, but also whether inference is done exactly or approximately. These factors

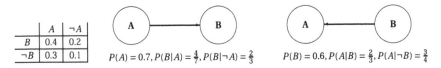

	A	$\neg A$
B	0.4	0.2
$\neg B$	0.3	0.1

$P(A) = 0.7, P(B|A) = \frac{4}{7}, P(B|\neg A) = \frac{2}{3}$

$P(B) = 0.6, P(A|B) = \frac{2}{3}, P(A|\neg B) = \frac{3}{4}$

Figure 3 Causal versus correlation: two ways of modelling the same distribution in a Bayesian network (note that ¬A is mathematical notation for not-A)

determine what exactly one can expect from the final model. The rich class of models that ML supports also creates a *bias-variance trade-off*, which intuitively says that one can either: (i) choose for very general models, but then the variance in the results of that model is large; or (ii) one can choose more specific models (biased by preferences or prior knowledge) and get a lower variance, but maybe the model does not fit the underlying characteristics of data anymore. The search process for models itself influences the final model, since usually there is no guarantee we get the best model possible, but only good in the 'vicinity' of models we have visited during the search. For example, take a look at Figure 3. Both small networks model the same distribution that is depicted on the left, but differ in the connection structure. Since this can happen in such small models, one can imagine that small differences in how the search progresses can generate different networks in the end.

One final thing to bear in mind is that models are trained using a *global* score, that is, the model is judged on how well it predicts *on average*. This means that predictions for any single individual may be wrong; something to consider when it comes to profiling (what do we do if the model predicts the individual to have some property with only probability 0.6; do we act upon this?).

Comprehensibility, transparency, visualisation, automation

Instead of *privacy enhancing technologies*, Hildebrandt and Koops (2010) advocate *transparency enhancing technologies* (TETs) to aid in developing ambient law. In the context of ML, several developments are relevant for enabling TETs.

Comprehensibility of what is being learned has always been somewhat neglected in ML and only occasionally is it discussed explicitly (Džeroski and Lavrac 2001: section 15.6). In general it is accepted that neural networks are less comprehensible and Bayesian networks and relational representations support *understanding* of what has been learned in human understandable terms. However, care must also be taken with these models. For humans, huge sets of hundreds of rules are very hard to inspect visually, especially when their predictions are combined probabilistically in complex ways. Furthermore, humans have a built-in bias to interpret models in a *causal way*. Look again at Figure 3. An arrow from *A* to *B* immediately triggers a causal interpretation that *A causes B*, but in fact this arc only indicates a dependency, and we can also place the arrow the other way around.

A very relevant development in the direction of TETs may come from *experiment databases* (Vanschoren 2010). The goal of such databases is to store, in addition to data themselves, the used *algorithms, settings and parameters* and *results* of experiments in ML. The main goal is to be able to *compare* algorithms more carefully and to not repeat experiments that have been done over and over again by many scientists. Recent efforts have been made towards developing *query languages* to ask any question about experiments or to find *relevant* experiments and results in case we want to relate them to our own experiments. A similar goal is reported in the work on the robot scientist we discussed earlier: by making *everything* explicit (data, hypotheses, algorithms, parameters and results) in formal languages, one can make the whole process of learning from data *transparent* and *reusable*.

Feedback, active learning and adaptive behaviour

So far, we have mainly dealt with the situation where there is *some* data set and we want to build a model out of it. However, if models function as profiles, presumably something is going to be *done* with the information drawn from the model (see also Hildebrandt 2008: section 2.4.4). For example, if the model represents information about customers in a webshop, the model can be used to target specific users to receive advertisements, that is, to *personalise* the advertising strategy (Pariser 2011). This, in turn, can trigger the population of customers to change – either customers coming and going, or by customers changing their behaviours – and this, in turn, may require rebuilding the model because it is outdated. In other words, profiling generates models, and actions based on these models will change the behaviour of individuals. For this reason, models will (have to) change and this *feedback loop* will continue.

With respect to *acting* upon the data, the ML subfield of *reinforcement learning* (RL) (Wiering and van Otterlo 2012) studies learning techniques with such feedback loops. A typical toy domain in RL is a *maze*. A *policy* represents the behaviour of a robot moving through the maze and, based on this policy, the robot will visit parts of the maze. Once it modifies its behaviour (its policy), the parts of the maze the robot visits will change, and this again drives a new modification of the behaviour and so on. An important characteristic of RL is a *reward function*, which drives behaviour modifications. Our maze robot will receive rewards for reaching the exit and for using fewer steps. The feedback the robot receives about its 'progress' in learning how to behave is scarce (that is, it does not receive specific instructions on how to get out, but only some feedback of how it is doing) and delayed (good initial steps will only be rewarded when it finally exits the maze). Translating this to a profiling case in a webshop, the rewards can come from customers ordering products, and the actions are advertisements and so on. An *adaptive system* could learn a model of its customers (as discussed throughout this chapter) and, based on that learning, it could act,[19] receive feedback and possibly modify its behaviour. Many techniques in RL exist for learning behaviour policies with or without explicitly learning models, and they could provide another interesting direction for ambient intelligence (cf Søraker and Brey 2007).

In the same direction, the advent of *probabilistic programming languages* is very relevant. At the crossing of probabilistic and relational ML, RL and even robotics, programming languages are developing that support learning.[20] As an example, take the following (made-up) program fragment:

p:= P(customer X buys product Y | X browsed through web pages Z and W)
IF p > 0.70 THEN place_advertisement_discount(page_top, product_X)
r:= profit_product_X - advertisement_cost
...

Both *p* and *r* are *parameters* of the program that are not available when writing the program. The program itself expresses the knowledge available at that time, and the parameters are *autonomously learned* from data when the program becomes active. A parameter such as *p* can come from, for example, a Bayesian network as the one we have discussed in this chapter, since most of these languages are based on the same probabilistic graphical models. A program can contain several *choice points*, that is, places where the program can select one of several actions, which can be learned through RL (cf van Otterlo 2009; Simpkins et al 2008). Several probabilistic relational learning systems are being expanded into such fully adaptive, probabilistic programming languages (Poole 2010). Profiling *programs*, programmed in such languages will eventually have full autonomy[21] in gathering, analysing and exploiting data, and it is especially here where new TETs are required.

Conclusions

This chapter is about a machine learning view on profiling. We have discussed representations and algorithms for learning models of user behaviours, which we have framed as activity recognition, an active branch of machine learning. We have discussed some descriptive models in more detail to highlight vital issues in the process of learning about, and prediction of, users and their behaviours. An important conclusion is that since there are many biases and choices involved when learning models from data, care must be taken as to the conclusions that can be drawn from these models.

Two directions are, in our opinion, particularly interesting to look at in the future when it comes to privacy issues in profiling. The *transparency* issue is important and it is interesting to note that some ML efforts seem to be focused on transparency, albeit often for different reasons. In many other cases, transparency seems to be a paradoxical issue: on the one hand, transparency in experiments gives the opportunity to *relate, reuse* and *explain* yet, on the other hand, the success of Google – for example – makes comprehensibility and transparency less relevant since 'big statistics' can solve many problems in searching for the right web page and translating texts. A second direction to keep an eye on when it comes to privacy and profiling are adaptive programming languages. Fully automated profiling machines are intriguing, yet they require new ways of monitoring to keep track of who they are influencing and why they are doing so.

Notes

* The author would like to thank Christophe Costa Florencio for interesting discussions, links and feedback on a draft of this chapter. Also many thanks go to Mireille Hildebrandt and Katja de Vries for feedback and discussions. A first version of this chapter was presented at the philosophers' reading panel at the Computer Privacy and Data Protection Conference (Brussels 2011), while the author was working as a post-doctoral in the machine learning group, department of computer science at the Katholieke Universiteit Leuven (Belgium). Subsequent ideas were presented at the CTIT annual symposium in Enschede and the Data Wars event in Newcastle (both in 2011). A follow-up article, extending the ideas on feedback, reinforcement learning and automated profiling was presented at the Amsterdam Privacy Conference (October 2012).

1 See also the interesting novel by Baluja (2011).

2 Different terms, such as *ambient intelligence* and *ubiquitous computing* are used in the literature. Here it suffices to think of any environment in which information about users' behaviours is being automatically processed.

3 In the author's presentation at the workshop (Computer Privacy and Data Protection Conference, Brussels 2011) that formed the basis of this present volume, the link between automated profiling and computational art was made. Both areas raise similar philosophical questions about the authenticity, ownership and value of profiles/artworks. Space prohibits further elaboration here, but the interested reader can start with the article by Rinaldo (1998). A related legal point of view, concerning copyright law, was described by van Dijk (2010).

4 See the hilarious movie *Kitchen Stories* (2003).

5 See the movie *Das Leben der Anderen* (2006).

6 Internet services are most often not really free; one pays with information (Sobiesk and Conti 2007).

7 See the movie *Minority Report* (2002).

8 See the movies *EyeBorgs* (2009), *1984* (1984) and *Enemy of the State* (1998).

9 'Profiles discovered by these techniques may not be anticipated, desired or politically correct but modern algorithms do not (yet) have the power to care' (Anrig et al 2008).

10 See Barbaro and Zeller Jr (2006) and http://en.wikipedia.org/wiki/AOL_search_data_scandal (accessed 30 October 2012).

11 The success of search engines such as Google and many other applications in activity recognition show that much can be done by 'just' correlation patterns. See 'The petabyte age' (*Wired* July 2008), the 2010 report on 'Big data' (Bollier and Firestone 2010) and several special issues of magazines such as the *The Economist* (see eg the issue of 27 February 2010 on 'The data deluge'). Modelling and predicting behaviour based solely on externally observable features resembles the behaviourism movement in psychology in the first half of the 20th century. 'A much simpler solution [simpler than equating the mind with the brain] is to identify the mind with the [physical] person. Human thought is human behavior. The history of human thought is what people have said and done' (Skinner 1976). Behaviourists argued, because it was absolutely impossible to look inside someone's brain to find out *why* some behaviour comes about, that psychology should only be concerned with *externally observable features of behaviour*. Stipulating higher order motivations, reasons, goals, intentions and the like are merely speculation about the reasons for certain behaviour. Of course, one could object that, contrary to animals, which are not capable of verbal explanations or introspection, humans are not complete black boxes because they can *talk about* their motivations and perform *introspection* on what is on their mind (a capacity pivotal to the work of 'introspectionist' psychologists at the end of the 19th and the beginning of the 20th centuries). However, according to behaviourist psychology introspection is not a suitable method to undertake repeatable, falsifiable science. The behaviourist movement in psychology is mirrored in AI by movements such as *behaviour-based* approaches and *new* AI, and also *reinforcement learning*. These directions often place a particular emphasis on *not representing*, or *reasoning* about, *intentions*, *goals*, *motivations* or *inner states*, but instead focus on how predictions and behaviours directly follow from data. This is unlike other trends in AI where the goal is – on the contrary – to model *cognitive belief states* explicitly (see Langley et al 2009). It is a good idea to bear in mind that many of the current techniques in data science which we describe here can in principle be applied in both contexts, although we lean slightly towards the behaviourist approaches.

12 See more on this in the book by Hildebrandt and Gutwirth (2008c), specifically the chapters by Hildebrandt (2008), Hildebrandt and Gutwirth (2008b) and Anrig et al (2008).

13 Many toy examples in graphical models are aimed at *diagnostic reasoning* about machines. The example here stems from Nilsson (2010).

14 And this becomes even worse for non-Boolean features, for example *number of children*. The number of combinations is n^k for k features that can each take on n values.

15 A parent of a node N is a node which has an arrow pointing towards N, and the children of node N are all the nodes that have N as parent.

16 This website features clusterings of music artists that are 'close' to one searched for. See http://www.music-map.com/ (accessed 30 October 2012).

17 Derived from a catch phrase 'Computer says no' from the British comedy series *Little Britain*.

18 See further Tversky and Kahneman (1981); Paulos (1988) and Gonick and Smith (1993).

19 Some of this was illustrated in van den Broeck et al (2010), only there the model was given beforehand and not learned.

20 Mitchell (2006), one of the principal actors in current ML, lists this as one of the strategic directions in ML.

21 For cinematic inspiration of possible consequences, see the movies *Wargames* (1983), *2001: A Space Odyssey* (1968), *Eagle Eye* (2008) and *EyeBorgs* (2009).

References

Alpaydin, E. (2004) *Introduction to Machine Learning*, Cambridge, MA: MIT Press.

Anrig, B., Browne, W. and Gasson, M. (2008) 'The role of algorithms in profiling', in Hildebrandt, M. and Gutwirth, S. (eds) *Profiling the European Citizen: Cross-disciplinary perspectives*, Dordrecht: Springer: 65–87.

Baluja, S. (2011) *The Silicon Jungle: A novel of deception, power, and internet intrigue*, Princeton: Princeton University Press.

Barbaro, M. and Zeller Jr, T. (2006) 'A Face is Exposed for AOL Searcher No. 4417749', *New York Times*, 9 August.

Bollier, D. and Firestone, C. M. (2010) *The Promise and Peril of Big Data*, Washington, DC: Aspen Institute.

Broeck, G. van den, Thon, I., van Otterlo, M. and de Raedt, L. (2010) 'DTProbLog: A Decision-Theoretic Probabilistic Prolog', in *Proceedings of the Twenty-Fourth AAAI Conference on Artificial Intelligence (AAAI-10)*, Menlo Park: AAAI Press: 1217–22.

Cao, L. (2006) 'Activity Mining: Challenges and Prospects', in *Proceedings of ADMA (Advanced Data Mining and Applications)*, Berlin: Springer: 582–93.

Damen, D. and Hogg, D. C. (2009) 'Attribute Multiset Grammars for Global Explanations of Activities', paper presented at the British Machine Vision Conference (BMVC), London, September 2009.

Dijk, N. van (2010) 'Auteursrecht in profielen', *Computerrecht* 35, 53–61.

Džeroski, S. and Lavrac, N. (eds) (2001) *Relational Data Mining*, Berlin: Springer.

Gonick, L. and Smith, W. (1993) *The Cartoon Guide to Statistics*, New York: HarperCollins.

Hildebrandt, M. (2008) 'Defining profiling: a new type of knowledge', in Hildebrandt, M. and Gutwirth, S. (eds) *Profiling the European Citizen: Cross-disciplinary perspectives*, Dordrecht: Springer: 17–45.

Hildebrandt, M. and Gutwirth, S. (2008a) 'Concise conclusions: citizens out of control', in Hildebrandt, M. and Gutwirth, S. (eds) *Profiling the European Citizen: Cross-disciplinary perspectives*, Dordrecht: Springer: 365–68.

Hildebrandt, M. and Gutwirth, S. (2008b) 'General introduction and overview', in Hildebrandt, M. and Gutwirth, S. (eds) *Profiling the European Citizen: Cross-disciplinary perspectives*, Dordrecht: Springer: 1–13.

Hildebrandt, M. and Gutwirth, S. (eds) (2008c) *Profiling the European Citizen: Cross-disciplinary perspectives*, Dordrecht: Springer.

Hildebrandt, M. and Koops, B. J. (2010) 'The Challenges of Ambient Law and Legal Protection in the Profiling Era', *Modern Law Review*, 73: 428–60.

Josephson, J. and Josephson, S. (1994) *Abductive Inference: Computation, philosophy, technology*, Cambridge: Cambridge University Press.

King, R. D., Oliver, J. R. S. G., Young, M., Aubrey, W., Byrne, E., Liakata, M., Markham, M., Pir, P., Soldatova, L. N., Sparkes, A., Whelan, K. E. and Clare, A. (2009) 'The Automation of Science', *Science*, 324(5923): 85–89.

Koller, D. and Friedman, N. (2009) *Probabilistic Graphical Models: Principles and techniques*, Cambridge, MA: MIT Press.

Langley, P., Laird, J. E. and Rogers, S. (2009) 'Cognitive Architectures: Research issues and challenges', *Cognitive Systems Research*, 10(2): 141–60.

Le, T. L., Boucher, A., Thonnat, M. and Bremond, F. (2010) 'Surveillance Video Retrieval: What we have already done?', in *Proceedings of the Third International Conference on Communications and Electronics (ICCE)*, Nha Trang, Vietnam.

Liao, L., Fox, D. and Kautz, H. (2005) 'Location-based Activity Recognition', in *Proceedings of the Nineteenth Annual Conference on Neural Information Processing Systems (NIPS-2005)*, Whistler, BC.

Mitchell, T. M. (1997) *Machine Learning*, New York: McGraw-Hill.

Mitchell, T. M. (2006) 'The Discipline of Machine Learning', Technical Report CMU-ML-06-108, U.S.A.

Neudecker, S. (2010) 'Die Tricks der Anderen', *Zeit Wissen*, June 2010.

Nilsson, N. J. (2010) *The Quest for Artificial Intelligence*, Cambridge: Cambridge University Press.

Pariser, E. (2011) *The Filter Bubble: What the Internet is Hiding from You*, London: Penguin Press.

Paulos, J. A. (1988) *Innumeracy: Mathematical Illiteracy and its Consequences*, New York: Vintage Books/Random House.

Perkowitz, M., Philipose, M., Fishkin, K. P. and Patterson, D. J. (2004) 'Mining Models of Human Activities from the Web', in *Proceedings of the 13th international conference on World Wide Web, WWW*: 573–82.

Poole, D. (2010) 'Probabilistic programming languages: independent choices and deterministic systems', in Dechter, R., Geffner, H. and Halpern, J. (eds) *Heuristics, Probability and Causality: A tribute to Judea Pearl*, Los Angeles: College Publications: 253–69.

Poole, D., Smyth, C. and Sharma, R. (2009) 'Ontology Design for Scientific Theories that Make Probabilistic Predictions', *IEEE Intelligent Systems*: 27–36.

Raedt, L. de (2008) *Logical and Relational Learning*, Berlin: Springer.

Rinaldo, K. E. (1998) 'Technology Recapitulates Phylogeny: Artificial life art', *Leonardo*, 31(5): 371–76.

Schölkopf, B. and Smola, A. J. (2002) *Learning with Kernels*, Cambridge, MA: MIT Press.

Simpkins, C., Bhat, S., Isbell, C. L. and Mateas, M. (2008) 'Adaptive Programming: Integrating Reinforcement Learning into a Programming Language', in *Proceedings of the Twenty-Third ACM SIGPLAN International Conference on Object-Oriented Programming, Systems, Languages, and Applications (OOPSLA)*: 603–614.

Singla, P., Kautz, H., Luo, J. B. and Gallagher, A. C. (2008) 'Discovery of Social Relationships in Consumer Photo Collections using Markov Logic', in CVPR Workshop on Semantic Learning and Applications in Multimedia, *IEEE Computer Vision and Pattern Recognition (CVPR) Workshop 2008: Semantic Learning and Applications in Multimedia*: 1–7.

Skinner, B. F. (1976) *About Behaviorism*, New York: Vintage Books.

Sobiesk, E. and Conti, G. J. (2007) 'The Cost of Free Web Tools', *IEEE Security & Privacy*, 5(3): 66–68.

Søraker, J. H. and Brey, P. (2007) 'Ambient Intelligence and Problems with Inferring Desires from Behaviour', *International Review of Information Ethics*, 8(1): 7–12.

Sowa, J. F. (1999) *Knowledge Representation: Logical, philosophical, and computational foundations*, Stamford, CO: Thomson Learning.

Torre, I. (2009) 'Adaptive Systems in the Era of the Semantic and Social Web, a Survey', *User Modeling and User-Adapted Interaction*, 19(5): 433–86.

Turaga, P., Chellappa, R., Subrahmanian, V. S. and Udrea, O. (2008) 'Machine Recognition of Human Activities: A survey', *IEEE Transactions on Circuits, Systems and Video Technology*, 18(11): 1473–88.

Tversky, A. and Kahneman, D. (1981) 'The Framing of Decisions and the Psychology of Choice', *Science*, 211(4481): 453–58.

van Otterlo, M. (2009) *The Logic of Adaptive Behavior*, Amsterdam: IOS Press.

Vanschoren, J. (2010) 'Understanding Machine Learning Performance with Experiment Databases', unpublished PhD thesis, Department of Computer Science, Katholieke Universiteit Leuven, Belgium.

Vries, K. de (2010) 'Identity, Profiling Algorithms and a World of Ambient Intelligence', *Ethics and Information Technology*, 12(1): 71–85.

Warner, M. and Stone, M. (1970) *The Data Bank Society: Organizations, computers and social freedom*, London: Allen & Unwin.

Wiering, M. A. and van Otterlo, M. (2012) *Reinforcement Learning: State-of-the-art*, Berlin: Springer.

Witten, I. and Frank, E. (2005) *Data Mining: Practical machine learning tools and techniques*, San Francisco: Morgan Kaufmann.

Yang, Q. (2009) 'Activity Recognition: Linking low-level sensors and high-level intelligence', in *IJCAI 2009. Proceedings of the 21st International Joint Conference on Artificial Intelligence*: 20–25.

Zamyatin, Y. (1924/1993) *We*, New York: Penguin Classics.

Part 2

Anticipating machines

3

Abducing personal data, destroying privacy

Diagnosing profiles through artefactual mediators

Lorenzo Magnani

Knowledge as a duty and its limitations

One of the aims of this chapter is to convince readers that knowledge has to become a duty in our technological world.[1] Thus far in my attempt to do so, I have to combine ethics, epistemology and cognitive science. An important issue arises from the fact that technological advances[2] have given greater value to external things – both natural and artificial – and while this may seem to bode ill for human beings, I believe we can use these things as moral media-tors[3] that serve a sort of 'copy and paste' function: we can take the value[4] of, say, a morally important artefact and transfer it to a person. Using moral mediators in this way, however, will require the construction of vast new body of knowledge, a new way of looking at the world. Moral mediators play an important role in reshaping the ethical worth of human beings and collectives and, at the same time, facilitate a continuous reconfiguration of social orders geared toward rebuilding new moral perspectives. Finally, thinking in terms of cognitive capacities, a human being can be considered a kind of 'thing' that can incorporate information, knowledge, know-how, cultural tradition etc, just as cognitive objects such as books, PCs or sculptures do. Unfortunately, human beings are sometimes assigned less value than things: moral mediators can help us redefine people as worthy of new moral consideration. As I will explain below – at least in the perspective of our current morality of freedom and of the politics of constitutional democracies – various artefacts that affect privacy play the role of moral mediators too, because they can lead to positive moral expected effects, for example by improving some services, social perfor-mances etc. Unfortunately, they can mediate violence too, sometimes beyond the intentions of their creators, when for example they destroy part of that ownerships of our destinies which we, human beings who live in constitutional democracies, like.[5]

In my recent book *Morality in a Technological World* (Magnani 2007), I have extensively illustrated that improving human dignity in our technological era requires that we enhance free will, freedom, responsibility and ownership of our destinies. To do so, it is absolutely necessary to respect knowledge in its various forms, but there are other ideas to consider as well: first, knowledge has a pivotal role in anticipating, monitoring and managing the hazards of technology; and, second, it has an intrinsic value that must be better understood, as do general information and metaethics themselves. Knowledge is duty, but who owes it to whom? And is it always a right as well as an obligation?

In some cases, information gathering is not the innocuous endeavour it may seem to be, and we must acknowledge that knowledge as a duty has certain limitations. I contend that when too much knowledge about people is contained in external artificial things, human beings' 'visibility' can become excessive and dangerous. Does the right to knowledge trump all other rights? If not, how do we reconcile the concept of knowledge as a duty with the notion that some kinds of knowledge must be restricted? Where do we draw the line?

Modern technology has precipitated the need for new knowledge; it has brought about consequences of such magnitude that old policies can no longer contain them. As Hans Jonas (1974) has observed, we cannot achieve a relevant, useful new body of ethics by limiting ourselves to traditional ethics: he points out that Immanuel Kant, for example, assumed that 'there is no need of science or philosophy for knowing what man has to do in order to be honest and good, and indeed to be wise and virtuous' (Kant 1964: 72). Kant also says: '[ordinary intelligence] can […] have as good a hope of hitting the mark as any philosopher can promise himself' (ibid: 72), and goes on to state that: 'I need no far-reaching ingenuity to find out what I have to do in order to possess a good will. Inexperienced in the course of world affairs, and incapable of being prepared for all the chances that happen in it' (ibid: 70). I can still ascertain how to act in accordance with moral law. Finally, Kant observes that even if wisdom 'does require science', it 'in itself consists more in doing and in not doing than in knowing' and so it needs science 'not in order to learn from it, but in order to win acceptance and durability for its own prescriptions' (ibid: 73). Jonas (1974: 8) concludes: 'Not every thinker in ethics, it is true, went so far in discounting the cognitive side of moral action.'

But Kant made his declarations at a time when today's technology was unimaginable and his notion that knowledge is simple and readily available to all people of good will is not sufficient anymore. In spite of Kant's declaration that wisdom and virtue are all one needs to make moral choices, decision-making must be accompanied by *knowledge* that allows us to understand increasingly complex problems and situations. And the knowledge involved should be not only scientific, but also human and social, embedded in reshaped 'cultural' traditions. The 'neighbour ethics' (Jonas 1974: 9) of justice, charity, honesty etc is no longer adequate for modern needs because such local action is overcome by collective action that creates consequences outside a proximate sphere – the results of an act are often spatially or temporally distant from the site where it is executed. To meet the new causal scale of individual and collective actions, a new long-range ethics of responsibility has to be built, one that is capable of dealing with the new global condition of human life.

As global stakes grow higher, knowledge becomes a more critically important *duty* than ever before and must be used to inform new ethics and new behaviours in both public policy and private conduct. This means that existing levels of intelligence and knowledge in ethics are no longer sufficient; today, ethical human behaviour requires that we assume long-term responsibility commensurate with the scope of our power to affect the planet, a power that has grown exponentially over the years.[6]

Discovering profiles: diagnosing the invisible

Even though producing knowledge is an important goal, actually doing so in certain circumstances is not always a welcome prospect: we must be cautious when dealing with issues of identity and cyberprivacy, where the excessive production and dissemination of knowledge can be dangerous, at least in the perspective of our current morality of freedom and of the politics of constitutional democracies.

The ethical problem of privacy is related to the theoretical problem of identity. Neuroscientists have discovered that some modular processors do not extract processes from the environment but, rather, from the subject's own body and brain. The brain contains multiple representations of itself and of the body, like the body's physical location in space, thanks to continuously updated somatic, kinesthetic and motor maps (Damasio 1999). The brain also contains the presentation of identity, a narrative autobiography encoded in episodic memory and higher cognitive functions such as action, perception, verbal reasoning and a 'theory of mind' that help to interpret other people's behaviour. It can be hypothesised that all these modules operating simultaneously in the conscious workspace account for the subjectivity of the self and its own identity. Once available in the conscious workspace, these modules' activity could be inspected by other processes, thus setting the stage for reflexive and higher order consciousness.[7]

Hence, it seems that our consciousness is formed in part by representations about ourselves that can be stored outside the body (narratives that authenticate our identity, various kinds of data), but much of consciousness also consists of internal representations about ourselves (a representation of the body and a narrative that constructs our identity) to which other people do not have access. We rarely transfer this second type of representation onto external mediators, as we might with written narratives, concrete drawings, computational data and other configurations. Such internal representations can be also considered a kind of information property (moral capital) that cannot be disseminated – even to spouses, since the need for privacy exists even between husband and wife. There are various reasons for withholding such representations: to avoid harm of some kind, for example, or to preserve intimacy by sharing one's secrets only in love or friendship. But perhaps the most deleterious effect of the loss of privacy is its impact on free choice. The right to privacy is also related to the respect for others' agency, for their status as 'choosers'; indeed, to respect people is also to concede that it is necessary to take into account how one's own decisions may affect the enterprises of others.

Scapegoating through profiling

First of all, profiling can be seen as the latest sophisticated powerful tool for intensively scapegoating a person or a group of persons: the scapegoat is a typical moral/religious mechanism of ancient groups and societies, where a paroxysm of violence would tend to focus on an arbitrary victim and a unanimous antipathy generated by 'mimetic desire' (and the related envy) would grow against him. Following Girard (1986, 1977) we can say that, in the case of ancient social groups, the extreme brutal elimination of the victim would reduce the appetite for violence that had possessed everyone just a moment before, leaving the group suddenly appeased and calm, thus achieving equilibrium in the related social organisation (a sacrifice-oriented social organisation may be repugnant to us but is no less 'social' just because it is rudimentary violence).

When we lose ownership of our actions, we lose responsibility for them, given the fact that collective moral behaviour guarantees more ownership of our destinies and involves the right to own our own destinies and to choose in our own way. When too much of our identity and data is externalised in distant, objective 'things', for example through automated profiling (knowledge discovery in database (KDD), of which data mining[8] (DM) is a part), the possibility of being reified in those externalised data increases and our dignity/ autonomy subsequently decreases and refined *discriminations* are also favoured. Indeed, the resulting profiling is often applied to a person because her data match the profile, so diagnosing her life styles, preferences, dispositions to risk, earning capacities and medical aspects. As I have anticipated, I think that, in principle, profiling furnishes the latest most sophisticated hidden way of socially intensively scapegoating a person (or a group of persons), for example through continuous unfair discrimination and masking: '[...] in the case of KDD the hypothesis emerges in the process of data mining and is tested on the population rather than a sample. [...] when trivial information turns out to correlate with sensitive information, an insurance company or an employer may use the trivial information to violently exclude a person without this being evident' (Hildebrandt 2008: 55). It is also because of the opacity of the computational processes that leave us completely unaware, that some of our interests can be at stake.

The ostracism and stigmatisation of individuals and minorities could increase and generate an explicit loss of freedom. Moreover, less choice may exist because of an implicit loss of freedom: for example, technology may one day lead a person to say 'I am no longer free to simply drive to X location *without leaving a record*', an idea explored further below. Less privacy could also mean the loss of protection against insults that 'slight the individual's owner-ship of himself' (as happens in the case of prisoners or of slaves); consequently, people will say *mine* with less authority and *yours* with less respect. Indeed, when we lose ownership of our actions, we lose responsibility for them, given the fact that morality involves the right decently to possess own our own des-tinies and to choose in our own way. Finally, the risk of infantilising people increases, as does the likelihood of rendering them conformist and conven-tional, and they are, as a result, faced with a greater potential for being oppressed. Given these possibilities, it is apparent that privacy is politically linked in many ways to the concepts of liberalism and democracy (Reiman 1995: 35–44).

By protecting privacy, however, we protect people's ability to develop and realise projects in their own way. Even if unlicensed scrutiny does not cause any direct damage, it can be an intrusive, dehumanising force that fosters resentment in those who are subjected to it. We must be able to ascribe agency to people – actual or potential – in order to conceive of them as fully human. It is only when our freedom is respected and we are guaranteed the chance to assume responsibility that we can control our lives and obtain what we deserve.

Abducing/inducing from private data

Cyber-warfare, cyber-terrorism, identity theft, attacks on abortion providers, Holocaust revisionism, racist hate speech, organised crime, child pornography and hacktivism – a blend of hacking and activism against companies through their websites – are very common on the internet (van den Hoven 2000: 127). As a virtually uncontrollable medium that cuts across different sovereign countries, cyberspace has proved to be fertile ground for new moral problems and new opportunities for violence and wrongdoing, mainly because it has created new moral 'ontologies' that affect human behaviour by generating conflicts and controversies.

Beyond supports of paper, telephone and media, many human interactions are strongly mediated and potentially recorded through the internet. At pre-sent, identity acquires a wide meaning. It must be considered in a broad sense: the amount of data about us as individuals is enormous, and it is all stored in external things/means. This repository of electronic data for every individual human, at least those in rich countries, can be described as an external 'data shadow' that, together with the biological body, forms a kind of cyborg that identifies us or potentially identifies us. The expression 'data shadow' was coined in Sweden in the early 1970s: it refers to a true, impartial image of a person from a given perspective (Gotterbarn 2000: 216).[9]

More than in the past, much of the information about human beings is now simulated, duplicated and replaced in an external environment. The need of the modern state for the registration of its citizens – originally motivated by tax obligations and by subscription in the national army – appears excessive. Moreover, as Hildebrandt (2008: 55) describes, corporate and global govern-ance demand new sophisticated means for identification:

> Supposedly justified by an appeal to security threats, fraud and abuse, citizens are screened, located, detected and their data stored, aggregated and analysed. At the same time potential customers are profiled to detect their habits and preferences in order to provide for targeted services. Both industry and the European Commission are investing huge sums of money into what they call Ambient Intelligence and the creation of an 'Internet of Things'. Such intelligent networked environments will entirely depend on real time monitoring and real time profiling, resulting in real time adaptation of the environment.

Indeed, ambient intelligence (AmI) is supposed to turn the offline world online.[10] We will not have to provide a deliberate input, because we are read by the environment that monitors our behaviour, diminishing human inter-vention as far as possible.

The activity of profiling is a massive *abductive/inductive* activity of new know-ledge production, basically performed by machines and not by organisms.[11] These machines are computational programs – which take advantage of vari-ous abductive[12] and inductive inferential procedures – 'trained' to recover unexpected correlations in masses of data aggregated in large databases and aimed at diagnosing individual profiles. These machines do not simply permit the making of queries in databases, summing up the attributes of predefined categories, but they provide an abductive or inductive generation of suitable knowledge about individuals, that is extracted from data.[13] It is extremely important to note that we cannot reflect upon the way that profiling impacts our actions because we have no access to the way they are produced and used (Hildebrandt 2008: 58).

Abducing/inducing from private data through profiling is fruitful. For example: 'Business enterprise is less interested in a foolproof registration of the inhabitants of a territory. Its focus is on acquiring relevant data about as many customers and potential customers as possible as part of their marketing and sales strategies' (Hildebrandt 2008: 56). Customers have to be persuaded and to this aim they are interested in a refined type of categorisation more than in the identification of a particular customer.

Profiling and the rule of law

Hildebrandt usefully contends that there is a deep impact of profiling 'on human identity in constitutional democracy'. In this perspective, we can say that the protection of democracy is equivalent to the need of promoting what is sometimes called cyberdemocracy. This impact jeopardises the so-called *rule of law*, which instead protects human identity as fundamentally *under* determined: 'This requires us to foster a legal-political framework that both produces and sustains a citizen's freedom to act (positive freedom) that is the hallmark of political self-determination, and a citizen's freedom from unreasonable constraints (negative freedom) that is the hallmark of liberal democracy' (Hildebrandt 2008: 57). Rule of law, Hildebrandt reminds us, relates to a *text* depending on writing ('an affordance of the printing press'), and so it is mediated by a very simple and ancient artefact: it is well known that rule of law aims both at protecting human rights and at limiting governments. Profiling challenges the interplay between negative and positive freedom, which, to be preserved, need that transparency which solely can provide those knowledge contents which renders individuals' actions and deliberations based on conscious reflections, autonomously, adequately and responsibly done. Unfortunately, in presence of the current profiling activities, we do not have any access to knowledge that conditions those choices. The following are some obvious consequences: (i) we think we are alone but we are watched by machines (and this will be more than evident in the case of the possible effects coming out of AmI; Hildebrandt 2007, 2009b); and (ii) we 'think we are making private decisions based on a fair idea of what is going on, while in fact we have no clue as to why service providers, insurance companies or government agencies are dealing with us the way they do' (Hildebrandt 2008: 61).

Various technological progresses will create an even worse situation and not only in the perspective of identity and privacy. What will happen when a silicon chip transponder, once surgically implanted into a human being, can transmit identifying data such as one's name and location through a radio signal? Of the many, many possibilities, one of the more benign is that it may render physical credit cards obsolete. And what will be the result when a transponder directly linked with neural fibres in, say, one's arms, can be used not only to generate remotely controlled movement for people with nerve damage, but also to enhance the strength of an uninjured person? For the blind, extrasensory input will merely be compensatory data, but for those with normal sight it will be a powerful 'prosthesis' that turns them into 'super-cyborgs' with tremendously powerful sensory capabilities. What about the prospect of 'hooking up' a nervous system to the internet? It will revolutionise medicine if it is possible to download electronic signals that can replace disease-causing chemical signals. It is worth remembering that the human nervous system is, by nature, electro-chemical – part electronic, part chemical (cf Warwick 2003: 135).

When delegating information or tracing identity, human beings have always used external mediators such as pictures, documents, various types of publication and fingerprints etc, but those tools were not simultaneously electronic, dynamic and global, as is the case with the internet and other technological devices and at their level it was always possible to delete records, because they were not strongly shared across contexts. Where we exist cybernetically in cyberspace is no longer simple to define, and new technologies of telepresence and ambient intelligence will continue to complicate the issue.

New moral ontologies/new human beings: biologically local and cybernetically global

In general, this complex new 'information being' involves new moral ontologies. We can no longer apply old moral rules and old-fashioned arguments to beings that are both biological (concrete) and virtual, physically situated in a three-dimensional *local* space but potentially 'existing' also as 'globally omnipresent' information packets (Schiller 2000). It is easy to materialise cybernetic aspects of people in three-dimensional local space, even if it is not quite as spectacular as in old *Star Trek* episodes, when Scottie beamed the glimmering forms of Captain Kirk and Mr Spock from the transporter room to the surface of an alien planet. Human rights, the notion of care, obligation and duty, have to be updated for these cybernetic human beings. These notions are usually transparent when applied to macro-physical objects in local spatio-temporal coordinates. According to van den Hoven 2000: 131), they suddenly become obscure, however, in cyberspace:

> What is an agent? What is an object? What is an *integrated product*? Is that one thing or two sold together? What is the *corpus delicti*? If someone sends an e-mail with sexual innuendo, where and when does the sexual harassment take place? Where and when it is read by the envisaged addressee? Or when it was typed? Stored on the server? Or as it was piped through all the countries through which it was routed? And what if it was a forwarded message?

In the era of massive profiling, privacy cannot be reduced to the mere non-disclosure of personal data, as a mere private good, because personal data remain out there, hidden in the cybernetic space. Privacy has to be also considered a democratic good: in this perspective citizens' freedom does not have to be silently constrained thanks to the structural/hidden moral (and/or legal) normative effects induced by profiling technologies. The common view about the efficacy of simply 'hiding personal data' is mistaken: this does not protect from group profiling and its 'candid' effect on our choices.

Moreover, a loss of privacy also implies a loss of security, given the fact that individual identity becomes more vulnerable. I have to stress the fact that a loss of privacy also generates an unequal access to information, which can promote a market failure, as Hildebrandt usefully notes: a market segmentation where companies can gain profit from a specific knowledge and/or unequal bargaining positions and consent based on ignorance. Indeed, people do not have access to the group profiles that have been inferred abductively or inductively by a mass of data gathered and do not have any idea on how these profiles can impact our chances in life. Hildebrandt nicely concludes: 'As for profiling, privacy and security both seem to revolve around the question "who is in control: citizens or profilers?" But again control is often reduced to hiding or disclosing personal data and this does not cover privacy and security as public values' (Hildebrandt 2008: 63). As I will illustrate in the following sections, new profiling technologies, fruit of a gigantic abductive/inductive increase of 'knowledge' about human beings, paradoxically threaten to increase our *moral ignorance*. I have previously pointed out that the idea of 'knowledge as a duty' is relevant to scientific, social and political problems, but it is even more important – as I will soon illustrate – when we are faced with reinterpreting and updating the ethical intelligibility of behaviours and events that can generate dangers. Obviously, information has an extraordinary instrumental value in promoting the ends of self-realisation and autonomy, but it can jeopardise or violate various aspects of our individual and social life which, for example, we morally or politically value very highly. For example, we value 'democracy' and, at the same time, we clearly see that profiling could threaten it. The question is, do we have an appropriate knowledge able to describe how profiling menaces democracy so that we can also build and activate suitable counterbalances?

In general, the new moral issues of the cyberage are well known. Some problems, such as financial deception and child abuse, were perpetrated for years via traditional media and have become exacerbated by the internet. Other issues arose as a result of new technology – problems including hacking, cracking and cooking up computer viruses or the difficulties created by artificial intelligence artefacts, which are able to reason on their own (Steinhart 1999). Also in need of attention is the proliferation of spam. The utility of spamming clashes with the time spent in data trash and garbage of the recipient: in this sense it can be said that spamming externalises costs.

Yet another challenge is the huge problem of the digital divide, for while millions of people are active cyborgs, a gulf has opened between them and others who number in the billions. Members of the latter group come from both rich and poor countries and they have not attained cyborg status. A further split, at least inside the 'cyborg community', occurred because of the way technology dictates the speed, ease and scope of communication; the dominance of certain text features creates an unfair playing field, and the disparity between computer users with the most sophisticated equipment and those with more modest systems indicates that we are far from the ideal of an unmediated internet. And the list continues: professional abuses, policy vacuums, intellectual property questions, espionage, a reduced role for humans – all of these things create further moral tangles. Finally, if we consider the internet as a global collection of copying machines, as Mike Godwin (1998) contends, huge copyright problems arise.[14]

In light of my motto 'knowledge as a duty', the internet and the new computational tools make available many goods that are critical for human welfare by increasing access to information and knowledge regarding people's biological needs: food, drink, shelter, mobility and sexuality. It also serves their rational aspects by providing information, stimulating imagination, challenging reason, explaining science and supplying humour, to cite a few examples (van den Hoven 2000). If the internet's power, fecundity, speed and efficiency in distributing information are universally acknowledged, moral problems immediately arise, related to distortion, deception, inaccuracy of data, copyright, patents and trademark abuses (Goldman 1992; Mawhood and Tysver 2000).[15]

Let us return to the problem of privacy. We must safeguard freedom of information and, at the same time, preserve privacy, the right to private property, freedom of conscience, individual autonomy and self-determination.[16] The problem is, how can traditional laws of our constitutional democracies protect people's privacy, given the fact that profiling technologies – as I will soon explain – cannot be touched by laws as we traditionally intend them? Harm to others through internet and other computational tools is often simply invisible (or it cannot be tracked) and we do not possess either knowledge about its ways of occurring or, of course, laws able to limit it in an more efficacious way.

Even in the complicated world of cyberspace, however, Mill's principle still establishes the moral threshold, in this case in the sense that only the prevention of harm to others justifies the limitation of freedom (but, how to weigh and balance harms or freedoms?): 'The only freedom which deserves the name, is that of pursuing our own good in our own way, so long as we do not attempt to deprive others of theirs, or impede their efforts to obtain it' (Mill 1966: 18). Mill also observes that truth emerges more easily in an environment in which ideas are freely and forcefully discussed. I will address the problem of morally and legally contrasting abuse at the level of privacy in the following sections.

Cyberprivacy: extending the 'extended mind' through profiling

How new knowledge can jeopardise privacy ...

In the previous section, I have explained how new profiling technologies, fruit of a gigantic abductive/inductive increase of 'knowledge' about human beings, paradoxically threaten to increase our *moral ignorance*. I have previously pointed out that the idea of 'knowledge as a duty' is relevant to scientific, social and political problems, but it is even more important when we are faced with reinterpreting and updating the ethical intelligibility of behaviours and events which can generate dangerous consequences. In sum, profiling technologies are in tune with my motto 'knowledge is a duty', because they increase knowledge thanks to the abductive/inductive capacity of rendering visible the invisible, but they also violate autonomy, security and freedom etc. How can we contrast these effects we dislike and that we perceive as violent and dangerous? My answer is that, thanks to a further production of knowledge able to reinterpret and update the ethical intelligibility of those violent processes and events, a new knowledge can also furnish the condition of possibility of effective legal remedies.

An organism and its environment co-evolve each other. Profiling is thus a crucial general *cognitive* sign of life, because it consists of a repeated identification of risks and opportunities by an organism in its environment (Hildebrandt 2008: 58): 'Interestingly enough, such organic diagnostic profiling is not dependent on conscious reflection. One could call it a cognitive capacity of all living organisms, without thereby claiming consciousness for an amoeba. One could also call it a form of intelligence based on the capacity to adapt: monitoring and testing, subsequent adaptation and repeated checking is what makes for the difference between the living and the inorganic world. This is what allows any organism to maintain its identity in the course of time, detecting opportunities to grow and spread as well as risks that need to be acted upon.'

In sum, profiling is a diagnostic cognitive activity that produces important knowledge contents, made available in various ways to organisms. The externally distributed resources – as, for example, identity marks – have culturally specific different degrees of stability and so various chances to be reinternalised, varying from the very stable and reliable, as in words and phrases of 'natural' language and certain symbols, to others which are more evanescent and transient. Only when they are stable can we properly speak of the establishment of an 'extended mind', as Wilson and Clark contend. Finally, internal and external resources (that is, neural and environmental) are not identical but complementary – I have already said that in this sense human beings can be appropriately considered 'cyborgs' (Clark 2003).

I have also already illustrated that the 'cyborg' comprises a vast quantity of external information and that it is possible to 'materialise' many of our cybernetic aspects; at home, I can, in principle,[17] print out a picture of you as well as gather information about your sexual, political and literary preferences based on records of your online purchases. Consequently, those aspects are not only available to the person they concern; because they are potentially 'globally omnipresent', everyone can, in theory, see them. We must note that computer technology also distances the human body from the actions performed, and because it is an automating technology, it has a great potential to displace human presence.

Philosophically, the problem of privacy is classically related to the so-called 'panopticon' effect. The panopticon, conceived by Jeremy Bentham in 1786, was an architectural design for prisons that allowed just a few guards to keep an eye on a great many convicts. The structure was a round, multi-storey building with each floor's cells arranged in a circle around a hollow core. Rising from ground level in the centre, in a round atrium, was a guard tower with windows facing out toward the cells. Because each cell was illuminated by a window to the outside and the cell's inner wall consisted only of bars, guards could easily monitor the prisoners, every one of whom was completely visible at all times. Michel Foucault described the panopticon as a metaphor of the 'mechanisms of large-scale social control that characterize the modern world' (Foucault 1979; see also Reiman 1995). Of course, a person's being on display is enough by itself to effect social control: many psychological studies have observed that when people believe they are visible to others, they behave differently from the way they do when they believe they are out of view. Foucault considered the practices of medicine, psychology and sex education to be forms of social control 'because they create a world in which the details of our lives become symptoms exposed to a clinical *gaze* – even if not actually looking' (Reiman 1995: 29).

The internet can be seen as a modern panopticon that makes us all visible to anyone in a position to see. There is a tremendous amount of information on the net: on display are census data, addresses, credit card purchases, credit histories, medical information, employment histories, evidence of intimate relationships, indicators of religious inclinations – the list could go on and on. But unlike Bentham's prison, where prisoners could be watched only from a single point – the central guard tower – we can be, in principle, 'viewed'[18] from billions of sites, for all it takes is a computer with an internet connection. Computer networks have no centres and almost any portion can operate as an autonomous whole, which is also what makes controlling the network so difficult and de facto impossible. As I have already illustrated, a detailed computational 'shadow' of a private life can easily be built by collecting information that is available online.

There are those who maintain that the more privacy we have, the harder it is for society to gather information needed to apprehend and punish criminals, although I am sceptical about that assertion. Members of society must be protected not only from being seen[19] but also from feeling visible, and both conditions allow us to see privacy either as a basic right that some people are deprived of, or, even more importantly, as a method of controlling who may have access to us (Fried 1984). Some ethicists contend this second idea of privacy leads to anomalies: for example, the moral right to privacy has to be limited to 'my' right that others be deprived of their access to me. Nevertheless, we certainly want to establish laws that protect privacy and guarantee its status as both a moral and a legal right, even (and especially) in the era of the so-called 'information panopticon'(Fried 1984: 32–e4).[20]

Philosophy's notion of the fundamental elements of privacy is clearly evoked by John Stuart Mill: 'The only part of the conduct of anyone, for which he is amenable to society, is that which concerns others. In the part which merely concerns himself, his independence is, of right, absolute. Over himself, over his own body and mind, the individual is sovereign' (Mill 1966: 14).[21]

Most authors agree that a cyberdemocracy must be established to emphasise the role of civil rights and responsibility in cyberspace. Johnson's argument about the role of internet technology in promoting democracy concludes in an enigmatic way: the internet 'has the capacity for hegemonic as well as democratic relationships'. She goes on to pose many provocative questions: (1) how is internet development related to the digital divide? (2) Does the internet move toward private interests and market focus? (3) Can the participation it guarantees influence decision-making processes? (4) Does the internet threaten the autonomy and democratic status of nations? (5) To what extent is there privacy on the internet and to what extent is it a medium of surveillance? It seems the internet is in the service neither of enhancing democracy nor of promoting global democracy (Johnson 2000: 190–96).

Finally, we can distinguish two kinds of privacy violation: the first involves disseminating intimate information to a general audience without the consent of the person involved (Elgesem 1994)[22] and the second – it is the case of profiling – occurs when such personal information[23] is used to make decisions about the individuals involved without their involvement, possibly to harm them, more or less intentionally. There is always a conflict between privacy and freedom of information.[24] Medical information, while rarely disseminated, can become emotionally charged, for a person may feel lost, unprotected and vulnerable if the information is in fact spread. Health records may be communicated to others in certain circumstances, as in the case of epidemiological research, which is possible only when medical information about subjects is gathered and examined by scientists. Even in this case, however, participants' privacy can be protected by assigning them pseudonyms. To conclude, it really does seem that privacy can be considered both an intrinsic and an instrumental value essential to democracy, autonomy and liberty (cf Tavani 2002; Johnson 1994).

The availability of too much personal information through profiling increases our vulnerability to all kinds of danger, so protective measures must be instituted; contrariwise, however, monitoring the communications of others contradicts the universal right to privacy. Although there are some cases when too much privacy can be catastrophic – when families hide abuse against women and children, for instance – the cyberage renders privacy increasingly important. Heightened privacy poses its own difficulties, of course, bringing challenges that include greater costs as well many new needs – the need for developing new ethical and technical knowledge, establishing new political priorities and passing new laws.

The current problem is that profiles have no clear status: the situation in Western countries presents many puzzling cases, which depict a general lack of awareness of their real ways of affecting our lives: '[...] today's technological and organisational infrastructure makes it next to impossible seriously to check whether and when the directive is violated, creating an illusion of adequate data protection' (Hildebrandt 2008: 65). This implies that technological and organisational infrastructure de facto implement *moral axiologies* constituting new frameworks, which affect human habits, regulate behaviours and at the same time these technologies *cannot* be controlled by the current democratic legal systems just because of their own structure, which is characterised by impenetrability. Technologies invite certain behaviours and inhibit others, or even enforce certain behaviours while prohibiting others.

I am convinced that current political powers in Western countries have already started to exploit this despotic aspect of the new technologies almost everywhere. Here is an example, even if not related to the problem of privacy: the previous Berlusconi Italian government used various informational technologies – for example at the level of Ministry of University, which implemented centralised complicated web systems worthy of a police system – to enforce its own government policies, because the government probably saw the technological tools as proper extensions of its exercise of power. De facto the government embedded legal norms in technological devices trying to sidestep the checks and balances supposedly inherent in legal regulation. In sum 'legal' normative effects embedded in technology go beyond what has been legitimately adopted through the democratic decision of the parliament. Those embedded norms *are not legal* but merely the product of more or less aggressive and incompetent Rome governmental bureaucracies, which produce relevant normative effects without the real approval of the parliament and without the awareness of both parliament and citizens.

... How new techno-knowledge can counter privacy abuse

To avoid becoming victims of the normative effect of new technologies my moral motto 'knowledge as a duty' is still applicable. New intellectual frameworks have to be built, as soon as possible. For example it is necessary to acknowledge that legal norms aiming at defending privacy have to be 'incorporated' in the profiling technological tools themselves. As Hildebrandt (2008) explains:

> We are now moving into a new age, creating new classes of scribes, demanding a new literacy among ordinary citizens. To abstain from technological embodiment of legal norms in the emerging technologies that will constitute and regulate our world, would mean the end of the rule of law, paving the way for an instrumentalist rule by means of legal and technological instruments. Lawyers need to develop urgently a hermeneutic of profiling technologies, supplementing their understanding of written text. Only if such a hermeneutic is in place can we prevent a type of technologically embodiment of legal norms that in fact eradicates the sensitive *mélange* of instrumental and protective aspects that is crucial for the rule of law.

New technical and scientific knowledge, together with an improvement of ethical and institutional capacity, are simply urgent. It is only through the acknowledgement of the necessity of embodying legal norms in new technological devices and infrastructures that we can avoid 'the end of law as an effective and a legitimate instrument for constitutional democracy' (Hildebrandt 2009a: 443).

Hildebrandt (2009a) illustrates some new interesting perspectives. The so-called RFID technologies should include the 'adoption of design criteria that avoid risks to privacy and security, not only at the technological but also at the organisational and business process levels'. Constructive technology assessment (CTA) represents a case for 'upstream' involvement in technological design, that is, not installing ethical commissions after the technology is a finished product but getting involved at the earliest possible stage of technological design. I have repeatedly observed in *Morality in a Technological World* that designers' good intentions do not determine the actual consequences and affordances of a technology. Nevertheless, privacy-enhancing technologies (PETs), aimed for example at hiding of data (anonymisation) and use of pseudonyms, could moderate privacy risks. Finally, 'Countering the threats of autonomic profiling citizens will need more than the possibility of opting out, it will need effective transparency enhancing tools (TETs) that render accessible and assessable the profiles that may affect their lives' (Hildebrandt 2008: 67). When detected, the actual unexpected negative consequences and affordances of technology can be 'intentionally' counterbalanced.

This new cognitive/ethical potential has to elevate cognition from the implicit and unperceived to the explicit, which will allow us to understand technological processes: once they are organised into an appropriate hierarchy, they can be more readily managed. In doing so, the implementation of PETs and TETs still requires intentionality and free will and, consequently, 'moral responsibility'.

The concept of so-called 'integrative cognitivism' is linked to the theory of 'actor network: in keeping with Giddens's (1990) and Rowlands's (1999) perspectives. Allenby (2005) concurs with recent research in cognitive science which indicates that the mind is *extended* in external objects and representations; I maintain that our status as 'cyborgs' is due in part to the modern human being's extended mind. I have already said that the mind is extended, as is the intentionality of individuals, which, once it has affected a complex system, can become distorted, complicated, combined and confused, as is also true in the case of identity and privacy. Integrative cognitivism holds that the mind is always hybrid – not only in the case of modern human beings – as is expressed in an act of cognition during this interplay between internal processes and the external materiality of structures. We are cyborgs because of our ancestors' continuous – and evolutionarily successful – offloading of cognitive functions into the external environment and of their subsequent reinternalisation of those functions when possible and useful.

In summary, it is surely important to stress the importance of two ideas when discussing intentionality[25] and free will in their relationships with technology:

- Free will is not only 'performable' because of external (political) and internal (spiritual) freedom (Allenby 2005: 329–30). At a more basic level, free will depends upon the extent of our scientific and ethical knowledge: we can hypothesise a kind of co-evolution between our brains and our ability to produce and disseminate knowledge that furnishes the all-important 'elbow room' (Dennett 1984: 109) that is critically necessary for free will.[26] Profiling technologies, even if they are surely fruit of an extension of knowledge thanks to computational tools and models, they can paradoxically annihilate or weaken that 'elbow room' itself, leading to a restriction of autonomy, security and freedom, as I have illustrated.
- Some researchers maintain that intentionality and free will are expressed through and constrained by objective systems that, as integrative cognitivism teaches us, are in turn themselves affected by the freely made decisions of those who use the systems, and these systems are complex and constantly changing. They think that individuals' intentionality and free will are the 'ultimate source' of contingencies of human-affected systems, such as, for example, technologies that involve a sort of 'derivative intentionality' beyond what was originally planned. The internet is a particularly good example of this: people are the 'ultimate source' of this system's potential for good or ill when they use free choice in constructing new profiling technologies, for example.

I think this attitude misrepresents the *autonomous* and *general* role played by external computational materialities and underestimates their intrinsic features' ability to constrain human cognitive acts through a kind of hybrid interplay between internal and external. This materiality, when affected by human cognition and action, becomes a *mediator* that can exhibit unexpected moral and/or violent outcomes. Mediators are also related to implicit ways of moral acting, which I called 'templates of moral doing' (Magnani 2007: ch 6). What I call 'morality through doing' is the capacity human beings have to act morally – and implicitly – through doing, without any precise intellectual awareness, as is sometimes the case in the ethics of care. This 'acting morally through doing' often consists in building external structures and materialities that can mediate positive moral outcomes, even unexpected ones.[27] Of course, the same structures and materialities can mediate effects that are instead perceived as violent by the people affected by them.

To conclude, I certainly think that the mediated intentionality expressed in large and complex artefactual cognitive systems reminds us that we should not evade moral responsibility, but I would further clearly emphasise that circumventing such responsibility arises from a lack of a commitment to producing suitable knowledge able to manage their negative consequences. As a result, modern people are often jeopardised by the unanticipated, global-scale outcomes of localised individual intentions and this gap between local intentions and global consequences derives from using systems (technologies, for instance) that are only energised by that intentionality itself, as in the case of profiling technology. Fully understanding our various cognitive systems will help us to avoid damage to the earth, which is why I strongly support the motto 'knowledge as a duty'.

Who owns our own destinies? Privacy, intimacy, trust

Inadequate privacy surely also injures self-esteem and assaults the feeling of 'human dignity' as long as this lack is a clear threat to individual 'liberty' (Bloustein 1984: 160). We have said that the human 'cyborgs' are designated as such because they are composed of a huge quantity of electronically incorporated external information about their identity. Externalising information about ourselves in 'things' that are just 'out there', which, of course, makes that information available to others, also puts into jeopardy very important ends and relations including respect, love, friendship and trust.[28] These concepts, through which we express some of the more sophisticated aspects of 'human animals', are simply inconceivable without privacy (Fried 1984: 205).

If we consider privacy to be the ability to control information and knowledge about ourselves, it is obvious – as illustrated by the panopticon effect – that we are less free when we are observed or if we believe we are being observed. For example, electronic monitoring drastically reduces the power we have over information about ourselves: 'monitoring obviously presents vast opportunities for malice and misunderstanding on the part of the authorised personnel. For that reason the subject has reason to be constantly apprehensive and inhibited in what he does' (Fried 1984: 216).

Moreover, because intimacy is the conscious sharing of information about ourselves that is typically not revealed at all, privacy is the means to create what has been called the 'moral capital' that we spend, for example, in love and friendship. Privacy grants control over information so that we can preserve intimacy. Even between husband and wife, the restraints of privacy hold; although marriage implies a voluntary renunciation of private information, one spouse never knows what the other has chosen not to share.

If we consider trust to be the expectation that another person will behave morally (that is, by sharing a common moral axiological background), privacy becomes essential. To foster trust not all information need be shared: a person cannot know that she is trusted unless she has the right to act without constant surveillance; only then can she freely choose to honour or betray the trust and it is privacy that furnishes that fundamental right.

So in order to engage in intimate relationships such as love, friendship and trust, we must reveal some of ourselves, but if this information is seen by too many others, it loses its intimate nature so that love, friendship and trust are threatened. It now appears clear that having no control over information about ourselves has a deleterious effect on love, friendship and trust, and is, consequently, an assault on our liberty, personality and self-respect.

Consequently, privacy can be defined as the protection against interference with a person's way of realising and developing her interests, in terms of practical objectives of merely shaping one's own identity over time. By protecting privacy, we preserve the ability to develop and realise projects in our own ways. If respect for people is related to the respect for their rights, privacy becomes paramount. A monitored individual is indeed inclined to 'give himself away' (Fried 1984: 218), and so he is compelled to appear false, cold and unnatural. This can affect the attitude of other people whose esteem, love and friendship he desires.[29]

Conclusion

Contrary to Kant, who believed 'there is no need of science or philosophy for knowing what man has to do in order to be honest and good', I think ethics and decision-making should *always* be accompanied by suitable knowledge related to the situations at hand. If we want knowledge to be considered a duty, we must commit ourselves to generating, distributing and using knowledge in service of personal, economic, social and democratic development. The vital importance of knowledge means that we must use great care in its management and distribution and there are several transdisciplinary issues related to this challenge: from promoting creative, model-based and manipulative thinking in scientific and ethical reasoning to deepening the study of 'epistemic' and 'moral mediators'; from the interplay between unexpressed and super-expressed knowledge and their role in information technology to the shortcomings of the existing mechanisms for forming rational and ethical argumentations. A lack of appropriate knowledge creates a negative bias in concrete moral deliberations and is an obstacle to responsible behaviour, which is why I have emphasised the potential benefits of new embodied methods of implementing ethical and legal 'tools' such as PETs and TETs, and of acknowledging the new status of artefacts as 'moral and legal carriers'.

I have repeatedly also said that the proliferation of information carries many risks, primarily in the areas of identity and cyberprivacy. The internet and various databases contain an astounding volume of data about people, creating for every individual a sort of external 'data shadow' that identifies us or potentially identifies us and the possible consequences must be examined. To avoid being ostracised or stigmatised, people must be protected not only from being seen but also from 'feeling' too visible, which impairs the ability to make choices freely. And when sensitive information about a person is properly shielded, he or she is much less susceptible to exploitation and oppression by those seeking to use data unscrupulously.

Notes

1 The motto 'knowledge as a duty' indicates a proposed general philosophical imperative, which invites people to adopt a more systematic commitment to various kinds of knowledge (scientific, ethical etc) and to a better management of knowledge in the various circumstances of individual and social life. It refers to a general duty that does not specify particular duties to generate, internalise, protect, store or share knowledge; in sum, it is an invitation to give more intrinsic value to the role of knowledge in our technological world, following the tradition that derives from the scientific revolution and Enlightenment (more details are illustrated in Magnani (2007)). It is obvious that if we appropriately take into account our *bounded rationality* and *relative autonomy*, instead of assuming sovereignty and radical freedom of choice, the philosophical motto 'knowledge as duty' must be further qualified – not only from the philosophical perspective – and so our trust in those 'mediators' that provide us with knowledge that is appropriate and morally desirable in particular endeavours.

2 Of course technologies are primarily tools to advance the interests of people.

3 Only human acts of cognition can add worth to or subtract value from an entity and that revealing the similarities between people and things can help us to attribute to human beings the kind of worth that is now held by many highly valued non-human things. This process suggests a new perspective on ethical thinking: indeed, these objects and structures can mediate moral ideas and recalibrate the value of human beings by playing the role of what I call *moral mediators*. What exactly is a moral mediator? As I explain (in chapter 6 of Magnani 2007), I derived the concept of the moral mediator from that of the epistemic mediator, which I introduced in my previous research on abduction and creative and explanatory reasoning. First of all, moral mediators can extend value from already prized things to human beings, as well as to other non-human things and even to 'non-things' such as future people and animals. We are surrounded by human-made and artificial entities, whether they are concrete objects, eg a hammer or a PC or abstractions such as an institution or society; all of these things have the potential to serve as moral mediators. For this reason, I say that it is critically important for current ethics to address not only the relationships among human beings, but also those between human and nonhuman entities. Moreover, by exploiting the concepts of 'thinking through doing' and of manipulative abduction, I have illustrated that a considerable part of moral action is performed in a tacit way, so to say, 'through doing'. Part of this 'doing' can be considered a manipulation of the external world in order to build various moral mediators that function as enormous new sources of ethical information and knowledge. I call these schemes of action 'templates of moral doing'.

4 On the intrinsic moral value of some artefacts cf Magnani (2007).

5 I have explained the strict relationship between morality and violence in my book (Magnani 2011).

6 Ideally, this duty is envisaged as a universal duty owed to all knowledge and information by all agents. The question is whether it has to be considered an example of a 'perfect universal duty' because it also has a corresponding right – that is, the right to information and knowledge. Of course, the duty in question is highly circumstantial: I addressed this last problem in the section 'The Right and the Duty to Information and Knowledge' (Magnani 2007: ch 4).

7 Cf Fletcher et al (1999); Gallese et al (1996); Weiskrantz (1997), quoted in Dehaene and Naccache (2001).

8 Risk assessment, credit scoring, marketing, anti-money laundering, criminal profiling, customer relationship management, predictive medicine, e-learning and financial markets all thrive on data mining techniques, which reflect a type of knowledge construction based on various types of computation.

9 Cf also the amazing example of the 'pizza profile' memorised in the pizza parlour caller ID, illustrated in Moor (1997).

10 'If your "Ambient Intelligent Environment" caters to your preferences before you become aware of them, this will invite or even reinforce certain behaviours, like drinking coffee that is prepared automatically at a certain hour or going to sleep early during week days (because the central heating system has lowered the temperature). Other behaviours may be inhibited or even ruled out, because the fridge may refuse a person another beer if the caloric intake exceeds a certain point' (Hildebrandt 2009a: 452).

11 On abduction and induction from a cognitive, epistemological and computational perspective, cf Magnani (2009: ch 2).

12 Traditionally, abduction refers to that cognitive activity accounting for the introduction of new explanatory hypotheses in science or in diagnostic reasoning (for example in medicine). Abduction is the process of *inferring* certain facts and/or laws and hypotheses that render some sentences plausible, that *explain* or *discover* some (eventually new) phenomenon or observation; it is the process of reasoning in which explanatory hypotheses are formed and evaluated. There are two main epistemological meanings of the word abduction: (i) abduction that only generates plausible hypotheses ('selective' or 'creative'); and (ii) abduction considered as inference 'to the best explanation', which also evaluates hypotheses. To illustrate from the field of medical knowledge, the discovery of a new disease and the manifestations it causes can be considered as the result of a creative abductive inference. Therefore, 'creative' abduction deals with the whole field of the growth of scientific knowledge. This is irrelevant in medical diagnosis, where instead the task is to 'select' from an encyclopedia of pre-stored diagnostic entities. A full illustration of abductive cognition is given in Magnani (2009).

13 Cf van Otterlo's contribution in this volume (Chapter 2).

14 Cf also the classical Johnson (1994) and Stallman (1991). The range of ethical problems that have been generated by computer ethics is so large that some authors have maintained that it is a 'unique' field of applied ethics in the sense that it might happen its ethical issues to be unique (on the 'uniqueness debate' cf Tavani 2002). Certainly computer ethics is a wonderful example of moral progress both in terms of new moral issues/objects and new moral principles.

15 On the internet's retention of information in corporations, governments and other institutions, cf Davis and Splichal (2000).

16 The internet and the so-called 'Intelligent Vehicle Highway Systems' (IVHS) have also created 'external' devices that challenge our established rights to privacy, making it necessary clearly to define and shape new moral ontologies. Recently, ECHELON, the most powerful intelligence-gathering organisation in the world, has garnered attention as it has become suspected of conducting global electronic surveillance – mainly of traffic to and from North America – which could threaten the privacy of people all over the world. The European Union parliament established a temporary committee on the ECHELON interception system (1999–2004) to investigate its actions. The 2001 draft report 'on the existence of a global system for the interception of private and commercial communications (ECHELON interception system)' can be found at http://cryptome. org/echelon-ep-fin.htm (accessed 30 October 2012).

17 Of course, if I have the resources to invest in the relevant software, as is the case for large companies.

18 Profilers see much more than what my friends on Facebook see. It is important to distinguish between the data that everybody can see because a person published them and the profiles that are harvested by DM technologies on the basis of data I leaked inadvertently.

19 In a way it is a good thing if I feel visible, since then at least I am aware of being tracked and traced. We are not looking for ways to make people transparent while at the same time they do not feel visible. This is actually one of the problems of data mining: people are not at all aware of the extent to which they are visible.

20 Cf also Edgar (1997) and Tribe (2000).

21 Other aspects and benefits of privacy, such as promoting mental health and autonomy are illustrated in Gavison (1984).

22 On the role of cookies, sniffers, firewalls, data encryption, filtering systems, digital signatures, authentication and other technical tools to threaten or to protect privacy, cf the original analysis given by *Beckett* (2000); *Weckert* (2000) and *Spinello* (2000).

23 Profiling – on the contrary – allows such targeting without the use of 'such personal information'.

24 Obviously there is 'always' a conflict if we think that freedom of information refers to any information dissemination by anybody to anybody. As a human right freedom of information is a contested concept that usually refers to disclosure of information to nourish public debate on *relevant* issues. In that case, there need not be a conflict. It will depend on the particular situation whether there is a conflict.

25 I am not referring to intentionality in the phenomenological (philosophical) sense of the term but in the common sense meaning of being deliberate or purposive.

26 See the sections 'Tracking the External Word' and 'Tracking Human Behavior' in Magnani (2007) ch 3.

27 Cf also the section 'Moral Agents and Moral Patients' in Magnani (2007) ch 6, where I discuss moral mediators and what is called surrogate intentionality.

28 An example of externalising information is provided by van Wel and Royakkers (2004), who deeply investigate the possible negative impact of web data mining over privacy.

29 Moor (1997) adds another justification of privacy, beyond the one in terms of control/restricted account I am adopting here: privacy is also justified as an

expression of the core values that all normal humans and culture need to survive: life, happiness, freedom, knowledge, ability, resources and security. In this sense, privacy is justified as an essential member of the central framework of values for a computerised society.

References

Adam, A. (2002) 'The Ethical Dimension of Cyberfeminism', in Flanagan, M. and Booth, A. (eds): 159–74.

Allenby, B. (2005) 'Technology at the global scale: integrative cognitivism and Earth systems engineering and management', in Gorman, M. E., Tweney, R. D., Gooding, D. C. and Kincannon, A. P. (eds) *Scientific and Technological Thinking*, Mahwah, NJ and London: Erlbaum: 303–43.

Beckett, D. (2000), 'Internet technology', in Langford, D., (ed.) Internet Ethics, St. Martin Press: New York, pp. 13–46.

Benn, S. (1984) 'Privacy, freedom, and respect for persons', in Schoeman, F. (ed.) *Philosophical Dimensions of Privacy: An anthology*, Cambridge: Cambridge University Press: 223–44.

Bloustein, E. J. (1984) 'Privacy as an aspect of human dignity', in Schoeman, F. (ed.) *Philosophical Dimensions of Privacy: An anthology*, Cambridge: Cambridge University Press: 158–202.

Bynum, T. W. and Rogerson, S. (eds) (2004) *Computer Ethics and Professional Responsibility*, Malden, MA: Blackwell.

Clark, A. (2003) *Natural-Born Cyborgs. Minds, technologies, and the future of human intelligence*, Oxford and New York: Oxford University Press.

Compaine, B. M. (2001) *The Digital Divide. Facing a crisis or creating a myth?*, Cambridge, MA: MIT Press.

Damasio, A. R. (1999) *The Feeling of What Happens*, New York: Hartcourt Brace.

Davis, N. D. and Splichal, S. L. (2000) *Access Denied. Freedom of information in the information age*, Ames, IA: Iowa State University Press.

Dehaene, S. and Naccache, L. (2001) 'Towards a cognitive neuroscience of consciousness', in Dehaene, S. (ed.) *The Cognitive Neuroscience of Consciousness*, Cambridge, MA: MIT Press: 1–37.

Dennett, D. (1984) *Elbow Room. The variety of free will worth wanting*, Cambridge, MA: MIT Press.

Dibbel, J. (2001 [originally published in 1993]) 'A rape in the cyberspace', in Micah Hester, D. and Ford, P. J. (eds) *Computers and Ethics in the Cyberage*, Upper Saddle River, NJ: Prentice Hall: 439–52.

Edgar, S. L. (1997) *Morality and Machines: Perspectives in computer ethics*, Sudbury, MA: Jones and Bartlett.

Elgesem, D. (1994) 'Privacy, respect for persons, and risk', in Hester D. Micah and Ford, P.J., eds., (eds) (2001) *Computers and Ethics in the Cyberage*, Upper Saddle River , NJ: Prentice Hall: pp 256–277.

Flanagan, M. and Booth, A. (eds) (2002) *Reload. Rethinking women + cyberculture*, Cambridge, MA: MIT Press.

Fletcher, P. C., Happé, F., Frith, U., Baker, S. C., Donlan, R. J., Frackowiak, R. S. J. and Frith, C. D. (1999) 'Other Minds in the Brain: A functional imaging study of theory of mind in story comprehension', *Cognition*, 57: 109–28.

Foucault, M. (1979) *Discipline and Punish: The birth of the prison*, translated by A. Sheridan, New York: Vintage Books.

Fried, C. (1984) 'Privacy', in Schoeman, F. (ed.) *Philosophical Dimensions of Privacy: An anthology*, Cambridge: Cambridge University Press: 202–22.

Gallese, V., Fadiga, L., Fogassi, L. and Rizzolatti, G. (1966) 'Action Recognition in the Premotor Cortex', *Brain*, 119(2): 593–609.

Gavison, R. (1984) 'Privacy and the limits of law', in Schoeman, F. (ed.) *Philosophical Dimensions of Privacy: An anthology*, Cambridge: Cambridge University Press: 346–402.

Giddens, A. (1990) *The Consequences of Modernity*, Stanford, CA: Stanford University Press.

Girard, R. (1977) *Violence and the Sacred*, Baltimore, MD: Johns Hopkins University Press.

Girard, R. (1986) *The Scapegoat*, Baltimore, MD: Johns Hopkins University Press.

Godwin, M. (1998) *Cyber Rights. Defending free speech in the digital age*, Toronto: Random House.

Goldman, A. (1992) *Liaisons. Philosophy meets the cognitive and social sciences*, Cambridge, MA: MIT Press.

Gorman, M. E., Tweney, R.D., Gooding, D. C., and Kincannon, A. P. (eds) (2005) *Scientific and Technological Thinking*, Mahwah, NJ and London: Erlbaum.

Gotterbarn, D. (2000) 'Virtual information and the software engineering code of ethics', in Langford, D. (ed.) *Internet Ethics*, New York: St. Martin Press: 200–219.

Hildebrandt, M. (2007) 'A vision of ambient law', in Brownsword, R. and Yeung, K. (eds) *Regulating Technologies*, Oxford: Hart: 175–91.

Hildebrandt, M. (2008) 'Profiling and the Rule of Law', *IDIS*, 1: 55–70.

Hildebrandt, M. (2009a) 'Technology and the End of Law', in Keirsbilck, B., Devroe, W. and Claes, E. (eds) *Facing the Limits of the Law*, Heidelberg/Berlin: Springer: 1–22.

Hildebrandt, M. (2009b) 'Profiling and AmI', in Rannenberg, K., Royer, D. and Deuker, A. (eds) *The Future of Identity in the Information Society*, Heidelberg and Berlin: Springer: 273–310.

Hoven, J. van den (2000) 'The internet and varieties of moral wrongdoing', in Langford, D. (ed.) *Internet Ethics*, New York: St. Martin Press: 127–57.

Johnson, D. G. (1994) *Computer Ethics*, Englewood Cliffs, NJ: Prentice Hall, 2nd edition.

Johnson, D. (2000) 'Democratic values and the internet', in Langford, D. (ed.) *Internet Ethics*, New York: St. Martin Press: 181–99.

Jonas, H. (1974) 'Technology and responsibility: reflections on the new tasks of ethics', in *Philosophical Essays: From ancient creed to technological man*, Englewood Cliffs, NJ: Prentice Hall: 3–30.

Kant, I. (1964) *Groundwork of the Metaphysics of Morals*, New York: Harper & Row, 3rd edition (reprint of the 1956 edited and translated by H. J. Paton, Hutchinson & Co., Ltd, London); originally published 1785.

Magnani, L. (2007) *Morality in a Technological World. Knowledge as Duty*, Cambridge: Cambridge University Press.

Magnani, L. (2009) *Abductive Cognition. The epistemological and eco-cognitive dimensions of hypothetical reasoning*, Heidelberg and Berlin: Springer.

Magnani, L. (2011) *Understanding Violence. The intertwining of morality, religion and violence: A philosophical stance*, Heidelberg and Berlin: Springer.

Mawhood, J. and Tysver, D. (2000) 'Law and internet', in Langford, D. (ed.) *Internet Ethics*, New York: St. Martin Press: 96–126.

Mill, J. S. (1966) *On Liberty* (1859), in *On Liberty, Representative Government, The Subjection of Women*, Oxford: Oxford University Press, 12th edition: 5–141.

Moor, J. H. (1997) 'Towards a Theory of Privacy in the Information Age', *Computers and Society*, 27: 27–32.

Reiman, J. H. (1984) 'Privacy, intimacy, personhood', in Schoeman, F. (ed.) *Philosophical Dimensions of Privacy: An anthology*, Cambridge: Cambridge University Press: 300–16.

Reiman, J. H. (1995) 'Driving to the Panopticon: A philosophical exploration of the risks to privacy posed by the highway technology of the future', *Computer and High Technology Law Journal*, 11(1): 27–44.

Rowlands, M. (1999) *The Body in Mind*, Cambridge: Cambridge University Press.

Schiller, H. J. (2000) 'The global information highway', in Winston, M. E. and Edelbach, R. D. (eds) *Society, Ethics, and Technology*, Belmont: Wadsworth/Thomson Learning: 171–81.

Spinello, R. A. (2000), 'Information integrity', in Langford, D., (ed.) *Internet Ethics*, St. Martin Press: New York, pp. 458–480.

Stallman, R. (1991) 'Why software should be free', in Bynum, T. W. and Rogerson, S. (eds) (2004): 294–310.

Steinhart, E. (1999) 'Emergent Values for Automations: Ethical problems of life in the generalized internet', *Journal of Ethics and Information Technology*, 1(2): 155–60.

Tavani, H. (2002) 'The Uniqueness Debate in Computer Ethics: What exactly is at issue, and why does it matter?', *Ethics and Information Technology*, 4: 37–54.

Tribe, L. H. (2000) 'The constitution in cyberspace', in Winston, M. E. and Edelbach, R. D. (eds) *Society, Ethics, and Technology*, Belmont: Wadsworth/Thomson Learning: 223–31.

Warwick, K. (2003) 'Cyborg Morals, Cyborg Values, Cyborg Ethics', *Ethics and Information Technology*, 5: 131–37.

Weckert, J. (2000), 'What is new or unique about internet activities?', in Langford, D., (ed) *Internet Ethics*, St. Martin Press: New York, pp. 46–47.

Weiskrantz, L. (1997) *Consciousness Lost and Found: A neuropsychological exploration*, New York and Oxford: Oxford University Press.

Wel, L. van and Royakkers, L. (2004) 'Ethical Issues in Web Data Mining', *Ethics and Information Technology*, 6: 129–40.

4

Prediction, pre-emption, presumption

The path of law after the computational turn

Ian Kerr[1]

> For the rational study of law the blackletter man may be the man of the present but the man of the future is the man of statistics and the master of economics.
>
> Oliver Wendell Holmes Jr, 'The Path of Law' (1897)

Introduction

When I was first asked for a contribution to this volume, I decided to challenge myself to a game of *Digital Russian Roulette*. I wondered what result Google's predictive algorithm would generate as the theoretical foundation for the article that I was about to write on predictive computational techniques and their jurisprudential implications. Plugging the terms: 'prediction', 'computation', 'law' and 'theory' into Google, I promised myself that I would focus this chapter on whatever subject matter popped up when I clicked on the 'I'm Feeling Lucky' search feature.

So there I was, thanks to Google's predictive algorithm, visiting a Wikipedia page on the jurisprudence of Oliver Wendell Holmes Jr (Wikipedia 2011). Google done good. Perhaps America's most famous jurist, Holmes was clearly fascinated by the power of predictions and the predictive stance. So much so that he made prediction the centrepiece of his own prophecies regarding the future of legal education: 'The object of our study, then, is prediction, the prediction of the incidence of the public force through the instrumentality of the courts' (Holmes 1897: 457).

Given his historical role in promoting the skill of prediction to aspiring lawyers and legal educators, one cannot help but wonder what Holmes might have thought of the proliferation of predictive technologies and probabilistic techniques currently under research and development within the legal domain. Would he have approved of the legal predictions generated by expert systems software that provide efficient, affordable, computerised legal advice as an alternative to human lawyers?[2] What about the use of argument schemes and other machine learning techniques in the growing field of 'artificial intelligence and the law' (Prakken 2006) – seeking to make computers, rather than judges, the oracles of the law?

Although these were not live issues in Holmes's time,[3] contemporary legal theorists cannot easily ignore such questions. We are living in the kneecap of technology's exponential growth curve, with a flight trajectory limited more by our imaginations than the physical constraints upon Moore's Law.[4] We are also knee-deep in what some have called 'the computational turn' wherein innovations in storage capacity, data aggregation techniques and cross-contextual linkability enable new forms of idiopathic predictions. Opaque, anticipatory algorithms and social graphs allow inferences to be drawn about people and their preferences. These inferences may be accurate (or not), without our knowing exactly why.

One might say that our *information society* has swallowed whole Oliver Wendell Holmes Jr's predictive pill – except that our expansive social invest-ment in predictive techniques extends well beyond the bounds of predicting 'what the courts will do in fact' (Holmes 1897: 457). What Holmes said more than a century and a decade ago about the 'body of reports, of treatises, and of statutes in the United States and in England, extending back for six hundred years, and now increasing annually by hundreds' (Holmes 1897: 457) can now be said of the entire global trade in personal information, fuelled by emerging techniques in computer and information science, such as KDD:[5]

> In these sibylline leaves are gathered the scattered prophecies of the past upon the cases in which the axe will fall. These are what properly have been called the oracles of the law. Far the most important and pretty nearly the whole meaning of every new effort of ... thought is to make these prophecies more precise, and to generalize them into a thoroughly connected system.

As we shall see, the computational axe has fallen many times already and will continue to fall.

This chapter examines the path of law after the computational turn. Inspired by Holmes's use of prediction to better understand the fabric of law and social change, I suggest that his predictive stance (the famous 'bad man' theory) is also a useful heuristic device for understanding and evaluating the predictive technologies currently embraced by public- and private-sector institutions worldwide. I argue that today's predictive technologies threaten due process by enabling a dangerous new philosophy of pre-emption. My con-cern is that the *perception* of increased efficiency and reliability in the use of predictive technologies might be seen as the justification for a fundamental jurisprudential shift from our current *ex post facto* systems of penalties and punishments to *ex ante* preventative measures that are increasingly being adopted across various sectors of society.

This shift could fundamentally alter the path of law, significantly under-mining core presumptions built into the fabric of today's retributive and restorative models of social justice, many of which would be pre-empted by tomorrow's actuarial justice.[6] Unlike Holmes's predictive approach, which was meant to shed light on the nature of law by shifting law's standpoint to the perspective of everyday citizens who are subject to the law, pre-emptive approaches enabled by the computational turn will obfuscate the citizen's legal standpoint. Pre-emptive approaches have the potential to alter the very nature of law without justification, undermining many of our core legal presumptions and other fundamental commitments.

In the section that follows, I lay out Holmes's view of law as a business focused on the prediction and management of risk. I suggest that his famous speech, 'The Path of Law', lays a path not only for future lawyers but also for data scientists and other information professionals. I take a deeper look at Holmes's predictive theory and articulate what I take to be his central contribution – that in order to understand prediction, one must come to acknowledge, understand and account for the point of view from which it is made. An appreciation of Holmes's predictive stance allows for comparisons with the standpoints of today's prediction industries. I discuss these industries later in this chapter, where I attempt to locate potential harms generated by the prediction business associated with the computational turn. These harms are then further explored, where I argue that prediction, when understood in the context of risk, is readily connected to the idea of pre-emption. I suggest that the rapid increase in technologies of prediction and pre-emption go hand in hand and I warn that their broad acceptance represents a growing temptation to adopt a new philosophy of pre-emption, which could have a significant impact on our fundamental commitments to due process. Finally, I conclude by reflecting on the path of law and its future in light of the computational turn.

Holmes's predictive stance

Before delving into the computational turn and its implications for due process, it is worth exploring Holmes's understanding of the general role that prediction plays in law. For, as I argue below, the juxtaposition between Holmes's predictive stance and the standpoint adopted by many of today's anticipatory algorithms throws into sharp relief the risk of harm potentially generated by the computational turn.

Understanding law as a business was unquestionably one of the principal messages of Holmes's 'Path of Law' speech (Gordon 2000: 11). In particular, Holmes believes that the business of law is to predict and thereby avoid risk. The goal of Holmesian prediction is highly pragmatic: lawyers do it to keep their clients out of harm's way. For the liberal-minded Holmes (1897: 458), that harm generally presents itself through state coercion:

> [t]he primary rights and duties with which jurisprudence busies itself again are nothing but prophecies ... a legal duty so called is nothing but

a prediction that if a man does or omits certain things he will be made to suffer in this or that way by judgment of the court; and so of a legal right.

It may be said that Holmes's predictive approach anticipates the *risk society* – what sociologist Anthony Giddens described shortly after the 100th anniversary of the publication of 'The Path of Law' as 'a society increasingly preoccupied with the future (and also with safety), which generates the notion of risk' (Giddens 1999).

Borrowing today's terminology, one might therefore say that Holmes reimagined law as the business of risk management. Not only did he invent the field but he also articulated its legal methodology. Although he did not use these words in 'The Path of Law', he recognised that published common law decisions could be used as the data points from which predictions about future risk avoidance could be generated. Demonstrating the instincts of today's data scientist, Holmes wondered: if prediction is the name of the game, what are the aspiring lawyers seated in this audience to do about the deluge of legal data accompanying what seemed like an exponential increase in the number of annually reported cases across the common law? Holmes stated (1897: 474):

> The number of our predictions when generalized and reduced to a system is not unmanageably large. They present themselves as a finite body of dogma which may be mastered within a reasonable time. It is a great mistake to be frightened by the ever-increasing number of reports. [...] I wish, if I can, to lay down some first principles for the study of this body of dogma or systematized prediction [...] for men who want to use it as the instrument of their business to enable them to prophesy in their turn [...].

Could there be a better call to arms than this for the budding field of legal informatics? Even Holmes could not have predicted the fallout from remarks of this sort – in or outside of the field of law.

After all, Holmes's central aim in the speech was 'to point out and dispel a confusion between morality and law' (Holmes 1897: 459). This, he thought, was crucial not only in a business context but also to ensure the proper study of law. Holmes hoped at the same time to expose the fallacy that 'the only force at work in the development of the law is logic' (Holmes 1897: 465). He wanted to replace the incumbent legal formalism and its syllogistic approach to legal education by offering a more robust and realistic method, recognising, as he famously put it, that '[t]he life of the law has not been logic; it has been experience. The law [...] cannot be dealt with as if it contained the axioms and corollaries of a book of mathematics' (Holmes 1881: 1).

I think it is safe to say that Holmes's predictive approach is closely linked to his disdain of natural law theory and its confounding of law and morals. As an adherent of the tradition of legal positivism, Holmes was of the belief that legal doctrine – duties and rights, for example – are not pre-existing moral objects but social constructs that have been posited by humans in order to achieve instrumental legal purposes.

Putting the cart before the horse – confusing legal and moral ideas – Holmes thought, undermines 'a right study and mastery of the law as a business with well understood limits, a body of dogma enclosed within definite lines' (Holmes 1897: 459). So important was this potential for confusion that Holmes constructed a perceptual device through which law could be identified and understood:

> If you want to know the law and nothing else, *you must look at it as a bad man*, who cares only for the material consequences which such *knowledge enables him to predict*, not as a good one, who finds his reasons for conduct, whether inside the law or outside of it, in the vaguer sanctions of conscience. (emphasis added)

Who exactly is this bad man and why does Holmes think *he* has a monopoly on legal understanding? In answering these questions, it is useful to remember that Holmes had already framed the business of prediction within the context of risk avoidance. Repeating his words, 'it becomes a business to find out when this danger is to be feared' (Holmes 1897: 457). According to Holmes:

> You can see very plainly that a bad man has as much reason as a good one for wishing to avoid an encounter with the public force, and therefore you can see the practical importance of the distinction between morality and law. A man who cares nothing for an ethical rule which is believed and practised by his neighbors is likely nevertheless to care a good deal to avoid being made to pay money, and will want to keep out of jail if he can.
> (Holmes 1897: 459)

> ...

> But what does it mean to a bad man? Mainly, and in the first place, *a prophecy that if he does certain things he will be subjected to disagreeable consequences* by way of imprisonment or compulsory payment of money.
> (Holmes 1897: 461, emphasis added)

It is worth noting that a careful reading of 'The Path of Law' reveals that Holmes's bad man is perhaps *not so bad* after all. Catherine Pierce Wells describes him as 'simply someone who does not share in the ideals that the laws represent. The bad man could, for example, be a feminist, a religious fundamentalist, an abolitionist, a black separatist, a gay activist or even a Moonie' (Wells 2000). Perhaps no one has put it better than William Twining, whose very thoughtful characterisation (1972: 280) paints the bad man as neither:

> [...] a revolutionary nor even a reformer out to change 'the system." The Bad Man's concern is to secure his personal objectives within the existing order as painlessly as possible; he is not so much alienated from the law as he is indifferent to all aspects which do not affect him personally. [...] Nor is he a subscriber to some perverse ethic which turns conventional morality upon its head. The Bad Man is amoral rather than immoral.

The implications of this 'pale, incomplete, strange, artificial man' (Twining 1972: 280) have been enormous (see eg Cooter 1998). Taking an economic perspective – seeing legal duties as disjunctive (either keep your contract or pay damages) rather than categorical (you have a duty to keep your contract) – Holmes's bad man 'eliminates the moral onus from his conduct' (Luban 2000: 39).

Having adopted a disjunctive view of legal duty, it is therefore a defining characteristic of Holmes's bad man that he desires to predict in advance the legal outcome of his future behaviour. Prediction allows him to choose a future course of action that best aligns with his own self-interest. Prediction allows him to decide whether to (dis)obey the law. It enables him to pre-empt unfavourable (il)legal outcomes when they are not to his advantage.

Holmes was telling a room packed full of aspiring lawyers that if they want a 'rationally motivated', 'precise' and 'predictable' understanding of what the law demands in any particular instance, they should not look at the matter from the perspective of classical analytic jurisprudence or – *Gott in Himmel* – through the lens of morality. Instead, they should imagine themselves in their offices with 'the bad man seated across the desk [...] and think of the matter from his point of view' (Luban 2000: 37). In so doing they will realise that to investigate law from this standpoint is really just to work out what clients need to know in order to make effective predictions regarding their future legal advantage (Twining 1972: 286).

Here, finally, we come to what I believe is the crux of the matter for Holmes. Plain and simple: when it comes to thinking about the law, the bad man offers an important *switch in standpoint*.[7] Through the eyes of the bad man (or, for that matter, the good citizen, who is likewise concerned with legal prediction),[8] Holmes encouraged his audience to shift perspectives from the traditional narrowness of the elite classical Victorian jurist to the standpoint of everyday citizens who are subject to the law and who therefore seek to predict the future consequences of their actions. Although he did not offer a comprehensive theory of legal prediction, Holmes taught us that predictions should be understood with reference to the standpoint of everyday people, from their point of view and their sense of purpose. These important lessons are often lost in contemporary discussions of prediction, where we pay disproportionate attention to outcome-oriented features such as accuracy, reliability and efficiency.

Holmes's predictive stance is invaluable as we start to ponder the computational turn. Where Holmes left off is precisely where we should begin. As a quick recap, Holmes told us that: (i) predictions are made by lawyers; (ii) predictions are made from the point of view of the client; (iii) clients use those predictions to avoid risk of future harm through state coercion; and (iv) the prophecies of what courts will do are to be found in legal reports, treatises and statutes and inferred by various legal methods. Extrapolating from this, when we assess some of today's predictive technologies, we ought to keep in mind the following questions: (i) who makes computational predictions? (ii) for whom and from what perspective are computational predictions being made? (iii) when and for what purposes? (iv) and on what basis and by what means? With these questions in mind, we move from Holmes's predictive theory to a more contemporary look at today's prediction industries.

Prediction industries

Like the Holmesian bad-man-on-steroids, we – consumers, citizens, corporations and governments in an *information society* – have come to rely on a host of computational software that can anticipate and respond to our future needs and concerns. It is instructive briefly to consider a few examples from both the private and public sectors.

I started this chapter with a reference to Google. Although we think of Google primarily as a search engine, its convergence of services is really more like a giant prediction machine. When you enter your search query, Google not only provides a list of websites related to your search terms, it also predicts which of those sites you will find the most relevant and lists them first (Google 2010a). It does so using a search algorithm that is based upon a series of secret factors, including a proprietary technology called PageRank (Brin and Page 2006). This ranking system generates search results from most likely to least likely, based on a series of votes.

A web page's votes are tabulated by calculating the number of pages linked to it multiplied by its own rank value. Like other 'democratic systems', this method has its shortcomings. PageRank might assume that any vote is valid, meaning that false, fake or misleading links apply equally.[9] As each clicked link has the potential to be someone's monetary gain, practices of cyber squatting or link renting corrupt search results (Wall 2004). In such cases, the top hit does not accord with Larry Page's vision of the perfect search engine. Instead, the equivalent of a virtual billboard appears: an advertisement on a link that scores a high ranking on Google's search result page.

As we have seen, the 'I'm Feeling Lucky' search is designed to save time by directing you straight to the page that Google predicts you were most likely looking for – the first result for your query (Google 2010b). Google has extended this use of key word-based prediction beyond the search engine. Google's AdSense and AdWords programs automatically display advertisements that the technology predicts will meet your interests, based on the information you provide to various Google programs, such as Gmail (Google 2010c) and, more recently, the social network known as Google+ (Google 2011b). Despite its enormous fame, like many of today's anticipatory algorithms, Google is a relatively opaque technology.

Other online companies similarly use predictive advertising technologies. Take for instance Amazon's popular 'recommendations' or iTunes's Genius. Amazon's predictive algorithm considers the items that you have previously purchased, rated or told Amazon that you own and compares this information with the same information from other users. Based on what those users have purchased, Amazon will 'predict' what related items you might like and will recommend them to you (Amazon 2011). iTunes's Genius is similar. It employs an algorithm to compare the songs in your iTunes library, and information about how frequently you listen to your songs, to the same information from other iTunes users. Based on that comparison, iTunes can predict and recommend new music that you might enjoy. And, of course, it gives you a direct link to the iTunes store (iTunes 2011; Mims 2010). Amazon and iTunes are certainly not the only online businesses using predictive algorithms to customise advertising to internet shoppers.[10]

The social network Facebook has further expanded on these predictive data mining techniques through its Open Graph and instant personalisation technologies (Facebook 2011; Facebook Developers 2011). Instead of relying on the information that a user provides to one website, say for instance the internet movie database IMDb, Open Graph connects the user's online information across a host of websites by adding the user's IMDb 'likes' to her Facebook profile.[11] Facebook advertisers can then better predict the interests of that user and target advertising accordingly. Open Graph also allows different websites that have partnered with Facebook to predict a user's preferences based on the information contained on the user's Facebook profile. A partner website can then use this Facebook profile information to customise what the user sees and hears when browsing their site.[12] Open Graph can be thought of as Facebook's answer to Google Streetview – just as the relationship between physical objects on the street can be mapped by way of special cameras and software that can stitch the pieces together in a seamless whole, so too can the data points of people's personal information and preferences on Facebook be connected in ways that create a larger graphical understanding of their social landscape, allowing for a broader range of predictions to be made about individuals and groups.

Loyalty cards, match-making websites and bankcard monitoring similarly try to predict habits and create customer profiles in order to determine what promotions, personal connections or cautions are applicable to specific clients. The prediction industry is by no means limited to the private sector.

Governments have many uses for predictive profiling systems as well. Perhaps the most widely known application of prediction occurs at airports and other border crossings.

For example, there are many passenger safety systems in place in airports around the world that demand additional screening from identified individuals or that prevent travellers from flying altogether. As I shall discuss further below, Canada's Passenger Protect program relies on predictive intelligence from the Canadian Security Intelligence Service and Royal Canadian Mounted Police to produce a computerised passenger database, which it calls the Specified Persons List (Transport Canada 2009). Individuals who are deemed to pose a threat to airline security are placed in the database (Government of Canada 2010). The system is designed to ensure that the individuals are identified before they have the opportunity to board an aircraft. The system is similar to the US No-Fly List and other systems employed elsewhere (see eg Federal Bureau of Investigation 2010; Transportation Security Administration 2010).

The reliability of such algorithms has been widely decried; systems such as Soundex and CAPPS II are now defunct owing to inaccuracy rates as high as 85 per cent (Moore 2007). Many newborn and deceased individuals have also somehow made their way onto no-fly lists. While officials claim that listing such individuals reduces incidences of misused identity, critics claim that the bureaucracy is too slow to respond (Zetter 2010). Memorably, Senator Ted Kennedy was briefly grounded because of confusion caused by a 'name likeness' with someone on the US No-Fly List (Henry and Ahlers 2004). To this day, there does not seem to be a compelling reason to have detained one of America's most well known senators. Furthermore, reports suggest significant challenges associated with profiling terrorists: a Dutch study showed no reliable indicators that could predict which individuals are likely to embrace Islamic radicalism (Whitlock 2007).

This brief set of descriptions and anecdotes offers a snapshot of the broad range of predictive technologies and techniques employed in the public and private sectors. Unlike legal prediction *à la* Holmes's bad man, computational prediction does not adopt a singular or even uniform predictive stance. To demonstrate this point and consider some of its consequences, it is useful to return to the generalised questions extrapolated from Holmes's work as discussed above.

Who makes computational predictions?

Locating the author(s) of a computational prediction is a difficult, sometimes awkward task. Prediction algorithms used by government agencies may be unavailable to the public for reasons of national security and public safety. Furthermore, many of the prediction algorithms and software applications discussed above are subject to copyright and trade secret laws, so the public cannot find out who wrote them, how they work or whether the assumptions upon which they are based are sound.[13] Difficulties in coming to know anything more about the author(s) of the prediction, let alone establishing a legal relationship with them, can be further complicated by the fact that private services are licensed to end users for only limited purposes. To complicate matters further, locating the author(s) of a computational prediction is sometimes awkward because the creator of the algorithm or software may not in any clear sense be the author of any particular prediction generated by the system. Intelligent agent software (Kerr 2004, 1999) and other innovations in the field of artificial intelligence enable 'autonomous' computer-generated operations that are distinct from the programs that set them in motion and are sometimes not even fully comprehended by the human beings who did the programming. Within the context of the computational turn, predictive techniques often have no human author; sometimes there is no one who is directly accountable for any particular machine-generated prediction (Solum 1992).

For whom and from whose perspective?

Recall that for Holmes the role and task of legal prediction is intimately and inextricably connected to the standpoint of those on whose behalf the predictions are made. The predictive stance for Holmes requires lawyers to adopt the perspective of their clients in order to promote their future interests, regardless of their moral stance. The same is untrue for most computational prediction systems. Unlike lawyers, who are bound by fiduciary duties, computational prediction providers are not usually seen as entering into personal relationships with their clients. The word *client* (which historically connotes one being under the protection and patronage of another) in this context is a misnomer. Here, the parties do not know each other. Neither does one protect the other. The so-called 'client' is in truth little more than a data subject, whose actual perspective is never considered.[14] An automated system simply collects data about the data subject and runs its algorithm(s).

Unlike lawyers or other professionals, computational prediction systems do not generate relationships of trust and therefore do not attract special duties of care in any traditional sense.[15] Rather, the duties between the parties – merely contractual in nature – are carefully circumscribed in the prediction provider's mass market end user licence agreement (EULA). These EULAs are typically one sided, generally quite restrictive and often require the data subject to waive various rights to privacy and due process. Unlike the solicitor–client relationship, these EULAs ensure that the parties remain at arm's length (see eg the Terms and Conditions provided at iTunes 2010). Although the services provided are often thought of as 'free', in the sense that they do not cost money, the personal information that is collected and used in exchange for the prediction service is often so valuable that it is the basis of the entire business model.[16]

In many cases, the prediction service is little more than an appendage to a broader range of sales and services provided, none of which involves taking into account the standpoint or future interests of the data subject. At best, there is a willingness to stroke certain consumer preferences in exchange for valuable personal information, the implications of which are usually obfuscated and unclear from the perspective of the data subject. For example, the predictive recommendations made by Amazon or iTunes are less about serving clients than they are about mining data about individual preferences in order to sell stuff. Unlike legal or medical predictions, which aim to benefit the well being of the client or patient,[17] much of today's private sector prediction industries serve a broader corporate mandate that seeks first and foremost to benefit the information service provider.

Of course, the situation is even worse for computational systems designed to render predictions *about* data subjects. In contrast to Holmesian legal prediction, the entire basis of which was to shield citizens from the threat of state sanction, modern social sorting and profiling techniques such as no-fly lists are designed to promote corporate and state interests such as profit, prosperity, security and safety, often at the expense of any given citizen. As part of a broader adversarial system, technologies of this sort are meant to generate predictions entirely at odds with the interests of the data subjects, especially when they are presumed to be the 'bad man'. It is important to note that, unlike Holmesian prediction, these are *not* predictions about legal outcomes. For the most part, they are behavioural predictions about the supposed future conduct of individuals, often based on their past behaviour or their associations with other individuals and groups (McCulloch and Pickering 2009; Wilson and Weber 2008).

When and for what purposes?

Predictions are by definition anticipatory. To predict is to say or know something before it happens.[18] As we saw with Holmes, legal prediction allows a lawyer to anticipate the consequences of future courses of conduct in order to advise clients whether it is feasible or desirable to avoid the risk of state sanction. I will call predictions that attempt to anticipate the likely consequences of one's action 'consequential predictions'.

With this definition, one sees right away that many of the predictive technologies discussed above are of a different sort. When I ask iTunes's Genius to anticipate which songs I will like, the system is not generating predictions about my conduct or its likely consequences. Rather, it is trying to stroke my preferences in order to sell me stuff. Much of the prediction business is focused on predictions of this sort, which I shall refer to as 'preferential predictions'. Like the lawyer's consequential predictions, preferential predictions are meant to increase a person's future options, but in a more materialistic way and usually from the perspective of the seller.

There is a third form of prediction exemplified by a number of the technologies that form part of today's prediction industries. Unlike consequential and preferential predictions, 'pre-emptive predictions' are used to diminish a person's future options. Pre-emptive predictions assess the likely consequences of (dis)allowing a person to act in a certain way. Immediately, one should recognise that these predictions do not usually adopt the perspective of the actor. Pre-emptive predictions are mostly made from the standpoint of the state, a corporation or anyone who wishes to prevent or forestall certain types of action. Pre-emptive predictions do not assess an individual's actions but whether the individual should be permitted to act in a certain way. Examples of pre-emptive prediction techniques include a no-fly list used to preclude possible terrorist activity on an airplane, or a regionally coded DVD that automatically scrambles the North American display of movies bought in Europe (thus pre-empting presumed copyright infringement).

These three categories of prediction – consequential, preferential and pre-emptive – are not meant to provide an exhaustive list of all possible predictive purposes. But, as I will articulate in the sections that follow, understanding these different predictive purposes will help to locate the potential harm of various predictive technologies associated with the computational turn.

On what basis and by what means?

The question 'on what basis and by what means are computational predictions made?' is, for the most part, best left to the chapter in this volume written by data scientist van Otterlo (Chapter 2). The reason for this is not only because of the technical nature of the answers to such questions but also because of how little is publicly known about the means by which some of the more significant examples of computational predictions are made. As mentioned above, it is important to recognise that the basis and means by which particular predictions are generated are often developed in a context where secrecy is tantamount to the success or profitability of the product. I challenge any technologist in the world not involved in the development or maintainance of such systems to detail *exactly* how Google's secret algorithm works publicly or how the US Terrorist Screening Centre's No-Fly List is computed.[19]

This attempt to provide even basic answers to the question ('on what basis and by what means?') and the three questions that preceded it leads me to end this discussion of the inquiry with a circumlocution of Holmes's great opening line in 'The Path of Law':[20] When we study predictive algorithms we are studying a mystery, *not* a well known profession.

Prediction and pre-emption

The power of today's predictive techniques and their potential for harm are perhaps best understood in the context of risk. Earlier in this chapter I mentioned that Holmes's predictive approach anticipates the *risk society*. When sociologist Ulrich Beck coined this term in the 1990s, he was not suggesting that society is more risky or dangerous nowadays than it was before. Instead, he set out to describe the manner and extent to which modern society is organised in response to risk.

Beck believes (1992: 19) that, in modern society, 'the social production of wealth is systematically accompanied by the social production of risks' and that, accordingly:

> ... the problems and conflicts relating to distribution in a society of scarcity overlap with the problems and conflicts that arise from the production, definition and distribution of techno-scientifically produced risks.

On Beck's account, risk and prediction are interrelated concepts. He subsequently defined risk as 'the modern approach to foresee and control the future consequences of human action' – which he believed to be the 'unintended consequences of radicalised modernization' (Beck 1999: 3).

Holmes saw this connection as well, contending that prediction is a means of avoiding risk. Much like Beck, Holmes had also recognised that the production of risk is lucrative. It is therefore no surprise that Holmes used the legal device of contract to illustrate both prediction and risk as valuable commodities. When we create a contract, we obtain benefits in exchange for undertakings; we get something now with a probability of being forced to pay for it later. In other words, we create risk – we mortgage our future selves in favour of our present selves. Legal prediction is a highly valued commodity for clients who seek to avoid or mitigate future legal risk. At the same time, the production of legal risk (for example, the creation of a contract or the assumption of debt) is invaluable to both lawyers and their clients.

Taken together, Holmes and Beck help to demonstrate the clear connection between risk and prediction. To put it bluntly, prediction industries flourish in a society that is organised in response to risk. This is because prediction often precipitates the attempt to pre-empt risk.

The relationship between prediction and pre-emption was of less import to Holmesian society than it is to the risk society. Holmes's preoccupation was the power of the state over individuals, which generated an interest in what I have called consequential predictions: predictions about the likely (legal) consequences of the bad man's actions.

By contrast, in a society that is organised in response to risk – where *anyone* can be the bad man – there is a heightened interest in pre-emptive predictions: predictions that assess the likely consequences of (dis)allowing a person to act in a certain way. Given the above analysis regarding the relationship between risk and prediction, it stands to reason that the escalating interest in (pre-emptive) predictions will provide the justification for new forms of social pre-emption. In much the same way that Holmesian clients use legal prediction to pre-empt future legal risk, governments, corporations and individuals will use predictive technologies in order to pre-empt or forestall conduct that is perceived to generate social risk.

The Specified Persons List mentioned above provides an illustration. With an increased (perception in the) ability of government agencies successfully to predict which individuals will pose a threat to national security, this deeply controversial list[21] catalogues an inventory of individuals who are pre-empted from boarding a commercial aircraft for travel in or out of the country. Canada's Passenger Protect system, implemented in 2007, pre-empts from flight anyone on the Specified Persons List, that is, anyone 'who may pose an immediate threat to air security' (Government of Canada 2010). The means of predicting who poses a risk sufficient to pre-empt them from flying includes a (partially) computer-generated assessment of:

- past history with regards to acts of violence, terrorism, criminal acts and/or convictions, active association with known or suspected terrorists and/or terrorist groups and their personal history of terrorist acts
- the individual's intent with regards to engaging in a hostile act that may involve or threaten transportation or aviation
- the individual's capability based on their knowledge, abilities and/or experience, which may be used to threaten or harm aviation or transportation.

Prior to the development of this list, those perceived to be high-risk individuals were still free to travel – unless there were reasonable and probable grounds to believe that the high-risk individual was actually in the process of committing an offence. A no-fly list pre-empts the need for any such evidence. In the risk society, prediction replaces the need for proof.

Although nascent, the private sector also has a deep interest in the development and use of pre-emptive technologies. A typical example is the growing use of digital locks to pre-empt unauthorised individuals (read: high-risk hacker types) from accessing copyrighted works. Prior to the development of these digital technologies, the entire system of copyright was premised on the notion that individuals are free to consume intellectual works and free to copy and share them within the limits of copyright law – without ever asking for anyone's prior permission to do so. Under the old system, copyright owners also had the right to sue anyone that they believed to be infringing their copyright. But they *did not* have the legal right or technological power to pre-empt access to the work altogether. Now they have both. First, they have the technological capability to wrap digital locks around digital content so that only those with prior authorisation can access it (Stefik 1997, 1996). Second, in many jurisdictions, this form of technological pre-emption is in fact state sanctioned. Not only is pre-emption legally permitted – in many countries there are laws that prohibit tampering with the digital lock – even if the lock-breaker has proprietary reasons for doing so and never intended to infringe copyright in the process (Kerr 2010, 2005). This state-sanctioned pre-emption of access to digital content has a tremendous impact on various rights and freedoms, including access to information, freedom of expression, privacy, encryption research, freedom to tinker and education, as well as copyright's delicate balance between owner and user rights.

Of course, similar pre-emptive techniques can be employed beyond the copyright sector. They can be used to prevent a broad range of activities limited only by the technological imagination, from drinking and driving (O'Donnell 2006) to filtering out sounds that are not part of the prepaid bundle of services subscribed to by a patient with cochlear implants (Kerr 2011).

It is tempting to view the broad adoption of the above technologies in both the public and private sector as evidence of a potential shift towards a new philosophy of pre-emption – what two authors recently styled the 'duty to prevent' (Feinstein and Slaughter 2004). Perhaps the best illustration of this philosophical shift is the legal and technological approach to counter-terrorism, exemplified by what has become known in international law as the 'Bush Doctrine'. President Bush first publicly discussed pre-emption in a speech at West Point on 1 June 2002:

> If we wait for threats to fully materialize, we will have waited too long. ...
> We must take the battle to the enemy, disrupt his plans, and confront the
> worst threats before they emerge...our security will require all Americans
> to be forward-looking and resolute, to be ready for preemptive action
> when necessary to defend our liberty and to defend our lives.
>
> (United States Military Academy 2002)

Those who subscribe to the philosophy of pre-emption believe that '[p]erpetrators of terrorist attacks now operate from a dispersed and invisible transnational network – terrorists are "here, there and everywhere"' (Nabati 2003: 779).[22] Here, the terrorist is the ubiquitous bad man. Whereas the word 'criminal' connotes a person who has committed a crime at some point in the past, the future threat of the terrorist looms large. According to McCulloch and Pickering (2009: 630), in other words, the terrorist concept is inherently pre-emptive:

> Countering terrorism is uniquely suited to a shift to pre-crime frameworks because the term 'terrorism' itself is pre-emptive, existing prior to and beyond any formal verdict.

McCulloch and Pickering's reference to pre-crime frameworks is of course an allusion to Philip K. Dick's famous 1956 short story *The Minority Report* (Dick 1956). Dick imagines a future society that has fully embraced the philosophy of pre-emption. The pre-emption of crime is made possible through the technological mediation of three mutant precogs who, together, form a prediction machine able to forecast future outcomes with stunning accuracy and reliability. Blurring the lines between deterrence and punishment, the pre-crime system pre-emptively incarcerates individuals whenever the pre-cogs predict that they will commit a future crime. This predictive system replaces the traditional criminal justice system of discovering a crime and its perpetrator *ex post facto*, presuming the accused's innocence, then, through due process, establishing guilt and, finally, issuing an appropriate punishment. Like the no-fly list, we see that prediction replaces the need for proof.

Whether Dick was himself predicting the future or providing its blueprints by way of a self-fulfilling prophecy, modern data mining techniques are already being used to carry forward this pre-emption philosophy (Steinbock 2005; Beecher-Monas 2003). For example, Richard Berk, Professor of Statistics and Criminology at the Wharton School, University of Pennsylvania (University of Pennsylvania 2011) has developed an anticipatory algorithm that sifts through a database of thousands of crimes and uses algorithms and different variables, such as geographical location, criminal records and ages of previous offenders, to come up with predictions of where, when and how a crime could possibly be committed and by whom (Watson 2010). Versions of this technology have already been adopted in Baltimore and Philadelphia to predict which individuals on probation or parole are most likely to murder and to be murdered (Bland 2010). Washington DC has recently implemented a newer version of the software, which will identify individuals most likely to commit crimes other than murder.

Although the 'pre-crime' concept is not directly at play, Professor Berk's anticipatory software is already being used to help determine how much supervision parolees should have based on predictions about how they are likely to behave in the future. Professor Berk says the program will also play an invaluable role in future determinations for bail and sentencing hearings (Bland 2010). For better or for worse, his software, which merely computes statistical probabilities, is already pre-empting the life chances and social opportunities of thousands of data subjects across various jurisdictions in a very real way. And Professor Berk's software is not the only game in town – there are a growing number of similar systems in use throughout the United States and the United Kingdom.[23]

Reports such as these are often exaggerated and even more often used to prophesy the coming era of *The Minority Report*, and the idea that we are 'sleepwalking into a surveillance society'.[24] This is not my purpose. The more modest claim that I have tried to articulate in this section is that prediction, when understood in the context of risk, is easily connected to the idea of pre-emption. If this is correct, it should therefore come as no surprise that technologies of prediction and pre-emption go hand in hand. This is not because they are somehow inevitably linked but simply because, as Holmes told his audience so long ago: 'people want to know under what circumstances and how far they will run the risk of coming against what is so much stronger than themselves, and [...] to find out when this danger is to be feared' (Holmes 1897: 457).

A careless and excessive adoption of the pre-emption doctrine could have a significant impact on our fundamental commitments to justice and due process, unravelling many core presumptions that stitch together the very fabric of our legal system. In the next section I highlight a few key threads and show how they might be unknotted by today's predictive and pre-emptive techniques.

How prediction and pre-emption undermine due process

The coupling of pre-emptive goals with predictive techniques, discussed in the previous section, signals an important concern shared by many who study the relationship between law and technology. Technologists have the ability to impose upon the world norms of their own making – promulgated not through democratically enacted legal code but through the oligarchy of software code (Lessig 2006; Reidenberg 1998). Left unchecked, predictive and pre-emptive technologies provide tremendous power to programmers and those who utilise their technologies. They are able to use software to regulate human behaviour and make key decisions about people without the usual legal checks and balances furnished in real space. Artificial intelligence pioneer, Joseph Weizenbaum, was not kidding when he once said that: '[t]he computer programmer is a creator of universes for which he alone is responsible. Universes of virtually unlimited complexity can be created in the form of computer programs' (Weizenbaum 1976). From a broad legal and ethical perspective, problems are sure to arise when anticipatory algorithms and other computational systems import norms that undermine the due process otherwise afforded to citizens by law (Hildebrandt 2008). In the final two sections of this chapter, I consider – à la Weizenbaum – whether predictive programs have the potential to rewrite the code of the legal universe by reprogramming some of its core normative presumptions.

If the legal universe has a 'prime directive' (Joseph 1975), it is probably the shared understanding that everyone is presumed innocent until proved guilty. This well known legal presumption is usually construed, narrowly, as a procedural safeguard enshrined in criminal and constitutional law (Quintard-Morenas 2010; Schwikkard 1998). However, it can also be understood as a broader moral claim, the aim of which is to provide fair and equal treatment to all by setting boundaries around the kinds of assumption that can and cannot be made about individuals. These boundaries are intended to prevent certain forms of unwarranted social exclusion (Ericson 1994; Gandy 1993).

In the context of criminal procedure and administrative law, the systematic safeguards underlying this broader understanding of the presumption of innocence generally include: timely and informative notice of a hearing; an ability to know the case against you; a fair and impartial hearing; an opportunity to respond; an ability to question those seeking to make a case against you; access to legal counsel; a public record of the proceedings; public attendance; published reasons for the decision; and, in some cases, an ability to appeal the decision or seek judicial review (Friendly 1974–1975). Although European tradition historically labelled these rights under the heading of 'equality of arms' (Wasek-Wiaderek 2000), many common law and civil law jurisdictions now refer to this bundle of normative legal rights and presumptions as 'due process' (Shipley 2008).

Due process is primarily understood as a creature of public law. However, much of the private sector is imbued with a corollary set of presumptions and safeguards with similar aims and ambitions. Indeed, there are many parallels between the duties owed by the state to its citizens and the duties owed by corporations to employees and customers.[25] A host of legal and ethical norms in the private sector mirror due process guarantees in public law. These are usually expressed in the form of: a right to full information; a right to be heard; a right to ask questions and receive answers; and a right of redress. Basic rules of fairness such as these are often adopted or otherwise imposed upon the private sector – even where criminal and constitutional due process rights are not in play.

For example, in the North American workplace, prospective employees – even if never hired – are entitled to fair treatment during the recruiting process.[26] Among other things, this means that in order to ensure that job applicants perceive the hiring process as fair, employers need to offer interviewees an opportunity to: demonstrate their knowledge and skill; be evaluated only on relevant skills; ask questions about the selection process; receive timely and informative feedback on the decision-making process; challenge its outcomes etc (Gilliland 1995). Because hiring is among the most fundamental of decisions made about a person in our society, something like due process is required to ensure that people are treated fairly. Principles of this sort are meant to provide job applicants with the opportunity to participate and be heard, ensuring that hiring decisions are not made on the basis of faulty predictions or presumptions, so that no one is unfairly pre-empted from employment.

A second example occurs in private sector data protection practices implemented throughout Europe, Canada and in various sectoral laws in the US (FTC 2007). Originally promulgated as guidelines by the OECD (OECD 1980), most of these laws are also founded on basic principles of fairness – sometimes known as 'fair information practice principles'. In much the same way that due process requires notice prior to a trial or administrative hearing, fair information practice principles require data subjects to be notified about information sharing practices[27] prior to decisions about the collection or disclosure of their personal information. With the aim of achieving 'informational self-determination' (German Data Forum 2010: 632–33; Federal

Constitutional Court of Germany 1983), data subjects are provided timely and affordable means of access to data collected about them and are likewise permitted to contest its accuracy (FTC 2007). Where self-regulatory models fall short, data subjects are usually entitled to various means of enforcement and redress – including private rights of action enforced by courts or administrative bodies (FTC 2007).

A number of broader due process values underlie the data protection model, including openness, accountability, consent, accuracy of information and reasonable limits on collection and use (Personal Information Protection and Electronic Documents Act, SC 2000, c 5: Schedule 1). Among other things, the embedding of these values into the data protection model seeks to ensure that information will not be used out of context to make unwarranted presumptions or predictions that could unfairly implicate the life chances or opportunities of data subjects (Nissenbaum 2009). More and more, private sector entities are being called upon to develop due process-friendly procedures aimed at ensuring fairness to individuals about whom personal information is collected, used or disclosed. This has resulted in the adoption of similar due process guidelines by the United Nations and throughout Europe and North America for a broader range of consumer protection issues (see eg Massachusetts Office of Consumer Affairs and Business Regulation 2011; European Commission 2005; United Nations 2003; Consumer Protection Act, SO 2002, c 30: Schedule A (Ontario)). Some academics have further argued that we need a special regime to extend due process requirements to systems operators on the internet, recognising that the actions of system operators 'can become the occasion for substantial injustice if [...] imposed without adequate cause or without the use of procedures that give the user (and, perhaps, the cybercommunity) a chance to be heard' (Johnson 1996).

At its core – whether in the public or private sector, online or off – the due process concept requires that individuals have an ability to observe, understand, participate in and respond to important decisions or actions that implicate them.

Of course, these rights are precisely what some predictive and pre-emptive technologies seek to circumvent. To take one recent example, the State of Colorado recently implemented a Benefits Management System (CBMS) that uses predictive algorithms to automate decisions about an individual's entitlement to Medicaid, food stamps and welfare compensation (Citron 2007–2008: 1256). Historically, important decisions of this sort were administrative decisions subject to due process. But this is no longer so. In fact, the entire point of automated systems such as CBMS is to streamline or eliminate administrative process in order to maximise efficiency and reduce transaction costs (Hammons and Reinertson 2004). Used with increasing frequency by governments and the private sector, such systems minimise or in many cases remove human beings from the decision-making process altogether – not merely the human decision-makers but also the subjects of these decisions. This becomes deeply problematic when automated systems go awry, as was the case with the CBMS. Owing to hundreds of programming errors in the translation of the state's benefits rules into computer code, CBMS issued hundreds of thousands of erroneous Medicaid, food stamps and welfare eligibility decisions, negatively affecting the lives of an even greater number of people than would have been affected by a slower, human-run system (Booth 2011; Smith 2006).

In her extremely thoughtful article entitled 'Technological Due Process', Professor Danielle Citron very convincingly demonstrates the dangers of such predictive and pre-emptive technologies: they undermine notice requirements, obfuscate the right to be heard and thwart participation and transparency in a rapidly eroding public rule-making process (Citron 2007–2008). Professor Citron provides some well tailored solutions, advocating a new model of technological due process. Drawing on the rules-versus-standards literature in US administrative law, she offers surrogate rules to prevent errors and increase transparency, accountability and fairness. She also considers new standards that might be encoded into the software to prevent arbitrary decision-making. Her overarching aim is to find a means of protecting due process 'without forgoing the benefits offered by computerized decision systems' (Citron 2007–2008: 1313).

Embedding pragmatic solutions into the architecture of new and emerging technologies on a case-by-case basis is a popular approach in the privacy field (Information and Privacy Commissioner of Ontario 2011). But what of the potentially deep systemic problems sure to arise as we scuttle the justice system in favour of efficient actuarial models, as we shift away from law's foundational commitment to righting wrongs, opting instead for the adoption of technological systems that prevent and preclude them? Are there not reasonable limits to the kinds of thing that institutions should be allowed to presume and predict about people without their involvement or participation? To what extent and by what means should institutions be permitted to organise in relation to such presumptions and predictions?

The path of law after the computational turn

Contemplating these difficult questions, it is useful to return one last time to Holmes's approach to legal prediction. Recall that one of Holmes's most important contributions to jurisprudence was his recognition that *point of view* matters. Understanding law from the point of view of the bad man or his lawyer – who seek nothing other than accurate predictions about what courts will do in fact – is *in fact* an endorsement of due process.[28] After all, it is not possible for legal subjects or their counsel to make predictions about what courts or tribunals will do without the ability to observe, understand, participate in and respond to the decision-making process. Due process is a prerequisite of legal prediction. Yet, due process is precisely what is thwarted when the predictive focal point shifts from the law's rules and decisions to its subjects.

As discussed earlier in this chapter, the computational turn has not only improved our ability to make consequential predictions about what courts will do but it has also vastly expanded the capability for producing preferential and pre-emptive predictions about people. Such predictions are now used routinely by institutions with financial or security related interests for social sorting and actuarial decision-making. Holmes's original vision of human beings making predictions about institutions for individual benefit has rapidly given way to a very different model: machines making predictions about individuals for the benefit of institutions. Except in the most perverse sense, this is no longer a client- or citizen-centric approach.

In either case, if one essential element of any just decision-making process is its predictability, then it must be possible for the subjects of those predictions – whose life chances and opportunities are in the balance – to scrutinise and contest the projections and other categorical assumptions at play within the decision-making processes themselves. While this should by now be an obvious point in the context of law courts and regulatory tribunals, as I suggested in the previous section, similar considerations apply in a number of private sector settings. Such considerations will become increasingly significant in both public and private sector settings, especially in light of our emerging understanding that: '[t]he application of probability and statistics to an ever-widening number of life-decisions serves to reproduce, reinforce, and widen disparities in the quality of life that different groups of people can enjoy' (Gandy 2009; see also Hildebrandt 2010).

The threats to due process posed by the computational turn should therefore cause grave concern not only to Holmes's bad man, but also to everyone else seeking to avoid unfair treatment in public and private decision-making. Unfortunately, Holmesian positivism offers little in the way of protection. Having bathed the law in 'cynical acid' (Holmes 1897: 462), cleansing it of any and all moral stain, Holmes undermines any normative basis of complaint for citizens who wish to ensure predictability and fairness in decisions being made about them.

This did not go unnoticed by subsequent jurists. Lon Fuller, for example, sought a corrective through the refinement of eight fundamental 'principles of legality' required to ensure predictability and fairness in the bumbling decisions of an imaginary law-maker named Rex (Fuller 1964: 33). According to Fuller's famous postulation, legal rules and decision-making systems must be: (i) sufficiently general; (ii) publicly promulgated; (iii) sufficiently prospective; (iv) clear and intelligible; (v) free of contradiction; (vi) sufficiently consistent over time; (vii) not impossible to comply with; and (viii) administered so that individuals can abide by them (Fuller 1964: 75). For Fuller, these due process-type principles are absolutely foundational. As he put it (Fuller 1964: 39):

> A total failure in any one of these eight directions does not simply result in a bad system of law; it results in something that is not properly called

a legal system at all, except perhaps in the Pickwickian sense in which a void contract can still be said to be one kind of contract.

Some commentators have questioned whether these eight principles provide an 'inner morality' of law, as Fuller contended (see eg Kramer 1998; Dworkin 1965; Hart 1958). Other jurists have addressed the more specific question of whether Fuller's principles demonstrate a necessary connection between law and morality, *contra* Holmes's separability thesis (Simmonds 2007). These important philosophical questions notwithstanding, perhaps the more appropriate reading of Fuller in the present context – one that Holmes surely could have lived with – is simply that Fuller reinforces predictability as an essential legal attribute, postulating a number of necessary preconditions for the possibility of predictability and fairness in law and in life. Even the bad man needs King Rex to promulgate and adhere to basic due process principles in order to secure personal objectives and avoid risk within the existing legal order.

When considering the future path of law, it is crucial to see that the computational turn threatens the bad man (and everyone else) in this very respect. The computational turn provokes various questions about whether our jurisprudential aspirations of predictability and fairness remain viable in the face of a generalised institutional adoption of anticipatory algorithms and other actuarial approaches of the sort discussed in this chapter. Or, to use Fuller's parlance instead, whether a broad uptake of predictive and pre-emptive approaches across the social order might reach a tipping point wherein our systems of social control could no longer properly be called a 'legal system'.

I have suggested that an increasing institutional use of predictive and pre-emptive technologies facilitates the first steps away from our current *ex post facto* systems of penalties and punishments towards a system that focuses on *ex ante* preventative measures. If this approach were to be generalised across various key institutions, it would threaten core rights and presumptions essential to our retributive and restorative models of social justice. Indeed, a shift of this nature could quite plausibly risk a 'total failure' of several of Fuller's eight principles of legality. It would likewise sabotage Holmesian prediction. Recall one last time that Holmes believed that predictions should be understood with reference to the standpoint of everyday people, made from their point of view and operationalised with their sense of purpose in mind. This important insight has been eclipsed by today's outcome-oriented prediction industries, which tend to use people as mere means to their institutional ends. Although accuracy, reliability, efficiency and the bottom line are laudable social goals, this approach ignores the insight underlying the presumption of innocence and associated due process values – namely, that there is wisdom in setting boundaries around the kinds of assumption that can and cannot be made about people.

Given the foundational role that due process values play in our legal system, a lingering question is therefore whether law ought to set reasonable limits on the types of presumption and prediction that institutions are permitted to make about people without their involvement or participation. And, if so, how? Although questions of system design will continue to be important in promoting technological due process, it is no substitute for addressing important threshold questions about the broader permissibility of prediction, pre-emption and presumption in the face of the computational turn. I hope that this chapter inspires further research in this regard.

Notes

1 I would like to thank Mireille Hildebrandt, Solon Barocas and Katja de Vries for their very special invitation and for their extremely insightful comments on an earlier draft. I would also like to thank the Social Sciences and Humanities Research Council and the Canada Research Chairs programme for their generous contributions to the funding of the research project from which this chapter derives. Special thanks to Katie Szilagyi, Sinziana Gutiu, Charlotte Freeman-Shaw, Stephanie Low and Andrew Bigioni for their brilliance and for the high quality of research assistance that they so regularly and reliably provide. Saving the best for last, my extreme gratitude goes out on this one to Kristen Thomasen – anthropologist, superstar law student and proud owner of these fine footnotes – for her generosity of spirit, her unrelenting passion in everything she does, her uncanny ability to find a nano-needle in a haystack, her deep inquisitiveness and her continuing quest for 'seriousness of craft', which she has not only cultivated for herself but, through collaboration, inspires in others.

2 Advertising for programmes such as Quicken Legal Business Pro tells potential consumers that one does not require an attorney to run a small business, as all the required paperwork is included with the software package (Nolo 2010).

3 Although his contemporaries, Warren and Brandeis, had recognised the future implications of foundational information technologies, such as snapshot photography, a decade earlier (Warren and Brandeis 1890).

4 More than 40 years ago, Intel co-founder Gordon Moore observed that computer processing power had doubled about every two years from 1957 to 1965 and predicted that it would continue to do so until at least 2020 (Moore 1965). In his Law of Accelerated Returns, futurist Ray Kurzweil predicted that this trajectory will continue to evolve across new paradigms in computing once the physical limitations of the integrated chip have been exhausted (Kurzweil 2001).

5 KDD is the acronym for knowledge discovery in databases. This field seeks to make sense of data by applying algorithms that identify patterns and extract useful knowledge from databases. See eg Fayyad, Piatetsky-Shapiro and Smyth (1996).

6 The actuarial approach to criminal justice seeks to anticipate crime and 'shifts away from a concern with punishing individuals to managing aggregates of dangerous groups' (Freeley and Simon 1992: 449).

7 I borrow this phrase from William Twining.

8 As Twining points out, '[t]here may also be occasions when the Good Citizen can be said to have a moral duty to predict the likely consequences of his actions. The difference between the Bad Man and the Good Citizen does not rest on the latter's indifference to prediction, but on the former's indifference to morality' (Twining 1972: 282).

9 Google is, however, constantly reworking its search algorithm in an effort to counteract these shortcomings (Google 2011a).

10 For instance, predictive recommendations are also popular on social network Facebook, internet radio site Pandora.com and movie streaming site Netflix.com. See eg Iskold (2007).

11 The visitor to the site may express approval for a movie by clicking a 'Like' button associated with that specific movie. The movie will then be added to the visitor's Facebook profile as a movie that she likes (Facebook Developers 2010).

12 Current partner websites include search engine Bing, travel website TripAdvisor, TV recommendations website Clicker, movie review site Rotten Tomatoes, document collaboration site Docs.com, internet radio site Pandora, restaurant review site Yelp and online reading site Scribd (Facebook 2011).

13 This problem is not limited to the private sector. Where private companies create algorithms for government agencies, the same protections might apply (Citron 2007).

14 Except perhaps from the standpoint of some social category to which they are presumed to belong, whether or not they actually belong (Hildebrandt and Gutwirth 2008).

15 Elsewhere I have argued that we ought to consider online service providers as fiduciaries when they are the stewards of our personal information (Kerr 2001).

16 It is valuable not only to other private sector partners but also to public sector entities, which will pay vast sums for it in order to build databases for their own KDD applications. KDD in government and industrial applications is specifically geared towards enabling better decision-making or better delivery of services. This can permit governments to make decisions based on scientific or statistical support.

17 For example, diagnosis decision support software allows physicians to enter a patient's symptoms into the program and the software will 'predict' and display potential diagnoses (see eg Isabel Health Care 2011; Nolo 2010).

18 *The Oxford English Dictionary* (2nd edn) *sub verbo* 'prediction'.

19 Google has consistently rejected calls to make its search algorithm public or to implement 'neutral search' rules that would be regulated by a government or other oversight body (Mayer 2010).

20 'When we study law we are not studying a mystery but a well-known profession.'

21 As one commentator has put it, the enumerated individuals are somehow so dangerous that they are not allowed to fly, yet so innocent that they are permitted to roam Canadian streets freely (Kutty 2007).

22 Or, as the then US Secretary of Defence, Donald Rumsfeld, put it: 'We know where they are. They're in the area around Tikrit and Baghdad and east, west, south and north somewhat' (United States 2005: 25716).

23 Such as Memphis Police Department's use of IBM's new Blue CRUSH (Crime Reduction Utilizing Statistical History), an analytics software system that predicts

trends, allocates resources and identifies 'hot spots' to reduce crime rates (SPSS 2011). Researchers from Queen's University Belfast have added CCTV cameras to the equation, using ISIS (Integrated Sensor Information System) computer vision technology in order to 'profile individuals to see if they pose a risk and then to check for patterns of behaviour that may be suspicious or anti-social' (Centre for Secure Information Technologies 2011; Alleyne 2009).

24 This idea was raised by British Information Commissioner, Richard Thomas, when expressing his concern about government proposals for national identification cards and population databases (Ford 2004).

25 Corporations may owe legal duties to customers and employees, as elaborated below with respect to data protection legislation, or they may owe a normative duty to treat customers and employees fairly lest they develop a bad business reputation or lose customers (see eg Donoghue and de Klerk 2009; Gilliland 1995).

26 Job applicants may have legal entitlements to fair treatment (for instance, human rights legislation can prohibit certain criteria from being considered in the hiring process, see eg Ontario's Human Rights Code, RSO 1990, c H. 19: s 5(1)) as well as normative entitlements to fair treatment (Gilliland 1995).

27 Not merely pertaining to whom the information will be shared but, also, the uses to which the data will be put, the steps taken by the data collector to ensure confidentiality, security, integrity and the quality of the data (see eg OECD 1980: Part II; PIPEDA 2000).

28 I owe this brilliant insight to the wonderful Mireille Hildebrandt.

References

Alleyne, R. (2009) 'Artificially Intelligent CCTV Could Prevent Crimes Before They Happen', available at http://www.telegraph.co.uk/science/6222938/Artificially-Intelligent-CCTV-could-prevent-crimes-before-they-happen.html (accessed 3 June 2011).

Amazon (2011) 'Recommendations', available at http://www.amazon.com/gp/help/customer/display.html?ie=UTF8&nodeId=13316081 (accessed 2 June 2011).

Beck, U. (1992) Risk Society: Towards a new modernity, London: Sage.

Beck, U. (1999) World Risk Society, Malden, MA: The Polity Press.

Beecher-Monas, E. (2003) 'The Epistemology of Prediction: Future dangerousness testimony and intellectual due process', Washington & Lee Law Review, 60: 353–416.

Bland, E. (2010) 'Software Predicts Criminal Behaviour: Program helps law enforcement determine who is most likely to commit crime', available at http://abcnews.go.com/Technology/software-predicts-criminal-behavior/story?id=11448231&page=1 (accessed 3 June 2011).

Booth, M. (2011) 'Colorado Computer Benefits System Cited in Federal Audit for "Serious" Ongoing Problems', available at http://www.denverpost.com/news/ci_18424589 (accessed 29 July 2011).

Brin, S. and Page, L. (2006) 'The Anatomy of a Large-Scale Hypertextual Web Search Engine', available at http://infolab.stanford.edu/~backrub/google.html (accessed 2 June 2011).

Centre for Secure Information Technologies (2011) Queen's University Belfast, available at http://www.csit.qub.ac.uk/ (accessed 29 July 2011).

Citron, D. K. (2007–2008) 'Technological Due Process', *Washington University Law Review*, 85: 1249–313.

Cooter, R. D. (1998) 'Models of Morality in Law and Economics: Self-Control and self-improvement for the "bad man" of Holmes', *Boston University Law Review*, 78: 903–30.

Dick, P. K. (1956) 'The Minority Report', *Fantastic Universe*, 4(6): 4–35.

Donoghue, S. and de Klerk, H. M. (2009) 'The Right to be Heard and to be Understood: A conceptual framework for consumer protection in emerging economies', *International Journal of Consumer Studies*, 33: 456–67.

Dworkin, R. M. (1965) 'The Elusive Morality of Law', *Villanova Law Review*, 10: 631–39.

Ericson, R. V. (1994) 'The Decline of Innocence', *University of British Columbia Law Review*, 28: 367–83.

European Commission (2005) 'Consumer Protection in the European Union: Ten basic principles', Brussels: Directorate-General for Health and Consumer Protection, available at http://ec.europa.eu/consumers/cons_info/10principles/en.pdf (accessed 29 July 2011).

Facebook (2011) 'Instant Personalization', available at http://www.facebook.com/instantpersonalization/ (accessed 13 June 2011).

Facebook Developers (2010) 'Like Button', available at http://developers.facebook.com/docs/reference/plugins/like (accessed 13 June 2011).

Facebook Developers (2011) 'Open Graph Protocol', available at http://developers.facebook.com/docs/opengraph/ (accessed 13 June 2011).

Fayyad, U., Piatetsky-Shapiro, G. and Smyth, P. (1996) 'From Data Mining to Knowledge Discovery in Databases', *AI Magazine*, 17: 37–54.

Federal Bureau of Investigation (2010) 'Frequently Asked Questions', available at http://www.fbi.gov/about-us/nsb/tsc/tsc_faqs (accessed 2 June 2011).

Federal Constitutional Court of Germany (Bundesverfassungsgericht) decision of 15 December 1983, reference number: 1 BvR 209, 269, 362, 420, 440, 484/83, available at http://zensus2011.de/uploads/media/volkszaehlungsurteil_1983.pdf (accessed 29 July 2011).

Federal Trade Commission (FTC) (2007) 'Fair Information Practice Principles', available at http://www.ftc.gov/reports/privacy3/fairinfo.shtm (accessed 29 July 2011).

Feinstein, L. and Slaughter, A. (2004) 'Duty to Prevent', *Foreign Affairs*, 83: 136–50.

Ford, R. (2004) 'Beware Rise of Big Brother State, Warns Data Watchdog', available at http://www.timesonline.co.uk/tol/news/uk/article470264.ece (accessed 3 June 2011).

Freeley, M. and Simon, J. (1992) 'The New Penology: Notes on the emerging strategy of corrections and its implications', *Criminology*, 30: 449–474.

Friendly, H. J. (1974–1975) 'Some Kind of Hearing', *University of Pennsylvania Law Review*, 123: 1267–317.

Fuller, L. (1964) *The Morality of Law*, New Haven, CT: Yale University Press.

Gandy, O. H. Jr (1993) *The Panoptic Sort: A political economy of personal information*, Boulder, CO: Westview Press.

Gandy, O. H. (2009) *Coming to Terms with Chance: Engaging rational discrimination and cumulative disadvantage*, Burlington, VT: Ashgate.

German Data Forum (2010) *Building on Progress: Expanding the research infrastructure for the social, economic and behavioural sciences*, vol 2, Farmington Hills, MI: Budrich UniPress Ltd, available at www.ratswd.de/publ/KVI/Building_on_Progress_Band_II.pdf (accessed 29 July 2011).

Giddens, A. (1999) 'Risk and Responsibility', *Modern Law Review*, 62: 1–10.

Gilliland, S. W. (1995) 'Fairness from the Applicant's Perspective: Reactions to employee selections procedures', *International Journal of Selection and Assessment*, 3: 11–19.

Google (2010a) 'Technology Overview', available at http://www.google.com/corporate/tech.html (accessed 13 June 2011).

Google (2010b) 'Features: 'I'm feeling lucky', available at http://www.google.com/support/websearch/bin/answer.py?hl=en&answer=30735 (accessed 13 June 2011).

Google (2010c) 'Ads in Gmail and Your Personal Data', available at http://mail.google.com/support/bin/answer.py?hl=en&answer=6603 (accessed 13 June 2011).

Google (2011a) 'Finding More High-Quality Sites in Search', available at http://google blog.blogspot.com/2011/02/finding-more-high-quality-sites-in.html (accessed 1 August 2011).

Google (2011b) 'The Google+ Project', available at http://www.google.com/+/learn-more/ (accessed 29 July 2011).

Gordon, R. W. (2000) 'Law as a Vocation: Holmes and the lawyer's path', in Burton, S. J. (ed.) *The Path of Law and its Influence: The legacy of Oliver Wendell Holmes Jr*, New York: Cambridge University Press.

Government of Canada (2010) 'Passenger Protect', available at http://www.passenger-protect.gc.ca/specified.html (accessed 2 June 2011).

Hammons M. and Reinertson, K. (2004) 'New Benefits System Well on its Way', *Rocky Mountain News Archive*, available at http://nl.newsbank.com (accessed 29 July 2011).

Hart, H. L. A. (1958) 'Positivism and the Separation of Law and Morals', *Harvard Law Review*, 71: 593–629.

Henry, E. and Ahlers, A. (2004) 'Kennedy: Airline security risk?', available at http://www.cnn.com/2004/ALLPOLITICS/08/19/kennedy.airlines/index.html (accessed 2 June 2011).

Hildebrandt, M. (2008) 'Legal and Technological Normativity: More (and less) than twin sisters', *Techné: Journal of the Society for Philosophy and Technology*, 12(3): 169–83.

Hildebrandt, M. (2010) 'Proactive Forensic Profiling: Proactive criminalization', in Duff, R. A. Farmer, L., Marshall, S. E., Renzo, M. and Tadros, V. (eds) *The Boundaries of the Criminal Law*, New York: Oxford University Press: 113–37.

Hildebrandt, M. and Gutwirth, S. (2008) *Profiling the European Citizen: Cross-Disciplinary perspectives*, Dordrecht: Springer.

Holmes, O. W. Jr (1881) *The Common Law*, Boston, MA: Little, Brown & Co.

Holmes, O. W. Jr (1897) 'The Path of Law', *Harvard Law Review*, 10: 457–78.

Information and Privacy Commissioner of Ontario (2011) 'Privacy by Design', available at http://privacybydesign.ca/ (accessed 29 July 2011).

Isabel Health Care (2011) 'The Diagnosis Checklist', available at http://www.isabelhealthcare.com/home/default (accessed 2 June 2011).

Iskold, A. (2007) 'The Art, Science and Business of Recommendation Engines', available at http://www.readwriteweb.com/archives/recommendation_engines.php (accessed 2 June 2011).

iTunes (2010) 'Terms and Conditions', available at http://www.apple.com/legal/itunes/ca/terms.html#ITUNES (accessed 2 June 2011).

iTunes (2011) 'iTunes A to Z', available at http://www.apple.com/itunes/features/#genius (accessed 2 June 2011).

Johnson, D. R. (1996) 'Due Process and Cyberjurisdiction', *Journal of Computer-Mediated Communication*, available at http://jcmc.indiana.edu/vol2/issue1/due.html (accessed 29 July 2011).

Joseph, F. (1975) *Star Trek Star Fleet Technical Manual*, New York: Ballantine Books.

Kerr, I. (1999) 'Spirits in the Material World: Intelligent agents as intermediaries in electronic commerce', *Dalhousie Law Journal*, 22: 189–249.

Kerr, I. (2001) 'The Legal Relationship Between Online Service Providers and Users', *Canadian Business Law Journal*, 35: 419–58.

Kerr, I. (2004) 'Bots, Babes and the Californication of Commerce', *University of Ottawa Law and Technology Journal*, 1: 285–324.

Kerr, I. (2005) 'If Left To Their Own Devices: How DRM and anti-circumvention laws can be used to hack privacy', in Geist, M. (ed.) *In the Public Interest: The future of Canadian copyright law*, Toronto: Irwin Law.

Kerr, I. (2010) 'Digital Locks and the Automation of Virtue', in Geist, M. (ed.) *From 'Radical Extremism' to 'Balanced Copyright': Canadian copyright and the digital age*, Toronto: Irwin Law.

Kerr, I. (2011) '2.50 for an Eyeball and a Buck and a Half for an Ear: Artificial organs as mass market consumer goods', available at http://www.nyu.edu/media.culture/kerr.mov (accessed 29 July 2011).

Kramer, M. (1998) 'Scrupulousness Without Scruples: A critique of Lon Fuller and his defenders', *Oxford Journal of Legal Studies*, 18: 235–63.

Kurzweil, R. (2001) 'The Law of Accelerating Returns', available at http://www.kurzweilai.net/the-law-of-accelerating-returns (accessed 2 June 2011).

Kutty, F. (2007) 'Canada's Passenger Protect Program: Too guilty to fly, too innocent to charge?' Submission by the Canadian Council on American Islamic Relations to the Passenger Protect Program: Identity Screening Regulations, available at http://papers.ssrn.com/sol3/papers.cfm?abstract_id=962797 (accessed 2 June 2011).

Lessig, L. (2006) *Code: Version 2.0*, New York: Basic Books.

Luban, D. (2000) 'The Bad Man and the Good Lawyer', in Burton, S. J. (ed.) *The Path of Law and its Influence: The legacy of Oliver Wendell Holmes Jr*, New York: Cambridge University Press.

Massachusetts Office of Consumer Affairs and Business Regulation (2011) 'Consumer Bill of Rights', available at http://www.mass.gov/?pageID=ocamodulechunk&L=5&L0=Home&L1=Government&L2=Our+Agencies+and+Divisions&L3=Division+of+Professional+Licensure&L4=Consumer+Fact+Sheets&sid=Eoca&b=terminalcontent&f=dpl_consumer_consumer_bill_of_rights&csid=Eoca (accessed 29 July 2011).

McCulloch, J. and Pickering, S. (2009) 'Pre-Crime and Counter-Terrorism: Imagining future crime in the "war on terror"', *British Journal of Criminology*, 49: 628–45.

Mayer, M. (2010) 'Do Not Neutralize the Web's Endless Search', reprint from *The Financial Times*, available at http://googlepublicpolicy.blogspot.com/2010/07/our-op-ed-regulating-what-is-best-in.html (accessed 2 June 2011).

Mims, C. (2010), 'How iTunes Genius Really Works: An Apple engineer discloses how the company's premier recommendation engine parses millions of iTunes libraries', available at http://www.technologyreview.com/blog/mimssbits/25267/ (accessed 2 June 2011).

Moore, G. (1965) 'Cramming More Components onto Integrated Circuits', *Electronics*, 38: 114–117.

Moore, J. (2007) 'Are You on the No Fly List, Too?', available at http://www.huffingtonpost.com/jim-moore/are-you-on-the-no-fly-lis_b_42443.html (accessed 2 June 2011).

Nabati, M. (2003) 'International Law at a Crossroads: Self-Defense, global terrorism and preemption (a call to rethink the self-defense normative framework)', *Transnational Law & Contemporary Problems*, 13: 771–802.

Nissenbaum, H. (2009) *Privacy in Context: Technology, policy, and the integrity of social life*, Palo Alto, CA: Stanford University Press.

Nolo (2010) 'Quicken Legal Business Pro 2011', available at http://www.nolo.com/products/quicken-legal-business-pro-SBQB.html (accessed 2 June 2011).

O'Donnell, J. (2006) 'Will Autos Some Day have Breathalyzers?' *USA Today*, available at http://www.usatoday.com/money/autos/2006-04-24-breathalyzer-usat_x.htm (accessed 2 June 2011).

Organization for Economic Cooperation and Development (OECD) (1980), *OECD Guidelines on the Protection of Privacy and Transborder Flows of Personal Data*, available at http://www.oecd.org/document/57/0,3746,en_2649_34255_1815186_1_1_1_1,00.html (accessed 29 July 2011).

PIPEDA (2000) *Personal Information Protection and Electronic Documents Act*, S.C. 2000, c. 5, Schedule 1, <www.privcom.gc.ca/legislation/02_06_01_01_e.asp>

Prakken, H. (2006) 'AI & Law, Logic and Argument Schemes', *Augmentation*, 19: 303–316.

Quintard-Morénas, F. (2010) 'The Presumption of Innocence in the French and Anglo-American Legal Traditions', *American Journal of Comparative Law*, 58: 107–49.

Reidenberg, J. (1998) 'Lex Informatica: The formulation of information policy rules through technology', *Texas Law Review*, 76: 553–84.

Schwikkard, P. J. (1998) 'The Presumption of Innocence: What is it?', *South African Journal of Criminal Justice*, 11: 396–408.

Shipley, D. E. (2008) 'Due Process Rights before EU Agencies: The rights of defence', *Georgia Journal of International and Comparative Law*, 37: 1–51.

Simmonds, N. E. (2007) *Law as a Moral Idea*, New York: Oxford University Press.

Smith, J. (2006) 'Audit: Costly errors in computer system for benefits had high mistake rate', *Rocky Mountain News*, A4, cited in Citron, D. K. (2007–2008) 'Technological Due Process', *Washington University Law Review*, 85: 1249–313.

Solum, L. B. (1992) 'Legal Personhood for Artificial Intelligences', *North Carolina Law Review*, 70: 1231–87.

SPSS (2011) 'IBM SPSS Podcast', available at http://www.spss.com/10/memphis-police/ (accessed 3 June 2011).

Stefik, M. (1996) 'Letting Loose the Light: Igniting commerce in electronic Publication', in *Internet Dreams: Archetypes, myths, and metaphors*, Cambridge, MA: MIT Press.

— (1997) 'Shifting the Possible: How trusted systems and digital property rights challenge us to rethink digital publishing', *Berkeley Technology Law Journal,* 12: 137–60.

Steinbock, D. J. (2005) 'Data Matching, Data Mining, and Due Process', *Georgia Law Review*, 40: 1–84.

Transport Canada (2009) 'Passenger Protect Program', available at http://www.tc. gc.ca/eng/mediaroom/backgrounders-b06-a003e-1847.htm (accessed 2 June 2011).

Transportation Security Administration (2010) 'Secure Flight Program', available at http://www.tsa.gov/what_we_do/layers/secureflight/index.shtm (accessed 2 June 2011).

Twining, W. (1972) 'The Bad Man Revisited', *Cornell Law Review*, 58: 275–303.

United Nations – Department of Economic and Social Affairs (2003) *United Nations Guidelines for Consumer Protection*, New York, United Nations, available at www. un.org/esa/sustdev/publications/consumption_en.pdf (accessed 29 July 2011).

United States (2005) *Congressional Record*, 151(19).

United States Military Academy (2002) 'President Bush Delivers Graduation Speech at Westpoint', available at http://georgewbush-whitehouse.archives.gov/news/ releases/2002/06/20020601-3.html (accessed 2 June 2011).

University of Pennsylvania (2011) 'Richard Berk', available at http://www-stat.whar ton.upenn.edu/~berkr/ (accessed 3 June 2011).

Wall, A. (2004) 'Search-Marketing Info: Above the fold', available at http://www. search-marketing.info/linking-campaign/renting-links.htm (accessed 2 June 2011).

Warren, S. D. and Brandeis, L. D. (1890) 'The Right to Privacy', *Harvard Law Review*, 4: 193–220.

Wasek-Wiaderek, M. (2000) *The Principle of 'Equality of Arms' in Criminal Procedure under Article 6 of the European Convention on Human Rights and its Functions in Criminal Justice of Selected European Countries: A comparative view*, Leuven Law Series 13, Leuven, Belgium: Leuven University Press.

Watson, S. (2010) 'Pre-Crime Technology to be Used in Washington D.C.', available at http://www.prisonplanet.com/pre-crime-technology-to-be-used-in-washing-ton-d-c.html (accessed 3 June 2011).

Weizenbaum, J. (1976) *Computer Power and Human Reason: From judgment to calculation*, San Francisco: W. H. Freeman.

Wells, C. P. (2000) 'Oliver Wendell Holmes, Jr., and William James: The bad man and the moral life', in Burton, S. J. (ed.) *The Path of Law and its Influence: The legacy of Oliver Wendell Holmes Jr*, New York: Cambridge University Press.

Whitlock, C. (2007) 'Terrorists Proving Harder to Profile', available at http://www. washingtonpost.com/wp-dyn/content/article/2007/03/11/AR2007031101618. html (accessed 2 June 2011).

Wikipedia (2011) 'Prediction Theory of Law', available at http://en.wikipedia.org/ wiki/Prediction_theory_of_law (accessed 2 June 2011).

Wilson, D. and Weber, L. (2008) 'Surveillance, Risk and Preemption on the Australian Border', *Surveillance & Society*, 5: 124–41.

Zetter, K. (10 March 2010) 'No Fly List Includes the Dead', available at http://www. wired.com/threatlevel/2010/03/no-fly-list-includes-the-dead (accessed 2 June 2011).

5

Digital prophecies and web intelligence

Elena Esposito

Intelligence without consciousness

Smart environments, e-learning, predictive machines, intelligent devices: many of the themes and projects that have recently been discussed in the context of telematics and cybernetics bring again to the fore the by now classical issue of the intelligence of machines. Can intelligence be artificial, and what is intelligence in general? For a long time the first question overshadowed the second and research dealt predominantly with the localisation of intelligence. As we know it, intelligence must be attributed to someone, and apparently this someone must be a consciousness, which however can also be artificial. The problem was then first of all to find a consciousness or its (perhaps 'weak' or imperfect) surrogates. The scientific studies and big projects on expert systems and artificial intelligence (AI) focused their attention more towards consciousness than intelligence.

Today this focus on consciousness is challenged. This challenge is not posed by theory but rather by practice. For example, industry seems to be more interested in the construction of environments that act in a smart way than in the artificial reproduction of a centralised consciousness. This is not just a small lexical shift from the search for the consciousness of machines; rather, it signals a change of attitude of a wider scope. As long ago as 1984 John Gage of Sun Microsystems uttered the much quoted formula 'the network is the computer', shifting the focus from individual consciousness to communication and recognising implicitly the approach always claimed by sociological systems theory.[1]

Consciousness, natural but also artificial, has as its first feature that of being obscure and wanting to remain so: the psychic system of an individual is a black box, inaccessible from the outside and largely also from within; it processes thoughts and feelings that are only its own and derive from the uniqueness of its perspective. The modern notion of individuality is based precisely on the originality of a specific way of perceiving the world, its objects and other observers within it: 'the world seen from a specific point' (Luhmann 1989b: 214). If we could reproduce consciousness artificially we should reproduce this impenetrability first: a consciousness thinks what it thinks and cannot be controlled or even read from the outside. Many projects involving the autonomous learning capacity of machines (beginning with the pioneering projects on neural networks) seem to recognise this condition, which is actually the paradox of designing something one does not know. From a communication point of view, however, the problem is more radical: if we could ever succeed in building an autonomous consciousness, it would be obscure and unpredictable, and the constructor might not be in control, because the consciousness-machine would not necessarily follow the constructor's directions (otherwise it would not be a consciousness).

Put in this way, the issue does not seem to have a way out. However, things change if one switches to communication. The only form of transparency is achieved through communication, when consciousness translates its thoughts in a form that can be offered to other observers. This is how black boxes influence and understand each other – only in the indirect and highly mediated form permitted by common participation in communication, when one listens to what the others say (or write, or somehow communicate) and translates it into one's own thoughts. With regard to AI this then implies that we must shift the focus from the single information processing centre to the connection that circulates communication. In the field of cybernetics, this is reflected by a shift from the single computer to the network that connects computers with each other: the World Wide Web as a World Wide Computer where intelligence is not located anywhere in particular, and which produces information that cannot be traced back to any of the (natural or artificial) conscious entities participating in it (Carr 2008: 9ff, 108ff, 213ff). This is the move that seems to be made with the introduction of formulas such as 'cloud computing' or 'semantic network', where the connection not only serves to circulate information generated and processed elsewhere (in consciousness or in computers) but where the connection itself produces its own meanings and a specific form of intelligence. When one leaves the reference to consciousness and turns to the unique and gigantic operating system involving the internet, its services, devices such as satellites, all the connected PCs and even (for some observers) the minds of the users, it could be argued that the web is the real outcome of the projects of artificial intelligence (AI).[2] More soberly, others are questioning the practical implications of this transformation in the economic or in the legal field: the new forms of production and distribution, the revision of the traditional forms of copyright and the problems of accountability when communication involves artificial entities that cannot be traced back to the responsibility or the intention of anyone (Koops, Hildebrandt and Jaquet-Chiffelle 2010; Benkler 2006). Cybernetic intelligence, if there is any, is produced by the network.

In this chapter, I try to analyse the structures and the consequences of this intelligence, which works and is interesting precisely because it is different from the natural one and does not try to reproduce its structures and procedures – it succeeds by difference and not by analogy. In the next section, I describe how a network is able to function without a central project or unit of control, namely when the fast increase of data produces structures that, in turn, allow the management and selection of these same (or other) data. These structures produce meanings, but do not depend on the intention or on the consciousness of anyone (they have not been thought by anyone); they result *a posteriori* from the very functioning of the net. If thereby, as some contend, a new intelligence is generated, it is an intelligence working very differently from the natural one we are familiar with; I then go on to discuss the features of such intelligence: it relies on explanations that do not refer to causes but to correlations, works on the surface, proceeds from the past to the future and has a perfect memory. But these features, often presented as very innovative, actually faithfully reproduce the procedures of a divinatory rationality, which guided the decisions and the orientation in the world of ancient societies, referring to a perfectly determined world ruled by divine intelligence. This analogy can be traced back to the fact that, in both cases, referring to the network and referring to divine wisdom, one is confronted with a logic that greatly exceeds human capabilities and cannot be perfectly understood. Studying divinatory practices, developed and refined over the course of millennia, one can get many hints to understanding the logic of the web and its mechanisms. But the theological setting, which was at the base of divination and made it work, has irreparably changed with the passage to modernity; this is the reason why today the 'divinatory' logic of the web leads to the emergence of problems relating to the autonomy of subjects and the openness of the future. These problems are expressed in widespread concerns about the diffusion of the web: the defence of privacy and the freedom of self-determination. Finally, I suggest how these concerns might be approached when the point of departure is not the analogy but the difference between net intelligence and individual consciousness.

Self-regulation without control

The problem of defining intelligence remains, also when we are dealing with a cybernetic intelligence: in this distributed and impersonal form, what is intelligence? How should we understand an intelligence that is not localised in the mind or in consciousness?

What we observe is a production and management of information that cannot be properly attributed to anyone but emerges from the web as a whole. This emergent order was not designed in advance and cannot be centralised (Benkler 2006: 16, 320), because it derives from the circularity of a mechanism where the search for information produces extra information which, in turn, regulates itself. In part this additional information is intentionally provided by the users, who in the context of web 2.0 are at the same time, and on the same channel, producers and consumers of content: Wikipedia results notoriously from the coordinated but uncontrolled actions of millions of users, producing jointly (with corrections and integrations) a text that cannot be properly attributed to anyone, but is more reliable, complete and up-to-date than traditionally authored encyclopedias (as shown by the continual comparisons with the Encyclopaedia Britannica, which all in all confirm Wikipedia as the winner: Bauerlein 2012; Giles 2005). The same happens with the video and audio contents offered spontaneously by users in circuits including YouTube or with the reviews provided on almost everything: books, records, but also home appliances, shops, hotels and restaurants (eg Amazon, Kelkoo, eBay or TripAdvisor). Together with its contents the web offers criteria for the selection of these contents. In centralised mass media, information overload creates major problems. In contrast, when the digital information overload increases in the decentralised architecture of the web the problem and the remedy coincide: with the increase of data there is also an increase in tools and filters to select data.

The most interesting aspect of this self-regulation without control, however, concerns the criteria and guidelines that are generated from the information supplied by people without their intention or even their consciousness, that is, the information that does not derive from communications but simply from data – information that is generated by the machine through its processing mechanisms, without anyone ever having produced it or even having thought the corresponding meaning. We can think of the messages on Amazon informing us that users who have purchased a particular book have appreciated (or at least bought) specific other books (although they never thought of suggesting the same purchase to others). Or we can recall the number of different recommendations for our tastes and preferences that the network seems to be able to transmit, or other complicated inferences derived from the work on the web connecting various sources, including user behaviour, such as location data captured by GPS sensors, mobile phones and the like. This information was not communicated by anyone (unlike a review put on the web by a user, maybe anonymous) but was derived by special algorithms that sift through data scattered on the net looking for additional information (with data mining and machine learning techniques).

A classic but not exhaustive example is the PageRank algorithm used by Google to explore the web, starting from links made by users and interpreting them as signs of interest for the content of a given site (weighed on the basis of their relevance, following the model of academic referees). Users use Google to get information about the contents of the web, while their searches provide Google with materials to orient later searches, classifying sites for relevance depending on values obtained from the search behaviour of previous users. Searches not only generate information that a user might look for, they also constitute new information, allowing search engines to build structures that organise the overall traffic of information. One can go even further, as profiling practices do, and use the finest mathematical techniques to derive correlations or patterns from the mass of available data, in order to identify particular individuals or groups (Hildebrandt and Gutwirth 2008; see also van Otterlo in this volume); and since each of us continuously provides data to the web, researching contents but also writing messages, making phone calls or using a GPS navigator, this 'secondary' information multiplies without pause, increasing at the same time the mass of data and the complexity of the criteria for filtering and selecting them. Something similar happens in financial markets that have been using, over the last few decades, computer techniques to derive indications of the trends of future behaviour from the past behaviour of the markets. The so-called 'implied volatility' is not meant to provide a measure of the direction of market movements (whether they will be increasing or decreasing) but of their instability (whether they will be turbulent or stable, risky or relatively reliable) (Esposito 2011).

The web can be explored in order to obtain guidelines concerning the web itself, to find models of users or of the general public, or to seek directions on an uncertain and unpredictable future. In all cases, however, this circular mechanism seems to have the great advantage of turning the excess of information, affecting modern society since the diffusion of the printing press, from a problem into an opportunity: the growth of content on the web improves and makes the mechanisms for discriminating between various content more reliable. Rather than being overwhelmed by the 'data deluge', Google's search engine thrives on the information increase, because it activates a new form of 'intelligence' that is different and almost alternative to the one still guiding centralised mass media (where the increase of data means an increase in complexity and often in confusion). In mass media that function according to a centralised model, order must have an addressee and a reference: that is, they have to involve one or more conscious entities and a plan developed by someone – therefore these centrally organised mass media can never escape the suspicion of manipulation, which implicitly accompanies each of their communications.[3] The disruption of order simply means disorder, and requires some other criterion in order to regain control. Google, on the contrary, is not led by any project or by any order given in advance, and strictly speaking guarantees no control: it offers, however, an order that works merely on the basis of these assumptions, and works the better the more it abandons any link with a centralised project, because it delegates the production of information to a widespread 'intelligence' that cannot be localised.[4]

Sense production a posteriori

One could say that these kinds of distributed mechanism radicalise the original project of the internet, conceived explicitly as a network without a centre and without a top, turning this lack of unitary order into an element of strength and robustness. At the inception of the internet, a few decades ago, the motivation was strategic–military (it is difficult to destroy an entity that can be reproduced from every one of its points). Today the motivation is to work with a mechanism that regulates itself by giving up regulation – and thereby paradoxically seems to become intelligent.

If one wants to derive a criterion from this way of functioning, one has to consider that the criteria one infers are always criteria a posteriori, radically different from the ones that guide and orient action and communication. Within the functioning of the web 'sense' is a deduction, not a premise. Think again of Google: the advantage over competing search engines is that it is not driven by a categorisation fixed in advance, wherein the various contents have to fit. This is what all previous search engines such as Altavista, Lycos, or even Yahoo! were trying to do: they started from an order and tried to make an order out of it (Battelle 2005). Google goes backwards, tracking and reviewing the links arriving at each site. This analysis of links is not meant to disclose anything but to produce a posteriori what then becomes the geography of the web: the order is obtained from disorder. The placement of objects into a category emerges 'after the fact', measured by the incoming links. There is no reason why a specific content is rated in a certain way and is presented as 'more interesting' than others – the reason is produced later, when a given site becomes more interesting as a result of the actions that qualified it as such. It is not sense that guides the actions of the search engine or of the data mining techniques – they would be hopelessly slow and too inefficient. These techniques rather look at purely quantitative data, at statistics or correlations. Sense emerges afterwards, as a result of the information obtained and transmitted. It is as if you did something first and only later, looking from a distance, you grasped its sense.[5]

In this way of operating Google is not alone. In fact, many of the most successful projects operating on the web share, more or less consciously, the same attitude. I have already mentioned the models used by financial markets to guide investment decisions. Financial markets are seemingly overwhelmed by an unmanageable excess of data. This data excess is further multiplied enormously by the digitalisation of markets, allowing for an infinity of virtually simultaneous operations, which largely take place outside the regulated markets (over-the-counter transactions). The calculus of implied volatility with the Black-Scholes formula for pricing options (Black and Scholes 1981), for instance, also creates sense a posteriori, projecting past uncertainty into the future, and transforming the opacity of markets into a source of information. By applying the formula that predicts the evolution of the markets backward (to the known data), one infers (again a posteriori) a measure which estimates their orientation, which should allow one consciously to project one's investments (MacKenzie 2006). One derives from the past an indication about the unknown future. When many operators are guided by these kinds of indication, they confirm their effectiveness a posteriori. As MacKenzie says, a formula, which at the start was completely unrealistic, is made real a posteriori through the actions of these operators.

Very well known and much discussed[6] is also Craig Vender's project for genome sequencing. Anderson (2008) takes Vender's project as a model for scientific research starting neither from models nor from a priori hypotheses, but from the processing power of computers and from an enormous amount of data. The objective is to obtain additional data that one will use later to infer information: for example, to 'discover' that a formerly unknown gene sequence must represent a new species – and to ask what its features may be. According to this approach even science proceeds a posteriori: it starts from correlations and patterns found out in the mass of available data and looks for an order that must be explained.

In all these cases, one is dealing with 'semantic networks' that produce meanings but are not meaningful from the start and cannot be driven by meanings, even if they generate an order and govern the circulation of information. It is obvious, however, that this information must be handled differently from the current one: it does not make much sense to interpret this information as one interprets communication, starting from the intentions and the sense intended by the one uttering it (incorporated in the model or in the theory that guides the exploration of the world and the obtaining of data). Now sense comes after information: it is a matter of information that has not been issued by anyone and cannot be attributed to any consciousness, even if it is not random at all and provides significant indications. How must this be understood? Does it still make sense to deal with it by means of categories, for example with scientific theories and techniques, elaborated to handle communication?

The structures of web intelligence

Very provocatively, Anderson (2008) answers no, and sets the guidelines of what should be the new intelligence – an intelligence independent of consciousness and of meanings that guide the search for and the processing of information in the new mediated and interconnected mode. To date scientific logic has relied on causal reasoning, and reached explanations when it succeeded in connecting an event (as an effect) to the underlying causes – the more precise and determinate this finding of causes, the better the explanation. Therefore we needed theories that guided the explanation and the search for causal connections. All this would no longer be necessary, superseded by technological progress that provides massive amounts of data and a high capacity to process them,[7] until 'the numbers speak for themselves', with no need for theories or models. From data processing one derives correlations and patterns that reveal the structure and the order of the universe at stake. The order of the universe at stake can be learnt and studied: one infers knowledge with no need of a theory directing it, one explains the world with no need to know the underlying causes. If the underlying causes raise interest (and *only* if they raise interest) one can study them later. The implicit assumption is that theories (and meanings) are needed only when one has limited processing capabilities, as a kind of shortcut that saves one the trouble of a punctual examination of all cases and eventualities. One could say, with George Spencer Brown, that a proof is only needed when one is not able to provide a demonstration (Spencer Brown 1972: 93ff). To show the validity of a theorem there are two roads: either one examines all possible cases and assignments of value to calculate the result (in this case one demonstrates), or one constructs a proof that shows (in a much more economical way) that with those premises there can be only one result. According to Anderson (2008), now that the processing power and the amount of data are potentially unlimited, there is no need to prove anything anymore and we just have to demonstrate. We can calculate all combinations and all possibilities, until the result emerges from the numbers and from their correlations. Demonstration supersedes proof as correlations supersede causes. Scientific thought (as well as all other areas of society oriented to finding causes, such as the legal system) should adapt to this new technological landscape.

Abandoning proof in favour of demonstration would of course have consequences, for example, for the classic distinctions between problem and solution, and between question and answer (not by chance taken from the model of communication): first you identify a problem and then you search for the explanation; first you ask the questions and then you formulate the answer. Today, according to, for instance, Nicholas Carr (2008: 220ff), in the web the order is reversed and intelligence lies in finding problems from solutions. The overabundance of available data already contains all solutions that can be achieved, even without having explicitly defined the problem. Once more the model is Google, which gets answers from the internet for unclearly asked questions, or perhaps even for questions that have not been asked at all: you do not need to know what to look for to be able to find it, you just let the machine do its work.[8] Again the temporal order is reversed and the future is already contained in the past: the web computer is an 'anticipation machine' (Carr 2008: 220ff), which prefigures our choices without even needing to forecast them. The web computer does not need to know our preferences or our guidelines, it does not need to know the user's consciousness (it has no contact with the user); it simply derives patterns from previous choices of that user or of others connected with him by additional processing (profiling and the like). The problems are derived retrospectively from the solutions, or are not even identified. Problems and questions are needed by consciousness in order to understand the processing of information, that is, they are still linked to human intelligence – but web intelligence, implicit in the complex of links and programs, works in another much more powerful way.

The web, some say, works at the surface and with speed, surpassing what Sherry Turkle described a few years ago as the replacement of the 'modern' schema of the interpretation of meanings by the 'post-modern' schema which does not need any depth and does not reward it (Turkle 1995). Turkle illustrated this shift by opposing IBM to Mac aesthetics, where the first corresponded to the first phase of knowledge of informatics. Because IBM gave access to source codes, enabling and encouraging this descent to lower layers, a programmer who was able to operate at all levels of the functioning of the machine, from hardware to higher programming languages, had advantages in efficiency and control over a programmer whose knowledge was limited to the higher levels. The ability to go deep was rewarded, as modern culture rewards those who do not stop at appearances and are able to investigate causes and meanings. In contrast, the attitude prefigured by Mac, which later spread to much of digital culture, favours those who use all their capabilities on the surface (Apple traditionally gave no access to source codes, that is, to deeper levels), looking for connections and references with no care for causes or for the deep architecture of the system. One could say it is an attitude that recognises and accepts an underlying mystery it does not care to clear, preferring to investigate the accessible surface layers. In the actual use of the network, consistency and depth are no longer values. This has been criticised with much alarm by Nicholas Carr (2008), for whom surface seems to be the equivalent of superficiality, of a new dangerous inconsistency and unconsciousness in the relationship with information.[9]

Whatever the evaluation, the new intelligence of the network – including all data and all links between data – seems to be the technological realisation of a perfect memory that knows everything and does not forget anything. With such storage and processing capacity another traditional priority is reversed: since antiquity remembrance was what one wanted to achieve and forgetting was what one wanted to limit. The *ars memoriae* and all related mnemonic technologies were originally used merely to save as much content as possible from the inexorable process of forgetting: humans have limited ability to retain information, so normally one forgets; opposing this trend requires energy and attention, as well as more and more complex equipments – for instance writing and printing (Esposito 2002). But the intelligence of the web does not have these limitations and does not forget anything: the default value is no longer forgetting but remembering, in the sense that a specific decision is needed in order to forget, choosing to erase certain content (from large databases as well as from our files or email lists); without a decision everything is preserved (Mayer-Schönberger 2009). The problem is rather to succeed in forgetting when we consider it necessary; one would like to achieve forgetting and to limit remembrance. As in other contexts, the problem is to produce randomness in a totally determined machine. To generate randomness has become much more difficult and expensive than to produce order, as forgetting has become much more complex and expensive than remembering.

The structures of divinatory intelligence

The intelligence of the network, then, operates on the surface, works with correlations, gives answers from which the questions can be derived and has a perfect memory. The authors describing these developments in more or less emphatic tones tend to highlight their innovative aspects, linked to exceptional developments in digital technologies. These are undeniable, but if one describes the overall features of this alternative form of information processing, as I tried to do in the previous paragraphs, one can see that maybe it is not totally new. Curious analogies emerge with a rationality that is indeed an alternative to the logic of modern society, but is not new or unknown to Western civilisation – it has indeed ruled Western society for several millennia. We seem to face a form of non-modern, but not necessarily post-modern rationality; maybe for certain aspects we should even retrieve the characteristics of a pre-modern culture. I refer to the culture of divination, as it was produced by ancient societies in the Middle East or in Greece, and which was developed in very elaborate ways in the Chinese world.[10]

Interestingly, many or nearly all the features of the form of 'intelligence' which seems to operate in the web re-propose the logic of a divinatory culture. This divinatory logic is anything but an irrational and primitive approach to the world: although its criteria and techniques are profoundly different from those of the scientific attitude, they are extremely refined. Not by chance divination has accompanied the development of Western culture until the establishment of a scientific attitude in the first modernity, which for the first time refused divination as superstition and irrationality. The logic of divination is not only different from scientific logic, but also the assumptions and the image of the world legitimating its plausibility differ – in the wording of systems theory, one could say that the logic of divination is based on a different order of observation.

What are the structures of divinatory logic? It is primarily a logic based on necessity, where chance does not exist and where even linear cause/effect relations to explain the events are lacking; much more important are relations of homology and correlation between things and events, referring to the ordered structure of the universe (Vandermeersch 1974: 27ff; Vernant 1974: 14ff). All phenomena appear as signs of each other and not as consequences (or effects) of previous facts; each one could in principle explain all the others and the links of progression turn into relationships of symmetry. These signs can be inscribed in objects of any kind, from the flight of birds to the shape of minerals or the movements of the clouds – they can also be produced specifically for the purpose of obtaining omens, as configurations of liver of sacrificial animals, smoke figures or traces of oil in water. Temporal configurations also turn into spatial configurations, that is, into correlations: as the four seasons correspond to the four cardinal points, and the history of a country to its topography, so the life of an individual corresponds to the shape of his or her body and an individual's fate is inscribed in the order of things. Instead of causality a general synchronicity[11] operates that gives a profoundly different meaning to the prediction of the future: it is not a matter of foreseeing a future that does not yet exist, but of revealing the necessity inscribed in the order of things, of indicating favourable or unfavourable moments and the conditions that determine the success of a project (which, however, cannot be governed).[12] One can read the present, the past or the future interchangeably, because each of them (if correctly interpreted) reveals the same logic and the same order.

This world devoid of chance cannot be read by chance: one needs a very refined and very elaborate technique to get away from the excess of significance of the world and from the 'hypertrophy of actuality' (Luhmann 1989a: 134). The divinatory reading of signs was reserved for persons living at a distance from the normality of everyday life: priests or monks, who were different from common communication partners and who themselves were not observed as observers. This is how the enormous complexity of divinatory procedures developed, controlled in every detail and deprived of any discretion, even if in our view they have no logical strength. Divination is led by a technique that, as in the case of science or law (Bottéro 1974: 131, 1987: 157ff.), is first of all needed to break the symmetry and the substantial immobility of a world where everything is connected with everything else. Technique is required to introduce chance into this universe without chance, or – as Vernant (1974: 15) says – to introduce 'game' into the system, and then to develop procedures that reveal experimentally the necessity in the order of things. Even when the beginning is random, as in the launch of coins in the I-Ching or in the production of forms with oil in water, it is not a matter of investigating this contingency or going back to the causes, but of remaining at the surface to investigate its configurations. In China, this even led to the development of an 'experimental semiology' that generates and formalises its signs (connected with augural formulas), identifies correlations, combines and manipulates them with each other to produce a divinatory arithmetic and then a divinatory algebra – always meant to read the meaning of the universe (Vandermeersch 1974). The aim is to seduce the world to speak, translating its structures in forms meaningful to man, increasingly complex and articulated as the technique is developed. The result is a 'random mechanism able to learn from itself' (Luhmann 1997: 237), all the more significant because the contingency of the starting point is absorbed into the superior necessity of the process.

What are the analogies with the intelligence of the web? First, the absence of chance, that the computer does not know. Chance, where needed, must be produced artificially with 'random generators' or other devices. The world of the machine is not only devoid of chance but also of sense, that is, of the reference to a deep level of meanings and understandable reasons – because the machine has nothing to understand, and always remains on the surface. The same happens in the culture of divination, which makes no claim to understand the profound meaning of things, reserved for God and forever inaccessible to humans, and moves on the surface, trying to grasp indications of the general order of things out of the forms and their regularity. Distributed web intelligence does the same, searching for correlations and pure forms, and manifesting an order it does not care to understand – and it does this with a highly controlled and formalised technique, where formalisation seems to have a value in itself. Like the logic of divination, the logic of the web does not proceed linearly from the past to the future, from cause to effect, from question to answer, but subverts the sequence in a substantial synchronicity, where the past can give indications for the future, because both should correspond to the same logic and the same formal criteria. Finally, in both cases information is not attributed to communication: one does not communicate with the machine as one does not communicate with the oracle. These do not express their thoughts and do not involve their consciousness, but merely reveal information enclosed in the order of things, which is interpreted in order to solve its obscurity, not to understand what the one (oracle or computer) who uttered it had in mind.

Perfect memory and its problems in an undetermined world

Why do we find these analogies between divinatory and web logic? How can we explain the similarity between two forms of rationality separated by millennia, especially after a few centuries of scientific logic oriented to the search for causes and led by theories and methods? What do these interpretative universes have in common, and what distinguishes them from scientific rationality?

First of all, they both refer to an entity possessing such wealth of information and endowed with such processing capabilities and calculating power to seize connections and correlations, that the reasoning of this entity is completely inaccessible to the human mind. In one case, this concerns a superior divine intelligence; in the other the vast power of the web. In the divine view as well as in the logic of computers, everything is connected to everything else – for those who have the ability to see and understand it. Even time is only a perspective illusion, due to the limitations of the human mind that can see only a portion of divine eternity, whereas to a divine entity past, present and future appear as contemporary and without any obscurity.[13] Forgetting is a problem (and a need) only for humans: the machine, as God, does not forget anything and preserves all data and information – as well as the connections with any other data and information. Contingency is the human dimension, arising from the inability to grasp the deep links between things: superior wisdom sees a world guided by necessity.

For the ancient mentality, facing a world still ruled by theological references, this was sufficient, and divination had no problems with irrationality. In contrast, scientific mentality requires the identification of causes, because God is no longer considered as making punctual intervention in all the affairs of the world, and the 'book of nature' must not be read in accordance with the Holy Scriptures but with Nature's laws and mechanisms (Eisenstein 1979). Explaining a phenomenon through the analogy with an astral configuration, with no indication of understandable and verifiable causal relations, becomes superstition and irrationality. The modern scientific approach requires theories that propose assumptions, and methods that allow putting these assumptions to the test in the world so that they can be verified or confuted – in order to arrive at the explanations that make this world understandable and allow effective projects. These explanations are imperfect and improvable, hence always contingent: necessity is not needed and not interesting, also because the world constantly changes with the passage of time and with the participation of observers. The modern world is made first of observers and of relations between observers, not of immutable and independent objects.[14]

This is not the place to deepen the epistemological issues concerning modern science, already the subject of heated debate. What interests me here is to observe the conditions it stems from: the idea of a world that must be explained in an understandable and verifiable way, not appealing to an incomprehensible superior wisdom. The plausibility of divination was based on the trust in a general order of the cosmos; since modernity our society lives in a disordered and not necessarily rational world. Even though the web makes use of a form of intelligence that is radically different from the one heralded by modern science, the era of the web shares the fundamental experience of disorder and contingency with modernity. This leads to a series of problems that divinatory culture did not know: does it make sense to think that the web computer investigates the ultimate sense of things, a kind of infinite wisdom that captures the necessary order in the universe? And to whom should it be attributed? It is not enough to say, with Chris Anderson (2008), that those who work in the web do not need ontologies if the operations presuppose an ultimate order: a very strong ontology that is not questioned. With the aggravating circumstance that while the divine order was by definition wise and admirable (that is, good), there is neither a guarantee that the order of the web is not 'bad' nor a guarantee that we can trust it.

The main problems, however, are not ontological but rather practical: the intelligence of the web does not always work. In all applications of the logic of the web issues emerge for which we seem to lack adequate conceptual tools. First of all, there is the issue of circularities: the financial crisis has highlighted how the techniques used to minimise risks have actually multiplied them dramatically, leading to an uncontrollable circuit of trading with increasingly risky outcomes. The calculus of implied volatility and the corresponding portfolio of planning techniques did not work, precisely because they failed to take the inevitable disorder of markets into account. The techniques used to draw conclusions about future trends based on the past did not consider that the future reacts also (and most of all) to attempts to predict it. Therefore the investment choices change simply because of the spread of models that should describe them.[15] Profiling techniques seem to take account of this circularity, that is, of the effects that their use has on the individuals and groups they want to describe (van Otterlo in this volume); but of course it is always possible that individuals will react not so much to the information contained in the profile but to profiling itself, which is rejected as such – and then there are no learning techniques that can avoid the self-defeating effect of attempted classification (up to the trivial case where the user refuses to buy the books recommended by the web precisely because they are recommended).

Prophecy did not have these problems, because it was based on the assumption of an already decided future that could not be altered by human activities – not even by those who try to oppose it. The utterance of the oracular response became a factor that contributed to its realisation (think of Oedipus), while the obscurity of the response allowed people to blame the interpretation when the response apparently did not come true: one did not understand correctly, but the oracle was right. This determinacy of the future is now completely implausible: the future of the modern world, and also of the post-modern one, is open and develops from human actions; it cannot be known in advance because it does not yet exist. The machine foresees only what can be expected on the basis of past logic, even if (as in the models of risk management) it considers the multiplicity of possible future courses, admitting that today one cannot know which of them will occur (open future). What escapes, however, is precisely the real future: the one that will become real reacting to our attempts to predict it and is therefore inherently unpredictable (it is none of those considered by the models). The circularity of the forecast tends to self-defeat (as in the case of financial markets) or in any case leads to enormous management problems.

Not recognising communication, the logic of the machine does not recognise the inherent indeterminacy of the social world, which cannot be known because it continuously reproduces its own uncertainty – and this is the problem of the application of profiling procedures. It is not a matter of the quantity of information, but precisely of circularity. The other (in sociological terms: the alter ego) cannot be known, not because one lacks a sufficient ability to process information, but precisely because the most relevant information is lacking – the information arising from the fact that the behaviour of the other depends on one's own behaviour, which tries to orient to this other. The technical term is double contingency, which expresses the basic problem (and the fascination) of the social dimension (Luhmann 1984: ch 3). This double contingency is completely inaccessible for the machine, which produces at most a mirroring of simple contingency[16] and reconstructs a model of the user based on past data and the available correlations – but without the ability to take into account the circular mechanism producing the authentic insurmountable unpredictability of subjects, who react to the very model that should describe them and thus orient their behaviour.

Freedom as the increase of possibilities

This insurmountable unpredictability is basically the mystery that we do not succeed in handling in our relationship with the web. In the ancient view, mystery was the guarantee of the rationality of the procedure. The procedure was considered convincing and reliable precisely because it reflected man's inability to understand the logic of the world – God cannot be brought back to the level of human abilities. In fact, there was no mystery to preserve and to protect (it protected itself): even the obscurity was only a human illusion, because for a superior mind everything would have been clear and understandable. Today we are again facing a mystery: the functioning of the web that no human rationality can fully grasp (and precisely therefore it is useful and interesting). Contrary to the ancient setting there is now no higher rationality that understands it, and it is possible there is indeed nothing to understand. This mystery – delegated to the machine – does not offer any guarantee of rationality; it is disturbing rather than reassuring, and threatens to lead to a general unintelligibility and a total loss of control.

It is not by chance that many of the problems related to the web centre precisely around control. A mysterious and incomprehensible web or, if you want, a true AI, cannot be controlled. On the contrary: the general rule of the network is to 'lose control' (Anderson 2006: 221), and this renunciation should lead to a different form of order– we saw it in all structures of the network intelligence. The incomprehensible world faced by divination could not be controlled either, but then there was no need, because the control was due to an infinitely wiser superior entity. Today we cannot refer to this wisdom and the lack of control is much more worrying, especially in cases where it meddles in areas where the only form of wisdom still recognised and understandable operates: that of the individual mind, with its limited intelligence that is increasingly different as to its logic and its proceedings from the alleged web intelligence (which does not even pretend to be a consciousness – not even an artificial one).

The more disturbing topic, notoriously, involves the protection of privacy (and its derivative issues). In its original formulation, privacy concerned the right of the person to prevent information regarding him or her to be handled by others without consent.[17] Today this meaning is obviously obsolete, since most of the information circulating on the web is not only totally unknown to the person concerned (since it is machine generated and produced by any possible data), but also unknown to any other (if not to the machine). One does not understand how the person could give consent, or what can replace consent in the new technological situation.

The difference concerns technology. The very concept of privacy (which has not always existed) is related to communication technologies, and in particular to the diffusion of the printing press – the very concept of privacy would not have been plausible before. With the printing press, the first mass medium in the strict sense, a genuine public dimension, anonymous and impersonal, was born and at the same time its opposite was born: a private dimension, individual and personalised.[18] With the advent of the printing press the need to protect the private sphere arises; that is, the need to avoid a situation where the public dimension totally absorbs the private and constrains private autonomy.

If too many things about a citizen are disclosed in public without authorisation and control, private life no longer has any discretion. This is the real reason why we do not want private images or confidential conversations to be published: not because there is necessarily anything to hide,[19] but because later we will also have to consider these images or conversations in our private field. Their publication will restrict our freedom within the private domain, where we will not be able to do some things or do them the same way anymore (and this may even result in our anticipation, meaning that we cannot act in certain ways even in advance, if there are no adequate mechanisms to protect privacy) (Rodotà 2005: 13–18). The possibilities available in private are reduced to the public image. What we want to protect, in fact, is not so much privacy but rather the distinction between private and public sphere.

With the printing press the problem that has guided our analysis arose: the information overload that turns the excess of memory into a problem, which requires a solution. Many concepts, tied to a particular technological situation, are no longer adequate when technology changes, together with its impact on society and on semantics: notions such as privacy and memory are certainly useful and relevant, and also in reference to communication on the web, but they should be redesigned to reflect the new communication situation – or, if you like, the functioning of a different intelligence.

Today, when mass culture switches to 'massively parallel culture' (Anderson 2006: 184), the intelligence of the web seems to have found an answer to the problems of information overload, making the excess of data (the data deluge) its own solution: data, as we have seen, are generated together with the structures that help to manage and select them, and the more the data increase the more the selection mechanisms become efficient. The problem has been known since antiquity and connected with the eternal search for an *ars obliviona-lis* (Eco 1987): a technique that allows learning to forget, as the *ars memoriae* teaches how to remember. The difficulty, however, is that the search for an *ars oblivionalis* is self-contradictory, because it would be a procedure to remember to forget – and was in fact never developed. Mnemotechnics itself recognised that the only effective way to increase forgetting was to multiply the range of available memories (Weinrich 1996). As sociological systems theory argues, memory is made not only of remembrance, but basically of the distinction between remembrance and forgetting. Memory increases when both sides of the distinction increase: one remembers more and forgets more (Esposito 2008). One could say that the excess of remembrance is produced together with forgetting, that is, with the ability to overlook all the data that are not relevant.[20] The perfect memory of the web should then work perfectly: it remembers more and forgets far more than any previous memory.

In the case of privacy, things seems more problematic, even if the concept has a similar structure and a similar history as the issue of information overload. Applying the same reasoning we should say that the privacy of the person increases when its public exposure increases, namely that the interiority of individuals becomes more and more inaccessible when the amount of publicly available personal data increases. In fact, since modernity the mystery of the universe has moved into individuals: the real obscurity to be respected and to be recognised is the black box of the individual psyche, which is not and should not be understood thoroughly by anybody (not even by the subject at stake). The mystery is the originality and indeterminacy of the individual, a mystery that nobody wants to give up, not even in one's communication with others. In a sense, it is true that this obscurity increases with the participation in a networked communication: as long as the mass media operated as a shared social memory, one could at least know the presuppositions that everyone referred to in the construction (through conformity or through deviance) of one's individuality.[21] The greater the mass and the variety of information available in public, the higher the possible varieties of individual minds. Today the fragmented and decentralised personalised media allow almost no deduction of what happens in the minds of the participants, if not for the few mass aspects that are still shared by everyone. It may be that these psychic processes take place increasingly on the surface and do not permit the construction of an authentic critical sense,[22] but undoubtedly they are increasingly separated from the public dimension – the individual is increasingly public (think only of social networks) and increasingly inaccessible (private) at the same time.

It is clear that this is not enough to reassure those who are worried about the consequences that the growth of the web may have on individual freedom and autonomy. Both in the case of privacy and in the case of forgetting the solution is not reassuring, because it refers to an intelligence now completely separated from the 'natural' one and from the rationality of individuals – and not necessarily rational. The increasing impenetrability of individuals does not necessarily mean increased freedom or creativity, and we know that the web's form of forgetting does not imply that people do not have constraints – indeed they must continually cope with a past reviewed and revised by the network and with their public image that does not correspond to their private identity (for instance, in the much discussed cases in which a person is denied a job because of an old picture on the web, maybe showing him when drunk or encouraging class struggle). If we want them to be effective, however, the defence of privacy and the defence of the freedom of the future from the constraints of the past should be placed at the same level of complexity as the AI they are threatened by, which does not work as human consciousness. It is not effective to criticise this AI by taking consciousness as a reference: rather one should stress the difference and not claim that the network functions as a consciousness.

The policy on privacy, then, should use the same divinatory or para-divinatory structures working in the web: we must learn to control the lack of control, to increase data as a condition for being able to select them, to elaborate forms and meanings that are independent from sense but allow us to build a sense a posteriori; we must acquire the ability to stay on the surface – precisely because this way we can defend a different sense, that goes in depth, identifies causes, operates with meanings and has a limited processing power. The protection of forgetting, as we have seen, seems to work better when it multiplies data than when it tries artificially to erase some portions: because erasing memories, as we know, always means that one remembers to forget – it increases remembrance, not forgetting. Presumably, then, it will also be convenient to operate in this way in the case of privacy, building opportunities rather than imposing prohibitions – increasing data to react to the increase of data. So understood, the defence of privacy is not so much about putting barriers to the data accessible on the web, but rather about trying to make everything accessible – however, the obtained information should not restrict the possibilities of a person to act. We should not keep a secret, but preserve a mystery: the mystery of the black box of the individual psyche. Although the network provides a profile, this should not affect the possibility that in the future one makes different choices – that is, keeping the future open, even and precisely if it depends on the past. This is the real problem of the defence of privacy, which should be faced for example by a substantial increase of the amount of profiles and the ability to construct them. That is something we can work on, for example with models of consumers who change their behaviour because the network forces them to observe themselves with its recommendations, or with privacy defence techniques that increase the data about each person to such an extent that it becomes difficult to obtain univocal indications.[23] The individual would then keep the freedom to make choices, without being too much constrained by the individual's past and public image. The operational sense of privacy would be preserved, without opposing the functioning of the web, but rather exploiting the operations of the network and utilising them according to a different logic.

Notes

1 Which explicitly takes the (still very controversial) decision to locate consciousness in the environment of the system of society, whose elements are communications (Luhmann 1997: ch 1).
2 See Kelly (2010, 2005). According to Pierre Levy (1997) the technical infrastructure of cyberspace constitutes the 'hypercortex' of a new form of collective intelligence.
3 According to Luhmann (1996), the suspect of manipulation is the original sin of the system of mass media – the sin that can never be cancelled or overcome.
4 As we will see later on, this of course does neither mean that there are no constraints for the user nor that information cannot be used by someone for specific (commercial or other) purposes; it simply means that it is a deeply different form of control.

5 A practice well known to the theory of organisation, which has long recognised paradoxes and their function: see Weick (1995).

6 In a famous article, which was a common point of reference at the workshop (Computer Privacy and Data Protection Conference, Brussels 2011) that formed the basis of this present volume, Anderson (2008) comments on Craig Vender's project for genome sequencing.

7 Thanks again to the possibilities offered by models such as cloud computing, allowing for the exploitation of the exceeding computational capacity of connected computers, that have been chronically under-utilised since the spread of PCs. In the new forms of connection this unused capacity is made available to other projects and other computing needs, optimising the performances of the mega-computer of the web. The techniques of virtualisation even overcome the constraints of technological compatibility, since special software is able to simulate all the components of the systems operating in digital mode: see Carr (2008: 71ff).

8 Think of the function of 'Instant', which offers autocomplete suggestions as soon as you type the first letters or words of your search query.

9 This is the topic of Carr (2010), already revealed by the title: *The Shallows*.

10 Not devoid of interest to our theme, addressed to communications technologies, is the link between divination and orality: these techniques were diffused in societies that, even if they knew writing, subordinated (not alphabetical) written communication to oral communication. China cannot be considered a society without writing, and ancient Mesopotamia as well, but they never developed a fully phonetic writing. A large body of material on this subject can be found in Vernant et al (1974).

11 Jung's well known issue (Jung 1952a, 1952b).

12 It is not by chance that the analogy with Chinese thought has often been observed: see more recently Jullien (1996).

13 In the classic definition of Plato: the 'moving image of eternity': Timaeus: 37ff.

14 For the position of constructivism see Luhmann (1988, 1990).

15 MacKenzie (2006) speaks of 'counter-performativity'.

16 We can maybe talk of virtual contingency (Esposito 1993) – the one that is searched for by, for instance, the models of genetic programming and by the (by now) classical research on neural networks. These models seek to realise a learning capability by incorporating a certain indeterminacy into the program, which via the interactions with other programs of a 'population' should produce an unpredicted and always flexible order. While virtual contingency might involve two (or more) contingencies recognising and influencing each other, this does not necessarily entail the circularity of the authentic double contingency that is present in profiling. Double contingency is expressed in the formula 'I do what you want if you do what I want' (Luhmann 1984: 166) – and raises the question 'Who begins?' It is a radical and inherently paradoxical contingency, because the possibilities arise precisely in the circular mutual dependency of the 'subjects'.

17 Standard reference is Warren and Brandeis (1890).

18 Here the standard reference is Habermas (1962).

19 As Ian Kerr (Chapter 4 in this volume) argues with reference to the figure of the 'bad man'.

20 The concerns of those who would like to protect the ability to forget (Mayer-Schönberger 2009) should be placed at this level.
21 This is the reason why cultural industry appeared so threatening.
22 As Carr (2010) fears.
23 The procedures of obfuscation described by Brunton and Nissenbaum (Chapter 7 in this volume) offer an illuminating example.

References

Anderson, C. (2006) *The Long Tail. How endless choice is creating unlimited demand*, London: Random House.
Anderson, C. (2008) 'The End of Theory: The data deluge makes the scientific method obsolete', *Wired*, 16.
Battelle, J. (2005) *The Search: How Google and its rivals rewrote the rules of business and transformed our culture*, London: Portfolio.
Bauerlein, M. (2012) 'Authority Figures', *The Chronicle*, 18 March.
Benkler, Y. (2006) *The Wealth of Networks: How social production transforms markets and freedom*, New Haven, CT and London: Yale University Press (It.tr. *La ricchezza della Rete. La produzione sociale trasforma il mercato e aumenta la libertà*, Milano: EGEA, 2007).
Black F. and Scholes M. (1981) 'The Pricing of Options and Corporate Liabilities', *Journal of Political Economy*, 8: 637–54.
Bottéro, J. (1974) 'Sintomi, segni, scritture nell'antica Mesopotamia', in Vernant, J. P., Vandermeersch, L., Gernet, J., Bottéro, J., Crahay, R., Brisson, L., Carlier, J., Grodzynski, D. and Retel Laurentin, A. (eds) *Divination et Rationalité*, Paris: Seuil (It.tr. *Divinazione e razionalità*, Torino: Einaudi, 1982): 73–124.
Bottéro, J. (1987) *Mésopotamie. L'écriture, la raison et les dieux*, Paris: Gallimard.
Carr, N. (2008) *The Big Switch. Rewiring the world, from Edison to Google*, New York and London: Norton (It.tr. *Il lato oscuro della Rete. Libertà, sicurezza, privacy*, Milano: RCS Libri, 2008).
Carr, N. (2010) *The Shallows. What the internet is doing to our brains*, New York and London: Norton.
Eco, U. (1987) 'An Ars Oblivionalis? Forget it!', *Kos*, 30: 40–53.
Eisenstein, E. L. (1979) *The Printing Press as an Agent of Change. Communications and cultural transformations in early-modern Europe*, Cambridge: Cambridge University Press.
Esposito, E. (1993) 'Der Computer als Medium und Maschine', *Zeitschrift für Soziologie*, XXII (5): 338–54.
Esposito, E. (2002) *Soziales Vergessen*, Frankfurt a.M.: Suhrkamp.
Esposito, E. (2007) *Die Fiktion der wahrscheinlichen Realität*, Frankfurt a.M.: Suhrkamp.
Esposito, E. (2008) 'Social Forgetting: A systems-theory approach', in Erll, A. and Nünning, A. (eds), *Cultural Memory Studies: An interdisciplinary and international handbook*, Berlin and New York: de Gruyter: 181–89.
Esposito, E. (2011) *The Future of Futures. The time of money in financing and society*, Cheltenham: Edward Elgar.
Giles, J. (2005) 'Internet Encyclopaedias go Head to Head', *Nature*, 438: 900–901.
Habermas, J. (1962) *Strukturwandel der Öffentlichkeit*, Neuwied: Luchterhand.
Hildebrandt, M. and Gutwith, S., (eds) (2008) *Profiling the European Citizen. Cross-Disciplinary Perspectives*, Dordrecht: Springer.

Jullien, F. (1996) *Traité de l'efficacité*, Paris: Grasset & Fasquelle (It.tr. *Trattato dell'efficacia*, Torino: Einaudi, 1998).

Jung, C. G. (1952a) 'Synchronizität als ein Prinzip akausaler Zusammenhänge', in *Gesammelte Werke*, Band 8, Olten: Walter-Verlag, 1971: 457–554.

Jung, C. G. (1952b) 'Über Synchronizität', in *Gesammelte Werke*, Band 8, Olten: Walter-Verlag, 1971: 555–66.

Kelly, K. (1997) 'New Rules for the New Economy', *Wired*, 9: 140–44 and 186–97.

Kelly, K. (2005) 'We Are the Web', *Wired*, 8.

Kelly, K. (2010) *What Technology Wants*, New York: Viking Books.

Koops, B. J., Hildebrandt, M. and Jaquet-Chiffelle, D. O. (2010) 'Bridging the Accountability Gap: Rights for news entities in the information society?, *Minnesota Journal of Law, Science & Technology*, 11: 497–561.

Levy, P. (1997) *L'intelligence collective. Pour une anthropologie du cyberspace*, Paris: La Découverte.

Luhmann, N. (1984) *Soziale Systeme. Grundriß einer alllgemeinen Theorie*, Frankfurt a.M.: Suhrkamp.

Luhmann, N. (1988) *Erkenntnis als Konstruktion*, Bern: Benteli.

Luhmann, N. (1989a) 'Geheimnis, Zeit und Ewigkeit', in Luhmann, N. and Fuchs, P. *Reden und Schweigen*, Frankfurt a.M.: Suhrkamp: 101–37.

Luhmann, N. (1989b), 'Individuum, Individualität, Individualismus', in *Gesellschaftsstruktur und Semantik. Studien zur Wissenssoziologie der modernen Gesellschaft* vol 3, Frankfurt a.M.: Suhrkamp: 149–258.

Luhmann, N. (1990), *Die Wissenschaft der Gesellschaft*, Frankfurt a.M.: Suhrkamp.

Luhmann, N. (1996) *Die Realität der Massenmedien*, Opladen: Westdeutscher.

Luhmann, N. (1997) *Die Gesellschaft der Gesellschaft*, Frankfurt a.M.: Suhrkamp.

MacKenzie, D. (2006) *An Engine, Not a Camera. How financial models shape markets*, Cambridge, MA: MIT Press.

Mayer-Schönberger, V. (2009) *Delete: The virtue of forgetting in the digital age*, Princeton: Princeton University Press (It.tr. *Delete. Il diritto all'oblio nell'era digitale*, Milano: Egea).

Plato (1903) *Timaeus*, ed. John Burnet. Oxford: Oxford University Press.

Rodotà, S. (2005) *Intervista su privacy e libertà*, Roma-Bari: Laterza.

Spencer Brown, G. (1972) *Laws of Form*, New York: Julian Press.

Turkle, S. (1995) *Life on the Screen. Identity in the age of the internet*, New York: Simon & Schuster.

Vandermeersch, L. (1974) 'Dalla tartaruga all'achillea (Cina)', in Vernant, J. P., Vandermeersch, L., Gernet, J., Bottéro, J., Crahay, R., Brisson, L., Carlier, J., Grodzynski, D. and Retel Laurentin, A. (eds) *Divination et Rationalité*, Paris: Seuil (It.tr. *Divinazione e razionalità*, Torino: Einaudi, 1982): 27–52.

Vernant, J. P. (1974) 'Parole e segni muti', in Vernant, J. P., Vandermeersch, L., Gernet, J., Bottéro, J., Crahay, R., Brisson, L., Carlier, J., Grodzynski, D. and Retel Laurentin, A. (eds) *Divination et Rationalité*, Paris: Seuil (It.tr. *Divinazione e razionalità*, Torino: Einaudi, 1982): 5–24.

Vernant, J. P., Vandermeersch, L., Gernet, J. Bottéro, J., Crahay, R., Brisson, L., Carlier, J., Grodzynski, D. and Retel Laurentin, A. (eds) (1974) *Divination et Rationalité*, Paris: Seuil (It.tr. *Divinazione e razionalità*, Torino: Einaudi, 1982).

Warren, S. and Brandeis, L. (1890) 'The Right to Privacy', *Harvard Law Review* 4: 193–200.

Weick, K. E. (1995) *Sensemaking in Organizations*, Thousand Oaks: Sage.

Weinrich, H. (1996) *Gibt es eine Kunst des Vergessens?*, Basel: Schwabe & Co.

Yates, F. A. (1966) *The Art of Memory*, London: Routledge & Kegan Paul (It.tr. *L'arte della memoria*, Torino: Einaudi, 1993).

6

The end(s) of critique

Data behaviourism versus due process

*Antoinette Rouvroy**

Introduction

Operations of collection, processing and structuration of data for purposes[1] of data mining and profiling, helping individuals and organisations to cope with circumstances of uncertainty or relieving them from the burden of interpreting events and taking decisions in routine, trivial situations have become crucial to public and private sector activities in domains as various as crime prevention, health management, marketing or even entertainment.[2]

The availability of new ICT interfaces running on algorithmically produced and refined profiles, indiscriminately allowing for both personalisation (and the useful, safe and comfortable immersion of users in the digital world)[3] and pre-emption (rather than regulation) of individual and collective behaviours and trajectories appears providential to cope with the complexities of a world of massive flows of persons, objects and information, and to compensate for the difficulties of governing by the law in a complex, globalised world. The implicit belief accompanying the growth of 'big data' is that, provided one has access to massive amounts of raw data (and the world is actually submersed by astronomical amounts of digital data), one might become able to anticipate most phenomena (including human behaviours) of the physical and the digital worlds, thanks to relatively simple algorithms allowing, on a purely inductive statistical basis, the building of models of behaviours or patterns without having to consider either causes or intentions. I will call 'data behaviourism' this new way of producing knowledge about future preferences attitudes, behaviours or events without considering the subject's psychological motivations, speeches or narratives, but rather relying on *data*. The 'real time operationality' of devices functioning on such algorithmic logic spares human actors the burden and responsibility of transcribing, interpreting and evaluating the events of world. It spares them the meaning-making processes of transcription or representation, institutionalisation, convention and symbolisation.

The question whether the pre-emptive powers of algorithms are overestimated, whether algorithms produce 'valid' predictions or not or, in other words, whether 'it works or not' is not really crucial for what I am interested in here, which is to say that, never mind the validity of all this, what counts most is to identify the extent to which relying on the apparent operationality of algorithms spares us a series of individual and collective perceptual, cognitive, evaluative, conventional, institutional, linguistic efforts or tasks, and at what price.

The impacts of the computational turn on governmentality are far from trivial. The constant 'adaptation' of environments to individual and collective 'profiles' produced by 'data intelligence' – be it called 'personalisation' or 'technology of security' – is an unprecedented mode of government.[4] The type of knowledge it consumes and produces, the modalities through which it impacts on individual and collective behaviours, the modes of individuation which may sway or resist algorithmic governmentality[5] deserve careful examination. The aim of this chapter is precisely to inaugurate such inquiry.

This chapter is thus about a vertiginous matter. Formulated as an inquiry about the state of knowledge, power and subjects after the computational turn, it turns out as a reformulation of the question of the possibility of critique, recalcitrance and subjectivation[6] in an epistemic and political universe gradually deserted by empirical experiment and deductive, causal logic, and with regard to a mode of government appearing to disregard the reflexive and discursive capabilities (as well as their 'moral capabilities') of human agents, in favour of computational, pre-emptive, context- and behaviour-sensitive management of risks and opportunities. In other words, I wonder whether it is still possible to practise critical thinking after a computational turn which, despite its pretences to 'objectivity', appears as a turning away from the ambitions of modern rationality anchored in empirical experiment and deductive – causal–logic, and, despite its promises of personalisation and better taking into consideration of individual merits, needs, abilities, preferences, does not address individuals through their reflexive capabilities or through their inscription within collective structures, but merely through their 'profiles'.

It will then be argued that what makes critique so difficult to practise vis-à-vis the computational turn we are now experiencing with the gradual and almost viral generalisation of data mining and profiling, is:

- first, the fact that it produces a zone where (constructed) reality and (background of) the world in all its spontaneity and uncertainty become indistinct
- second, the fact that the transversal dimension – essential in the scientific, the judicial and even the existential domains – of 'test', 'trial', examination', 'assessment' or '*épreuve*', or even 'experience', is rendered obsolete by real time, pre-emptive production of algorithmic reality
- third, the fact that algorithmic governmentality does not allow for subjectivation processes, and thus for recalcitrance, but rather bypasses and avoids any encounter with human reflexive subjects. Algorithmic

governmentality is without subject: it operates with infra-individual data and supra-individual patterns without, at any moment, calling the subject to account for himself.

The chapter will thus present a defence of all these things that usually appear as the weaknesses of regulation by the law and adjudication by the judicial system – that is, of the legal construction of reality – compared with regulation by the algorithms: ineffectivity, inefficiency, belatedness etc which are all 'creating' temporal space and (judicial) scene where meaning regains autonomy vis-à-vis the pure factuality of 'data behaviourism', where norms can be negotiated and contested, where (legal) subjects can materialise, building their motivations and, calling each other into account through language, create occasions for individual and collective individuations which are always deviations from known patterns and profiles.

The algorithmic production of 'reality': data behaviourism

Discovering a reality immanent to the data world

Each epoch has its own privileged ways of building evidence and rendering the world meaningful. As Pierre Legendre explains, the world is not given to man. Man can access the world only through the mediation of language, and thus representation (Legendre, 2001: 17). On the basis of *what is present and available to human senses*, representation attests to the presence of what is not immediately available to our senses: the (hidden) *causes* of phenomena, the psychological *motivations* of actions, their *potential* to develop into or give birth to other phenomena or actions, Boltanski (2009: 93–94) states in this respect an interesting distinction between 'reality' (the result of representation) and 'the world':

> The question of the relationship between, on one side, that which appears to hold firm, to be consistent, and, on the other side, that which is fraught with uncertainty and opens the way to critique, cannot be fully deployed if one situates oneself on the sole ground of reality. Indeed, in a two dimensional coordinate space, reality tends to be confused with what appears to stand in some way by its own strength, that is to say, with the order, and nothing then, allows to understand the challenges against this order, at least in its most radical forms. ... But talking of reality in these terms amounts to relativize its scope and thereby to suggest that it is detached from a distinct background that it does not exhaust. We will call this background the world, considered, to paraphrase Wittgenstein, as 'whatever happens'. One may, in order to render this distinction between

the 'reality' and the 'world' palpable, make an analogy with the way in which one can distinguish between risk and uncertainty. The risk, in so far as it is probabilizable, constitutes, precisely, one of the instruments invented in the XVIIIth century to construct reality. ... But all events are not controllable in the risk logic, so that an unknown portion of radical uncertainty remains. And, just as one can make the project of knowing and representing reality, the aim of describing the world, in what would be its totality, is not within the reach of anyone. Yet, something of the world manifests itself precisely each time events or experiences whose possibility ... or probability had not been inserted in the design of reality, arise in speech and/or surface in the field of individual or collective action.

The distance between 'the world' and 'reality', this 'unknown part of radical uncertainty' has always been a challenge for institutions and, at the same time, a precondition for the possibility of critique if, by critique we mean, like Foucault (1990): the virtue consisting in challenging the very categories through which one is predisposed to perceive and evaluate people and situations of the world, rather than merely judging them according to these very categories. Critique is:

> ... a practice that suspends judgment and an opportunity to practice new values, precisely on the basis of that suspension. In this perspective, critique targets the construction of a field of occlusive categories themselves rather than on the subsumption of a particular case under a pre-constituted category.

Data mining and profiling, building on the factual availability of enormous amounts of raw digital data, renovate a new 'truth regime' – which I call 'data behaviourism' – creating the widest possible zone of indistinction between reality and the world, and eroding the 'unknown part of radical uncertainty', thereby also reducing the scope of critique. As a consequence of the drive to automate the processes going from raw data to knowledge, what 'counts as real' is increasingly 'discovered' within the exponentially growing data warehouses. These data warehouses then 'stage' a digital version of the world, a world populated by the 'purely factual' profiles generated according to a process diagnosed by Alain Supiot (2010: 81) as the

> ... metamorphosis of all singular quality into measurable quantity whereby we are bound in to a speculative loop in which the belief in these numerical images replaces the contact with the reality that these images are meant to represent.

As already suggested, profiles appear – to the general public at least – as a 'spontaneous' germination[7] from the digital transcription and statistical analysis of 'reality' (through predictive data mining), resisting characterisation as either spontaneous or artefactual and bypassing human interpretation.[8] The use of data mining and profiling is usually justified by arguments of rationalisation. 'Crunching numbers' appears as a victory of rational thought over emotionally, politically, racially biased human perception.[9] With the computational turn, our relation to *knowledge* seems indeed to be changing. In 'Managing Information', a special report published by *The Economist* on 25 February 2010 (cited in Cukier (2010)), one reads that:

> ... epistemologically speaking, information is made up of a collection of data and knowledge is made up of different strands of information. But this special report uses 'data' and 'information' interchangeably because, as it will argue, the two are increasingly difficult to tell apart. Given enough raw data, today's algorithms and powerful computers can reveal new insights that would previously have remained hidden.

Data, information and knowledge are thus more or less taken to be the same things. Such 'knowledge' thus does not appear as a 'production of the mind', with all the artificiality and cognitive and emotional biases unavoidably connoting mental productions, but as always already 'given', immanent to the (digitally recorded) world, in which it is merely automatically 'discovered' or from which it literally flourishes thanks to algorithmic operations rendering invisible correlations operational.

To what category of sign or signal do the raw 'big data' forming the texture of algorithmic rationality belong? What is their relation with the 'things of the world' of which they are taken to be a 'sign' or a 'signal' of? Raw data do not resemble or keep even indirect physical bound with any thing of the world,[10] and they are not conventional symbols thereof either. It is, nevertheless, these massive amounts of raw data, these huge, constantly evolving, impersonal statistical data that today constitute 'the world' in which algorithms 'unveil' what algorithmic governmentality takes for 'the reality'. 'Reality' – that knowledge appearing to hold – does not seem to be produced anymore, but is always already there, immanent to the databases, waiting to be discovered by statistical algorithmic processes. Knowledge is not produced *about* the world anymore, but *from* the digital world. A kind of knowledge that is not tested-by or testing the world it describes and emanates from: algorithmic reality is formed inside the digital reality without any direct contact with the world it is aimed at representing. Rather than the validity of its predictive models,[11] it is its operationality, its plasticity, its contribution to the 'fluidification' of economic and social life (and thus of capitalism), its efficiency in sparing human agents time and effort in the interpretation and evaluation of persons and events of the world that characterise the 'intelligence' of 'big data'. Raw data function as deterritorialised signals,[12] inducing reflex responses in computer systems, rather than as signs carrying meanings and requiring interpretation. Everything goes as if meaning making was not necessary anymore,[13] as if the world was already, absent any interpretation, saturated with meaning.[14] As Neyrat (2011) writes:

> We wouldn't speak not because all would have been said, but would have been predicted, always already written, edicted, edited, but in a writing that would be the writing of things themselves. Not the signature of things, but rather the signs-things, and signosis, this disease of the nailed, fixed say, never removed from its eternity, stuck in a topos.

Atopy of algorithmic reality

That immanent knowledge is also atopic, in the sense that it is no longer linked to any temporal or geographical anchor. Blossoming from the eternal actuality of data warehouses, fed by data recorded from heterogeneous contexts, the productions of data behaviourism are at odds with the idea of 'interested' knowledge (Spinoza 1990), or of knowledge as enactment and result of power relations (Foucault 1990). Patterns discovered in data warehouses have an aura of 'pure' knowledge, autonomous vis-à-vis both powers and effects. Refining itself in real time, building and rebuilding itself from within the huge 'numerical memories' where every bit, never mind when and where recorded and stored, floats on the flat surface of pure actuality and pure presence,[15] the statistical body seems to have expurgated every bit of obscurity: everything being always available, it perfectly fits an aesthetics of full light and intemporal or achronological transparency. Therefore, the 'information' from which the new knowledge is produced will not be evaluated on the basis of traditional criteria of authenticity, historical coherence, or critical apperception, but merely on the merits of immediate operationality, plasticity, flexible adaptation to changing circumstances, and immediate availability.

This atopy sheds some doubts about the possibility of speaking of knowledge at all in this case if knowing, as Didi-Huberman (2009: 11) argues, requires 'taking position', that is:

> ... situating oneself two times at least, on the two fronts at least that each position comprises as any position is, necessarily, relative. It goes, for example with affronting something, but, in front of that thing, one must also take into account everything one leaves aside, the off-frame that exists behind us, that one may refuse but which, for a substantial part, affects our movement itself, thus our position. It also implies to situate oneself over time. Taking position, it is desiring, requesting something, it is situating oneself in the present and aiming at a future.[16]

A distinct usage of statistics

Data behaviourism is different from statistical quantification

'Data behaviourism' is very different from other 'governmental' strategies based on statistics, and which, most of the time, are systems of quantification, rendering heterogeneous situations and accomplishments *commensurable*. As explained by Desrosières (2010), benchmarking also contributes to reduce or manage uncertainty but is aimed at building and negotiating spaces of commensurability by reaching agreements about measurement procedures and allowing for an arbitration of means and finalities. 'Benchmarking' translates otherwise incommensurable objects or situations into numbers. Such mechanism of quantification solves a series of difficulties of evaluation (of human actions and productions). Quantification is a manner of building objects with an (ideally) negotiated, conventional value. The quantification process binds individuals together within a given system of evaluation and constrains them to use the 'language' of quantification in comparing their respective merits, needs etc. This makes of benchmarking a strategy perfectly articulated with the ideal of 'due process'.

Quantification logics create epistemic communities and enable human evaluation processes, whereas algorithmic reason simply exempts from the burden of creating any type of community, of organising interpretation or evaluation processes. The algorithmic rationality governing data mining and profiling processes and the logic of 'data behaviourism' carried thereby is simply at odds with the idea of (due) process or even, simply, with the idea of *appearance* (in laboratories, in courts etc) of actual persons, situations or objects. As will be developed further later on, algorithmic governmentality carefully avoids all types of confrontations, especially with those who are affected by its governmental effects. 'Data behaviourism' *spares* the burden of testing, questioning, examining, evaluating actual facts and persons of flesh and blood; it avoids making objects or persons *appear* in laboratories or in courts in order to test or question their causes or intentions.

Data behaviourism does not presuppose or test hypotheses about the world

Unlike other uses of statistics – like uses in epidemiology – data mining does not presuppose, or reinforce or invalidate any hypothesis about the world[17] but merely appears as an agnostic, pragmatic, highly operational and effective manner to structure, in an anticipative way, the possible field of actions of 'bodies'. This *agnosticism* contributes in making it appear both an *inoffensive* and a *universally valid* way of rendering the world meaningful. In particular, the 'dropping' of causality does not revive the deterministic metaphysics accompanying early uses of statistics, despite possible misinterpretations of the idea that in a data-rich environment such as ours, 'anything can be predicted' by 'crunching numbers' (Ayres 2007). The computational turn is in no way a return to the deterministic metaphysics accompanying the advent of statistics in the 19th century and exhibited for example in the writings of Laplace (1814) – defending the idea that human actions, even those that seem to result from chance or human liberty, are in fact governed by laws as necessary as the laws governing phenomena in physics – or Quetelet (1835) – who constructed the idea of 'the average man'. On the contrary, it is precisely *because* determinist thought no longer appears plausible at all and because human psychological motivations and singularities appear – maybe more than ever – incommensurable and unpredictable owing to the complexification and massification of flows of persons, data and objects that algorithmic systems of statistical profiling appear so appealing today, relieving human beings from the harsh tasks of interpreting and evaluating facts in an epistemic universe devoid of common testing and evaluation criteria.

The rate of intentionality, causality, experience and discourse have dropped

Betraying the ambitions of modern, deductive, rationality linking observable phenomena (that is, phenomena preselected as objects of observation and assessment in view of explicit and determined interests) to their causes, the 'algorithmic rationality' follows an inductive logic. Indifferent to the causes of phenomena, 'data behaviourism' is anchored in the purely statistical observation of correlations (independent from any kind of logic) among data collected in a variety of heterogeneous contexts. This does not mean, of course, that the computational turn has a direct impact on the empirical (in)existence of causal interactions between phenomena or on the nature and degree of intentionality or rationality of human actions.[18] I merely suggest, parallel to Benjamin's (2000: 115) observations with regard to experience:

> It is as if we had been deprived of a faculty of ours which seemed unalienable, the most ensured of all: the faculty to exchange experiences. One of the reasons of this phenomenon is obvious: the rate of experience has dropped. And it continues to fall indefinitely.[19]

Now, the *rates of causality and intentionality* – by 'rate' I mean our ability or willingness to *use* these categories to predict, regulate and give account of phenomena – have dropped as well. Sometimes, 'resources of meaning' become unavailable. Walter Benjamin, as long ago as 1933, identified the incapacity to transmit an experience, and thus the 'weakness of experience' as a consequence of the First World War (survivors of battlefields returned mute, not enriched with experience they could share, but impoverished by the 'irrepresentable').

The functioning of experience as resource for the production of meaning may also be impaired in situations where the 'truth value' attributed to experience or experiment decreases. Giorgio Agamben (2002: 26), for example, articulates the dropping of the rate of experience with the decline of the 'authority to speak':

> Because experience finds its necessary correlate less in knowledge than in authority, that is, in speech and narrative, today no one seems to have enough authority to guarantee an experience; should one have it, one would not be touched by the idea of establishing an experience on the ground of that authority. That which characterizes present time is on the contrary that all authority is grounded on what cannot be experienced; to an authority that would be legitimated merely by an experience, no one would grant any credit.[20]

In the context of data mining and profiling, the same thing happens: patterns and profiles are not merely competing with testimony, expertise, discourses of authority or confession; they make linguistic modalities of 'evidence' appear obsolete compared with the operationality, immediacy and objectivity of data behaviourism. If, therefore, the computational turn does not have any impact on the *phenomena* of causality and human agency and the reflexive capabilities it presupposes and leaves them untouched, it nevertheless deflects concerns or attentions away from these previously privileged perspectives of causality and intentional agency or individual and collective 'authority' (that is, for our purpose, the capability to 'author' one's actions, to have the 'authority' to give account of the meanings of one's actions).

The obsolescence of tests and challenges

The 'algorithmic reason', immanent to the digitally recorded 'real', escapes the types of trials, tests, examinations, experiments and other *épreuves* or challenges that usually appear essential to attest to the robustness, truth, validity or legitimacy of claims and hypotheses formulated about reality in the scientific, the judicial and even the existential domains (Ronell 2005). Data behaviourism simply appears to have rendered the *interpretive* time and space of *trial or process* irrelevant. It is a regime of truth evaluated against criteria of cost effectiveness and operationality. The computational turn thus attests to the decline of *interpretation* to the benefit of something much more immediate (and immediacy is one of the connotations usually attached to efficiency), which is statistical inference operated on the basis of correlations, while validation of patterns or profiles happen through a kind of 'backward performativity': anything that would happen and be recorded, never mind whether it fits a pre-existing pattern or profile or not, will contribute to the refinement and improvement of the 'statistical body', and will 'validate'[21] the methods of automatic interpretation or correlation to which they are subjected. This does not mean that systems are not checked at all, that they are not monitored so as to ensure that they perform in function of what they are supposed to achieve: it is simply that these kinds of check and test are confined to checking the system's operationality. The operationality, real time character, plasticity of the 'algorithmic reason' are at odds with the interruption, the distance and the delays that are the preconditions for a critical appraisal of any kind of produced knowledge. If 'predictive data mining' does not represent reality, its 'real time' operationality, the fact that decisions are increasingly taken on the basis of profiles, the relative performativity of these profiles, leads, de facto, to a situation of quasi-indistinction between algorithmically produced 'reality' and the 'world' from which it is supposed to emanate, whereas the *distinction*, the *non-coincidence* of things and their representations are necessary to leave open the space of critique.

This truth regime is often praised for its 'objectivity', rather than because it would have been 'robust' enough to pass the usual tests of scientific validity or political legitimacy. On the contrary, the 'force' of the knowledge produced by algorithms is proportional to the difficulty of submitting it to any convention of quantification, or to any kind of test. The 'force' of algorithmic governmentality is thus proportional to its 'non-robustness' (if one takes robustness to be the capacity to sustain challenges and critiques). This 'non-robustness' is also what makes the aesthetics of algorithmic governmentality: an aesthetic of fluidity, continuity, real time adaptation, immediacy, dynamism, plasticity, non-obtrusiveness, seamlessness etc. Compared with such a powerful aesthetics, human interpretation and subjective accounts of reality appear rather inaesthetic (time consuming, always belated, perhaps more authentic but less trustworthy, perhaps more critical but less operational etc).

Algorithmic governmentality

The spread of 'data behaviourism' accompanying the deployment of data mining and profiling systems in a diversity of applications inaugurates an unprecedented regime of power that I have previously called 'algorithmic governmentality'.

Algorithmic government is spectral

The focus on anticipation and pre-emption shifts the target of 'power' from actuality, and from the present wilderness of facts, to potentiality, to the risks and opportunities (which are the *virtual* dimension of what is here and now, that is, the portion of irreducible uncertainty that one has renounced trying to render commensurable),[22] the future which it tries to tame through anticipative framing of informational and physical contexts. 'Data behaviourism' is thus an anticipative coincidence with a 'real' that it is aimed at preventing and which, if the system works properly, will thus never happen[23] (this is the case when data mining and profiling are are used in security scenarios) or with a 'real' with which it will entertain relations of backwards performativity (or feedback loop performativity). The 'probabilistic subject' is not the same as the actual, experiential, present and sentient subject.

The algorithmic government thus contrasts with what we know about a neoliberal mode of government which produces the subjects it needs. Through the ubiquitous injunction – and its internalisation by subjects – of maximisation of performance (production) and enjoyment (consumption), neoliberalism produces 'hyper-subjects' having, as their normative horizon, the continuously reiterated project of 'becoming themselves', and passionately engaged in 'self-control', 'self-entrepreneurship' and 'self-evaluation'.[24] Algorithmic governmentality does not produce any kind of subject. It affects, without addressing them, people in all situations of possible criminality, fraud, deception and consumption, which are situations where they are not requested to 'produce' anything, and certainly not subjectivation. Rather, algorithmic governmentality bypasses consciousness and reflexivity, and operates on the mode of alerts and reflexes.

Unlike government by the law, algorithmic government affects potentialities rather than actual persons and behaviours

Classically, 'governing', that is, producing a certain 'regularity' of behaviours (among citizens, customers, patients, students, employees etc) consists – at least in liberal countries – in inducing individuals to choose, in the range of things they may do or may abstain from doing, those things which best fit the interests of the community. In *Nomography, or the Art of Inditing Laws*, Bentham (1843) explains the process through which compliance with the laws is produced:

> ... to be productive of any of the effects intended by it, the law of the legislator requires an appendage, which, for the production of its effects, is never needed by the head of a private family. With reference to the law just mentioned, this appendage may be styled the subsidiary law: of this subsidiary law, the business and object consist in the presenting to the party or parties subject, inducement directed to the purpose of producing on their parts compliance with the principal law.
>
> And here, then, we have existing on each occasion, in necessary connexion with one another, two distinct species of law; namely, 1. The principal, or say the direction-giving; 2. The subsidiary, or say the inducement-giving law.
>
> These distinct species of laws are addressed to two different classes of persons:—the direction-giving law is addressed to the person or persons

at whose hands compliance is constantly looked for in the first instance;—addressed always to a person, or set of persons other than the above, is the subsidiary, or say inducement-giving law.

This person, or set of persons, is different, according as the inducement employed by the lawgiver is of the nature of evil or of the nature of good.

If it be of the nature of evil, the inducement is styled punishment; and the sort of person to whom this subsidiary law is addressed is the judge: and the act which he is calculated to perform, in the event of non-compliance with the will expressed by the principal law, is an act of punishment—an act to which exercise is given by producing evil, or say pain, on the part of him by whom compliance with the will expressed by the principal law has failed to be made.

Such inducements/disincentives do not affect in any way the *potentialities* (or *puissance d'agir*) of individuals, of the persons to which the first type of laws is addressed.[25] Describing the 'potentialities of the legal subject' – that is, to describe the field of immune possibilities, of what remains immune from attunements by the law – would require a multi-level analysis. It should, on multiple levels, describe how the operations of the law impact on individual conducts. Legal commandments deserve much more careful attention than the attention I can devote to the topic in this chapter. Beyond the blunt statement that legal constraints are not the same as physical constraints or preconscious constraints – leaving individuals the ultimate choice to obey or disobey the law, be it at their own risks, distinctions exist in the law between 'rights to' and 'rights not to'. That the (presumed) calculating selves obey the law because, after rational deliberation, they believe that the disadvantages ensuing from the risk of being punished for disobedience if caught outweighs the gains or advantages he may expect from disobeying[26] does not by itself impact (increase or decrease) the individual *faculty* to comply or not to comply with the law. In the liberal legal system, the integration of the norm by the subjects presupposes and relies on their reflexive capabilities and their capacities to balance the expected pleasures and pains ensuing from either compliance with or violations of the laws. But choosing compliance does not affect their (theoretical and practical) faculty to breach the law. This 'potentiality', which is, according to Giorgio Agamben, a 'faculty', something that does not need being actualised in order to exist but that does not disappear either in case of actualisation,[27] may well be a crucial element to 'define' what subjectivity is about, in a perspective taking into account the inheritance of critical scholarship of the 1960s and 1970s. From then on, the 'subject' is not any more defined by his/her possibility of self-positioning, but by his/her capability continuously and interactively to discover a 'reality' in appropriate ways, a capability to be present in that reality; that is, to open and expose him/herself in it while maintaining him/herself as 'self', that is, as project to be and become him/herself (Haber 2007: 213). This is what the 'virtuality' of the subject is about, and one sees that virtuality is indeed paradoxically *definitional* of the subject.[28]

In situations where there is a (private or public) need or wish of 'government',[29] the 'success' of 'algorithmic reason' is proportional to its ability to help public and private bureaucracies *anticipating* what bodies and persons *could do*[30] by allowing them to *perceive* (rather than to understand) that which is not (yet) perceptible to ordinary senses without having either to test, experiment or interrogate material (human or non-human) bodies[31] or to rely on testimonies, confessions, expertise or other discourse of authority. The computational turn renders persons and situations immediately and operationally 'meaningful' through their automatic subsumption into (*future* opportunities or risk) patterns or profiles, without the interpretative detour of trial or process and even without concrete, material confrontation or encounter with the *actual* objects or persons concerned. These unprecedented algorithmic statistical practices combine with the contemporary dominance of new regulative principles (often inspired by a new set of fears of imminent 'catastrophes') such as precaution and risk minimisation, privileging detection, classification, anticipative evaluation and prevention or pre-emption of what bodies could do, over topical efforts to remedy the causes of sub-optimal actual, present situations.[32] Unlike government by the law, the 'force' of algorithmic government consists in separating subjects from their ability to do or to not do certain things. Its target – as its focus on prediction and pre-emption attests – is *contingency as such*, the conditional mode of the formula 'what a body *could* do',[33] whereas this conditional mode is definitional of *agency* as such:

> But what problems, what way of being, feeling and acting does the word *agency* sum up or signal? In what way could it help us? It could help us in suspending the metaphysical and scholastic opposition between liberty and necessity, in departing from the opposition between sociologies of determinism and philosophies of 'miracle', 'act' or 'event'. It could help us to refuse to perceive liberty as the other of power or domination. To not presuppose that liberty has its source in an absolutely sovereign subject. To think of liberty as production and as relation, and, indissociably, to think of liberty as productivity: as practical capability to be affected and produce effects. To orient thought towards an empirical, pragmatic approach of the question of emancipation: an art of *agency*.[34]

Algorithmic governmentality thus exhibits a new strategy of uncertainty management consisting in minimising the uncertainty associated with human agency: the capacity humans have to do *or not to* do all they are physically capable of. Effected through the reconfiguration of informational and physical architectures and/or environments within which certain things become impossible or unthinkable, and throwing alerts or stimuli producing reflex responses rather than interpretation and reflection, it affects individuals in their agency that is, in their *inactual, virtual* dimension of potentiality and spontaneity (which legal inducements and dissuasions leave untouched), including with regard to potential disobedience.

Applications such as dynamic biometrics, intelligent video surveillance, individualised recommendations systems, smart environments, ambient intelligence and autonomic computing appear, primarily, as solutions to an epistemic governmental problem: the radical indeterminacy and incommensurability of contexts and behaviours. Yet, these new kinds of statistical treatment of raw data, not less than 'classical' statistics (Dosrosières 2008), are at the same time 'cognitive interfaces' productive of specific kinds of 'operational knowledge' (in the case of data mining and profiling, probabilistic knowledge about intentions, propensities, preferences, risks and opportunities carried either by individuals or situations) and instruments of 'governmental' channelling (rather than regulating or coordinating) social activities and of guiding public interventions. This 'computational turn' upsets traditional modalities of political, legal and social production and enforcement of norms. As such, the resulting norms (patterns or profiles) elude usual tests both of epistemic validity and of political legitimacy, despite having, when embedded in systems of detection, classification and anticipative evaluation of human behaviours, governmental effects in the various spheres where they apply. This 'algorithmic governmentality' and its self-enforcing, implicit, statistically established norms emanating, in real time, from digitalised reality, contrasts with 'political governmentality' and the imperfectly enforced, explicit, deliberated character of laws resulting from time-consuming political deliberation. Therefore, depending on the context and circumstances, the adjunction or substitution of algorithmic governmentality with political governmentality may be felt as a welcome, cost-effective objectivation and automatisation of normative production and enforcement, or as a dangerous evolution towards further depolitisation of normative production and as a threatening erosion of the protective and recursive role of the judicial process.

Subject matter(s): potency

Algorithmic governmentality avoids all kinds of confrontation with human subjects

The pre-emptive character of algorithmic governmentality, the fact that it operates often at a preconscious stage (framing conducts by 'throwing alerts' – and nothing is less intentional (in the sense of conscious direction of attention) than being 'alerted' or having one's attention attracted by something) following the automatic and anticipative evaluation of what bodies could do (potentialities) rather than of what people are actually doing, the fact that profiling spares the burden of making persons appear as agents, leave no occasion for persons to become 'subjects' of algorithmic governmentality.

Algorithmic governmentality does not allow the process of subjectivation to happen, because it does not confront 'subjects' as moral agents (avoiding having to question them about their preferences and intentions, about the reasons and motivations of their actions) but attunes their future informational and physical environment according to the predictions contained in the statistical body. The only 'subject' algorithmic governmentality needs is a unique, supra-individual, constantly reconfigured 'statistical body' made of the infra-individual digital traces of impersonal, disparate, heterogeneous and dividualised facets of daily life and interactions. This infra- and supra-individual statistical body carries a kind of 'memory of the future', whereas the strategy of algorithmic governmentality consists in either ensuring or preventing its actualisation.

Algorithmic governmentality does not need to tame the wilderness of facts and behaviours; neither does it aim at producing docile subjects. One may even say – against part of the surveillance studies community – that algorithmic governmentality decreases the risks of anticipative conformity of behaviours or the chilling effects associated with ubiquitous surveillance. This is because, unlike 'visible', 'scopic' surveillance generating 'norms' which remain, broadly, intelligible to individuals, and available for them to compare and attune their behaviours, algorithmic governmentality carefully avoids any direct confrontation with and impact on flesh and blood persons. One may even say that algorithmic governmentality simply ignores the embodied individuals it affects and has as its sole 'subject' a 'statistical body', that is, a constantly evolving 'data body' or network of localisations in actuarial tables. In such a governmental context, the subjective singularities of individuals, their personal psychological motivations or intentions do not matter. What matters is the possibility of linking any trivial information or data left behind or voluntarily disclosed by individuals with other data gathered in heterogeneous contexts and to establish statistically meaningful correlations. The process bypasses individual consciousness and rationality (not only because operations of data mining are invisible, but also because its results are unintelligible for the instruments of modern rationality), and produces their 'effects of government' by anticipatively 'adapting' the informational and physical environment of persons according to what these persons are susceptible to do or wish to do, rather than by adapting persons to the norms which are dominant in a given environment.

Beyond the legal subject as functional fiction, rethinking the subject's potency

I do not intend to rehabilitate the autonomous, unitary, perfectly intentional and rational subject, the fundamental unit of liberalism. As for the 'subject' or the 'person', I hypothesise that there has never been anything to be nostalgic about. The rational, liberal, individual subject, or the autonomous legal subject have never been anything other than useful or even necessary functional fictions without empirical, phenomenal correlates, despite their merits and the fact that, in a series of domains, they need to be presupposed. However, the legal subject must be presupposed by the law, even though this subject is in no way an empirical entity. This is powerfully explained by Cléro (2007: 76):

> One may, for example, challenge the existence of the *I*, of *me*, challenge the characteristics one spontaneously or traditionally attach to *I* or *me*, that of being a substance, of being one, of existing individually and as a person, one may also refute the paralogisms which pretend to demonstrate its characters. And yet, one may use the fiction of the *me* in order to orient moral behaviours, finalize legal conducts, organize value systems. The person, challenged at the ontological level, is rehabilitated at the deontological level: is it reasonable? But, also: do we have the possibility to do otherwise? Could we, suddenly, reorganize our Law, our ethics, without the help of the notion of *person*, notwithstanding the weakness of its ontological value? Unable to operate such a change, I envision my life as the realization of my person, the life of others as worth promoting on the same ground or, at least, worthy of the same respect. Let's say that the notion of *person* is a fiction.

I thus happily endorse the anti-humanistic posture of Althusser (1971) (subjects are constituted through ideological interpellation, and do not pre-exist such interpellations), Butler (2005) (subjects constitute themselves by 'giving account of themselves', and it is this 'gesture' of 'giving account', not the 'truth' or 'falsity' of what they are telling, that constitutes the subjects) or – Derrida (1990),[35] according to whom the law presupposes and constructs the legal subject (one appears before the law with our will and imagination, but without the law we would not be subjects) or, more generally, in the only possible perspective taking into account the inheritance of the 1960s' and 1970s' critique:

> From now on, what we have to deal with is a subject defined not by the possibility of self-positing, but the continuous ability to interactively discover a reality, in ad hoc ways, and to be present in it while rendering this real present, or, said otherwise, to open and expose oneself in it while maintaining oneself as 'self', that is, as a project of being and becoming oneself.
>
> (Haber 2007: 213)

These 'pragmatic' accounts understand the 'self' as a process rather than a phenomenon, a process happening *between* individuals, in a space that both presupposes and constitutes 'the common'.[36] The self – as processes of subjectivation and individuation – is an interstitial matter and a contribution to the continuous, never achieved 'effort of individual and collective recomposition of the lost totality' – never mind the symbolic nature of such totality (Bourriaud 1994).

Understanding that the target of algorithmic governmentality is the *inactual, potential* dimensions of human existence, its dimensions of virtuality, the conditional mode of what people 'could' do, their potency or agency, allows us to understand what is at stake here: a deprivation which does not have as its opposite the possession of oneself.[37]

What we care about is certainly not a mythical transparency of the subject to himself, its pretended pre-existence, as a fixed entity, but rather the continuous processes through which *subjectivation and individuation occur* and thus the virtual and utopian dimensions of human existence.[38] Walter Benjamin described utopia as an excessive anticipation, or an anticipation always in excess, like the gesture of a child learning how to take things by throwing his hand towards the moon (Abensour 2010: 99). These sorts of gesture in excess are *designs*. They give shape to our projects. They draw *motives*. By these gestures, we also take 'position', that is, we situate ourselves, despite the atopy of algorithmic governmentality, we take consistence (both as physical entities and autobiographical trajectories) in an 'outside' opened by our gesture (or enunciation), as carriers of 'events' (which are nothing but the encounter of (unpredicted) circumstances and meaning-making gestures). 'Motivation' is the drawing of 'motive', the singularity of design, beyond truth and falsity. Taking position, making such gesture, does not so much require 'equal information', privacy or transparency enhancing technologies etc which keep us sealed inside the 'algorithmic reality', as it requires 'outer' spaces and time for heterogeneous modes of creation of reality.

Transparency enhancing technologies (TETs) and privacy enhancing technologies (PETs) etc pretend to empower individuals and allow for contestation but as they are operating 'within' algorithmic governmentality, they are disabled, because algorithmic governmentality is a mode of governmentality without negativity (no organisation of questioning or challenge of either cognitive or normative productions). There is simply no space nor time for contesting (even if one gets to the point where everything becomes transparent to everybody). Recalcitrance must come from outside, from 'consistent', that is, sentient bodies animated with a perceptive life (intensity) whose scope is not confined to the 'infosphere'.

How do we find an 'outside', an excess of the world over reality, a space of recalcitrance from which to gain solidity and to practise critique?[39] Rather than resurrecting personological approaches (epitomised by the possessive individualism of data protection regimes) which would be both ill grounded and ineffective, we should realise that the fundamental stake – what has to be preserved as a resource antecedent to both the 'subject' and sociality, as excess of the world over the algorithmic reality, is 'the common'; this 'in between', this space of common appearance (*comparution*) within which we are mutually addressed to each other. The mode of address that links us together is essentially linguistic.[40] Language is the polyphonic 'shape' of our togetherness, of our common projections of 'becoming'. 'But how could one come back to what has never been?', Frédéric Neyrat asked (2009: 54) in his beautiful book about Artaud and the 'Western spell':

> 'Here, it is not / drawing / in the proper meaning of the word, of some incorporation / of reality in the drawing',[41] it is not about incorporating a reality (the common), that would have been antecedent to the drawing, as this reality (of the common) is precisely that which is lacking.[42]

To the extent that subjects have to give account of themselves despite the fact that they may not have mastered the circumstances which have made them act in a certain way, the 'motive' or 'drawing' they 'make', does not 'represent' the antecedent reality as much as it opens new political possibilities at the very location where the limits of representation and representability are exposed: in this interstice between 'the world' and 'reality', and this is the 'outside' we were looking for (Butler 2000).

Here one perceives, at last, that 'due process', 'subjectivation' and 'critique' may well be three different names for the same exigency: we speak, precisely, because we are on the edge of the abyss, because no subject is antecedent to his enunciation, and thus, to rejoin a 'common' that is crumbling under our words, that is never securely acquired, that happens only as unexpected fulguration. The exigency is this one: convening this impersonal form of the common through a language which gives us individual and collective consistence – at safe distance from both algorithmic profiling and neoliberal injunctions of performance and maximisation of *jouissance*.

How then could we make use of the technologies of the information society so as to re-enchant the common? By making this re-enchantment of the common their primary goal, reconfiguring their design accordingly when needed, by protecting that goal by law, by pursuing that goal in our practices? 'Putting man in the machine', following Félix Guattari's (1977) invitation, could mean just this: producing interstices in which the common may happen – even if these interstices should interrupt or grip the fluidity of our techno-capitalist reality, thereby really producing crisis, at last, allowing for a recomposition of what, for human beings, for the common, appears a humanely consistent reality.

These consistencies need, in order to happen, heterotopic spatio-temporal spaces interrupting digital and capitalistic flows – such as the judicial, theatrical, literary, laboratory scenes. These scenes guarantee a certain heterogeneity of the modes of construction of realities against the ubiquitous deployment of an operational but 'neutralising' and meaningless algorithmic rationality.

Conclusion

Algorithmic government, failing to acknowledge anything other than infra-individual data and supra-individual profiles, and avoiding confrontations with subjects either physically or linguistically (testimony, avowal and other forms of biographical representation are becoming useless in the big data era), may be understood as the culmination of a process of dissipation of the institutional, spatial, temporal and linguistic conditions of subjectivation for the sake of the 'objective' and operational pre-emption of potential behaviours. An algorithmic government that frames the future, affecting individuals and groups on the mode of alert throwing and reflex responses but which never confront them or exposes itself to be challenged by human liberty eradicates the conditions of critique, deprives human beings of their fundamental potency, which is their capacity to emerge as individual and collective subjects in a 'common' that is interstitial between the world and reality. The very fundamental differences between government by law and government by algorithms are certainly that:

- the law preserves individual and collective agencies or potencies, whereas the pre-emptive stance of algorithmic government and its affectation of individuals either at a preconscious stage or by reconfiguration of their environments so that certain courses of action become impracticable, does not preserve such agency or potency
- because it organises the challenge of its own normative productions (through judicial process and legislative processes), the law opens time and spaces (with specific rituals etc.) interrupting the fluidity and real time metabolism of algorithmic processes, and provides a series of scenes where norms can be made visible, intelligible and contestable, where individual and collective subjects may become consistent and give shape to the common

Maybe more fundamentally, because it requires people to talk, to make use of language, after the facts, to recall, represent the facts, redraw the motives of their acts; the law (just as theatre, or literature) – especially in the context of judicial process – provides a scene where subjects perform their 'authorship', with an authority to speak, to give account of themselves. Becoming subjects, people thereby rehistoricise the time against the total synchronisation of a digital world space of which all points are all immediately contemporaneous (Fischbach 2011: 110–112) in a 'real time', depriving people from duration ('real time' is not a dimension of life, as life is always experienced over time and not as a juxtaposition of successive instances of 'now'). They contribute to a legal construction of reality at odds with the algorithmic construction of 'their' profiles, as well as with neoliberal productivity and enjoyment maximisations injunctions. These privileged (judicial, legislative, theatrical, literary) scenes are threatened today not by technologies (they could as well be used to re-enchant the common, facilitate enunciations and emancipation), but by that of which the success of algorithmic governmentality is but a symptom; a mode of government motivated almost exclusively by the goal of fluidification (or liquidation) of existences, requiring the suppression of all that would oppose the indistinctiveness of the world and a numerical, calculable reality. Realising the magnitude of the phenomenon, and finding, collectively, new configurations between human existence, the law and technologies, thes would be our tasks for the present and for the future, as there is no need of data mining to guess that these tasks are not meant ever to be achieved.

Notes

* I wish to express all my gratitude to Mireille Hildebrandt for her thoughtful and stimulating comments on this chapter, as well as for earlier enlightening conversations.
1 The term 'purpose' may appear counterintuitive in this context, speaking of data warehouses which, by definition, contain massive amounts of data collected in heterogeneous contexts, for a variety of initial purposes which, at the stage of storage in data warehouses, have become irrelevant. Unlike traditional statistics – which were performed in view of confirming or informing specific hypotheses about the 'real', or were performed by government officials in order for the state to gain specific and quantified knowledge of its human and material resources – the aim of data mining is much less pre-oriented towards any specific end.
2 The United States General Accounting Office (2004) defines data mining as 'the application of database technology and techniques (such as statistical analysis and modelling) to uncover hidden patterns and subtle relationships in data and to infer rules that allow for the prediction of future results. As has been widely reported, many federal data mining efforts involve the use of personal information that is mined from databases maintained by public as well as private sector organizations'. The objectives of data mining, according to the same report, include 'improving service or performance; detecting fraud, waste, and abuse; analysing scientific and research information; managing human resources; detecting criminal activities or patterns; and analysing intelligence and detecting terrorist activities'.
3 Farecast, for example, a part of Microsoft's Bing search engine, advises users about the optimal time to buy their airplane tickets, predicting when the prices are the lowest, by examining 225 billion flight and price records.
4 By 'government', I mean the practice of framing the fields of actions of others. 'Government' in this sense is not the monopoly of public authorities. Private actors – internet service providers, operators of search engines and social networks or, more generally, marketeers, employers, insurers, parents, school teachers etc, to the extent that they frame the possible field of perceptions and actions of others – govern.
5 For a detailed description of algorithmic governmentality, see Rouvroy and Berns (2010).
6 See for example Boltanski and Thévenot (2006).

7 Despite the fact that human intervention is of course involved in the initial design, training (in the case of learning algorithms) and supervision of algorithms, the nature and extent of this human intervention is gradually blurred with their growing 'autonomic' capabilities of algorithms.

8 On interpretation as essential role or function of humanities, and on the absolute necessity of thinking of interpretation as essential step in the production of knowledge, see Citton (2010).

9 See for example Zarsky (2011: 327): 'if data mining is accepted by the legislature, it might only require limited judicial review. This is as opposed to the use of profiles and field officer discretion, which calls for greater scrutiny.'

10 Events of the physical world may leave *traces* (footsteps, imprints in the sand, animals' or plants' pheromones left behind and acting as messages to the other individuals of the same species, photographic imprint of light on the photographic paper etc). These traces may well then be translated into data, but the data themselves are in no way *traces* by themselves. They may represent traces but are not in themselves an imprint of some event of the physical world on a reactive surface. Of course an objection could be raised on the ground that internet users 'leave traces' on the internet but here again, I would suggest that, because from an algorithmic point-of-view we do not exist *as subjects* in this context, but merely as *a trans-individual, continuously evolving network of data points*, the data we release on the internet, as soon as it is decontextualised, anonymised and aggregated with data released by others in a multitude of heterogeneous geographic and temporal contexts, *are not, individually, traces of us*, but function as pure 'signals' triggering different kinds of aggregations and reconstructions of operational meanings.

11 'Crunching numbers' may well be a 'new way to be smart' (Ayres 2007), but as crunching numbers merely provides a quantitative account of (potential) reality, the 'knowledge' it produces is unavoidably reductionist, 'only' taking into account aspects of the world which can be translated into data signals and enrolled in algorithmic calculation.

12 Signals can be calculated quantitatively, independent from their meaning (Eco 1976: 20). See also Genosko (2008).

13 My translation.

14 Algorithmic governmentality, then, appears as the perfect embodiment of the capitalist world whose texture is made of liberated flows of deterritorialised, decoded, neutralised signals. See Guattari (1977: 264).

15 This may even become truer in the era of cloud computing.

16 My translation.

17 'Profiling in the European Union: a high-risk practice', *INEX policy brief*, N.10, June 2010: 'while more classical statistical approaches aim at validating or invalidating proposed correlations believed to be pertinent answers to existing questions, with profiling there are no preliminary questions. The correlations as such become the "pertinent" information, triggering questions and suppositions' (Gonzalez Fuster, Gutwirth and Ellyne 2010).

18 And one may of course discuss whether causal relations do exist by themselves or are merely attributed by men, but this does not really matter for our current discussion, as the existence or inexistence of 'natural' causal relations is not affected by the computational turn.

19 My translation.
20 My translation.
21 This is not a true 'validation', however. True validation presupposes some external point from which the evaluation is performed. Here, 'validation' is immanent to the system awaiting validation.
22 Anything that is 'actual' is always surrounded by a cloud of virtual images. Pure actuality does not exist. See Deleuze and Parnet, 1996: 179.
23 This does not mean that the system will not detect false positives. Yet, the proportion of such false positives will be impossible to assess.
24 See Leblanc (2007).
25 See Hohfeld (1913).
26 There are of course many other reasons explaining compliance with the law, including the coherence between the legal content and social norms and expectations, habits, deference to authority etc.
27 See Agamben (2002).
28 On the virtual dimension of the subject, and its relation with collective utopia, see Rouvroy (2011b).
29 By 'government', I mean any action, performed by private or public agents, aimed at structuring or framing the possible field of actions of others, no matter for which specific purposes, and no matter the success or failure of such enterprise. Governing, thus, presupposes a certain amount of knowledge of what others 'could do', of what would deter them or incite them in behaving in certain ways or choosing certain trajectories rather than others. Alternatively, when such knowledge is unavailable – and it is increasingly unavailable given the dissipation of homogeneous social microcosms and the correlative decline of implicit social norms – 'governing' requires the deployment of new logics, strategies and tactics. My hypothesis is that the computational turn contributes to the renewal of these logics, strategies and tactics of government.
30 A project which would have seemed impossible to Spinoza. According to him: 'one does not know what a body can do.' See Spinoza (1990) and Deleuze (2003: 28).
31 In the context of machine learning, the 'tests' are not targeted at 'bodies' but at 'data'.
32 See, for example, Neyrat (2008).
33 Deleuze and Guattari (1980: 318, my translation): 'A body is only defined by longitude and latitude, that is, by the whole of material elements that belong to it under relations of movements and rest, speed and slowness (longitude), the whole of intensive affects it is capable of under a given power or degree of potency – or rather according to the limits of this degree.'
34 Vidal 2008: 17–23, my translation.
35 See also Sarat (1995).
36 For further elaboration of the idea that the common is both what is threatened by and the privileged resource for a critique of algorithmic rationality, see Rouvroy (2012).
37 The challenge also consists in finding a critical perspective after the decline of the concept of alienation. On this, see Haber (2007: 151).
38 For further developments around this idea see Rouvroy (2011b).

39 See Rouvroy (2011a).
40 Nancy (2010: 12): '*Le commun n'associe ni ne dissocie, il ne rassemble ni ne sépare, il n'est ni substance ni sujet. Le commun c'est que nous sommes – ce terme pris dans sa pleine teneur ontologique – dans le renvoi les uns aux autres (ici encore, laissons les autres existants). L'élément de ce renvoi est le langage. Celui-ci nous adresse les uns aux autres et nous adresse tous ensembles à ce qu'il fait essentiellement surgir: l'infini d'un sens que nulle signification ne remplit, et qui, cette fois disons-le, enveloppe avec les hommes la totalité du monde avec tous ses existants. … Le sens du monde n'est rien de garanti, ni de perdu d'avance: il se joue tout entier dans le commun renvoi qui nous est en quelque sorte proposé. Il n'est pas "sens" en ce qu'il prendrait références, axiomes ou sémiologies hors du monde. Il se joue en ce que les existants – les parlants et les autres – y font circuler la possibilité d'une ouverture, d'une respiration, d'une adresse qui est proprement l'être-monde du monde.*'
41 Artaud (2004:16) cited by Neyrat (2009: 54).
42 My translation.

References

Abensour, M. (2010) *L'homme est un animal utopique*, Paris: Les editions de la nuit.
Agamben, G. (2002) *Enfance et histoire. Destruction de l'expérience et origine de l'histoire*, Paris: Payot & Rivages.
Althusser, L. (1971) 'Ideology and Ideological State Apparatuses', in *Lenin and philosophy, and other Essays*, New York: Monthly Review Press: 127–186.
Artaud, A. (2004) *50 dessins pour assasiner la magie*, Préface d'Evelyne Grossman, Paris: Gallimard.
Ayres, I. (2007) *Super Crunchers: Why thinking-by-numbers is the new way to be smart*, New York: Random House.
Benjamin, W. (2000) *Oeuvres*, III, Paris: Gallimard.
Bentham, J. (1843) 'Nomography. The art of inditing laws', in *The Works of Jeremy Bentham*, published under the superintendence of his executor, John Bowring, Edinburgh: William Tait: 1838–43.
Boltanski, L. (2009) *De la critique. Précis de sociologie de l'émancipation*, Paris: Gallimard.
Boltanski, L. and Thévenot, L. (2006) *On Justification: economies of worth*, Princeton, NJ: Princeton University Press.
Bourriaud, N. (1994) 'Le paradigme esthétique', *Chimères* (21).
Bouveresse, J. (1993) *L'homme probable. Robert Musil, le hasard, la moyenne et l'escargot de l'histoire*, Paris: L'éclat.
Butler, J. (2000) *Antigone's Claim. Kinship between life and death*, New York: Columbia University Press.
—— (2005) *Giving an account of oneself*, New York: Fordham University Press.
Citton, Y. (2010) *L'avenir des humanités. Economie de la connaissance ou cultures de l'interpretation*, Paris: La découverte.
Cléro, J. P. (2007) 'Quelques difficultés symptomatiques de la théorie benthamienne des fictions', *Cahiers critiques de philosophie* (4).
Cukier, K. (2010) 'Data, Data Everywhere. Interview with Kenneth Cukier', *The Economist*, 25 February, available at https://www.economist.com/node/15557443 (accessed 30 October 2012).
Deleuze, G. (2003) *Spinoza. Philosophie pratique*, Paris: Editions de Minuit.

Deleuze, G. and Guattari, F. (1980) *Mille plateaux*, Paris: Editions de Minuit.

Deleuze, G. and Parnet, C. (1996) *Dialogues*, Paris: Flammarion.

Derrida, J. (1990) 'Force of Law: The "mystical foundation of authority"', *Cardozo Law Review* (11), 919–1045.

Desrosières, A. (2008) *Gouverner par les nombres. L'argument statistique II*, Paris: Presses de l'Ecole des Mines.

Desrosières, A. (2010) 'Est-il bon, est-il méchant? Le role du nombre dans le gouvernement de la cite néolibérale', communication at the workshop L'informazione prima dell'informazione. Conoscenza e scelte pubbliche, Université de Milan Bicocca, 27 mai 2010.

Didi-Huberman, G. (2009) *Quand les images prennent position. L'oeil de l'histoire*, I, Paris: Editions de Minuit.

Eco, U. (1976) *A Theory of Semiotics*, Bloomington: Indiana University Press.

Fischbach, F. (2011) *La privation du monde. Temps, espace et capital*, Paris: Vrin.

Foucault, M. (1990) 'Qu'est-ce que la critique?', Proceedings of the session of 27 May 1978, *Bulletin de la Société française de Philosophie*.

General Accounting Office (2004) '*Data Mining: Federal Efforts Cover a Wide Range of Uses*'. *Reports & Testimony* Newsletter, Stonehenge International.

Genosko, G. (2008) 'Banco sur Félix. Signes partiels a-signifiants et technologie de l'information', *Multitudes* (34): 63–73.

Gonzalez Fuster, G., Gutwirth, S. and Ellyne, E. (2010) 'Profiling in the European Union: A high-risk practice', *INEX policy brief*, (10).

Guattari, F. (1977) *Révolution moléculaire*, Paris: Recherches.

Haber, S. (2007) *L'aliénation. Vie sociale et expérience de la dépossession*, Paris: PUF.

Henman, P. (2011) 'Conditional Citizenship? Electronic networks and the new conditionality in public policy', *Policy & Internet*, vol 3, Issue 3, Article 5, available at http://www.psocommons.org/policyandinternet/vol3/iss3/art5/?sending=11513 (accessed 30 October 2012).

Hohfeld, W. (1913) 'Some Fundamental Legal Conceptions as Applied in Judicial Reasoning', *Yale Law Journal* (23): 16.

Laplace, P.-S. (1814) *Essai philosophique sur les probabilités*, Paris: Courcier.

Leblanc, G. (2007) *Les maladies de l'homme normal*, Paris: Editions du Passant.

Legendre, P. (2001) *De la société comme texte. Linéaments d'une anthropologie dogmatique*, Paris: Fayard.

Nancy, J.-L. (2010) *L'adoration (Déconstruction du christianisme, II)*, Paris: Galilée.

Neyrat, F. (2008) *Biopolitique des catastrophes*, Paris: MF.

Neyrat, F. (2009) *Instructions pour une prise d'âmes. Artaud et l'envoûtement occidental*, Paris: La Phocide.

Neyrat, F. (2011) 'Désajointement', *Variations*, (15), available at http://variations. revues.org/91 (accessed 30 October 2012).

Quetelet, A. (1835) *Sur l'homme et le développement de ses facultés, ou Essai de physique sociale*, Paris: Bachelier.

Ronell, A. (2005) *Test Drive*, Illinois: University of Illinois Press.

Rouvroy, A. (2011a) 'Epilogue – Technological mediation and human agency as recalcitrance', in Hildebrandt, M. and Rouvroy, A. (eds) *Law, Human Agency and Autonomic Computing. Philosophers of law meet philosophers of technology*, Abingdon: Routledge.

Rouvroy, A. (2011b) 'Governmentality in an Age of Autonomic Computing: Technology, virtuality and utopia', in Hildebrandt, M. and Rouvroy, A. (eds) *Law, Human Agency and Autonomic Computing. Philosophers of law meet philosophers of technology*, Abingdon: Routledge.

Rouvroy, A. (2012) 'Face à la gouvernementalité algorithmique, repenser le sujet de droit comme puissance', available at http://works.bepress.com/antoinette_rouvroy/43 (accessed 30 October 2012).

Rouvroy, A. and Berns, T. (2010) 'Le nouveau pouvoir statistique', *Multitudes*, 40: 88–103.

Sarat, A. (1995) 'A Prophecy of Possibility: Metaphorical explorations of postmodern legal subjectivity', *Law and Society Review*, (29)4.

Spinoza, B. (1990) *Ethique*, III, scolie 2, Paris: PUF.

Supiot, A. (2010) *L'esprit de Philadelphie. La justice sociale face au marché total*, Paris: Seuil.

U.S. General Accounting Office (2004) Data Mining: Federal Efforts Cover a Wide Range of Uses. GAO-04-548, Washington D.C.

Vidal, J. (2008) *La fabrique de l'impuissance. 1. La gauche, les intellectuels et le libéralisme sécuritaire*, Paris: Editions.

Zarsky, T. (2011) 'Governmental Data Mining and its Alternatives', *Penn State Law Review*, (116)2: 285–330.

Part 3

Resistance & solutions

7

Political and ethical perspectives on data obfuscation

*Finn Brunton and Helen Nissenbaum**

Asymmetries of data gathering and means of redress: the warrant for obfuscation

Our chapter, like all the others gathered in this volume, is written in light of the fact that computer-enabled data collection, aggregation and mining dramatically change the nature of contemporary surveillance. Innocuous traces of everyday life submitted to sophisticated analytics tools developed for commerce and governance can become the keys for stitching disparate databases together into unprecedented new wholes. These data are often gathered under conditions of profound power imbalance. What can we do when faced with these demands, which are often trivial but whose implications are profound, and which we may not be in a position to refuse?

Being profiled is the condition of many essential transactions, from connecting with friends in online social networks to shopping, travelling and engaging with institutions both public and private. Neither, as we shall discuss below, can we rely on law, technology or the scruples of the data gatherers. What we propose is an alternative strategy of informational self-defence, a method that acts as informational resistance, disobedience, protest or even covert sabotage – a form of redress in the absence of any other protection and defence, and one which disproportionately aids the weak against the strong. We call this method *obfuscation* and, in this chapter, we will argue for the political and ethical philosophy it expresses and embodies.

Obfuscation is the production of misleading, ambiguous and plausible but confusing information as an act of concealment or evasion. It is a term we use to capture key commonalities in systems ranging from chaff, which fills radar's sweep with potential targets; to the circulating exchanges of supermarket loyalty cards that muddle the record of purchases; to peer-to-peer file sharing systems such as BitTorrent, protecting their users from legal action by producing records of many IP addresses, only a few of which may be engaged in file sharing. Through these and other cases we can begin to clarify obfuscation among the other forms of resistance to surveillance, whether that surveillance takes the form of consumer data aggregation (for supermarkets, or by companies such as Acxiom), monitoring for intellectual property violations (at the behest of the Recording Industry Association of America (RIAA) and the Motion Picture Association of America (MPAA)), targeted advertising (by sites such as Google and Facebook) or police actions by repressive governments (which we will see addressed by obfuscation tactics within platforms for secure private conversation such as Tor).

We distinguish and evaluate different modes of obfuscation as well as motivations and power topologies of key actors: are obfuscation tactics typically the response of the weak against the strong, adopted by those outside circles of power and influence, or vice versa? Our political analysis of obfuscation also addresses normative questions of legitimacy, asking whether such 'smokescreens' to avoid monitoring are morally defensible – ever, never or sometimes? Under what conditions in the political landscape of surveillance are obfuscation's deceptive tactics acceptable? These can be deemed legitimate assertions of autonomy or problematic instances of economic free ridership (relying on others to be less conscientious in muddying their tracks and therefore better targets); they can be hailed as resistance to inappropriate monitoring or damned as the poisoning of wells of collective data. Obfuscation, as a tactic both personal and political, offers a platform for studying legitimate and problematic aspects of both surveillance and its opposition in an age of ubiquitous data capture.

In the context of this volume, we do not need to go out of our way to describe the problematic state of contemporary data gathering and analysis, but we do need to highlight the specific problems of asymmetry these practices, as a matter of fact, often involve. The most mundane points of contact with contemporary life implicate the involuntary production of data on our part: passing security cameras, withdrawing cash, making credit card purchases, making phone calls, using transit (with electronic ticketing systems such as MetroCards, FasTrak tags, Oyster, Octopus, Suica or E-ZPass) – to say nothing of using the internet, where every click and page may be logged and analysed, explicitly providing data to the organisations on whose systems we interact, as well as their associates. These data can be repackaged and sold, collected, sorted and acquired by a variety of means, and reused for purposes of which we, the monitored, know nothing, much less endorse (Gonzalez Fuster 2009). The unreliability of the businesses and public–private partnerships in the information industry gives data mobility still more sinister dimensions, as materials are stolen, leaked, sold improperly or turned to very problematic ends by governments – ChoicePoint's sale of 145,000 records to identity thieves being one particularly egregious example.[1] The nature of these businesses, acquiring new data sets to add to their existing collections, points to a final area of concern. Multiple databases consolidated and cross-referenced, with incidental details linking previously disconnected bodies of information, produce a far more significant whole than any one part would suggest: identities, tendencies, groups and patterns with both historically revelatory and predictive power.[2]

The asymmetry problems to which we alluded above are, first, an asymmetry of power: rarely do we get to choose whether or not we are monitored, what happens to information about us and what happens to us because of this information. We have little or no say when monitoring takes place in inappropriate contexts and is shared inappropriately with inappropriate others. The second asymmetry, equally important, is epistemic: we are often not fully aware of the monitoring, and do not know what will become of the information produced by that monitoring, or where it will go and what will be done with it.

Your data are not accumulated in neutral circumstances, whether surveillance occurs at the level of infrastructure with which you must participate, through forms that must be completed to receive essential resources, or onerous terms of service to which you must consent before you can use an online product that has become vital to doing business. The context is often one of major power imbalance, between individual consumers and major corporations, or citizens and governments. Obviously there is nothing inherently wrong with gathering and aggregating data on individuals – it is the lifeblood of the work of the epidemiologist, for example, and the starting point for many benefits of the networked society. It is in the combination of data gathering with authority and its arbitrary interests where problems may begin.

These problems continue once our data have been collected: we do not know whether whoever gathers them will repackage and resell them, whether they will become part of a schedule of assets after a bankruptcy or whether they will be collated by a private party such as ChoicePoint with public records for reassembly and used in a different context from the original point of provision. Data mining and related disciplines are complex and intellectually demanding; they often require resources of expertise, software and hardware that people outside large institutions do not possess. We do not have access to the other databases, or the techniques and the training in mathematics and computer science, to comprehend what can be done with seemingly trivial details from our lives and activities, and how they can provide more powerful, total and revealing analyses than we could have anticipated (Solove 2008; Reiman 1995). The inconsequential and even benign can quickly become the problematic and sinister.

Furthermore, we do not know what future techniques and databases will enable. Opportunities for the correlation of information tend to increase with time. Institutions very rarely voluntarily destroy materials with as much potential as a rich database and, as Templeton (2009) points out, the mechanisms to extract value from databases are only going to get better. Materials from very different contexts, created in conditions of many different norms – telephone call logs, geolocative data, purchase records whether in person or online, demographic and personally identifying information, products of the data generating machines that are social networking sites – can be combined, correlated and cross-referenced with less and less effort.

Finally, the gravity of the potential consequences of this mass of data is not easily perceived in the many small moments when we are faced with a decision about whether or not to comply, and give up information. The cost to any one individual at any one moment in time is generally very low, becoming apparent only in aggregate and over a longer period – at which point the moment to make a decision is already past. The disproportionate cost, at the moment when you want to join some friends on a social network, get health insurance or purchase airline tickets – or when you are obliged to provide some seemingly insignificant information while facing an asymmetry of power – does not become clear until it scales to the community and longer timescales, and this issue frames the politics of data gathering and analysis.

The lack of capacity to assess consequences that matter to us is deeply troubling. We do not know all that 'they' know about us, how 'they' come to know it or even who all the significant players might be. We cannot easily subject these players to symmetrical analysis: such organisations might operate under the veil of national security or proprietary trade secrets, and we probably would not have the methods or the training to do anything with their data if we could get our hands on them. As people whose data are being collected, what we know of the situation is problematic, and what we do not know is substantial.[3]

In theory, the ways out of our predicament of inescapable, ubiquitous, asymmetric collection and scrutiny of data are numerous and diverse, the palette of options familiar to anyone following the privacy debates: user opt-out, law, corporate best practice and technology. Each offers a prognosis for particular challenges, and each has shortcomings in relation to the asymmetries of data analysis. While useful for certain types of threat, each has not proved responsive to others, and all have particular short-term flaws, which could compound into a future that worries us. The first of these established – even reflexive – approaches is the most common counterargument to the two asymmetries, the opt-out argument, which puts the responsibility on the shoulders of individuals whose data are being gathered. The other three are classic long-term, slow-incentive structures for creating social change; their gradual pace, and investment in existing interests, makes them problematic for short-term protection and sets the stage for self-directed and individually introduced strategies such as obfuscation.

The steady rhetorical drumbeat in the discussion around data privacy is that refusal is a personal responsibility. If you are so offended by the way these companies collect and deploy your data, simply do not use their services – *opt out*. No one is forcing you. To which we reply: yes and no. Many of these systems are not mandatory yet (government systems and various forms of insurance being only two exceptions), but the social and personal cost of refusal is already substantial and, indeed, growing. We pay by loss of utility, efficiency, connection with others in the system, capacity to fulfil work demands, and even merely being able to engage in many everyday transactions. To rely entirely on personal choice is to leave all but the most dedicated and privacy obsessed at the mercy of more conventional means of regulation – or resistance.[4]

Why not rely on *corporate best practice*? Private sector efforts are hampered by the fact that companies, for good reasons and bad, are the major strategic beneficiaries of data mining. Whether the company is in the business of gathering, bundling and selling individual data, such as DoubleClick and ChoicePoint, or has relied on the data generated and provided by its customers to improve its operations, such as Amazon and Wal-Mart, or is based on user data-driven advertising revenue, or subcontracts the analysis of consumer data for purposes of spotting credit, insurance or rental risks, it is not in their interest to support general restraints on access to information.

Law and regulation, historically, have been central bulwarks of personal privacy, from the Fourth Amendment of the US Constitution to the European Union's data protection requirements and directives. While our laws will probably be the eventual site of the conversation in which we answer, as a society, hard questions about the harvesting and stockpiling of personal information, they operate slowly; and whatever momentum propels them in the direction of protecting privacy in the public interest is amply counterweighted by opposing forces of vested corporate and other institutional power, including governmental interests. In the meantime, and in the short term, enormous quantities of personal data are already in circulation, packaged, sold, provided freely and growing by the day.

Finally, there is great interest among the technical, particularly research, community in *engineering systems* that 'preserve' and 'enhance' privacy, be it in data mining, surfing or searching the web, or transmitting confidential information. Detecting data provenance, properly anonymising data sets, generating contextual awareness and providing secure, confidential communication: mechanisms supporting these goals pose technical challenges, particularly when embedded in the real world or when working against the grain of features native to infrastructural systems such as the web. Furthermore, no matter how convincing the technical developments and standards, adoption by key societal actors whose organisations and institutions mediate much data flow is another matter and fraught with politics.

Tools offered to the individual directly, such as Tor and other proxy servers, are praiseworthy and valuable but the fact remains that they are not widely understood or deployed outside the relatively small circles of those who are already privacy aware and technologically sophisticated. Additionally, there are utility costs: Tor can be slow, for example, and is blocked by many large websites. All privacy-protecting technologies entail trade-offs, and those required by robust approaches such as Tor have thus far kept their adoption relatively small.

We are not questioning the ability of law, the private sector and technology to provide relief to individuals from unfettered monitoring, gathering, mining and profiling. The benefits of the status quo to those on the other side of the power and epistemic asymmetries that define and entrench our predicament, however, will not be easily ceded and, even if ultimately they are, the wait for meaningful relief is likely to be long. Turning to obfuscation, therefore, is a way to take matters into our own hands in the interim. Before discussing how it addresses the specific problem of data gathering and analysis, we introduce obfuscation through an array of historical and contemporary examples so that we can see it as a general strategy, with many different forms, media and motives.

Obfuscation in practice: cases and examples

Obfuscation in its broadest and most general form offers a strategy for mitigating the impact of the cycle of monitoring, aggregation, analysis and profiling, adding noise to an existing collection of data in order to make the collection more ambiguous, confusing, harder to use and, therefore, less valuable. (We chose 'obfuscation' for this purpose because of its connotations of confusion, ambiguity and unintelligibility, seeking to distinguish it from other strategies involving concealment or erasure, such as cryptography.) Obfuscation, like data gathering, is a manifold strategy carried out for a variety of purposes, with a variety of methods and perpetrators. Obfuscators may band together and enlist others, or produce misleading information on their own; they might selectively respond to requests for information, or respond so excessively that their contribution skews the outcome. They may engage in obfuscation out of a simple desire to defend themselves against perceived dangers of aggregation, in resentment of the obvious asymmetry of power and knowledge, to conceal legitimate activities or wrongdoing or even in malice, to render the system of data collection as a whole worthless. This diversity of purposes, methods and perpetrators is reflected in the wide range of forms taken by obfuscation tactics.

These forms, across a range of media and circumstances, can be loosely clustered around four themes: time-based obfuscation, which relies on temporal limitations; cooperative obfuscation, requiring the 'network effect' of cooperation or collaboration by groups of obfuscators; selective obfuscation, interfering with data to conceal specific details while leaving others available; and ambiguating obfuscation, which renders data ambiguous and doubtful for future use.

Time-based obfuscation

Whereas some forms of obfuscation try to inject doubt into the data permanently, time-based obfuscation, in many ways the simplest form of the practice, adds need for an onerous amount of processing in a situation where time is of the essence. *Chaff* offers a canonical example: the radar operator of the Second World War tracks a plane over Hamburg, guiding searchlights and anti-aircraft guns in relation to a phosphor dot whose position is updated with each sweep of the antenna. Abruptly the plane begins to multiply, dots quickly swamping the display. The plane is in there somewhere, impossible to locate for the presence of all the 'false echoes'. The plane has released chaff, strips of black paper backed with aluminum foil and cut to half the target radar's wavelength, floating down through the air, thrown out by the pound and filling the system with signals. Chaff has exactly met the conditions of data the radar is configured to look for and given it more planes, scattered all across the sky, than it can handle. Knowing discovery to be inevitable, chaff uses the time and bandwidth constraints of the discovery system against it by creating too many potential targets (in this regard, Fred Cohen (2006: 646) terms it the 'decoy strategy', and we can indeed consider obfuscation as the multiplication of plausible data decoys).That the chaff only works briefly, as it flutters to the ground, and is not a permanent solution, is irrelevant under the circumstances; it only needs to work well enough for the time it will take the plane to get through.

Another contemporary example is the practice of *quote stuffing* in high-frequency trading (HFT). (To be clear, quote stuffing is still only a theoretical obfuscation project, a plausible explanation for recent bursts of anomalous activity on the stock market.) The rarefied world of HFT is built on algorithms that perform large volumes of trades far faster than humans, taking advantage of exceedingly minute spans of time and differences in price that would not be worth the attention of human traders, if it were even physically possible for them to act on the change in price before the advantage was gone. Analysts of market behaviour began to notice unusual patterns of HFT activity over the summer months of 2010 – bursts of quote requests for a particular stock, sometimes thousands a second. Such activity seemed to have no economic rationale, but one of the most interesting and plausible theories (Nanex 2010) is that these bursts are an obfuscation tactic in action: 'If you could generate a large number of quotes that your competitors have to process, but you can ignore since you generated them, you gain valuable processing time.' Unimportant information, in the form of quotes, is used to crowd the field of salient activity, so the generator of the unimportant data can accurately assess what is happening while making it more difficult for competitors to do so in time. The volume of trades creates a cloud of fog that only the obfuscator can see through. In the sub-split-second world of HFT, the act of having to observe and process this hiss of activity is enough to make all the difference.

Finally, two examples of time-based obfuscation in thoroughly concrete contexts. The affair of the 'Craigslist robber' offers a minor but illustrative example of obfuscation as a practice turned to criminal ends. At 11 am on Tuesday 30 September 2008, a man dressed as an exterminator in a blue shirt, goggles and a dust mask, and carrying a spray pump, approached an armoured car parked outside a bank in Monroe, Washington, incapacitated the guard with pepper spray, and took the money. When the police arrived, they found 13 men in the area wearing blue shirts, goggles and dust masks – a uniform they were wearing on the instructions of a Craigslist advertisement which promised a good wage for maintenance work, which was to start at 11:15 am at the bank's address. This incident is one of the few real world examples of a recurrent trope of obfuscation in movies and television: the many identically dressed actors or objects confusing their pursuers as to the valuable one. Obviously it will only take a few minutes to determine that none of the day labourers is the bank robber – but a few minutes is all the thief needs.

Much of the pleasure and challenge of poker lies in learning to read people and deduce from their expressions, gestures and body language whether they are bluffing, or pretending to hold a weaker hand in hopes of drawing a call. Central to the work of studying opponents is the 'tell', some unconscious habit or tic an opponent will display in response to a strong or weak hand: sweating, a worried glance, leaning forward. Tells play such a crucial role in the informational economy of poker that players will use *false tells*, creating mannerisms that may appear to be part of a larger pattern.[5] According to common poker strategy, the use of a false tell is best reserved for a crucial moment in a tournament, lest the other players figure out that it is inaccurate and turn it against the teller in turn. A patient analysis of multiple games could separate the true from the false tells, but in the time-bound context of a high-stakes game the moment of deception can be highly effective.[6]

Cooperative obfuscation

All of the cases described so far can be performed by a single actor (perhaps with some unwitting assistants), but other forms of obfuscation require the explicit cooperation of others. These obfuscatory cases have a 'network effect' of becoming more valuable as more people join. A powerful legend exemplifies this idea: the often retold, factually inaccurate story that the king and population of Denmark wore the Yellow Star to make it impossible for the occupying Germans to distinguish and deport the Jews. While the Yellow Star was not used in Denmark for fear of arousing more anti-German feeling, '[t]here were documented cases of non-Jews wearing yellow stars to protest Nazi anti-Semitism in Belgium, France, the Netherlands, Poland, and even Germany itself.'[7] The legend is a perfect story of cooperative obfuscation: a small group of non-Jews wearing the Yellow Star is an act of protest; a whole population, into which individual Jews can blend, is an act of obfuscation.

Loyalty card swapping pools provide another superb real world example. Quite quickly after the widespread introduction of 'loyalty cards', offering discounts to regular shoppers at grocery store chains, came card swapping networks, where people shared cards – initially in ad hoc physical meetings, and increasingly in large populations and over wide geographical regions enabled by mailing lists and online social networks – to obfuscate their data. Rob's Giant Bonus Card Swap Meet, for instance, started from the idea that a barcode sharing system could enable customers of the DC area supermarket chain to print out the barcodes of others, pasting them onto their cards (Carlson 2010). A similar notion was adopted by the Ultimate Shopper project, mailing stickers of a Safeway loyalty card barcode and creating 'an army of clones' accruing shopping data (Cockerham 2002). Cardexchange.org is devoted to exchanging cards by mail, presenting itself as a direct analogue to the physical meet-ups. These sites also act as clearing houses for discussion, gathering notes, blog posts, news articles and essays on loyalty cards, debating the ethical implications of various approaches and sharing theories and concerns. This is obfuscation as a group activity: the more who are willing to share their cards, the farther the cards travel and the more unreliable the data become.

Another form of collective obfuscation appears in the argument for participation in Tor. Tor is a system designed to enable anonymous use of the internet, through a combination of encryption and passing the message through many different independent 'nodes'. If you request a web page while working through Tor, your request will not come from your IP address, but from an 'exit node' on the Tor system, along with the requests of many other Tor users. Data enter the Tor system and pass into a labyrinth of relays, computers on the Tor network that offer some of their bandwidth for handling Tor traffic from others, agreeing to pass messages sight unseen. In return for running a Tor relay, as the FAQ (Tor Project, 2012) notes, 'you do get better anonymity against some attacks. The simplest example is an attacker who owns a small number of Tor relays. He will see a connection from you, but he won't be able to know whether the connection originated at your computer or was relayed from somebody else.' If you are on Tor and not running a relay, then an adversary will know you wrote the message you sent to him. But if you are allowing your computer to operate as a relay, the message might be yours or simply one among many that you are passing on for other people. Did it start with you or not? The information is now ambiguous, and messages you have written are safe in a flock of other messages you pass along.[8]

Selective obfuscation

All of the examples thus far have been about general methods of covering one's tracks. But what if you want your data to be useful without diminishing your privacy, or to interfere with some methods of data analysis but not others? This is the project of selective obfuscation. FaceCloak, for example, provides the initial steps towards an elegant and selective obfuscation-based solution to the problem of Facebook profiles. It takes the form of a Firefox plug-in that acts as a mediating layer between a user's personal information and the social networking site. When you create a Facebook profile and fill in your personal information, including details such as where you live, went to school, your likes and dislikes and so on, FaceCloak offers you a choice: display this information openly, or keep it private? If you let it be displayed openly, it is passed to Facebook's servers like any other normal data, under their privacy policy. If you want to keep those data private, however, FaceCloak sends them to encrypted storage on a separate server only to be decrypted and displayed for friends you have authorised, when they browse your Facebook page (using the FaceCloak plug-in.) Facebook never gains access to the data. Furthermore, by generating fake information for the data that Facebook requires of its profiles, FaceCloak obfuscates its method – the fact that the real data lie elsewhere – from both Facebook and unauthorised viewers. As it passes your real data to the private server, FaceCloak generates a gender, with appropriate name and age, and passes those to Facebook. Under the cover of this generated, plausible non-person, you can connect and exchange with your friends, obfuscating the data for all others.

The theoretical goal for selective obfuscation has been outlined from a policy perspective as obfuscating the data for certain users or the reconstruction of individual acts. In Gloria Gonzalez Fuster's recommendations for EU data processing, selective obfuscation is understood as limiting the data to primary processing: structuring the data such that they can be evaluated for their intended purpose, to which the data's subjects consent, but not for unanticipated analyses (Gonzalez Fuster 2009). In this scenario, data gathered for, say, a public health study would be suited to the process used for that study, difficult to use for other public health data mining and impossible to reprocess for any other purpose.

The work of Nam Pham and others (2010) on privacy-preserving participatory sensing shows us how this idea could work in practice, on an applied and mathematically sophisticated scale. Where a project such as FaceCloak obfuscates the data for all but an authorised few, private participatory sensing obfuscates them beyond a certain degree of specificity – the data work generally, but not for identifying or tracking anyone in particular. Vehicular sensors, for instance, which can be used to create a shared pool of data from which to construct maps of traffic or pollution, raise obvious concerns over location-based tracking. However, Pham and his colleagues demonstrate how to perturb the data, letting each vehicle continuously lie about its location and speed while maintaining an accurate picture of the aggregate.

Ambiguating obfuscation

Time-based obfuscation can be quickly seen through; cooperative obfuscation relies on the power of groups to muddy the tracks; selective obfuscation wishes to be clear for some and not others. Ambiguating obfuscation seeks to render an individual's data permanently dubious and untrustworthy as a subject of analysis. For example, consider the Firefox extension TrackMeNot, developed in 2006. Developed by Daniel Howe, Helen Nissenbaum and Vincent Toubiana, TrackMeNot was designed to foil the profiling of users through their searches. Our search queries end up acting as lists of locations, names, interests and problems, from which not only our identities can be determined but a pattern of our interests revealed regardless of whether our IP addresses are included. As with many of the previous cases of obfuscation, opting out of a web search is not a viable choice for the vast majority of users. (At least since 2006, search companies have been responsive, although only partially, to users' concerns over the logging and storage of search queries.) TrackMeNot automatically generates queries from a seed list of terms that evolve over time, so that different users develop different seed lists. TrackMeNot submits queries in a manner that tries to mimic user search behaviours. These users may have searched for 'good wi-fi cafe chelsea' but they have also searched for 'savannah kennels', 'exercise delays dementia' and 'telescoping halogen light' – will the real searchers please stand up? The activity of individuals is masked by that of many ghost queries, making a pattern harder to discern.

Similarly, BitTorrent Hydra fights the surveillance efforts of anti-file sharing interests, by mixing genuine requests for bits of a file with dummy requests. The BitTorrent protocol breaks a file up into many small pieces, so that you can share those pieces, sending and receiving them simultaneously with other users. Rather than downloading an entire file from another user, as with the Napster model, you assemble the file's pieces from anyone else who has them, and anyone who needs a piece you have can get it from you (Schulze and Mochalski 2009). To help users of BitTorrent assemble the files they want, the system uses 'torrent trackers', which log IP addresses that are sending and receiving files – if you are looking for these pieces of file x, users a to n, at the following addresses, have the pieces you need. Intellectual property groups, looking for violators, starting running their own trackers to gather the addresses so they could find major uploaders and downloaders of potentially copyrighted material. To protect BitTorrent users, Hydra obfuscates by adding random IP addresses to the tracker, addresses that have been used for BitTorrent connections at some point. This step means that, periodically, as you request pieces of the file you want, you will be directed to another user who does not actually have what you are looking for. It is a small inefficiency for the BitTorrent system as a whole, but it makes address gathering on the part of anti-piracy organisations much less useful. The tracker can no longer be sure that any one address was actually engaged in sharing any particular file. Hydra does not avert data collection, but contaminates the results, making any specific case problematic and doubtful.

CacheCloak, meanwhile, has an approach to obfuscation suited to its domain of location-based services (LBSs). LBSs take advantage of the locative technology in mobile devices to create various services. If you want the value of an LBS – say, to be part of the network that your friends are on so you can meet if you are nearby – then you will have to sacrifice some privacy and get used to the service provider knowing where you are. 'Where other methods try to obscure the user's path by hiding parts of it', write the creators of CacheCloak, 'we obscure the user's location by surrounding it with other users' paths' – the propagation of ambiguous data. In the standard model, your phone sends your location to the service and gets the information you requested in return. In the CacheCloak model, your phone predicts your possible paths and then fetches the results for several likely routes. As you move, you receive the benefits of locative awareness – access to what you are looking for, in the form of data cached in advance of potential requests – and an adversary is left with many possible paths, unable to distinguish the beginning from the end of a route, where you came from and where you mean to go, still less where you are now. The salient data, the data we wish to keep to ourselves are buried inside a space of other, equally likely data.

Finally, the technique of botnet-resistant coding operates on similar lines to quote stuffing. A botnet is a collection of malware-infected personal computers controlled by a remote attacker, using system resources or snooping for data. One of the more prolific of these botnets, known as Zeus, sits on the network looking for the patterns of data that suggest banking information; when found it sends the information – passwords, account details and so on – back to its controllers, who will use it to make bank withdrawals or commit other forms of identity theft. The defensive solution proposed is an obfuscation move: large quantities of completely plausible but incorrect information would be injected into the transactions between the user's computer and the bank. Banks would know how to filter the false information, because they have generated it, but not the botnet. Faced with this source of confusion, attackers either move on to easier targets or waste resources trying to find the accurate needle in a bank's haystack.

The politics and ethics of obfuscation: a 'weapon of the weak'?

The examples we have compiled show something of the broad range of obfuscation practices, from foiling statistical analysis and escaping visual sensing to thwarting competitors in the stock market. Some methods take advantage of human biases and others the constraints and loopholes of automated systems. Obfuscation is deployed for short-term misdirection, for legal deniability, to encourage an adversary to construct a flawed model of the world and to change the cost-benefit ratio that justifies data collection. The swathe of types, of methods, motives, means and perpetrators are not surprising considering that obfuscation is a reactive strategy and, as such, a function of as many types of action and practice as it is designed to defeat.

Despite this diversity, we would like to think that obfuscation will become a subject of interest for scientific study, to identify key variables and parameters, to understand the relationships among them and, ultimately, to quantify its value and optimise its utility. With encryption, for example, algorithms possess standard metrics based on objective measures such as key length, machine power and length of time to inform community evaluations of their strength. By contrast, the success of obfuscation is a function of the goals and motives of both those who obfuscate and those to whom obfuscation is directed, the targets. It simply has to be 'good enough', a provisional, ad hoc means to overcome the challenge that happens to be in its way.

Our task here, however, is not a scientific analysis of obfuscation but an ethical one. There are ways in which obfuscation practices can be unethical, but there are also mitigating conditions that we must consider and details we must resolve – and, along with those ethical particulars, there is a general political analysis to be made before we can claim a full understanding of obfuscation's moral and political dimensions. We discuss each, in turn, below.

Ethics of obfuscation

In 'A Tack in the Shoe' (2003), Gary Marx writes: 'Criteria are needed which would permit us to speak of "good" and "bad", or appropriate and inappropriate efforts to neutralise the collection of personal data.' If we accept that obfuscation works – that, even if weak, it can be a successful and consequential strategy – we must still ask whether it can be defended against charges that it is unethical. Although we are interested in the moral standing of particular uses of obfuscation, our central concern here is with the strategy of information obfuscation itself, whether structurally or inherently unethical. Thus, we address several of the most compelling issues that critics have raised.

Dishonesty

Implicit in obfuscation is an element of dishonesty – it is meant to mislead. Some people might balk at valorising any practice that systematises lying or deception. (Some obfuscation approaches, such as that of CacheCloak, work around this problem by remaining ambiguous instead of providing untrue information – but such an approach depends on an informational relationship where queries can be left vague.) These critics might prefer encryption (that is, hiding, a form of refusal) or silence to producing streams of lies. Whether lying, in general, can be morally justified is an exploration that clearly would take us too far afield from our subject, but that general discussion yields insights that are useful here. Except for the Kantian who holds that lying is always absolutely wrong (famously, prescribing a truthful answer even to the murderer seeking one's friend's whereabouts), in many analyses there are conditions in which the proscription of lying may be relaxed (Bok 1999). We must ask whether the general benefits of lying in a given instance outweigh harms, and whether valued ends are served better by the lie than truthful alternatives. There are many special circumstances in which lies may be excused; for example, if one is acting under duress or lying to one party to keep a promise to another.

Free riding

Obfuscation may involve two different forms of free riding, both of which take advantage of the compliance of others in the obfuscator's situation. Imperfect as it may be, obfuscation may raise the cost of data gathering and analysis just enough to deter the surveillant or divert him to other data subjects. These may overlap or coexist, but their distinct ethical values are clear. The first takes advantage of the willingness of others to submit to data collection, aggregation and analysis – no need to be faster than the predator so long as one is faster than other prey. It allows others to be victimised while one remains safe oneself, a safety that is the product, however indirectly, of the victimisation of others. The second involves enjoying the benefits provided by the data collector, without paying the price of one's data. (Loyalty card swapping pools are an instance, as participants enjoy the bounty of special offers while escaping the information pool that presumably supports them.)

Waste, pollution and system damage

A common critique of obfuscation is that it wastes or pollutes informational resources – whether bandwidth and storage, or the common pools of data available for useful projects.

In considering such accusations, we note that 'waste' is a charged word, implying that resources are used improperly, based presumably on an agreed-upon standard. This standard could be challenged; what is wasteful according to one standard might be legitimate use according to another. However, noise introduced into an environment is not only wasteful but may taint the environment itself. On a small scale, obfuscation may be insignificant – what can be the harm of marginal inaccuracy in a large database? On a large scale, however, it could render results questionable or even worthless. To take a recent case, the shopping logs of supermarket loyalty cards were used by the Centers for Disease Control and Prevention to identify a common purchase among a scattered group of people with salmonella, trace that purchase to the source and institute a recall and investigation, a socially valuable project which the widespread adoption of loyalty card swapping pools would have made much slower or even, theoretically, impossible (Mercer 2010).

Data aggregation and mining is used not only to extract social utility but to guide decisions about individuals. If introducing noise into a system interferes with profiling, for example, it might harm the prospects of individuals, innocent bystanders, so to speak. FaceCloak demonstrates this problem: '[F]or some profile information (eg an address or a phone number), it is ethically questionable to replace it with fake information that turns out to be the real information for somebody else' (Mercer 2010: 6). The risk is not only in the present, but also holds for future uses not yet foreseen, the nightmare of the regularly incorrect United States No-Fly List writ large, or the mistakes of police profiling software compounded by a large pool of alternate, inaccurate names, addresses, activities, search terms, purchases and locations. As a possible counterargument, however, if we believe that these databases and the uses to which they are put are malignant, this bug becomes a feature. A database laden with ambiguously incorrect material becomes highly problematic to act on at all.

Finally, waste includes the potential of damage, possibly fatal damage, to the systems affected by obfuscation. Consider quote stuffing in high-frequency trading, a move which, if broadly adopted, could actually overwhelm the physical infrastructure on which the stock exchanges rely with hundreds of thousands of useless quotes consuming the bandwidth. Any critique of obfuscation based in the threat of destruction must be specific as to the system under threat and to what degree it would be harmed.

Assessing the ethical arguments

The merits of each charge against obfuscation are not easily assessed in the abstract without filling in pertinent details — and these details make all the difference. The overarching question that drives this chapter is about obfuscation aimed at thwarting data monitoring, aggregation, analysis and profiling, so we confine our evaluation to this arena, drawing on the cases we introduced above. One consideration that is relevant across the board is ends; legitimate ends are necessary, although, clearly, not always sufficient. Once we learn, for example, that the Craigslist robber used obfuscation to rob banks or that quote stuffing could bring down the stock exchange, it hardly seems relevant to inquire further whether the lies or free riding were justifiable.

The judgment of ends can also take in questions about proportionality and not only whether an action in question is flatly right or wrong. The obfuscator running TrackMeNot may not disapprove of the ultimate purpose of Google's query logs but may consider the degree of surveillance too extreme. The company makes its revenue from advertising, and it is reasonable for it to serve keyword-specific ads automatically against a given query — but if the data mining begins to seem too personal, too precise, or is extended into a previously off-limits private domain and the user feels it is no longer fair or proportionate, he or she will begin using TMN. Astute businesses will be helped by paying attention to customers giving voice to their concerns through soft acts of protest such as these, which signal a need to bring a practice into line with consumer expectations and beliefs. These are not demands for total reinvention but the reassertion of more equitable standing.

Dishonesty

In cases such as TrackMeNot, CacheCloak, Tor relays and loyalty card swapping, the ethical arguments can become quite complex. To justify the falsehoods inherent in obfuscation, the ends must be unproblematic, and other aspects of the case taken into consideration – whether achieving the ends by means other than lying is viable and what claim the targets of falsehood may have to 'real' information. If individuals feel they have little chance of protection through law, technology and corporate best practice, as we discussed above, under duress and with little assurance that those extracting information can be trusted, the obligation to speak the truth is certainly lessened. Contrast this scenario with highly controlled environments, such as a courtroom, where myriad other constraints circumscribe the actions of all parties; we may still speak under duress but epistemic asymmetries are mitigated because of these other strictures of context.

Free riding

While deception may be justified by asymmetries of knowledge and power and the absence of alternatives, other critiques remain. The problem of free riding on the contributions of others casts obfuscation efforts in an unseemly light. The obfuscator is presented as not so much the rebel as the sneak, with an interest, however indirect, in the ignorance and foolishness of others: that they fail to 'game the system' as the obfuscator does. (A house's safety from theft, one might say, comes not only from a locked door but from other houses being left unlocked.) Against this charge we can bring in mitigating circumstances and specific details, as we did with dishonesty, but we can also draw on a broader argument which we make below, based in a Rawlsian analysis – free riding has a different ethical valence if it is available to all and disproportionately aids the weak against the strong. As long as the free rider is not actively attempting to keep others from enjoying the same benefit (as though hobbling others in the herd to make them more likely to be caught by predators), the ethical price of their actions is paid by supererogation. Obfuscators cannot be expected to imperil themselves solely because others are in peril; they cannot be morally obligated to starve simply because others are starving.

The second form of free riding – drawing on benefits provided by data collectors without paying the price of personal data – has a different moral pattern. Individuals using FaceCloak or CacheCloak, for example, may draw the ire of Facebook or location-based services because they are depriving these services of the positive externalities of personal information flows, which normally would enrich either their own data stockpiles or those of others to whom these data are sold or exchanged. It is not clear to us that companies are entitled to these externalities. At the very least, these relationships need to be examined from a broad societal perspective and the flow of costs and benefits (direct and indirect) explicitly recognised. If and only if it can be established that extracting the benefits offered by these services inflicts general, unacceptable costs, and not simply costs to companies, are there grounds to judge such free riding unethical.

Waste

Wastefulness is a charge that may be levelled against systems such as TrackMeNot that 'waste' bandwidth by increasing network traffic and 'waste' server capacity by burdening it with search queries that are not, in reality, of interest to users. A cost-benefit or utilitarian assessment directs us to consider the practical question of how severe the resource usage is. Does the noise significantly or even perceptibly undermine performance? In the case of search queries, which are short text strings, the impact is vanishingly small compared with the internet's everyday uses at this point, such as video distribution, online gaming and music streaming.[9]

Additionally, it is not sufficient to hang the full weight of the evaluation on degree of usage – it is necessary to confront normative assumptions explicitly. There is irony in deeming video streaming a *use* of network but a TrackMeNot-initiated search query a *waste* of network, or a TrackMeNot-initiated query a *waste* of server resource but a user-generated search for pornography a *use*. This claim makes sense, however, once we acknowledge that the difference between waste and use is normative; waste is use of a type that runs counter to a normative standard of desired, approved or acceptable use. The rhetoric of *waste*, however, begs to be scrutinised because, while it may be dressed up as an objective, definable concept, in many cases it is speakers who inject and project their perspectives or interests into defining a particular activity as wasteful.

Pollution and system damage

Data 'pollution' and the propagation of error and inaccuracy may be the trickiest issues of all, and reach to the heart of obfuscation. The intention behind inserting noise into the data stream is precisely to taint the resulting body. Yet there are various ways it can be tainted and some may be more problematic than others. One misspelt name does not a ruined database make; at what point does inaccurate, confusing and ambiguous data render a given project or business effectively worthless? Obfuscation that does not interfere with a system's primary functioning but affects only secondary uses of information might be fair.[10] Further, while some obfuscation practices might confuse efforts to profile individuals accurately, they may not render aggregate analysis useless, for example, as in the case of the work of Pham et al (2010) on perturbing individual data while retaining a reliable total picture.

Yet what if there is no getting around the noise? Where does this reality leave the ethical status of obfuscation? Is it acceptable to coerce people into providing data into the pool for the sake of another party, or even for the common good? And if they are coerced with no assurance as to how the information will be used, where it will travel and how it will be secured, are they not being asked to write a blank cheque with little reason to trust the cheque's recipients? These are akin to many ethical questions confronting individuals, both in relation to other individuals and to society and, as with those questions, there may be no general answers that do not call for further elaboration of the surrounding context. When pushed into a corner, in cases where dishonesty, free riding, resource consumption and data tainting cannot be denied, obfuscation nonetheless may pass the moral test. But establishing this status requires exploration of the specific and general obligations that the obfuscator may owe, whether securing freedom from the machinations of monitoring and analysis is justified and whether the obfuscator, having considered alternatives, is acting in earnest assertion of these freedoms. Explaining the calculus of those freedoms, and what liberties obfuscation defends, is our goal in the remainder of this chapter.

Politics of obfuscation

Reflecting on properties of obfuscation that are potentially morally problematic in the previous section, we found that none by itself implies that data obfuscation is inherently unethical. This finding is relevant to the inquiry of this section, in which we ask about the politics of obfuscation, namely what approach might a just society adopt toward data obfuscation, whether to ban or condone it, and by what lights. Inspired by Rawls's (1971) two principles, the first directs us to assess whether data obfuscation violates or erodes basic rights and liberties. If the reasoning above is sound, it seems there are no grounds to assert this categorically. Instead, the details of particular instances or types of instances will matter – for example, whether untruths or dissipation of resources abridge rights of those against whom obfuscation is practised, such as autonomy, property or security and, if they do, whether countervailing claims exist of equal or greater weight and legitimacy (of those who obfuscate), such as autonomy, fair treatment freedoms of speech and political association (that is, various freedoms associated with privacy protection).

Data obfuscation provides a particularly interesting case for Rawls's (1971) second 'maximin' principle. Setting aside instances of obfuscation, such as the Craigslist robber, which do not meet the requirements of the first principle, controversial cases may include some in which there are unresolved conflicting rights and liberties, and others in which respective claims are in conflict. The types of case described above include those in which, say, individuals seek cover through obfuscation for legitimate conditions or behaviours, thus denying positive externalities to data gatherers or that seek secrecy at a cost to the purity of a data pool. In paradigmatic instances, there are clear power differentials: individuals are reaching for obfuscatory tactics to avoid surveillance, profiling and manipulation, in general, to remain out of reach of a corporate or government actor.

Although obfuscation can be used by the more powerful against the less powerful, there are usually more direct ways for the more powerful to impose their will on the less powerful. Because obfuscation is not a strong strategy, it is only very rarely adopted by powerful actors – and then usually to evade notice by other powerful actors, as in the case of shell companies created to deter journalists and regulators, or the phenomenon in the Guatemalan secret police of multiple 'red herring' evidence plants and false testimonies to suggest that any final determination of what took place in a crime will be impossible (Goldman 2007). There is less need for stronger actors to resort to obfuscation because they have better methods available if they want to hide something – such as secret classifications, censorship and the threat of state violence.

For those who are generally less well off, less politically powerful, not in a position to refuse terms of engagement, technically unsophisticated, without the background in computing to use protections such as encryption, for those who need discounts at the supermarket, free email and cheap mobile phones, obfuscation can be a salve. It can avail some measure of resistance, obscurity and dignity. In this way, obfuscation fits into the domain that James C. Scott describes as 'weapons of the weak', the domain of dissimulation, slow-downs, petty theft, gossiping, foot dragging and other forms of resistance on the part of deeply disempowered actors (in the case of Scott's analysis, agrarian peasants) on the wrong side of severe power asymmetries. These are people without the possibility of armed revolt, without law or legislature on their side – what remains to them is 'passive noncompliance, subtle sabotage, evasion, and deception', terms that nicely capture the dimensions of obfuscation (Scott 1987: 31). As Anatole France put it: 'The law, in its majestic equality, forbids the rich as well as the poor to sleep under bridges and steal bread.' For those whose circumstances and necessity oblige them to give up their data – those who most need the shelter of the bridge, however ad hoc and unsatisfying it may be compared with a proper house – obfuscation provides a means of redress and, as such, is politically justified.

Although these political asymmetries are due in part to traditional sources of power differentials, such as influence, money, social class, education, race and so on, epistemic asymmetries, as discussed above, are also enormously consequential in contemporary, data driven societies. We may reach for obfuscation to shake off unwanted coercive influences, but we may do so simply because we are in the dark; we know that information about us is not disappearing but we know not where it is going nor how it has been or will be used. We are reaching for it to avoid or neutralise a lurking but ill-understood threat. In pushing against not so much the exercise of power and coercion but the threat of it, we are acting against what Philip Pettit might call domination, which he defines as the capacity to interfere in another's choices on an arbitrary basis (Pettit 1997). From the perspective of the individual on the other side of the epistemic asymmetry, the capacity of those who create and act on profiles of us that they have generated by gathering, aggregating and mining data may seem quite arbitrary.

Rawls's maximin principle demands that a just society opts for 'the alternative the worst outcome of which is superior to the worst outcomes of the others' (Rawls 1971: 153). Because data obfuscation offers a means to the less well off to assert their will against the more well off and powerful, banning data obfuscation either directly or indirectly by supporting measures coercing individuals to provide sound information, in our view, would violate the maxi-min principle. Where the obfuscator acts earnestly to resist the machinations of monitoring and analysis, obfuscation thus enables acts of reasonable and morally sound disobedience.

Among the toughest challenges to obfuscation are those that point to free riding and database pollution. The obfuscator is faulted for being unwilling to pay the cost for a benefit to him or herself, or for obstructing potential benefits to society at large by being unwilling to pitch in. Although these charges are worth taking seriously, so also is a caution that Jeremy Waldron issues in his discussion of a post-9/11 world in which citizens are expected to accept a rebalancing of security and liberty in favour of the former. Whenever there is talk of achieving a balance among social goods requiring that one be traded off against another, among other objections to such trade offs, one is that all too often we fail to take into consideration that costs and benefits are unevenly distributed (Waldron 2003). It may simply not be the case that *we* collectively give up a certain measure of freedom in return for *our* collective greater safety but that the loss of liberty is concentrated on a small sub-set of our society, who take a massively disproportionate loss for the possible benefit to us as a whole (from which 'they', who lose so much more of their liberty, are now excluded) or for those of us in a different sub-set. According to Waldron, we, collectively, may accept this unfair trade-off because, in aggregate, we do not feel the sting very much.

In cases of data obfuscation where we might be inclined to cite free riding or data pollution, Waldron's caution must not be ignored. In these cases, obfuscation might be legitimate acts of resistance by some, carrying the burdens of dataveillance disproportionately, for the sake of others, or for the sake of us all. Obfuscation may be an appropriate response, because it is disproportionately advantageous to the more vulnerable actor against the less vulnerable. Compared with the price of refusal and the difficulties of complete concealment, obfuscation is a relatively simple and intuitive way for the individual to resist, allowing both compliance and protest at the same time.

Conclusions

Obfuscation, as we have presented it here, is at once richer and less rigorous than academically well established methods of digital privacy protection, such as encryption. It is far more ad hoc and contextual, without the quantifiable protection of cryptographic methods. It is often haphazard and piece-meal, creating only a temporary window of liberty or a certain amount of reasonable doubt. It is for precisely those reasons that we think it is a valuable and rewarding subject for study. Politically, as long as the ends are sound and we take care to avoid certain methods, obfuscation can be a force for good in our contemporary culture of data. These moves are a valuable resource in the defence of our privacy and freedom of action. We have provided an outline of the family, a number of examples, the parameters for quantification and improvement, and a view of the political and ethical problems it creates, as well as arguments in its favour. Now, we hope the community of privacy researchers and activists will help to expand this idea. We face a number of further questions, beginning with one scientific, one moral and one technical:

- Is it possible to create a meaningfully quantified science of obfuscation? Can we optimise different obfuscation tactics for different scenarios, and find weak points in the overall strategy?
- Does our description of obfuscation as a viable and reasonable method of last-ditch privacy protection lead to the same political problems created by other systems of privacy preserving technology and possibilities such as opt-out – that is, putting the responsibility back on the private user and side-stepping the need to create a mature civil society around managing data?
- Are there methods for counter-profiling – figuring out how the profilers work to fine-tune our data strategies and how best to stymie them – that could be incorporated into the project of refining obfuscation?

Under duress, in the face of asymmetry, innovative methods for drawing the contextual lines of information flow will emerge; people will create models of informational security and freedom from invasive analysis, irrespective of claims profit-seeking CEOs make about 'human nature' and the transformations of privacy. Obfuscation is often cheap, simple, crude and clever, rather than intelligent and lacks the polish or freedom from moral compromises that characterises more total privacy solutions. Nonetheless it offers the possibility of cover from the scrutiny of third parties and data miners for those without other alternatives. It is the possibility of refuge when other means fail, and we are obliged both to document it and to examine whether it can be made stronger: a more effective bulwark for those in need.

Notes

* This project was researched and written with funding from AFSOR: MURI (ONR BAA 10-002), NSF:PORTIA (ITR-0331542) and NSF-CT-M (CNS-0831124) grants. We are grateful for their support. This work benefited enormously from

the invaluable help and insights of members of the Privacy Research Group at NYU and audiences at Computers, Privacy and Data Protection 2011 and the European Association for the Study of Science and Technology 2010, where developing versions of this work were presented. We would also like to thank Solon Barocas, Ian Kerr and Mireille Hildebrandt for their astute comments, feedback and advice. We are indebted to Luke Stark for providing outstanding research assistance and editorial work.

1 The sale is well documented by the account in CSOonline, http://www.csoonline. com/article/220340/the-five-most-shocking-things-about-the-choicepoint-data-security-breach (accessed 30 October 2012), and the reactions by the FTC and ChoicePoint have been collected in the Privacy Rights Clearinghouse 'Chronology of Data Breaches' (see under 15 February 2005): http://www.privacyrights.org/ar/CPResponse.htm (accessed 30 October 2012). This incident led to the thought-provoking 'Model Regime of Privacy Protection' proposed by Daniel Solove and Chris Jay Hoofnagle; see Solove and Hoofnagle 2005.

2 In making this argument we are drawing on our descriptions of this problem with reference to the received notion of privacy in Nissenbaum (1999, 1998).

3 As one among many possible examples of our ignorance of the future uses to which our data may be put — whether it is records sold by an unscrupulous employee or left in a cab on a USB drive — see the business of scraping social network sites for their data, which can be bundled, sold and used without our ever being aware or giving consent to this use: http://www.readwriteweb.com/archives/bulk_social_data_80legs.php (accessed 30 October 2012). For analysis of this situation from a specifically legal perspective, see Hildebrandt (2008) and Zarsky (2005).

4 Any real opt-out policy would also have to offer the granularity of the process of aggregation and analysis itself, allowing you to make choices that lie between the extremes of refusal and compliance. An opt-out of consequence would enable the receipt of certain benefits in return for a degree of use; data that could be gathered or deployed only in certain contexts or for certain purposes, for a set period of time etc. This does not presently exist, and implementing it relies heavily on the diligence and good behaviour of private corporations. See Barocas and Nissenbaum (2009) for an instance of this problem of consenting to data use after the fact.

5 An anecdotal account of false tells from poker player Phil Hellmuth, from Navarro (2006), can be found online at http://southerngaming.com/?p=62 (accessed 30 October 2012).

6 It is interesting to imagine a poker strategy based around more extensive use of obfuscation — a player generating a constant stream of mannerisms and typical tells, so that anything involuntary is difficult to parse out — but it would probably be so irritating as to get a player ejected!

7 To be clear, that the specific case of the Danes and the Yellow Star is fictional in no way detracts from their heroic wartime history of helping Jews hide and escape.

8 As the FAQ (Tor Project, 2012) points out, as a practical matter this may not make a difference to a truly empowered adversary with complete oversight of the traffic moving onto and off your relay — a person who has agents on all sides of you and knows what has been passed and what has not.

9 Some of the quantitative analysis for network and server usage, respectively, will differ for the different 'uses', but the point of the normative argument stands.

10 Again, see the analysis in Gonzalez Fuster (2009), which provides a cogent explana-
    tion of an argument for the process of making data fit for an intended, 'primary' use
    and unfit for further 'secondary' – and non-consensual – uses.

References

Albrecht, K. and Mcintyre, L. (2006) *The Spychips Threat: Why Christians should resist RFID and electronic surveillance*, Nashville, TN: Nelson Current.

Alexander, J. and Smith, J. (2010) 'Disinformation: A taxonomy', University of Pennsylvania Department of Computer and Information Science Technical Report No MS-CIS-10-13.

Barocas, S. and Nissenbaum, H. (2009) 'On Notice: The trouble with notice and consent', Proceedings of the Engaging Data Forum: The First International Forum on the Application and Management of Personal Electronic Information, Cambridge, MA, October 2009.

Bok, S. (1999) *Lying: Moral choice in public and private life*, New York: Vintage, updated edition.

Carlson, R. (2010) 'Rob's Giant BonusCard Swap Meet', available at http://epistolary. org/rob/bonuscard/ (accessed 25 October 2010).

Cockerham, R. (2002) 'The Ultimate Shopper', available at http://www.cockeyed. com/pranks/safeway/ultimate_shopper.html (accessed 19 October 2010).

Cohen, F. (2006) 'The Use of Deception Techniques: Honeypots and decoys', in Bidgoli, H. (ed.) *Handbook of Information Security*, vol. 3, New York: Wiley & Sons.

Duhigg, C. (2009) 'What Does Your Credit-Card Company Know About You?', *New York Times*, 12 May.

Goldman, F. (2007) *The Art of Political Murder: Who killed the bishop?*, New York: Grove.

Gonzalez Fuster, G. (2009) 'Inaccuracy as a Privacy-Enhancing Tool', *Ethics and Information Technology*, 12: 87–95.

Hildebrandt, M. (2008) 'Profiling and the Rule of Law', *Identity in the Information Society* (IDIS), 1: 55–70.

Howe, D. and Nissenbaum, H. (2009) 'TrackMeNot: Resisting surveillance in web search', in Kerr, I., Lucock, C. and Steeves, V. (eds) *Lessons from the Identity Trail: Anonymity, privacy, and identity in a networked society*, Oxford: Oxford University Press.

Jackson, J. (2003) 'Cards Games: Should buyers beware of how supermarkets use "loyalty cards" to collect personal data?', *Baltimore City Paper*, 1 October.

Lessig, L. (2008) 'Prosecuting Online File Sharing Turns a Generation Criminal', *US News & World Report*, 22 December.

Lieber, R. (2009) 'American Express Kept a (Very) Watchful Eye on Charges', *New York Times*, 30 January.

Lund, J. and Deak, I. (1990) 'The Legend of King Christian: An exchange', *New York Review of Books*, 29 March.

Luo, W., Xie, Q. and Hengartner, U. (2009) 'FaceCloak: An architecture for user privacy on social networking sites', Proceedings of 2009 IEEE International Conference on Privacy, Security, Risk and Trust (PASSAT-09), Vancouver, BC, August 2009: 26–33.

Marx, G. (2003) 'A Tack in the Shoe: Neutralizing and resisting the new surveillance', *Journal of Social Issues*, 59.

Mercer, D. (2010) 'CDC uses Shopper-Card Data to Trace Salmonella', *Bloomberg BusinessWeek*, 10 March.

Meyerowitz, J. and Choudhury, R. R. (2009) 'Hiding Stars with Fireworks: Location privacy through camouflage', MobiCom'09, Beijing.

Nanex LLC (2010) 'Analysis of the "Flash Crash": Part 4, Quote stuffing, a manipulative device', 18 June 2010, available at http://www.nanex. net/20100506/FlashCrashAnalysis_Part4-1.html (accessed 26 November 2010).

Navarro, J. (2006) *Phil Hellmuth Presents Read 'Em and Reap: A career FBI agent's guide to decoding poker tells*, New York: Harper.

Netter, S. (2008) 'Wash. Man pulls off robbery using Craigslist, pepper spray', *ABC News*, 1 October.

Nielsen, A. (1952) *What's New in Food Marketing and Marketing Research: An address to grocery manufacturers of America at Hotel Waldorf-Astoria*, New York, 12 November, 1951, Chicago: A. C. Nielsen Co.

Nissenbaum, H. (1998) 'Toward an Approach to Privacy in Public: The challenges of information technology', *Ethics and Behavior*, 7: 207–219; reprinted in Spinello, R. A. and Tavani, H. T. (eds) (2001) *Readings in CyberEthics*, Sudbury: Jones and Bartlett.

Nissenbaum, H. (1999) 'The Meaning of Anonymity in an Information Age', *The Information Society*, 15: 141–44; reprinted in Spinello, R. A. and Tavani, H. T. (eds) (2001) *Readings in CyberEthics*, Sudbury: Jones and Bartlett.

Pettit, P. (1997) *Republicanism: A theory of freedom and government*, Oxford: Oxford University Press.

Pfaffenberger, B. (1992) 'Technological Dramas', *Science, Technology & Human Values*, 17: 282–312.

Pham, N., Ganti, R. K., Uddin, Y. S., Nath, S. and Abdelzaher, T. (2010) 'Privacy-Preserving Reconstruction of Multidimensional Data Maps in Vehicular Participatory Sensing', WSN 2010: 7th European Conference on Wireless Sensor Networks.

Postman, N. (1990) 'Informing Ourselves to Death', Speech given at the German Informatics Society, Stuttgart, 11 October 1990, available at http:// w2.eff.org/Net_culture/Criticisms/informing_ourselves_to_death.paper (accessed 24 November 2010).

Ratcliff, R. A. (2006) *Delusions of Intelligence: Enigma, ultra and the end of secure ciphers*, Cambridge: Cambridge University Press.

Rawls, J. (1971) *A Theory of Justice*, Cambridge, MA: Belknap.

Reiman, J. (1995) 'Driving to the Panopticon: A philosophical exploration of the risks to privacy posed by the highway technology of the future', *Santa Clara Computer and High Technology Law Review*, 11: 27–44.

Rothschild, F. and Greko, P. (2010) 'Botnet Resistant Coding: Protecting your users from script kiddies', paper presented at The Next HOPE, New York, 16 July 2010, available at http://thenexthope.org/talks-list/ (accessed 15 October 2010).

Scott, J. C. (1987) *Weapons of the Weak: Everyday forms of peasant resistance*, New Haven, CT: Yale.

Schulze, H. and Mochalski, K. (2009) *Internet Study 2008/2009*, Leipzig: IPOQUE, available at http://www.ipoque.com/resources/internet-studies/internet-study-2008_2009 (accessed 5 September 2010).

Soghoian, C. (2009) 'Manipulation and Abuse of the Consumer Credit Reporting Agencies', *First Monday*, 14.

Solove, D. (2008) 'Data Mining and the Security-Liberty Debate', *University of Chicago Law Review*, 74: 343.

Solove, D. and Hoofnagle, C. (2005) 'A Model Regime of Privacy Protection (Version 2.0) (5 April 2005)', GWU Legal Studies Research Paper No 132, available at http://ssrn.com/abstract=699701 (accessed 13 November 2010).

Stead, W. W. and Lin, H. S. (eds) (2009) *Computational Technology for Effective Health Care: Immediate steps and strategic directions*, Committee on Engaging the Computer Science Research Community in Health Care Informatics, National Research Council of the National Academies, Washington, DC: National Academies Press.

Subramani, M. (2004) 'How do Suppliers Benefit from Information Technology Use in Supply Chain Relationships?', *MIS Quarterly*, 28: 45–73.

Templeton, B. (2009) 'The Evils of Cloud Computing: Data portability and single sign on', 2009 BIL Conference, Long Beach, California, available at http://www.vimeo.com/3946928 and http://www.acceleratingfuture.com/people-blog/2009/the-evils-of-cloud-computing/ (accessed 5 October 2010).

Tor Project (2012) 'FAQ: Running a Tor Relay' available at https://trac.torproject.org/projects/tor/wiki/doc/TorFAQ (accessed 8 January 2012).

Waldron, J. (2003) 'Security and Liberty: The image of balance', *Journal of Political Philosophy*, 11: 191–210.

Wohl, R. (1996) *A Passion for Wings: Aviation and the western imagination, 1908–1918*, New Haven, CT: Yale.

Wohl, R. (2005) *The Spectacle of Flight: Aviation and the western imagination, 1920–1950*, New Haven, CT: Yale.

Zarsky, T. (2005) 'Online Privacy, Tailoring and Persuasion', in Strandburg, K. J. and Stan Raicu, D. (eds) *Privacy and Identity: The promise and perils of a technological age*, New York: Kluwer Publishing.

8

On decision transparency, or how to enhance data protection after the computational turn

Bert-Jaap Koops

Introduction

In the past decades, technology has fundamentally changed the landscape of data processing. We have seen the rise of the 'database nation', a society that increasingly depends on private and public databases to make decisions (Garfinkel 1999). Simultaneously, the 'network society' emerged as a new, global form of social organisation based on technical, organisational, economic and socio-cultural networks (Castells 1996). These have merged to develop vastly increasing – and increasingly complex – interconnections between data processors and their databases that facilitate public policy and business processes. Combining and analysing data sets through data mining and profiling has become daily practice (Murphy 2010; Hildebrandt and Gutwirth 2008).

The expansion and linkage of databases closely relates to sociological trends: the rise of risk governance (Renn 2008) as an overarching paradigm for regulation in the risk society, a culture of fear and a culture of control in which safety has become an overarching end in itself (Furedi 2006). 'Spatial controls, situation controls, managerial controls, system controls, social controls, self-controls – in one social realm after another, we now find the imposition of more intensive regimes of regulation, inspection and control' (Garland 2001: 194–95). Database and profiling technologies are a key enabling factor in the move towards risk governance to control risks, which at the same time stimulate the further development of these technologies. This amalgam of socio-technical trends establishes a 'computational turn' in societal organisation, in which decisions are taken on the basis of large-scale, complex and multi-purpose processes of matching and mining enormous amounts of data.

The computational turn challenges the current framework of data protection, which was established in the 1970s to early 1990s of the 20th century. Are the pillars of the data protection framework robust enough to resist the tremblings and quakes of 21st century data processing? Perhaps a different approach, or at least a different emphasis in our focus, is needed to meet the computational turn with effective forms of data protection. In this chapter, I will discuss such an alternative approach, one that focuses less on data minimisation, user control and procedural accountability, but instead directs its arrows at the outcome of computation-based decision-making: the decision itself. Making decisions that affect individuals more transparent is a different way of forcing powerful data processors to be careful and fair in their decisions, regardless of how exactly data were collected, processed and mined. Transparency is a key concept in modern governance and, although this does not imply we should regard it as the holy grail of governance (Hood and Heald 2006), it does provide a fruitful perspective with which to approach data protection (Gutwirth and de Hert 2008).

The aim of this chapter, then, is to discuss decision transparency as a productive approach to data protection after the computational turn. Does a focus on decision transparency have the potential to enhance data protection, perhaps more so than a focus on user control and procedural accountability that lies at the heart of the mainstream approach to data protection? I will start with a discussion of the limitations of current data protection, and then provide a theoretical perspective on decision transparency by applying the conceptual framework of David Heald on transparency relations to explain data processing relationships. To illustrate how the theoretical approach could be effected in practice, the chapter then describes existing models of transparency in legal, social and technical regulatory measures and how these models could enhance downwards transparency in illustrative cases of commerce, government service provisioning and law enforcement. The chapter concludes by arguing that the mainstream approach to data protection should be offset with increased attention for decision transparency.

The limitations of current data protection

The current approach to data protection as enshrined, in particular, in the Data Protection Directive,[1] is built on several pillars. These can be summarised, with reference to the commonly accepted basic data protection principles outlined in the OECD Guidelines, as a focus on data minimisation (collection limitation, purpose specification, use limitation), data security (quality and security safeguards), user involvement (openness, individual participation) and accountability.[2] The database age, with its computational turn, fundamentally challenges these pillars on which the data protection framework is built.[3]

A first challenge is that the relationship between privacy risks and the concept of personal data – data relating to an identifiable individual – is unclear (Robinson et al 2009: 27–28), and may become increasingly difficult to establish. While the Data Protection Directive (DPD) focuses on the risks associated with processing personal data, the risks associated with the computational turn do not necessarily involve personal data. Data mining and profiling also pose risks to individuals, but the DPD does not apply to substantial parts of profiling applications (Hildebrandt 2008b).

Second, if the DPD does apply to modern day data processing, the principle of purpose limitation (specifying a purpose and subsequently limiting processing to that purpose, or to purposes 'not incompatible' with the specified purpose) hardly works. The principle sits at odds with a database world in which function creep is becoming a household word. Function creep indicates the situation 'when a system developed for a particular purpose comes to be used for, or to provide the underpinnings for other systems that are used for, different purposes' (Curry et al 2004: 362). As a Council of Europe consultation document observes: '[i]n today's context, personal data is commonly used for purposes that go far beyond what may have been initially foreseen, far beyond what may be compatible with the initial purpose of the collection' (Council of Europe 2011). Moreover, function creep and knowledge discovery in databases also imply that, increasingly, data are used across contexts (commerce, public service provision, health, law enforcement, national security), where they lose the social norms associated with intra-context processing of data. Decontextualisation of data also provides new risks that are not well addressed by the current data protection framework (cf Nissenbaum 2010).

Third, data minimisation is not what we see in practice in the database age; quite the contrary. The zettabyte of information that is produced every year (that is, 10^{21} bytes, roughly a stack of DVDs from Earth to the moon and back) (IDC 2010) ends up in all kinds of database. A report commissioned by the Dutch Data Protection Authority estimated that the average Dutch citizen is included in 250–500 databases, or in up to 1000 databases for more socially active people (Schermer and Wagemans 2009) (see for similar accounts Murphy 2010; Solove 2004; Garfinkel 1999). Much of the information in these databases is not produced by web users themselves, at least not actively and knowingly (Mayer-Schönberger 2009: 88–90); more data are nowadays created *about* individuals than *by* individuals. In other words, our 'digital shadow' has outgrown our 'digital footprint' (IDC 2010). It is unsurprising, then, that the major review report of the DPD noticed that 'substantial dissatisfaction also exists ... on the processes that the Directive has provided to make these [substantive data protection] principles a reality, and on the question of whether these processes are effective' (Robinson et al 2009: 38). Another review observed that '[a]lthough these new [data protection] rights have been enshrined in legislation, their application remains limited, if not non-existent' (Poullet 2006: 208). Altogether, there is a wide discrepancy between the law in the books and the law in action.

This is partly due to the fourth issue, namely that accountability has severe shortcomings in the present age. The model of accountability – a division of responsibility between data controller, data processor and data subject – does not function well. The important role attached to self-regulation and co-regulation to make the principles work in different contexts and concrete settings has not come off the ground, while supervision by data protection authorities has limitations attributable to their hybrid tasks or shortage of powers or capacity (Purtova 2011: 166, 176–78; Robinson et al 2009: 35–37).

Fifth, the ideal of user involvement has little thrust in practice. Even as a privacy scholar, I myself have no idea which data are stored about me, as a reasonably socially active person, in an estimated 500+ databases (Schermer and Wagemans 2009), let alone that the average citizen will be aware of all the data 'out there'. People also have little awareness of their data protection rights, and very seldom ask data controllers for access (Poullet 2006: 208). They do not read privacy policies, which are theoretically meant to inform them of data processing but in practice serve as documents written by lawyers for lawyers (Robinson et al 2009: 28–29). This also implies that user consent, which is one of the possible legitimating grounds for data processing, and particularly relevant in the commercial sector, has limited meaning in practice (Robinson et al 2009). And if this already applies to current internet applications with online privacy statements, user involvement and consent become even more problematic in situations where people are continuously profiled and proactively served by ambient intelligence (AmI) applications (Hildebrandt 2008c).

Finally, data security is also under pressure, owing not only to the problem of prevalent attacks on and leakages from databases, but also because of increasing difficulty in dealing with outdated or inaccurate data. The rights of access, correction and erasure may work well for correcting a misspelt name in a data record, but effectively having incorrect records removed from databases requires a huge effort (see for example Nationale ombudsman 2009). More importantly, the risk for individuals of the computational turn resides in out-of-context, incomplete or partially polluted databases being mined to make inferences, against which a right to have 'incomplete or inaccurate' data corrected or erased (Article 12(b) DPD) can hardly be invoked. The risk of false positives and false negatives, which is one of the main ways in which individuals can suffer harm from predictive computations, is also not addressed by classic individual participation rights.

These challenges to the current data protection framework warrant the conclusion that the framework, constructed in the 1980s and 1990s, no longer functions as intended after the computational turn of the 21st century. We live as digital persons in databases, but as persons of flesh and blood we are hardly aware of what happens, and we have woefully little control over the way our digital personae and data shadows are being treated. The pillars of data minimisation, user participation, data security and oversight have become eroded.

Of course, the challenges to data protection have not gone unnoticed to policy-makers. Significantly, however, the current line of thinking for reviewing the Data Protection Directive assumes that the basic, substantive data protection principles are still valid, but that they need to be better implemented and that enforcement needs to be stepped up (European Commission 2010; Robinson et al 2009: vii). This translates into a focus on strengthening individuals' rights and enhancing controllers' accountability, among other things through promoting 'privacy by design' (European Commission 2010). The draft General Data Protection Regulation (GDPR) that is to replace the DPD, in its version of January 2012,[4] contains several elements aimed at enhancing the transparency of data processing; for example, the requirement to 'have transparent and easily accessible policies with regard to the processing of personal data and for the exercise of data subjects' rights' (proposed Article 11(1) GDPR). Particularly relevant is the new requirement that in case of certain automated decisions based on profiling, data controllers must inform data subjects with 'information as to the existence of processing for [an automated decision] and the envisaged effects of such processing on the data subject' (proposed Article 20(4) GDPR). This could be a significant, perhaps 'revolutionary', step forward in trying to level the playing field in profiling practices, as it requires ex ante specification of effects the controller aims at as well as *ex ante* reflection on unintended but foreseeable side-effects (Hildebrandt 2012: 51). However, this is process transparency, not outcome transparency and, moreover, a form of *ex ante* transparency, as the intention of the provision is to inform data subjects in advance that some form of automated decision-making will occur on the basis of their personal data, thus helping them to make informed choices in giving consent or exercising other data protection rights. It is doubtful whether the existing challenges relating to informational control by data subjects can be addressed by their being informed ex ante of 'envisaged effects' of the automated decision-making, particularly since the more general challenge of providing information about data processing to data subjects in a meaningful way (for example, through privacy policies) remains hard to tackle. (It should also be noted that the scope of Article 20 GDPR is restricted to decision-making processes that are fully automated; in many profiling contexts, such as the government licensing and law enforcement applications I discuss below, profiling will have some element of human intervention in the decision-making process, which leaves Article 20 inapplicable. Moreover, Article 20 is restricted to situations where the decision has legal effects or 'significantly affects' individuals, and it remains to be seen how many online profiling practices meet the threshold of 'significantly' affecting someone in the sense of this provision.) Overall, the transparency enhancing elements of the proposed General Data Protection Regulation seem good additions to update the regulatory framework, from the perspective of trying to strengthen user control and accountability for data processing. But the fact that people have little control over the way their digital personae and data shadows are being treated in the first place still remains a huge challenge that a comprehensive, data minimisation-based approach does little to address in practice. It is questionable whether clinging to the overall data protection framework and attempting to strengthen user control is a good strategy, if the pillars sustaining the framework are eroding.

Therefore, although elements of the current approach could prove effective, a more fruitful strategy than the comprehensive *ex ante* regulation in data protection might be to focus on targeted *ex post* regulation in the form of decision transparency.

Theoretical reflections on transparency

Heald's anatomy of transparency

Transparency is a characteristic of objects, organisations and processes that are, metaphorically speaking, 'allowing light to pass through so that the objects behind can be distinctly seen', resulting in their being 'open to public scrutiny'.[5] Transparency is associated, and sometimes equated, with openness, but it has a wider implication than merely being open: transparency also comprises simplicity and comprehensibility. Where openness contrasts with secrecy, transparency contrasts with complexity and disorder besides secrecy (Heald 2006).

To get more grip on what transparency is about, I follow David Heald's anatomy of transparency. Heald (2006) distinguishes four directions and three aspects, or dimensions, of transparency. The directions of transparency lie on two axes: vertical (upwards and downwards) and horizontal (inwards and outwards). On the vertical axis, Heald applies the perspective of the object being transparent or not, that is, whether the object of scrutiny can be seen by the party above or below. Thus, transparency upwards means that the object is visible from above and can be seen by those looking down: 'the hierarchical superior/principal can observe the conduct, behaviour, and/or "results" of the hierarchical subordinate/agent'. Transparency downwards is when the object can be seen from below, by those looking up, that is, 'when the "ruled" can observe the conduct, behaviour, and/or "results" of their "rulers"' (Heald 2006: 27). On the horizontal axis, transparency outwards exists when an organisation can observe what happens outside the organisation, and transparency inwards is when those outside can look inside the organisation (Heald 2006: 28).

Relevant dimensions of transparency consist of three dichotomies (Heald 2006: 29–35):

- event versus process transparency, that is, whether the input or output or end result is transparent or whether the process of producing a result is transparent
- transparency in retrospect versus transparency in real time
- nominal versus effective transparency, that is, whether something 'looks' transparent according to some measurement, or whether it effectively *is* transparent; the latter requires that there 'be receptors capable of processing, digesting, and using the information'.

These distinctions provide a useful framework for analysing transparency. As the often used metaphor of sunlight for transparency – 'sunlight is the most

powerful of all disinfectants' – suggests, transparency can purge away con-
taminations, but there is also a risk of over-exposure (Heald 2006: 40). Since
transparency is not intrinsically good or bad, and usually considered an instrumental rather than an intrinsic value (Heald 2006: 40), introducing transparency requires careful reflection on how much transparency is needed for which
purposes, in which variety, and by which means.

Transparency, privacy and due process in data protection

If we apply the anatomy of transparency to current data protection, the limitations of the data protection framework (as discussed above) can be put into
perspective. Vertical transparency is the major axis along which data protection is formed.[6]

Transparency upwards ('rulers' observing the 'ruled') is large and comprehensive, and still increasing, judging from the body of literature on the demise
of privacy and the rise of the surveillance state (see, among many others, House
of Commons Home Affairs Committee 2008; Murakami Wood 2006; Koops
and Leenes 2005; Sykes 1999). Public and private organisations can look into
both the events and the processes (behaviour) of individuals, increasingly in
(near) real time (which will be almost default if the vision of AmI becomes a
reality). According to many, this transparency is not only nominal (that is, the
ability to see things) but also effective (that is, actually seeing things and
acting upon that knowledge). The effectiveness of upwards transparency also
has a reflexive or foreshadowing aspect, in that the knowledge of possibly being
watched can have a panoptic effect on individuals who may change their behaviour accordingly (Koops 2010; Mayer-Schönberger 2009: 111–112). The level
of transparency upwards has led several authors to conclude that we live in a
transparent or glass society (Kohnstamm and Dubbeld 2007; Brin 1998).

This should be offset by transparency in the other direction. Data protection is, to a large extent, precisely intended to make the processing of data by
'rulers' (data processors) transparent, and therefore controllable, to the 'ruled'
(data subjects) (Gutwirth and de Hert 2008: 282). However, as we saw earlier,
the level of downwards transparency is limited in practice. The data protection requirements focus on process transparency but hardly on event transparency, so that scrutiny of the outcome of organisational data processing (for
example, decisions made about consumers or citizens) remains narrow. The
transparency is also restricted in time, focusing on *ex ante* (obligations to
notify to a data protection authority) and *ex post* (informing and providing
access to data subjects), thus offering little in terms of real time transparency.
Most importantly, the transparency can be said to be almost exclusively nominal, but not effective. The data processing may be open in the sense of accessible, but that does not make it transparent, as it lacks simplicity and
comprehensibility. The DPD review report's assessment of privacy policies or
privacy statements is illustrative of the DPD's transparency requirements

being nominal instead of effective: it 'is predominantly targeted to meet any applicable legal transparency requirement, rather than serving a real transparency benefit towards the consumer' (Robinson et al 2009: 29).

Taken together, this implies that current data protection can offer only limited protection to citizens to address privacy and due process concerns. Informational privacy, which is the most important dimension of privacy after the computational turn, lies at the intersection of privacy and data protection, requiring a careful combination of sufficient restrictions on upwards transparency (since privacy is an opacity tool, Gutwirth and de Hert 2008: 282) and sufficient room for downwards transparency. This balance is currently, however, skewed: organisations can look down on subjects much more than subjects can see what is happening in organisations.

As a consequence of this imbalance, due process is also threatened. Due process broadly refers to the possibility of contesting the way one is treated by the state or similarly powerful organisations. With limited downwards transparency, data subjects often do not know how they are being treated in the first place, because they have few means of knowing which data (or data sets, or profiles) were used when decisions were taken about them and, even if they do know, they have little means – in the sense of effectively being empowered – of challenging the decision. This could be alleviated by oversight measures, but that also is limited in practice: data protection authorities, even if they have capacity and power to investigate, focus on how organisations meet with nominal transparency requirements, rather than on understanding how exactly data were used in organisational decision-making.

Clearly, then, rebalancing is needed. If we think of the window between data processors and data subjects in terms of translucency, we can envision two strategies for effecting a new balance. First, upwards transparency can be diminished, thus making the window more opaque for those above looking down. Second, downwards transparency can be enhanced, making the window more transparent for those below looking up.

Diminishing upwards transparency

Obscuring the sight of those above can take a variety of forms. The most obvious is to shield data, for example in the form of hiding the content of data (using cryptography), limiting the accessibility of data (setting browsers not to accept tracking cookies) and limiting the connectability of data (for example, through anonymisation or onion routers). Although the technologies for shielding data exist, they are not always easy or convenient to use and, by and large, current technological trends facilitate the ability for third parties to take knowledge of data much more than the ability for users to hide data (Koops 2009: 100–101).

Perhaps it is a more effective strategy not to shield data as such, but to make them less visible in other ways. For example, you can hide data among other data with steganography (for example, hiding text in a photo image) or by multiplying innocuous but relevant-looking other data (for example, adding automated signatures with national security buzzwords to jam intelligence interception systems). Or you can hide data by putting them in plain sight, as Angelina Jolie does by sharing (what she lets us believe to be) all her information with the public: 'If you seem to be hiding things, the press are obsessed with prying. As a result, choosing to be public in a culture of publicity can actually mean choosing privacy' (boyd 2010).

This strategy of 'data obfuscation' (Brunton and Nissenbaum in this volume) may be a better way, ultimately, to protect privacy than to try and prevent others from accessing personal data. Digital abstinence to prevent digital traces from being generated (Mayer-Schönberger 2009: 128–34) is not realistic in a computer-pervaded world; neither does it prevent others from generating information about you in the form of digital shadows. If people cannot control the data that float around about them, they could resort to creating other data to counterbalance their digital personae. A strategy of data obfuscation, which relies partly on tools of data maximisation, sounds counterintuitive to the data protection community, who still have their minds focused on data minimisation. Nevertheless, after the computational turn it may make sense to use a topsy-turvy approach to personal data that is much more in line with other developments in the data economy, such as crowdsourcing, file sharing, viral marketing and using free services in exchange for being profiled (cf Anderson 2009; Mason 2008). For example, the (too) often used example of a job interview in which the applicant is turned down because of some silly item on Facebook may currently be apt, but it will not necessarily apply in the future. In 10 years' time, prospective employers may well be suspicious of online paragons of virtue, and rather expect applicants to have a realistic online profile, including the odd embarrassments and youthful peccadillos. Moreover, you could also claim that a particular item, such as the drunken picture on Facebook, was a prank, a carefully crafted element in your life strategy of data obfuscation.

Nevertheless, as Brunton and Nissenbaum acknowledge (in this volume), data obfuscation also has its limitations, and it may be more of a last resort than a frontline strategy. We may sometimes succeed in making the window a little more opaque for scrutinising data processors above us, but much will still remain visible for those intent on looking down. To keep a check on data processors' power, therefore, the second element of rebalancing is also vital.

Enhancing downwards transparency

If transparency is at a low level, then introducing (more) transparency will bring benefits – allowing more sunlight to shine on something that is relatively dark will serve as a disinfectant without over-exposing the object

(Heald 2006). Since, as noted above, data protection has a relatively low level of downwards transparency, introducing more transparency is likely to improve the protection of data subjects. This has been forcefully argued by David Brin in *The Transparent Society*: 'we may not be able to eliminate the intrusive glare shining on citizens of the next century, but the glare just might be rendered harmless through the application of more light aimed in the other direction' (Brin 1998: 23). Being seen is less unnerving if you know that the same level of visibility is directed to those behind the cameras, the black-listers and the profilers (Bailey 2004: 186–87). This downwards transparency can ensure that those who take decisions about individuals become more accountable for those decisions.

Looking at the dimensions of transparency, it seems important that down-wards transparency consists not only of insight into the process – which most of current data protection provisions currently focus on – but also of insight into events, in particular the outcome of the process. After all, the outcome, typically in the form of a decision made about an individual (for example, denying or granting a service or offer, allowing or prohibiting entry) strikes at the core of the privacy and due process risks. Downwards transparency needs to be particularly focused on decision-making and decisions, allowing people to understand which data were used in which ways to come to the decision. Only then does the decision become contestable.

As to the second dimension, of time, the transparency needs to be effected at least in retrospect, given the focus on output transparency. Retrospective transparency can take the form of periodic audits, scrutinising how, in general, decisions are taken and individuals are treated. For individual cases, how-ever, such audits may provide insufficient redress, or come too late. Allowing retrospective transparency should therefore also be considered for concrete cases, that is, that each individual decision becomes transparent after it has been taken. This comes close to a form of real time transparency, particularly if profiling becomes so prevalent as to be ubiquitous and continuous (Hildebrandt 2008c).

Most importantly, looking at the third dimension, transparency needs to be effective rather than merely nominal. The 'transparency illusion' must be prevented, that is, when transparency appears to be increasing according to some measurement index, while the reality is different (Heald 2006: 34). Current data protection involves a substantial risk of triggering the transparency illusion, since it largely focuses on formal information provision, while little is actually done – or can practically be done – with the information (as discussed above). The missing element is the 'receptors capable of processing, digesting, and using the information' that is necessary for effective transparency (Heald 2006: 35). Data subjects and data protection authorities currently have limited capacity for understanding or using the information about actual data processing processes and, while this may be redressed to some extent, as is the intention of the DPD review, there may be inherent limitations as to what individuals or official supervisory bodies can do. We should also consider other parties who can function as 'capable receptors' of transparency information. Privacy advocacy groups play an important traditional role in this respect (Bennett 2008), but we can also think of 'unusual suspects', such as right-wing libertarian groups, consumer organisations and sectoral supervisory bodies (such as telecommunications authorities or government accountability offices) (Koops 2011). Or, in line with web 2.0 developments that parallel the computational turn, we could crowdsource the scrutiny and use of transparency information: 'the cameras *are* coming. You can rail against them, shaking your fist in futile rage at all the hovering lenses. Or you can join *a committee of six billion neighbors* to control the pesky things, making each one an extension of your eyes' (Brin 1998: 333, emphasis added).

Conclusion

The anatomy of transparency helps us to understand the challenge of data protection after the computational turn. We need to rebalance the relationship between data processing organisations and individuals, by recalibrating vertical transparency. This implies a dual strategy: diminishing upwards transparency, through shielding and obfuscating data, and enhancing downwards transparency, through introducing mechanisms for output, case-by-case or (near) real time, and effective transparency. This requires receptors who are capable of understanding transparency information and who are able to use it.

Both strategies have been outlined here on a conceptual level, and may be easier said than done. They need to be elaborated and made more concrete before we can say whether they have a chance of actually working to make data protection more effective after the computational turn. Since the first prong of the strategy, relying on data obfuscation, is elaborated by Brunton and Nissenbaum elsewhere in this volume, I will focus in the remainder of this chapter on the second strategy. How could downwards transparency be effected in practice?

Practical reflections on transparency

Models for downwards transparency

For effecting downwards transparency, all kinds of measure can be taken. These can be grouped into three categories of regulatory instrument: legal, social and architectural approaches. I will briefly illustrate each approach with some existing models for enhancing transparency. A fourth category would be an economic approach, that is, using competition or pricing mechanisms to stimulate downwards transparency. While in general businesses have some market incentive to be transparent about what they do in order to gain or maintain consumer trust and transparency about good corporate governance can be a competitive advantage in marketing, for example, sustainable products, there is not much literature that suggests that being (really) transparent about personal data handling practices is being used by businesses to gain a competitive advantage. Market incentives in themselves are unlikely to work for enhancing data protection; hence, economic incentives will have to be backed up by legislation (cf Lessig 1999b: 508: 'the market is able to constrain in this manner only because of other constraints of law and social norms'). Therefore, I will discuss economic approaches within the category of legislation.

First, in the legislative approach, we have several models that focus specifically on making governmental or corporate decision-making more transparent, in particular to make it more accountable. Perhaps the best known model is Freedom of Information Acts (FOIA), a type of legislation dating roughly from the 1980s and 1990s that forces governments to make available documents or records related to administration or public policy. This can be used by individuals to uncover the process leading up to certain decisions or policy measures. While all kinds of exception apply, depending on countries' specific legislation, FOIA are used frequently in most Western countries, in particular by the press and advocacy groups. Less prevalent but relevant as a model for decision-making transparency is legislation that requires government agencies to take decisions in open meetings. The US Government in the Sunshine Act of 1976 stipulates that 'every portion of every meeting of an agency shall be open to public observation', where a meeting refers to 'the deliberations ... required to take action on behalf of the agency where such deliberations determine or result in the joint conduct or disposition of official agency business'.[7] The sunshine is limited, however, by many exceptions, some of which are fairly broad and open formulated, such as when an open meeting would involve premature disclosure of information that would 'be likely to significantly frustrate implementation of a proposed agency action'.[8]

Transparency legislation has also been enacted to make corporations more transparent. The US Sarbanes-Oxley Act, for example, requires public companies (that is, companies with securities for sale to the public) to document in annual reports the management's assessment of the internal (financial) control system, which must contain 'an assessment ... of the effectiveness of the internal control structure and procedures of the issuer for financial reporting'.[9] In environmental law, legislation also requires companies to make available information about their processes and products; the EU REACH Regulation, for example, requires companies to submit data about the safety of chemicals they process to the European Chemicals Agency and it establishes a publicly accessible internet database on chemicals.[10] Labelling requirements in law, for example the obligation to mention whether genetically modified organisms or allergenic substances have been used in producing food, are another example of transparency legislation, partly to ensure product safety but also to enhance consumer choice. Transparency requirements in law, for example in European telecommunications law about traffic management practices, can also enhance product or service quality – interestingly, experimental research suggests that this effect might occur when some knowledgeable end users receive in-depth information rather than when all end users receive superficial information (Sluijs, Schrett and Henze 2011). This underlines the importance of identifying capable receptors of transparency information and indicates that, in data protection, transparency requirements should not necessarily focus on providing 'average consumers' with understandable information about data processing; it could be equally or even more relevant to provide in-depth information to knowledgeable users, for example, consumer associations or supervisory authorities.

Whereas the financial, environmental and some consumer-oriented transparency legislation is typically focused on process transparency, another model, in data protection legislation, is concerned more with outcome transparency. According to Article 12(a) DPD, each data subject has the right to obtain from the controller 'knowledge of the logic involved in any automatic processing of data concerning him at least in the case of the automated decisions referred to in Article 15(1)', that is, 'a decision which produces legal effects concerning him or significantly affects him and which is based solely on automated processing of data intended to evaluate certain personal aspects relating to him, such as his performance at work, creditworthiness, reliability, conduct, etc' (Articles 12(a) and 15(1) DPD). This element of data protection legislation would seem particularly suited to enhance outcome transparency after the computational turn, as it specifically addresses situations in which decisions are taken based on profiling. As Leenes (2008: 298) suggests, in these cases: 'transparency is required with respect to the relevant data and the rules (heuristics) used to draw the inferences. This allows the validity of the inferences to be checked by the individual concerned, in order to notice and possibly remedy unjust judgements.' However, the efficacy of Article 12(a) DPD is limited in practice, not only by respect required for trade secrets and intellectual property rights (recital 41 DPD), but also because 'the logic' behind profile-based decisions resides in algorithms that are incomprehensible to data subjects (and probably to data protection authorities as well). It is questionable whether profiling processes can be translated with sufficient clarity into ordinary language, that is, in terms that non-experts can understand what happens. Nevertheless, at least in theory, Article 12(a) DPD provides a relevant model for enhancing downwards transparency.

The second category of regulatory approaches are social models. A model that quite literally enhances downwards transparency is 'sousveillance': turning around surveillance to look back from below. This was developed and practised by Steve Mann and colleagues in a number of experiments, in which they, for example, walked into (CCTV-equipped) shops with cameras that were visibly mounted on their bodies, or covertly videotaped conversations with shop personnel about the shop's CCTV policy, and subsequently confronting the staff in public with the recordings (Mann et al 2005). Sousveillance is rooted in women's, civil rights and environmental movements, aiming to use confrontation to start a reflective dialogue with those in power, and also to make the passive public realise how their behaviour reinforces existing power structures. Thus, sousveillance should ultimately influence the public debate in such a way that an equilibrium is created between surveillance and sousveillance in 'coveillance' (Mann et al 2005) or 'equiveillance' (cf Ganascia 2010; Mann, Fing and Lo 2006). While sousveillance typically focuses on camera surveillance, where 'looking upwards' happens in relatively close proximity in physical space, the model can also be applied in virtual space. WikiLeaks is a good example of the internet community trying to make government decision-making more accountable by publishing government restricted-access documents – a social, underground, variant of the legal FOIA approach. Similar approaches are visible in crowdsourcing initiatives of public scrutiny, for example the GuttenPlag Wiki that allowed 'the crowd', that is, the internet community, collectively to find plagiarised text parts in German (now former) minister Zu Guttenberg's dissertation. By June 2011, the crowd had identified 1218 plagiarised fragments from 135 sources.[11] The force of crowdsourcing downwards transparency is that it need not necessarily be the individuals affected who look upwards, or supervisory authorities; in the logic of the 'long tail' (cf Anderson 2006) there is always someone somewhere in the internet community who looks upwards at particular instances of governmental or corporate decision-making and who can denounce unfair treatment in web 2.0's market place of public opinion.

The third category concerns technological approaches, that is, 'architecture' in Lessig's (1999a) terms or 'techno-regulation' in Brownsword's (2008) terms. As profiling techniques are a 'technological black box for citizens... the integration of legal transparency norms into technological devices that can translate, for the citizen, what profiling machines are doing should be given priority' (Gutwirth and Hildebrandt 2010: 39). This leads to the model of transparency enhancing technologies (TETs), a counterpart to privacy-enhancing technologies that do not focus on data minimisation but on minimising knowledge asymmetry. TETs basically aim to clarify for individuals how they are being profiled, based on which actions, and how this potentially affects them (Hildebrandt 2008a: 17–18). This could be done *ex ante* (enabling anticipation of profiling practices before data are processed by profilers) or *ex post* (informing about consequences once data have been revealed) (Hildebrandt 2008a: 50). An example of the latter is Amazon's book recommendation service, which sends messages with recommended books based on previous purchases. These messages contain a link to a page called 'improve your recommendations', where you can see which books were used to profile your reading interests, and which allows you to adjust the data used for profiling, for example by unselecting books that were gifts or which you prefer not to be used for future recommendations.

Applying the models to data protection problems

The models sketched in the previous section are ideal types, which in practice occur in many variants and hybrids. Crowdsourced transparency, for example, can use FOIA requests to obtain documents and transparency enhancing technologies are often combined with legal transparency rights. For enhancing downwards transparency in decision-making based on computational data processing, it is therefore useful to explore which combination of models could provide more effective data protection. This can best be done for concrete contexts, because the data protection challenges differ depending on the type of data, data processor and risks to data subjects.

The scope of this chapter does not allow, however, for a comprehensive discussion, which would involve an in-depth analysis of the ins and outs of many concrete contexts. Instead, for illustrative purposes, I will outline some possible ways in which decision transparency could be enhanced in three examples from different sectors: commerce, government services and law enforcement. The yardstick for achieving more transparency follows from our theoretical discussion: we strive for outcome (and not only process) transparency, retrospective transparency in (near) real time for individual cases and, most importantly, effective (and not only nominal) transparency, implying that there be receptors capable of understanding and using the information (as discussed above).

The first example is behavioural advertising: websites showing specific advertisements based on the website visitor's clickstream, search words, zip code or other data that the user has filled in on a web form. Two privacy and due process concerns in behavioural advertising are relevant here. First, it may lead to 'unanticipated encounters' in which consumers are confronted with undesirable or irritating information. This is not generally a serious threat (indeed, with personalised advertising undesirable confrontations may be less than with classic advertising), but it may become a problem if the targeted advertising is based on sensitive data (for example, sexual preference or health-related information) and, for example, 'in a household where multiple users access one computer, it may reveal confidential information about an individual to other members' (Federal Trade Commission 2007: 5). Second, businesses influence the horizon of consumers' interest, which is a form of agenda-setting of their preferences. This might lead to a loss of surprises, of variety, or of side-stepping into new areas of interest (Koops 2010: 1008).

To address these risks, the Federal Trade Commission (FTC) has recommended that every website collecting data for behavioural advertising provide 'a clear, concise, consumer-friendly, and prominent statement that (1) data about consumers' activities online are being collected at the site for use in providing advertising about products and services tailored to individual consumers' interests, and (2) consumers can choose whether or not to have their information collected for such purpose' (Federal Trade Commission 2007: 3).

This is a typically procedural, *ex ante* approach to transparency that risks being nominal rather than effective (for the same reason that privacy statements provide no effective transparency; see above). A more fruitful approach would seem to provide retrospective, event-based transparency by showing a clickable 'profiling flag' each time an advertisement is shown based on profiling. The user, thus alerted, could click the flag to see which data from the consumer were used, and which non-personal group profiles were triggered by those data, for the specific advertisement to be selected; Amazon's link to an 'improve your recommendations' page is an example of such a profiling flag. It is true that such a flag would not help in the case of a spouse being shown an advertisement based on his wife's earlier browsing for *The Joy of Lesbian Sex* – on the contrary, it could reveal more embarrassing information than if the profiling logic had remained opaque. However, in a system where behavioural advertisements are consistently flagged, people are probably much more aware of profiling systems using behavioural data, and hence would sooner use privacy-preserving technologies in case they do not want specific digital traces to emerge in future advertisements. This requires the availability and low-threshold usability of privacy-preserving tools such as an opt-out button on websites collecting behavioural data. An alternative option to prevent embarrassing advertisements from showing up could be to make behavioural profiling and advertising more transparent to other observers, such as supervisory authorities (for example, FTCs) or consumer associations, which could periodically scrutinise the profiling system to see whether sensitive data (such as sexual or health-related data) are being processed and, if so, make recommendations to prevent these from being used in personalised advertisements. In short, a combination of technological transparency tools (event-based flags and pages showing the data underlying behavioural advertisements) and corporate transparency legislation could make it clearer to web users when and why they are shown personalised advertising, which decreases the risks of embarrassments or horizon-closing agenda-setting for consumer interests. And, legally to reinforce the spreading of sunlight to more receptors, the logic-explaining obligation of Article 12(a) DPD could be extended from a user-triggered access right to a provider-focused information duty, so that businesses will not passively wait until consumers ask for logic, but actively have to show logic in each decision based on profiling. Some elements of this approach can be discerned in the proposed Article 20(4) of the GDPR, in controllers having to inform subjects of the existence of profiling-based automated decisions, but this is only a first step in the right direction: besides the limitations, noted above, in the scope of this provision, in its current form Article 20(4) refers to an *ex ante* obligation in the stage of data collection rather than a *ex post* obligation in the stage of taking concrete decisions.

A second example is government licensing, for example municipalities providing a licence for merchants to sell goods on the street on the occasion of a festivity. In current society, licensing increasingly relies on risk assessments, aiming to minimise possible threats to public security, and these risk assessments rely on mining databases from multiple sources, such as financial, social security, health and safety, and police records. Suppose that a head of state is visiting the festivity and that security services require a 'risk-free' zone of one kilometre around the VIP's trajectory. A Greek restaurant owner is surprised, and dismayed, that he is denied a licence for selling his food on the street. Due process requires that he knows the reason underlying the decision, so that he can challenge it if he thinks it unfair. But the authorities only tell him that his restaurant lies within the one kilometre zone and that he is considered a security risk based on their risk assessment. Here, decision transparency needs to enter the equation, in the form of understanding which data and which weight factors were responsible for the outcome. It may be undesirable that the entire process of the risk assessment is made transparent to individual applicants (as that could allow people with bad intentions to try to trump the data mining process by data obfuscation). How could transparency be enhanced otherwise?

One option is that the municipality reverse engineer the data mining and identify the 'guilty' piece(s) of data in the sources used and inform the applicant of these specific data; if it turns out, for example, that the decision was ultimately based on the criminal record of a conviction 20 years ago for possessing drugs, then the restaurant owner could challenge the decision in appeal, arguing that drug possession (moreover, in the distant past) is not a concrete security risk for the VIP's visit, and the decision could then be revised. This option requires that the system used for risk assessment is sufficiently transparent for its users, which may be the case for relatively simple analyses of multiple databases, but may be less so if advanced self-learning algorithms calculate risks based on complex combinations of factors. For the last cases, an alternative option is required, for example that independent third parties, such as government accountability offices, are given access to the risk-profiling system in periodic audits, hopefully allowing them to uncover the logic behind risk assessments so that they can explain how, in general, different types of datum from different kinds of source influence the outcome of decisions. This would provide another type of checks and balances on the fairness of profiling-based decisions. Thus, decision transparency in government licensing could be effected, first, by a legal obligation to inform the applicant that the decision was based on profiling and allowing the applicant to request information about the logic involved in the profiling and, second, by architectural safeguards in risk assessment systems that aim at making the profiling more transparent, for example by marking in which proportion the outcome was influenced by data from each data source fed into the system and marking data in those sources that were used in consecutive steps when the profiling algorithm was run. Periodic independent audits could supplement the accountability of the decision-making process. Whether these approaches would really work in practice remains to be studied, of course, and one can imagine that transparency measures would be resisted by authorities particularly in licensing decisions that touch upon public order and security. If that is the case, then merchants being denied licences could start a website asking the crowd to counter-profile the authorities responsible for licensing decisions or maintaining public order during the festivity. As likely as not, someone may find that some official who will shake the VIP's hand consumed drugs in the 1970s, or that a police horse at a previous festivity kicked someone into hospital when scared by a champagne bottle being uncorked. Publishing these findings, the merchants could raise a public debate on what exactly constitutes a risk to public order, which ultimately could incentivise the municipality to reverse some decisions if it cannot pinpoint and substantiate a clear risk for individual merchants.

A third example concerns the use of automatic number plate recognition (ANPR) for law enforcement purposes. ANPR uses cameras automatically to recognise number plates of passing vehicles. It is increasingly used in a generic way to monitor and store data about road traffic, for multiple purposes, for example to track stolen cars or number plate holders with unpaid fines or arrest warrants, but also as an intelligence source in case of crime investigation (Clarke 2010). This use of comprehensive law enforcement data mining fits well in the current logic of intelligence-led policing (Harcourt 2007). It presents different privacy and due process risks, however, from the previous example (where a clear and specific decision was involved, that is, granting or denying a licence) and the risks also differ from those in classic policing. Rather than focusing on prosecution, with the overarching risk of being wrongly convicted on the basis of faulty evidence, intelligence-led policing is not primarily targeted at conviction but at other, pre-emptive types of intervention, which involves vaguer, smaller and less definable risks (Koops 2009; Murphy 2008). For example, ANPR can be used to identify 'suspicious' car movements, based on profiles of drug traders or armed robbers, and then obstruct or subtly hinder the driver by stopping the car several times in purported road traffic controls. ANPR can also be used as intelligence in murder investigations, for instance to flag cars that were in the vicinity of the crime scene at the material time. In both cases, false negatives can cause nuisance or some harm to individuals, not in the sense that they risk being imprisoned on the basis of ANPR records, but in the sense of, for example, having to explain what they were doing then and there – to the police but possibly also to their spouses. Drivers could also be cast in a negative light when the police make enquiries with third parties, such as employers or neighbours, to find possible further clues about the licence plate holder.

Because of the multiple and indeterminate ways in which road vehicle movement data feed back into intelligence-led policing, it is more difficult here to provide for decision transparency than in the previous examples. There is, after all, not always a clear decision, but rather a blend of intelligence that 'led' the police onwards in some directions rather than others. Moreover, law enforcement, particularly in its early stages of investigation, is typically covert in nature. Nevertheless, upwards transparency should be improved in order to provide for due process, particularly because the classic checks and balances in criminal law are not tailored to these situations (Koops 2009; Murphy 2008). We should distinguish between situations in which a concrete police or judicial action is clearly based on ANPR data, and situations in which the connection between ANPR and actions is less clear. For the former type, similar measures could be taken as in the case of the Greek restaurant owner's licence decision, in that the driver or licence plate holder should be informed that his car was stopped or that his employer was interviewed on the basis of data mining that included ANPR data. This is feasible to do on the spot in the case of pre-emptive actions, such as taking a car from the road, but may be less feasible or desirable in the case of investigative actions where secrecy is required. In the latter cases, transparency should be provided more downstream, for example in a case file if it leads to prosecution, or in a notification to the individual once the investigation is suspended. Legislation already provides for similar notification duties in the case of covert surveillance, but experience shows that these are often not executed in practice (Beijer et al 2004: 145–47), for practical reasons but also perhaps because of an intrinsic resistance among police to openness. A more effective method may therefore be to look at other capable receptors than the individuals affected, such as independent supervisors. For example, the British Chief Surveillance Commissioner is authorised to audit the practice of the Regulation of Investigatory Powers Act 2000, which includes investigating a sample survey of concrete cases and publishing annual reports on the findings.[12] This does not provide transparency in each individual case, but rather a strong form of periodic *ex post* transparency, which may be the next best thing given the intrinsic difficulties of establishing real time individual transparency in intelligence-led policing. Independent auditing also seems an appropriate measure for effecting transparency in the second type of situations, in which the connection between ANPR and police or judicial actions is less clear, because in those situations it is almost impossible to provide case-by-case transparency as to which data contributed in which ways for specific decisions.

Nevertheless, some form of individual ex post transparency should be effected somehow, because generic auditing provides only general checks and balances that may not have any effect in relevant individual cases. Imagine, for example, that a particular car is flagged down based on ANPR data associated with a murder investigation. After investigating this lead further, by checking the licence plate holder's credentials and matching her personal details with other data from the investigation, the police decides not to follow up this lead as it has a low likelihood of success. However, the data are retained, because it cannot be definitively excluded that this car was involved in the murder. The data could then spread to other police databases, without the context of the initial investigation and the case-specific knowledge of the police officials. (Note that, in the United States alone, there are 2000 police databases, according to Murphy (2010); in Europe, the number will not be much lower, while there is also an increasing exchange of law enforcement data based on the principle of availability.)[13] This could well lead to future harm or nuisance to the licence plate holder, if she is involved in other investigations based on profiling in which the initial vehicle data are somehow used, in ways difficult to foresee. If she is interviewed by the police, or her car is stopped surprisingly often in road traffic controls, due process requires that somehow she be enabled to trace back her involvement to the initial ANPR flag and argue that she had nothing to do with that old murder case, and that she can have her record cleaned by removing the data from all police databases. This is particularly challenging to achieve (cf Nationale ombudsman 2009: about a Dutch victim of identity theft who could not have himself removed from police databases; Murphy 2010). Legal access rights and audit measures can do little to address this issue by themselves. To enable at least some form of transparency, technical measures will be required that flag ANPR (and other intelligence-led policing) data with meta data that allow them to be followed during their lifetime in police databases, similar to sticky policies in data protecting PETs (Karjoth et al 2002).

Conclusion

The computational turn of the 21st century implies large-scale, complex and multi-purpose forms of matching and mining zettabytes of data. I have argued that this fundamentally challenges the approach to data protection, given the limitations of the current data protection framework in practice, where purpose limitation, data minimisation, accountability, data security and the ideal of user involvement have little thrust in practice. As the pillars supporting the data protection framework are eroding, we need new approaches if we are to achieve real data protection in practice rather than merely on paper. In this chapter, I have discussed decision transparency as one such approach of enhancing data protection in the database age.

With the help of David Heald's directions and dimensions of transparency, we can see that the relationship between data processing organisations and individuals needs to be adjusted by recalibrating vertical transparency. This implies a dual strategy: first, diminishing upwards transparency, through shielding and obfuscating data and, second, enhancing downwards transparency, through introducing mechanisms for outcome (and not only process) transparency, retrospective transparency in (near) real time for individual cases and, most importantly, effective (and not only nominal) transparency. This requires receptors who are capable of understanding transparency information and who are able to use it.

Increasing downwards transparency can be achieved in a number of ways. We can draw inspiration from existing models in legislation, such as Freedom of Information and Sunshine Acts, product-labelling obligations and the Data

Protection Directive's requirement of providing the logic behind automated decisions; in social practices, such as sousveillance and crowdsourced transparency initiatives in web 2.0; and in architecture, with transparency enhancing technologies. A combination of such measures is likely to be required to address privacy and due process risks by enhanced transparency. As illustrated by examples from the fields of commerce, government service provisioning and law enforcement, capable receptors for transparency information can be found both among individuals affected by decisions and among supervisory authorities or other third parties. Since individuals do not always have the means to understand or act upon information, and in some contexts such as law enforcement individual transparency can be undesirable, there is a clear role for supervisors to supplement the transparency framework, in the form of independent audits and monitoring of data mining processes. The examples also suggest that legal rights and duties to establish and enforce decision transparency are not sufficient; technical measures are almost always needed in order for data to be traceable along the complex computational paths they take in data mining processes. And if the combination of legal and technical measures is not sufficient in concrete situations, people might take recourse to technology-facilitated social measures of transparency: sousveillance and web 2.0-enabled scrutiny of governmental and corporate decision-making. How exactly these measures could or should look like in actual practice is a matter for further analysis; I have attempted here only to provide a line of argument along which decision transparency can be further studied and developed.

Decision transparency in the form of increasing downwards transparency in decision-making is not inconsistent with the mainstream approach to data protection. Indeed, as illustrated in the example of behavioural advertising, transparency can only really help to protect individuals if they are empowered to control their data in some way. However, there is a significant difference in focus between decision transparency and the orthodox approach to data protection that is based on data minimisation and user involvement. As the computational turn erodes the capacity of individuals to control data that are being used in myriad ways, our focus should shift along with the computation towards the outcome: the decision rather than the process leading up to it. Investing in user control and procedural accountability for data processors, as the current revision[14] of the Data Protection Directive advocates (Reding 2011), is an appealing ideal but also has a flavour of fighting last century's battle. If we look ahead to the age after the computational turn, I would rather put my money on enhancing decision transparency, with a smart mix of legal and technical transparency measures, than on enhancing user control with a focus on privacy-enhancing technologies. In the 21st century, with its computational turn, data protection can no longer reside in the exclusive realm of informational privacy and self-determination; rather, it must be approached from the angle of due process and fair treatment in the database age. A focus on decision transparency has good potential to achieve just that.

Notes

1 Directive 95/46/EC [1995] OJ L281/31 of 24 October 1995.
2 See the basic principles of national application in the OECD Guidelines on the Protection of Privacy and Transborder Flows of Personal Data, 1980, http://www.oecd.org/document/53/0,3746,en_2649_34255_15589524_1_1_1_1,00.html (accessed 1 September 2012).
3 I will leave aside the problem of transnational data flows, which complicate matters even further. For the purposes of this chapter, the problems intrinsic to data protection within a jurisdiction suffice to illustrate my argument.
4 Proposal for a General Data Protection Regulation COM(2012) 11 final of 25 January 2012 http://ec.europa.eu/justice/data-protection/document/review2012/com_2012_11_en.pdf (accessed 1 September 2012).
5 Two definitions of 'transparent' in the Oxford English Dictionary.
6 Which is not to say that horizontal transparency is irrelevant; particularly in the context of web 2.0, where internet users upload information also about other people and may become data controllers themselves, effecting data protection is an important issue. In order not to complicate my argument in this chapter too much, I leave this issue aside.
7 5 USC 552b under (b) and (a)(2), respectively.
8 5 USC 552b(c)(9)(B).
9 15 USC §7262(a)(2).
10 Regulation (EC) 1907/2006 [2006] OJ L396 arts 118–119.
11 http://de.guttenplag.wikia.com/ (accessed 1 September 2012).
12 Regulation of Investigatory Powers Act 2000 ss 62–63.
13 See Framework Decision 2006/960/JHA of 18 December 2006 on simplifying the exchange of information and intelligence between law enforcement authorities of the Member States of the European Union [2006] OJ L386/89 of 29 December 2006.
14 Note 4.

References

Anderson, C. (2006) *The Long Tail: Why the future of business is selling less of more*, New York: Hyperion.
Anderson, C. (2009) *Free: The future of a radical price*, New York: Hyperion.
Bailey, D. (2004) *The Open Society Paradox: Why the 21st century calls for more openness – not less*, Washington, DC: Brassey's.
Beijer, A., Bokhorst, R. J., Boone, M., Brants, C. H. and Lindeman, J. M. W. (2004) *De Wet bijzondere opsporingsbevoegdheden – eindevaluatie*, Meppel: WODC/Boom Juridische uitgevers.
Bennett, C. J. (2008) *The Privacy Advocates: Resisting the spread of surveillance*, Cambridge, MA: MIT Press.
boyd, d. (2010) *The Future of Privacy: How privacy norms can inform regulation*. International Conference of Data Protection and Privacy Commissioners, Jerusalem.
Brin, D. (1998) *The Transparent Society: Will technology force us to choose between privacy and freedom?*, Reading, MA: Perseus Books.

Brownsword, R. (2008) *Rights, Regulation, and the Technological Revolution*, Oxford and New York: Oxford University Press.

Castells, M. (1996) *The Rise of the Network Society*, Malden, MA: Blackwell Publishers.

Clarke, R. (2010) *The Covert Implementation of Mass Vehicle Surveillance in Australia*, Wollongong, NSW, University of Wollongong Press: 47–61.

Council of Europe (2011) *Modernisation of Convention 108: Give us your opinion!*, Council of Europe.

Curry, M. R., Phillips, D. J. and Regan, P. M. (2004) 'Emergency Response Systems and the Creeping Legibility of People and Places', *Information Society* 20: 357–69.

European Commission (2010) *A Comprehensive Approach on Personal Data Protection in the European Union*, Brussels: European Commission.

Federal Trade Commission (2007) *Online Behavioral Advertising: Moving the discussion forward to possible self-regulatory principles*, Washington, DC, FTC.

Furedi, F. (2006) *Culture of Fear Revisited. Risk-taking and the Morality of Low Expectation*, London and New York: Continuum.

Ganascia, J.-G. (2010) 'The Generalized Sousveillance Society', *Social Science Information* 49: 489–507.

Garfinkel, S. (1999) *Database Nation. The death of privacy in the 21st century*, Cambridge: O'Reilly.

Garland, D. (2001) *The Culture of Control: Crime and social order in contemporary society*, Chicago: University of Chicago Press.

Gutwirth, S. and de Hert, P. (2008) 'Regulating Profiling in a Democratic Constitutional State', in Hildebrandt, M. and Gutwirth, S. (eds) *Profiling the European Citizen*, Springer, 271–93.

Gutwirth, S. and Hildebrandt, M. (2010) 'Some Caveats on Profiling', in Gutwirth, S., Poullet, Y. and de Hert, P. (eds) *Data Protection in a Profiled World*, Dordrecht: Springer, 31–41.

Harcourt, B. E. (2007) *Against Prediction: Profiling, policing, and punishing in an actuarial age*, Chicago: University of Chicago Press.

Heald, D. (2006) 'Varieties of Transparency', in Hood, C. and Heald, D. (eds) *Transparency. The key to better governance?*, Oxford: Oxford University Press, 25–43.

Hildebrandt, M. (ed.) (2008a) *D7.12: Behavioural Biometric Profiling and Transparency Enhancing Tools*. Frankfurt: FIDIS.

Hildebrandt, M. (2008b) 'Profiling and the Identity of the European Citizen', in Hildebrandt, M. and Gutwirth, S. (eds) *Profiling the European Citizen*: Springer, 303–26.

Hildebrandt, M. (2008c) 'A Vision of Ambient Law', in R. Brownsword and K. Yeung (eds) *Regulating Technologies*, Oxford: Hart Publishing, 175–91.

Hildebrandt, M. (2012) 'The Dawn of a Critical Transparency Right for the Profiling Era', in Bus, J., Crompton, M., Hildebrandt, M. and Metakides, G. (eds) *Digital Enlightenment Yearbook 2012*, Amsterdam, IOS press 41–56.

Hildebrandt, M. and Gutwirth, S. (eds) (2008) *Profiling the European Citizen. Cross-disciplinary perspectives*, Springer.

Hood, C. and Heald, D. (2006) *Transparency: The key to better governance?*, Oxford and New York: Oxford University Press.

House of Commons Home Affairs Committee (2008) *A Surveillance Society?* London: House of Commons: 117.

IDC (2010) 'The Digital Universe Decade', available at http://www.emc.com/collat eral/demos/microsites/idc-digital-universe/iview.htm (accessed 1 September 2012).

Karjoth, G., Schunter, M. and Waidner, M. (2002) *Platform for Enterprise Privacy Practices: Privacy-enabled management of customer data*, London: Springer Verlag.

Kohnstamm, J. and Dubbeld, L. (2007) 'Glazen samenleving in zicht', *Nederlands Juristenblad* 82: 2369–75.

Koops, B. J. (2009) 'Technology and the Crime Society: Rethinking legal protection', *Law, Innovation & Technology* 1: 93–124.

Koops, B. J. (2010) 'Law, Technology, and Shifting Power Relations', *Berkeley Technology Law Journal* 25: 973–1035.

Koops, B. J. (2011) 'The Evolution of Privacy Law and Policy in the Netherlands', *Journal of Comparative Policy Analysis* 13: 165–79.

Koops, B. J. and Leenes, R. (2005) '"Code" and the Slow Erosion of Privacy', *Michigan Telecommunications & Technology Law Review* 12: 115–88.

Leenes, R. (2008) 'Addressing the Obscurity of Data Clouds', in Hildebrandt, M. and Gutwirth, S. (eds) *Profiling the European Citizen*, Springer, 293–300.

Lessig, L. (1999a) *Code and Other Laws of Cyberspace*, New York: Basic Books.

Lessig, L. (1999b) 'The Law of the Horse: What cyberlaw might teach', *Harvard Law Review* 113: 501–46.

Mann, S., Fung, J. and Lo, R. (2006) *Cyborglogging with Camera Phones: Steps toward equiveillance*. Santa Barbara, CA: ACM: 177–80.

Mann, S., Nolan, J. and Wellman, B. (2005) 'Sousveillance: Inventing and using wearable computing devices for data collection in surveillance environments', *Surveillance & Society* 1: 331–55.

Mason, M. (2008) *The Pirate's Dilemma: How youth culture reinvented capitalism*, New York: Free Press.

Mayer-Schönberger, V. (2009) *Delete: The virtue of forgetting in the digital age*, Princeton: Princeton University Press.

Murakami Wood, D. (ed.) (2006) *A Report on the Surveillance Society. For the information commissioner by the surveillance studies network*, Wilmslow: Office of the Information Commissioner, available at http://www.ico.gov.uk/upload/docu ments/library/ data_protection/practical_application/surveillance_society_full_report_2006.pdf (accessed 1 September 2012).

Murphy, E. (2008) 'Paradigms of Restraint', *Duke Law Journal* 57: 101–91.

Murphy, E. (2010) 'Databases, Doctrine & Constitutional Criminal Procedure', *Fordham Urban Law Journal* 37: 803.

Nationale ombudsman (2009) *Herzien Openbaar rapport, verzoekschrift van de heer K.*, Den Haag: De Nationale ombudsman.

Nissenbaum, H. (2010) *Privacy in Context*, Stanford, CA, Stanford Law Books.

Poullet, Y. (2006) 'The Directive 95/46/EC: Ten years after', *Computer Law and Security Report* 22: 206–217.

Purtova, N. (2011) *Property Rights in Personal Data: A European perspective*. Tilburg: Tilburg University, PhD thesis.

Reding, V. (2011) 'The Upcoming Data Protection Reform for the European Union', *International Data Privacy Law* 1: 3–5.

Renn, O. (2008) *Risk Governance: Coping with uncertainty in a complex world*, London and Sterling, VA: Earthscan.

Robinson, N., Graux, H., Botterman, M. and Valeri, L. (2009) *Review of the European Data Protection Directive*, Santa Monica, CA: RAND.

Schermer, B. and Wagemans, T. (2009) *Onze digitale schaduw. Een verkennend onderzoek naar het aantal databases waarin de gemiddelde Nederlander geregistreerd staat*. Amsterdam: Considerati.

Sluijs, J. P., Schuett, F. and Henze, B. (2011) 'Transparency Regulation in Broadband Markets: Lessons from experimental research', *Telecommunications Policy* 35: 592–602.

Solove, D. J. (2004) *The Digital Person: Technology and privacy in the information age*, New York: New York University Press.

Sykes, C. J. (1999) *The End of Privacy*, New York: St Martin's Press.

9

Profile transparency by design? Re-enabling double contingency

Mireille Hildebrandt

Introduction

The technologies of machine learning render us transparent in a rather counterintuitive manner. We become *transparent* in the sense that the profiling software looks straight *through us* to 'what we are like', instead of making transparent 'what or who we are'. This reminds me of a cartoon that shows a couple, sitting up in bed – after the act – confronted with a voice-over that proclaims: 'I'm glad you enjoyed that. People who like that technique also enjoyed these other sexual techniques: …'.[1] It is interesting to note that the couple – who may have felt they had just had a unique experience – is brought down to earth with a reminder of the repetitive nature of human interaction. They are reduced to being like many others and invited to explore the consolidated repertoire of those who are like them. In machine learning jargon the couple is mapped to its 'nearest neighbours' and even if their 'k-anonymity' prevents their unique identification, they are machine readable in terms of their likeness to a 'cluster' of other couples.

Privacy advocates often focus on unique identification as the main attack on our privacy. Data minimisation and anonymity are often depicted as the prevalent strategies to protect what is understood to be the core of privacy: the need not to be singled out, not to be recognised as the unique individual person we hope to be. So-called user-centric identity management systems are developed to allow people to maintain contextual integrity, to restrict information flows within specific contexts and to manage the set of different roles they play in different environments such as work, leisure, home, school, sport, entertainment, shopping, health care and so on. The holy grail of this version of contextual integrity is unlinkability, a notion that refers to techniques that should disable cross-contextual aggregation of individual profiles. In line with this, user-centric identity management refers to the use of credentials or attributes instead of full identification, which means that access to specific services is gained by merely disclosing the relevant attribute of a person (for example, being over 18 years old, being female, being an employee, having paid for the service).

In the meantime, reality presents us with an incentive structure that encourages business models that thrive on *consent* to override the purpose limitation principle,[2] or on *anonymisation* that renders most of data protection legislation inapplicable.[3] Together, uninformed consent and anonymisation facilitate continuous and persistent interpenetration of contexts, enabling smart infrastructures to develop fascinating cross-contextual profiles of consumers and citizens, often creating new types of knowledge of cross-contextual behaviour. In an elucidating text Massiello and Whitten (2010) consider the high potential of function creep; they celebrate the reuse of data for unforeseen purposes that creates unexpected added value. This is assumed to create a win–win situation. Consumers find their desires satisfied before they become aware of them and advertising networks charge advertisers for the most precious scarce good of the information-driven society: human attention.

As indicated in the title, this volume seeks to flesh out the impact of data science on privacy and due process. In this chapter, I will focus on due process, understood in the broad sense of the effective capability to contest decisions that have a significant impact on one's life. To contest such decisions, a person must be aware of them and be able to foresee their impact. In that sense, due process seems to require transparency and/or knowledge symmetry. The research questions for this chapter are, first, how the application of data science challenges such transparency and, second, how we can reinvent it with regard to the proliferating machine-generated profiles that have an increasing influence on our lives.

In the following section, I will introduce the Deleuzian concepts of derealisation and virtualisation to elucidate what it is that profilers construct when they create large 'populations' of anonymous profiles that can be applied to large populations of individual human beings. Next, I will continue this line of thought and add the Deleuzian concept of the dividual, aligned with terms from the domain of computer science: data, data models, attributes, characteristics and properties. This should help to prepare the ground for an answer to the question of whether data science practices in the field of commerce and law enforcement afford virtualisation or merely derealisation. I then explore the notions of transparency and enlightenment, connecting them to Parsons's and Luhmann's concept of double contingency. This regards the double and mutual anticipation that is constitutive for self, mind and society. The concept refers to the fundamental uncertainty that rules human communication, creating the possibility for new meaning amidst inevitable but productive misunderstandings. It also refers to the need for socio-technical infrastructures that stabilise meaning among individual minds, notably language, writing, the printing press, hyperlinked digitisation and, finally, the hidden complexity of computational decision systems. I will engage with Stiegler's notion of tertiary retention and the need to reinvent what he terms 'introjection' in the digital age. He introduces these notions in a plea for a new enlightenment that should inform a new rule of law. Finally, I will argue that renegotiating a novel double contingency will require profile transparency at the level of the digital infrastructure. I conclude with a brief sketch of what this could mean, taking into account that transparency can never be complete. The Renaissance painting techniques of the *clair-obscur* provide a salient background for a discussion of the balance between knowledge requirements and our bounded rationality.

Through the looking glass: derealisation or virtualisation?

Data science can be seen as a derivative of *Artificial Intelligence: A modern approach* (AIMO, see Russell and Norvig 2009). It generates non-trivial information on the basis of statistical inferences mined from what has been called 'big data'. Some would claim that machines have 'come of age', generating types of pattern-recognition way beyond 'good old fashioned artificial intelligence' (GOFAI).[4] Inductive learning, bottom-up algorithms, contextual awareness and feedback mechanisms all contribute to a novel type of transparency, an invisible kind of visibility (Hildebrandt 2009), based on a continuous, pervasive, seamless stream of comparisons. Individuals are thereby represented as an assemblage of different roles that cut across large 'populations' of similar roles. The term population refers to a concept within the domain of statistics, where it denotes the complete set of phenomena that are under investigation, of which only a sample can be examined in detail. Statistics contains the rules along which the outcome of the study of the sample can be extrapolated or generalised to the entire set, the population. Data science seems to allow operations on a subset of a population that is far more extensive than a sample. Together with the mathematical complexity of the operations that can be performed by current computing systems, data science is capable of generating types of pattern recognition far beyond the reach of earlier statistical inference. In fact, unsupervised learning algorithms can generate, test and adapt hypotheses instead of merely confirming or refuting them. This is why Anderson (2008) spoke of the end of theory: he asserted that machine learning will soon be better at constructing and fine-tuning hypotheses than human beings will ever be. This is made possible by the fact that data mining operations are capable of working on unprecedented populations of data, creating what Amoore (2011) has coined 'data derivatives' that easily turn into new populations: resources for further research. Note that we are now speaking of generations of populations: starting from the original flux of lifeworld phenomena, followed by their translation into machine readable data models, followed by the inferred profiles (data derivatives), followed by the inferences that build on these first generation derivatives (constituting second generation derivatives). The original phenomena as framed by the mind of whoever designed the research is the first generation population, their translation into discrete data models is the second generation population, the first set of inferences is the third generation population and so on. The interesting and pertinent question is how fourth or fifth generation 'populations' connect with the first. And, of course, how all this connects with the population that constitutes human society.

In the present infosphere, the plethora of machine readable profiles do not offer the individuals to whom such profiles are applied a looking glass (that is, a mirror), where they can see how they are being matched against inferred profiles. Instead these profiles provide the company or authority who paid for the software with a way to reach out behind *their* looking glass, gazing straight through our condensed selves into the disentangled sets of 'similars', showing a maze of association rules that link us with – statistically – relevant lifestyles, demographic or geographic types, health risks or earning capacities. Just like in the famous story of *Through the Looking Glass, and What Alice Found There* (Carroll 1999), 'profiling machines' (Elmer 2003) open up an alternative world, basically consisting of simulations of our future states or behaviours. Profiling machines or 'inference engines'[5] thus function as a looking glass that provides an opportunity to peek into this alternative world. This enables the industry to calculate what profits can be gained from catering to consumers' inferred preferences, and similarly enables public authorities to calculate what types of offences may be committed where, when and possibly by whom – for example, social security fraud.

In principle, profiling systems could function as virtualisation machines in the sense of Deleuze's (1994) conceptualisation of the virtual.[6] To clarify what he means with the virtual I will build on the work of cyber-philosopher Lévy (2005, 1998), who elaborated Deleuze's notion of virtualisation for the digital age. Deleuze understands the *virtual* in relation to what he calls the *actual*, and opposes this pair to that of what he calls the *possible* and the *real*. For Deleuze, what is real is what exists. However, the real has two modes of existence: the virtual and the actual. His use of the terms of virtual/actual and possible/real may not be congruent with our common sense, but he derives them from an imaginative reconstruction of our philosophical tradition, thus shedding light on phenomena that our current common sense may not grasp. While drawing on medieval philosophy Deleuze re-engineers philosophical concepts, to provide the conceptual tools needed in the era of data derivatives (Lévy 1998: 23):

> The word 'virtual' is derived from the Medieval Latin *virtualis*, itself derived from *virtus*, meaning strength or power. In scholastic philosophy the virtual is that which has potential rather than actual existence. The virtual *tends* towards actualization, without undergoing any form of effective or formal concretization. The tree is virtually present in the seed. Strictly speaking, the virtual should not be compared with the real but the actual, for virtuality and actuality are merely two different ways of being.

There is – according to this particular understanding of the virtual – a crucial difference between the possible and the virtual (Lévy 1998: 24):

> The possible is already fully constituted, but exists in a state of limbo. It can be realized without any change occurring either in its determination or nature. It is a phantom reality, something latent. The possibility is exactly like the real, the only thing missing being existence. The realization of a possible is not an act of creation, in the fullest sense of the word, for creation implies the innovative production of an idea or a form. The difference between possible and real is thus purely logical.

The virtual, therefore, should not be compared to the real (since it is already real), but to the actual. Back to the seed (ibid):

> The seed's problem, for example, is the growth of the tree. The seed is this problem, even if it is also something more than that. This does not signify that the seed knows exactly what the shape of the tree will be, which will one day burst into bloom and spread its leaves above it. Based on its internal limitations, the seed will have to invent the tree, coproduce it together with the circumstances it encounters.

This implies that actualisation can be understood as the solution to a problem – a solution, however, that is never entirely determined by that problem since it requires a co-creation with its not entirely predictable environment. Whereas realisation is the *predetermined* concretisation of a possible (for example, execution of a computer program), actualisation is the production of a solution to a problem that entails a measure of uncertainty (neural networks hosting unsupervised algorithms?). In respect of data derivatives, the more interesting transition is the reversal of actualisation: virtualisation. Whereas 'actualization proceeds from problem to solution, virtualization proceeds from a given solution to a (different) problem' (Lévy 1998: 27). This move generates the generic set of problems that gave rise to the particular solution, and creates room for alternative solutions. Note that, for Deleuze, virtualisation is not a matter of derealisation. The art of virtualisation is to stick to the realm of the real, to resist moving back to a predefined set of possibilities that merely lack reality. Derealisation severely restricts the kinds of solution that can be generated, because it remains in the realm of necessity and mechanical application. By way of contrast, 'virtualization is one of the principle vectors in the creation of reality' (Lévy 1998: 27): by shifting from concrete solutions to virtual problems we create the precondition for novel acts of creation, generated in the course of novel types of actualisation.

The question at stake in this chapter is how we should understand the virtual machines,[7] inference engines or profiling technologies that 'look through' our selves at myriad potentially similar states or entities. Are they machines of virtualisation in the sense of Deleuze or machines of what he terms dereali-sation? Do they provide a range of overdetermined possibilities (in Deleuze's sense) or do they provide sets of virtuals that allow for novel, underdeter-mined actualisations? Is data science a science of derealisation or an art of virtualisation? If these machineries merely present us with endless variations of what is already present (derealisation) we may be strangled in the golden cage of our inferred preferences. If data science, however, triggers pools of unexpected similarities that evoke and provoke unprecedented articulations of self and other – we may be the lucky heirs to an extended domain of co-creation. In that case, the question becomes: who is cultivating this extended domain and who gets to pick its fruits?

Dividuals and attributes: possibles or virtuals?

From individual to dividual – and back?

There is a fascinating indifference with regard to individual persons in machine learning and other profiling technologies, summed up by Rouvroy (2011) under the heading of the 'statistical governance of the real'. Individuals seem to count only as a resource of data or as a locus of application; in a sense the individual has finally become what Deleuze (1992) famously coined an assemblage of 'dividuals'. As explained when discussing the concept of popu-lation, the aggregate that forms the basis of knowledge construction is not a mass of people but a 'bank' of assorted data, correlated in numerous ways by a variety of techniques. These data do not concern *in*dividuals, they are not necessarily meant to identify a unique person. Rather, they allow their mas-ters to connect the dots, generating a plethora of permutations and combina-tions (Deleuze 1992):

> We no longer find ourselves dealing with the mass/individual pair. Individuals have become 'dividuals,' and masses, samples, data, markets, or 'banks'.

The focal point of data science is not the indivisible person as the smallest unit in various types of populations: the individable *in*dividual. The focal point is the multiplicity of machine readable attributes used to assemble the various types of units that compose a variety of populations that are not necessarily 'made up' of people. Populations may for instance be populated with hair colour types, employment segments, health risks, security threats or other units of comparison. This, however, does not mean that the profiles mined from such data aggregates will not be applied to individual human persons.

In the Netherlands, a producer of adult diapers telephoned people on behalf of its pharmacy to inquire after their urine loss. Based on these inquiries, people were categorised as fitting various 'user profiles', which would be employed to decide on the compensation paid for incontinence diapers by their insurance company, which had asked the pharmacies for categorisation. The uproar this caused led to an immediate termination of the policy, with the Minister for Healthcare speaking out against commercial companies thus gaining access to sensitive data. The insurance company quoted the need to reduce costs as a reason for the construction of user profiles that determine the attribution of compensation (Pinedo 2012). We may guess that at some point the quantifiable level of incontinence can be inferred from the fusion of various databases, or from information gleaned from medically prescribed applications even if these were originally dedicated to other purposes,[8] creating dividuals depicting incontinence probability. Once this is possible, nobody has to phone patients or clients to remind them of their problem, and some would claim that the automation of profiling is therefore less invasive, while also more objective than human assessment. To the extent that such granular profiling informs automated or semi-automated decision systems we may have to learn to live with an extended family of dividuals that co-determine how government agencies, companies, health insurance and public utility providers 'read' us. These dividuals are not of our own making; we do not choose them and are hardly aware of their 'existence'. They are virtual in the common sense of not-physical or abstract; they depict the kind of profiles we fit at the level of statistical inferences and to the extent that they involve mechanical application dividuals seem to stand for derealisation in the sense of Deleuze's genealogy of the real. They form abstractions of an individual, based on the match between some of her attributes with profiles inferred from masses of attributes from masses of individuals. Profiling thus transforms the original 'mass' that is composed of a mass of 'individuals', into an aggregate of attributes that cut across and divide the *in*dividuals into their elements, characteristics, properties or attributes. As explained, these elements or properties are not given; they are *attributed* by whoever writes the algorithms of data analytics, taking into account that whatever dividuals are sought after they must be inferred from machine readable data by machine-readable algorithms.

To investigate whether – or in which types of case – the computerised gaze through the looking glass is a matter of derealisation or an act of virtualisation, we need to look into the subtle negotiations that determine the attributes filling the databases. We must take into account that such databases are often seen as equivalent with the population of statistical inferences. It is tempting to assume that 'big data' mining does not work with samples but with – nearly – complete populations, and this reinforces the assumption that inferred predictions are accurate, precisely because all data have been taken into account. This, however, is an illusion, as any machine learning expert can explain. The term 'attribute' is salient here, because it highlights the performative act of negotiating the types of data that will fill the databases, data servers and cloud computing systems on which data mining operations run. To demonstrate this point it is instructive to check the Wikipedia entries for the term 'attribute'. Wikipedia distinguishes between an attribute in research, philosophy, art, linguistics and computer science (Wikipedia contributors 2012a). In research, it qualifies an attribute as a characteristic of an object that can be operationalised by giving it a certain value (for example, yes/no, or blue/red/green/yellow or 1, 2, 3, 4) to allow for further data processing. Similarly, Wikipedia (Wikipedia contributors 2012b) qualifies a property in modern philosophy, logic and mathematics as an attribute (a quality) of an object, while this attribute may be considered an object in its own right, having various properties of its own. Numerous highly refined philosophical debates have assembled around the notion of property (essential or accidental, determinate or determinable, ontological or epistemological), which we need not enter here (Swoyer and Orilia 2011). What is relevant is the fact that attributes predicate a noun, qualifying and thus limiting its denotation. This implies that attributes are always attributes of something, even if that something is another attribute. In relational databases, attributes are used to define a property of an object or a class; to work with such attributes they are associated with a set of rules called operations, which define how they are computed within the relevant database. In a particular instance an attribute has a particular value. The class could for instance be 'woman', the attribute could be '> 40' (value: yes or no). Evidently we can imagine a class 'human being', with attributes 'sex' (value: man or woman) and 'age' (value: any number between 0 and 150). So, whether something is a class or an attribute depends on the structure of the database. We can easily think of attributes of attributes and various types of relationship between classes and objects that are defined in terms of required attributes. The crucial point here is the fact that attributes, characteristics or properties are not given, but attributed. The decision on which attributes define what classes, or for example the decision on what objects are defined as members of specific classes, has far reaching implications. It determines the scope and the structure of the collective that populates the database and this has consequences for the output of the operations that are performed on the database. For instance, to the extent that the output feeds into an assessment system or a decision system, the attributes and the way they structure the database co-define the output. The chosen data models thus co-define how the user of the system perceives and cognises her environment and how she will act, based on such perceptions and cognition. Especially in complex technological environments that integrate pervasive or even ubiquitous machine-to-machine communications that continuously assess the environment, machine learning will be based to a large extent on feedback loops between computing systems, potentially also grounding their key performance indicators on the output of a string of interacting inference machines. In that sense, computing systems may become increasingly self-referential, deferring to sub-systems or collaborating in the context of multi-agent systems capable of generating emergent behaviour. Much will depend, then, on the manner in which the flux of real life is translated into machine readable terms. Referring to the effects of the proliferation of information-processing machines on learning processes, Lyotard wrote – back in the 1980s (Lyotard 1984: 4):

> The nature of knowledge cannot survive unchanged within this context of general transformation. It can fit into the new channels, and become operational, only if learning is translated into quantities of information. We can predict that anything in the constituted body of knowledge that is not translatable in this way will be abandoned and that the direction of new research will be dictated by the possibility of its eventual results being translatable into computer language.

My point here is not that some types of knowledge are not translatable into computer language. This seems an obvious, although somewhat trivial observation. The same point can indeed be made for the script and the printing press, which require their own translations and – just like data-driven environments – require and produce a novel mind set as compared to a previous ICT infrastructure.[9] My point is that the flux of real life events can be translated into computational formats *in different ways* and that what matters is to what extent alternative translations produce *alternative outcomes*.[10] To come to terms with this we will have to find ways to play around with the multiplicity of dividuals that are used to profile us. Whereas we have learned to play around with written language, we may have more difficulty in achieving similar standards of fluency under the computational paradigm of proactive technological environments. This seems far more challenging, precisely because these environments outsource major parts of knowledge production and decision-making to complex interacting computing systems. Cognitive scientists claim that we are not hard-wired to understand statistics (Gigerenzer 1991), let alone to absorb the complexities of knowledge discovery in databases. Our bounded rationality seems to require hidden complexity and intuitive interfaces to come to terms with an environment that seamlessly adapts to our inferred preferences (Weiser 1991). This may, however, be a relief as well as a problem, depending on the extent to which we can guess what dividuality is attributed to us and how that may impact our life. The problem may seem to relate to the use of pseudonyms to separate contexts and roles, but the dividuals created by automated decision systems are not of our choice. They stand for the new stereotypes generated by our smart environments and could thus be termed artificial stereotypes, created by the unbounded computational irrationality of our environments – instead of being the result of the bounded rationality of human cognition.[11]

From disciplinary to control societies

Deleuze decribed the transformation of societies structured by practices of discipline into societies organised by practices of control. Inspired by Foucault (1995),

Deleuze's disciplinary societies are characterised by enclosed spaces (monasteries, prisons, schools, hospitals, factories) and regulated temporalities, organised in a manner that renders individual subjects observable and predictable, thus inducing a process of self-discipline that aligns their behaviour with the regularity of the average monk, inmate, student, patient or employee of the relevant rank. Control societies differ because their regulatory regime no longer depends on a stable separation of spaces or a predictable regulation of temporalities. Home, school, work and leisure increasingly overlap, both in space and in time. It is no longer the creation of the average individual subject that is at the heart of the mechanisms that produce modern or post-modern society. Instead, the individual is divided, mixed and mocked-up into a range of dividuals that are controlled by the invisible manipulation of complex data models. Deleuze in fact relates this to the further virtualisation of financial markets (ibid):

> Perhaps it is money that expresses the distinction between the two societies best, since discipline always referred back to minted money that locks gold as numerical standard, while control relates to floating rates of exchange, modulated according to a rate established by a set of standard currencies.

Floating exchange rates were of course just the beginning. By now we know that flows of money, interest, options, derivatives and futures are increasingly determined by the automation of machine readable inferences. And we are rapidly becoming aware of the complex feedback loops this entails between what Esposito (2011) has called the impact of the present futures on the future present. This may suggest that human subjects are progressively left out of the equation, but it is important to note that the automation ultimately concerns *inferences from* and *associations of* data points that are traces from human behaviours. The use of the plural in the term 'behaviours' is telling. It refers to the machine observable behaviour of persons, cut up into discrete data points that can be processed to compare and reconstruct dividuals, displaying a variety of probable future behaviours. The shift from a singular behaviour to a plurality of behaviours is significant; it alludes to the fragmentation and recombination that is typical for data mining operations and builds on the de- and re-contextualisation that is pivotal for pattern recognition in databases that have been fused (Kallinikos 2006).

Five assumptions of machine learning

Summing up, the architecture of the data models that forms the basis for mining operations is decisive for whatever outcome the process produces. On top of that, Sculley and Pasanek (2008) have suggested that data mining builds on five assumptions that are not necessarily valid.[12] In a salient article on 'Meaning and Mining: The impact of implicit assumptions in data mining for the humanities' — they point out that (1) machine learning assumes that the distribution of the probabilistic behaviour of a data set does not change over time, whereas a vigilant civil society and an individual may require and produce outliers, resisting such a fixed distribution (focusing on change and ambiguity rather than invariance over the course of time), (2) machine learning assumes a well defined hypothesis space because otherwise generalisation to novel data would not work, (3) for machine learning to come up with valid predictions or discoveries the data that are being mined must be well represented, avoiding inadequate simplifications, distortions or procedural artefacts, and (4) machine learning may assume that there is one best algorithms to achieve the one best interpretation of the data, but this is never the case in practice, as demonstrated by the 'no free lunch theorem' (which says there is no data mining method without an experimenter bias).[13] To illustrate their point they develop a series of data mining strategies to test Lakoff's claim about there being a correlation between the use of metaphor and political affiliation, both via various types of hypothesis testing (supervised learning methods) and via various types of clustering (unsupervised learning methods). They conclude that (ibid: 417):

> Where we had hoped to explain or understand those larger structures within which an individual text has meaning in the first place, we find ourselves acting once again as interpreters. The confusion matrix, authored in part by the classifier, is a new text, albeit a strange sort of text, one that sends us back to those texts it purports to be about.

In fact they continue (ibid):

> Machine learning delivers new texts — trees, graphs, and scatter-grams — that are not any easier to make sense of than the original texts used to make them. The critic who is not concerned to establish the deep structure of a genre or validate a correlation between metaphor and ideology, will delight in the proliferation of unstable, ambiguous texts. The referral of meaning from one computer-generated instance to the next is fully Derridean.

I will return to this point later in this chapter and briefly discuss a set of recommendations, provided by Sculley and Pasanek (2008), that should mitigate the risks generated by these assumptions.

Here I conclude that a closer look at the construction work needed to produce dividuals or data derivatives gives us some insight into the question of whether dividuals are virtuals or possibles. In management speak: we need tools that empower inhabitants to play around with their smart environments (dividuals as virtuals) rather than tools that manipulate them as mere resources for the computing systems that run the infrastructure, keeping them hostage to their inferred preferences (dividuals as possibles). The answer is that this will depend on whether the inhabitants of these new lifeworlds will be capable of figuring out how their dividuals determine what and how they can act upon that. As with all capabilities,[14] this does not merely depend on their intelligence. To bring them in a position from where they can interact with their own dividuals (deleting, modifying or enhancing them) they will need a legal and technical infrastructure that affords such reconfigurations. I will return to this later in the chapter, after investigating how pre-emptive computing upsets and disrupts one of the core assumptions of human intercourse, siding with Stiegler's call for a new enlightenment and a new rule of law.

Double contingency in the era of pre-emptive computing

In *Looking Awry*, Žižek (1991: 30) suggests that 'communication is a successful misunderstanding'. This may be the most salient summary of what is known as the concept of double contingency in sociology and philosophy, which denotes the most fundamental level of analysis concerning the coordination of human action.[15] Before fleshing out how data science practices may alter this 'primitive' of self, mind and society I will present a brief overview of the concept.[16]

The theorem of double contingency was first coined by Parsons (Parsons 1991; Parsons and Shils 1951), depicting the fundamental uncertainty that holds between interacting subjects who develop mutual expectations regarding each other in a way that objects do not. Pivotal here is that subjects must develop expectations about what the alter (the interacting subject) expects from them, to be able to 'read' their own interactions, and the same goes for their alter. The temporal dimension of interaction introduces a contingent and inevitable uncertainty about how the alter will understand one's action, knowing that the same goes for all interacting individuals. Parsons named this condition of fundamental uncertainty the double contingency of social interaction, highlighting the interdependence of the mutual expectations that provide a virtuous or vicious circle of iterative interpretation. Parsons basically builds on Mead's notion of the 'generalized other', that depicts the need to anticipate how others will understand us and how they will act upon our gestures, speech and actions. Mead and Morris (1962) explain this 'generalized other' with the example of a ball game that requires a player to internalise the positions of the other players with regard to each other, to the rules of the game and to herself, to be able to interact fluently and successfully as a player of that game.

In other work we have coined this mutual and co-constitutive set of anticipated expectations 'double anticipation' (Hildebrandt, Koops and de Vries 2009). We have argued that this is what enables and constrains human interaction, and elaborated how it co-constitutes individual identity. We draw on Ricoeur's (1992) *Oneself as Another*, which provides a penetrating analysis of human identity that seems pertinent for the issue of transparency in computationally enhanced environments. If the construction of identity depends on our capability to anticipate how others anticipate us, we must learn how to figure out the way our computational environment figures us out. Ricoeur discusses identity in terms of a relational self that must be situated on the nexus of the pair of continuity and discontinuity (diachronic perspective) and that of sameness and otherness (synchronic perspective). The most intriguing part of Ricoeur's analysis of human identity consists in his introduction of the concepts of *idem* (identical and identity, similarity and sameness, third person perspective) and *ipse* (self-hood, first-person perspective). In his account of personal identity, Ricoeur demonstrates how our understanding of self-identity is contingent upon our taking the role of the other (the second-person perspective) that eventually provides us with something like a third-person perspective on the self (cf also Mead's generalised other), which is constitutive for our developing 'sense of self' (first-person perspective).

Parsons was less interested in personal identity than in the construction of social institutions as proxies for the coordination of human interaction. His point is that the uncertainty that is inherent in the double contingency requires the emergence of social structures that develop a certain autonomy and thus provide a more stable object for the coordination of human interaction. The circularity that comes with the double contingency is thus resolved in the consensus that is consolidated in sociological institutions that are typical for a particular culture. Consensus on the norms and values that regulate human interaction is Parsons's solution to the problem of double contingency and thus also explains the existence of social institutions. As could be expected, Parsons's focus on consensus and his urge to resolve the contingency have been criticised for its 'past-oriented, objectivist and reified concept of culture' and for its implicitly negative understanding of the double contingency.

A more productive understanding of the double contingency may come from Luhmann (1995), who takes a broader view of contingency; instead of merely defining it in terms of dependency he points to the different options open to subjects who can never be sure how their actions will be interpreted. The uncertainty presents not merely a problem but also a chance; not merely a constraint but also a measure of freedom. The freedom to act meaningfully is constraint by earlier interactions, because they indicate how one's actions have been interpreted in the past and thus may be interpreted in the future. Earlier interactions weave into Luhmann's (1995) emergent social systems, gaining a measure of autonomy – or resistance – with regard to individual participants. Ultimately, however, social systems are still rooted in the double contingency of face-to-face communication.[17] The constraints presented by earlier interactions and their uptake in a social system can be rejected and renegotiated in the process of anticipation. By figuring out how one's actions are mapped by the other, or by the social systems in which one participates, room is created to falsify expectations and to disrupt anticipations. This will not necessarily breed anomy, chaos or anarchy, but may instead provide spaces for contestation, self-definition in defiance of labels provided by the expectations of others, and the beginnings of novel or transformed social institutions. As such, the uncertainty inherent in the double contingency defines human autonomy and human identity as relational and even ephemeral, always requiring vigilance and creative reinvention in the face of unexpected or unreasonably constraining expectations.

This is where Žižek's phrase comes in. By referring to communication as a misunderstanding, Žižek seems to acknowledge the inherent uncertainty that constitutes the meaning of our expressions. In a sense, we can never be sure whether what we meant to say is what the other understood. We can take the perspective of the other to guess how they took what we uttered, but this switch of perspective is always an anticipation, or an interpretation. It will create interstitial shifts of meaning between one utterance and another, even if the words are the same. However, Žižek also acknowledges that the misunderstanding that grounds our attempt to communicate is productive. Insofar as the attempt succeeds and communication 'works', meaning is created in between the black boxes that we are – thus also allowing us to reinterpret our own intended meanings. Our self-understanding emerges *in* and *from* this process of meaning attribution, contributing to a sustained practice that constitutes self, mind and society.

The question is what this means for self, mind and society in the era of pre-emptive computing. In his description of behavioural advertising McStay (2011: 3) speaks of the pre-emption of intention as a crucial characteristic of targeted advertising. More generally one can see that the original idea of ubiquitous computing, ambient intelligence (AmI) and the 'internet of things' relies on the same notion: we are being serviced before we have become aware of our need for such service. In other words, before we have formed an explicit or conscious intention, the computational layer that mediates our access to products or services acts upon the inferred intention. That includes, for instance, the personalisation of search engine results or the 'auto-complete' functions in mail programs. Some speak of digital butlers (Andrejevic 2002), who pre-empt the idiosyncratic urges of their masters without making a point of it: Jeeves revisited after the computational turn. Negroponte (1996: 149) explained the need for an *i*Jeeves in 1996:

> The idea is to build computer surrogates that possess a body of knowledge both about something (a process, a field of interest, a way of doing) and about you in relation to that something (your taste, your inclinations, your acquaintances). Namely, the computer should have dual expertise, like a cook, gardener, and chauffeur using their skills to fit your tastes and needs in food, planting, and driving. When you delegate those tasks it

does not mean you do not like to prepare food, grow plants, or drive cars. It means you have the option to do those things when you wish, because you want to, not because you have to.

Likewise with a computer. I really have no interest whatsoever in logging into a system, going through protocols, and figuring out your Internet address. I just want to get my message through to you. Similarly, I do not want to be required to read thousands of bulletin boards to be sure I am not missing something. I want my interface agent to do those things.

Digital butlers will be numerous, living both in the network and by your side, both in the center and at the periphery of your own organization (large or small).

It is important to acknowledge that we are already surrounded by cohorts of digital butlers and I dare say we are better off with them than without. My argument in this chapter is not one of techno-pessimism and I do not believe in a romantic offline past where all was better, more authentic or less shallow. However, to the extent that our computational environment provides for an external artificial autonomic nervous system we must come to terms with the implications. This 'digital unconscious' thrives on 'subliminal strategies' to cater to our inferred preferences,[18] as long as whoever is paying for the hardware and the software can make a profit. The element of pre-emption that is hardwired and softwired into the computational layers that surround us may be a good thing, but we must find ways to guess how they are guessing us. We must learn how to anticipate how these machineries are anticipating us. We must – in other words – reinvent a double contingency that reintroduces a successful misunderstanding between us and our computational butlers. If the misunderstanding fails, we may end up as their cognitive resources.[19]

A new enlightenment: tertiary retention and introjection

In a presentation at the World Wide Web Consortium (W3C), Stiegler (2012) has called for a new enlightenment, under the title of *Die Aufklärung in the Age of Philosophical Engineering*. The term philosophical engineering comes from an email by Berners-Lee, one of the founding fathers of the World Wide Web:[20]

Pat, we are not analyzing a world, we are building it. We are not experimental philosophers, we are philosophical engineers. We declare 'this is the protocol'. When people break the protocol, we lament, sue, and so on. But they tend to stick to it because we show that the system has very interesting and useful properties.

Philosophy was done with words, mediated by handwritten manuscripts and later by the printing press. Now, Berners-Lee writes, we do it by means of protocols that regulate online behaviours. He paraphrases Marx's famous Thesis XI on Feuerbach (Marx and Engels, 1998: 571): 'The philosophers have only interpreted the world in various ways; the point is to change it.' The point of Berners-Lee is that this is precisely what engineers do, whether they like it or not. He is calling on them to acknowledge their impact and – if I may summarise his position – to engineer for a better world, or at least to refrain from engineering a bad one.

In his presentation, Stiegler goes even further. He traces the role of technics (the alphabet, the printing press, the digital) in the construction of thinking, relating enlightenment thought to the workings of the printing press. His point is that the digital brain, constituted by what he calls the tertiary retention of the digital era, will not necessarily have the same affordances as the reading brain. If we want to preserve some of the affordances of 18th-century enlightenment that still inform our self-understanding, we must take care to engineer these affordances into the digital infrastructure. His main worry is that (ibid: 1):

> The spread of digital traceability seems to be used primarily to increase the heteronomy of individuals through behaviour-profiling rather than their autonomy.

Before explaining the notion of tertiary retention let me briefly reiterate that Stiegler emphasises that 'the web is a function of a technical system which could be otherwise' (ibid: 3), highlighting that whatever the present web affords may be lost if its basic structure is amended. This seems to accord with the idea that 'technology is neither good nor bad, but never neutral' (Kranzberg 1986). Although a technological infrastructure such as the printing press, electricity or the internet is not good or bad 'in itself', it has normative consequences for those whose lifeworld is mediated. It changes the constraints and the enablers of our environments, opening up new paths but inevitably closing down others. Whether that is a good thing is a matter of evaluation – and this will depend on what is gained and what is lost compared to a previous or alternative infrastructure. And, for whom.

The concept of tertiary retention builds on Husserl's (1964) understanding of memory. The first retention is that of perception, unifying the flux of impressions generated by one's environment into the experience of one's own perception. This first retention is entirely ephemeral: 'the perceived object only appears in disappearing' (ibid: 5). Secondary retention is the imprint 'in the memory of the one who had the experience, and from which it may be reactivated' (ibid: 6). Note that Stiegler does not speak of information retrieval, since we know that secondary retention is an ongoing process whereby each novel secondary retention and each reactivation transforms – however little – the initial secondary retention.[21] According to Stiegler, a tertiary retention is 'a spatialisation of time', meaning a transformation of 'the temporal flow of a speech such as the one I am delivering to you here and now into a textual space' (ibid: 4). In a way, this is a materialisation of the seemingly immaterial matter of time, although speech itself is obviously not immaterial (being produced by vocal organs disseminating sound waves etc). A tertiary retention, such as writing, printing on paper or on silicon chips externalises, spatialises and materialises the flux and the imprint of primary and secondary retention (ibid: 5):

> One can speak of a visibly spatialising materialisation to the extent that there is a passage from an invisible, and as such in-discernable and unthinkable material state, to another state, a state that can be analysed, critiqued and manipulated – in both senses that can be given to this verb, that is:
> 1. on which analytical operations can be performed, and intelligibility can be produced; and
> 2. with which one can manipulate minds – for which Socrates reproached the sophists in the case of writing, writing being the spatialisation of time of what he called 'living speech'.[22]

Such tertiary retention is called by the name of grammatisation, which, according to Stiegler (ibid: 4):

> describes all technical processes that enable behavioural fluxes or flows to be made discrete (in the mathematical sense) and to be reproduced, those behavioural flows through which are expressed or imprinted the experiences of human beings (speaking, working, perceiving, interacting and so on). If grammatisation is understood this way, then the digital is the most recent stage of grammatisation, a stage in which all behavioural models can now be grammatised and integrated through a planetary-wide industry of the production, collection, exploitation and distribution of digital traces.

Tertiary retention or grammatisation enables the sharing of content, of thoughts, of externalisations across time and space (Geisler 1985; Ricoeur 1973), across generational and geographical distances. It constitutes a transindividual retention that can survive the death of its author, but – as Stiegler emphasises – to empower individual persons it must be re-interiorised, re-individuated, reinforcing the capability 'to think for oneself' (ibid: 11). Here Stiegler paraphrases Kant's famous essay *Beantwortung der Frage: Was ist Aufklärung?* in which Kant calls on his reader to 'dare to think for themselves': *sapere aude!* Kant writes: 'have the courage to use your own mind' (Kant 1784: 481). This is what Stiegler is up to: we must preserve the particular dimensions of the bookish mind capable of arriving at such a thought. Instead of taking for granted that such thinking is the achievement of a disembodied transcendental ego (as Kant himself proposed), we need to investigate the grammatisation that is a condition for this type of thinking. This means, above all, that any tertiary retention that becomes entirely self-referential will be dead, and remain so 'if it does not trans-form, through a reverse effect, the secondary retentions of the psychical individual affected by this tertiary retention' (Stiegler 2012: 10). Today, neuroscience is capable of experimentally testing the 'constitution of the mind through the introjection of tertiary retentions' (ibid: 10), tracing the implications of reading and writing for the morphology and the behaviours of our brains (Wolf 2008). This way we can localise the correlates of capabilities such as reflection, consideration, deliberation and intentional action in what Wolf has called 'the reading brain'. If pre-emptive computational layers shortcut the introjection of tertiary retention, the point is reached that these layers are not merely our digital butlers but that we become their cognitive resource, part of their extended mind. Stiegler therefore concludes that the digital is like a *pharmakon*:[23] depending on its usage it may reinvent or destroy us. To prevent the digital brain from being short-circuited by *automata*, we must make sure that individual users of the internet have the capability to 'think for themselves' and know how to get their finger behind attempts to bypass the neo-cortex. Thus, a new enlightenment, a new transparency must be engineered. Words are not enough here.

A new rule of law: profile transparency by design

The computational turn is to be seen as a *pharmakon*. This will allow us carefully to distinguish between its empowering and destructive affordances. To the extent that the plethora of dividuals, data derivatives and other computational models create room for new actualisations, they are in the domain of virtualisation. But to the extent that the mass of inferences, profiles and automated decision systems pre-empt our intention they reduce to derealisations that stifle innovation and present us with nothing else than a sophisticated recalculation of past inclinations. To prevent the last and to preserve the first may require hard work and nothing can be taken for granted.

In this section, I will investigate what is required to reinstate the double contingency that constitutes self, mind and society – enabling us to guess how our computational environment anticipates our states and behaviours. This can be framed as a transparency requirement, but – taking note of the previous section – we must be cautious not to reduce transparency to a simple information symmetry. Such a symmetry will easily cause a buffer overflow:[24] the amount of information it would involve will flood our bounded rationality and this will enable manipulation by what escapes our attention. Although some would applaud the enlightenment of Descartes's *idées claires et distinctes*, others may point out that they generate over-exposure, wrongly suggesting the possibility of light without shadows. The metaphor of the buffer overflow actually suggests that we may require selective enlightenment, and are in dire need of shadows. The more interesting question, therefore, will be what should be in the limelight and where we need darkness. In Renaissance painting, the techniques of the *clair-obscur*, the *chiaroscuro*, the *hell-dunkel* were invented and applied to suggest depth, and to illuminate what was meant to stand out. By playing with light and shadow the painting could draw the attention of the onlooker, creating the peculiar experience of being drawn into the painting – as if one is standing in the dark, attracted by the light.

The computational turn invites us to reinvent something like a *clair-obscur*, a measure of transparency that enables us to foresee what we are 'in for'. This should enable us to contest how we are being clustered, correlated, framed and read, thus providing the prerequisites for due process. Therefore the question is how we can present the plurality of matching dividuals to the bounded rationality that constitutes our individuality. This should enable us to play around with our digital shadows, acquiring the level of fluency that we have learned to achieve in language and writing.

There are two ways of achieving such transparency. In terms of computer engineering one involves the front end of a system; the other the back end. The front end involves human–computer interaction (HMI), the back end concerns the computational operations, the hardware and the software that run the system. Neither can do without the other, and in fact they require human-machine interfacing (HMI).[25] There is an urgent need for intuitive interfaces that develop the *chiaroscuro* we need to frame the complexity that frames us (reinstating a new type of double contingency). To make sure that the interface does not obscure what requires our attention we need to achieve transparency about what actually happens in the back end. This involves the ability to check, test and contest the grammatisation that defines the outcome of computational decision systems. Such transparency may not fare well with current day business models, which thrive on trade secrets and intellectual property rights on data mining algorithms. It is, however, our only option to regain the introjection of tertiary retention, that is, to re-individuate the sets of proliferating dividuals that are used to *target*, *trade with*, or to *circumvent* our attention. As mentioned above, to make sure that the information that derives from testing computational mediations does not cause a buffer overflow with our bounded rationality, we must design an interface that manages a *clair-obscur*. And somehow, we will have to 'become grammatised' in the language of computational retention, to ground ourselves on the nexus of the front end and the back end. If we do not, we will lose the precious capability which Kant called on us to develop: to think for ourselves.

To achieve transparency about the back end of computational systems that profile us I return to the five recommendations provided by Sculley and Pasanek, as promised above. I adapt their recommendations, which were constructed for the domain of the digital humanities, to fit better the broader scope of marketing, law enforcement and the whole plethora of automated decision-making systems that co-define our lifeworld. For the original recommendations, see Sculley and Pasanek (2008).

First, a collaborative effort is required between the engineers, designers and users of the relevant computing systems and those whose capabilities will be affected (for instance, consumer organisations, citizens' juries, NGOs). All stakeholders should make the effort to clarify their assumptions about the scope, function and meaning of systems, as they are developed. After all, the construction of these systems concerns the architecture of the *polis*; it requires as much political participation as any other interaction with significant impact on third parties (Hildebrandt and Gutwirth 2007; Marres 2005; Dewey 1927).

Second, those using the systems for data mining operations should employ multiple representations and methodologies, thus providing for a plurality of mining strategies that will most probably result in destabilising any monopoly on the interpretation of what these systems actually do. This will clear the ground for contestation, if needed. Without an evidence-based awareness of the alternative outcomes generated by alternative machine learning techniques, data mining may easily result in holding people hostage to inferences drawn from their past behaviours. This would amount to derealisation instead of virtualisation. We can think of software verification, sousveillance or counterprofiling as means to prevent this. Searls's (2012) notion of vendor relationship management may be of help here, turning the tables on the mantra of customer relations management.

Third, all trials should be reported, instead of 'cherry picking' those results that confirm the experimenters' bias. At some point failed experiments can reveal more than supposedly successful ones. This is particularly important in a setting that generates automated decisions that impact the capabilities of groups as well as individuals. Especially with regard to prohibited or undesirable discrimination this seems important (Pedreshi, Ruggieri and Turini 2008). The imposition of documented auditability obligations on data controllers under the proposed EU General Data Protection Regulation (GDPR) confirms the import of situating the experimenters' bias. As indicated above, such bias is inevitable but this does not imply that any bias will do.

Fourth, whenever such impact is to be expected the public interest requires transparency about the data and the methods used, to make the data mining operations verifiable by joint ventures of – for example – lawyers and software engineers. This connects to the fifth recommendation, regarding the peer review of the methodologies used. The historical artefact of constitutional democracy feeds on a detailed and agonistic scrutiny of the results of data mining operations that can sustain the fragile negotiations of the rule of law. Without such a reappropriation or introjection of the tertiary retention of computational grammatisation, civil society will cease to exist.

Having started with a brief exploration of transparency of the back end, we now turn back to the front end. The recommendations summed up above focus on transparency about assumptions inscribed into the system, methods used and results obtained. Combinations of requirements, namely engineering, software verification and impact assessments regarding potential violations of fundamental rights should do at least part of the job here. Just as in the case of the back end total transparency is neither possible nor desirable. The challenge will be how to monitor compliance with, for instance, data protection legislation without posing new privacy risks, or how to prevent compliance models that create an illusion of compliance instead of the substance. This brings us to the front end. How to feed the results of critical and constructive discussions on the back end into the front end; how to provide consumers and citizens with the kinds of anticipation that nourish their capability to play with the system; how to engage the industry in a way that empowers it to invest in the kind of interfaces that take customers seriously as players instead of merely as cognitive resources for data mining operations? Do we need more icons instead of text? Must we design intelligent agents that are programmed on our behalf? Must we help customers to stop 'using' technology and start 'interacting' with it? Who is we? These are the hard questions, requiring the hard work.

The proposed GDPR introduces a right to profile transparency,[26] whenever automated decisions have a significant impact on the life of an individual, or legal effect. This right comprises the right to know about the existence of such a decision and the right to know the envisaged effects of the decision. This right falls within the scope of the obligation to implement data protection by design,[27] which requires those in charge of computational systems to implement appropriate technical and organisational measures and procedures to ensure that the processing will meet the requirements of profile transparency. The appropriateness is related to the technical state of the art and the economic feasibility. This seems a balanced and realistic challenge to invest in the development of both back end and front end transparency tools, notably at the interface between the two (Hildebrandt 2012). With this, I end this chapter on an optimistic note.

I return, nevertheless, to the enigma of the sphinx on the cover of this book. Oedipus is depicted in the *clearing* of the *clair-obscur*. He stands out strong, wilful and looks somewhat impatient. The sphinx stands in the shadow of a cave, potentially irritated that a trespasser has finally solved her riddle. However, although Oedipus may have solved the riddle, he cannot evade the fundamental fragility it foretells. Transparency tools can invent a new version of the double contingency that constitutes our world – they cannot resolve the fundamental uncertainty it sustains. On the contrary, these tools should help to reinstate this uncertainty, rather than the over-determination that the computational turn could otherwise enable.

Notes

1 Noise To Signal, RobCottingham.ca, A cartoon about social media, business and how we live and work in a digital world, see http://www.robcottingham.ca/cartoon/archive/2009-02-21-recommender/ (accessed 31 October 2012).

2 Note that in the EU context consent cannot overrule the purpose limitation principle. Consent is a ground for legitimate processing (Directive 95/46/EC art 7), but
such processing will have to comply with the norms for fair processing, of which
purpose limitation is one (ibid art 6). In the draft General Data Protection Regulation
(GDPR) it seems that data subjects can waive the right to purpose limitation with
regard to 'further processing' (secondary use); see art 6(4) of the draft GDPR as presented on 25 January 2012. Note that privacy policies or service licence agreements
often entail vaguely formulated indications of the purpose for which data may be
used, which seems equivalent to obtaining consent to overrule purpose limitation.

3 Data protection legislation is built on the concept of personal data, ie data that
relate to an identified or identifiable person (eg Directive 95/46/EC art 2). To the
extent that data are successfully anonymised the legislation does not apply.

4 I use the term 'machine' here in the broad sense of an artificial contraption that is
used as a tool to achieve certain goals by means of leverage (the lever), transformation of energy (steam engine) or automation (the computer). In reference to
machine learning as a branch of AI, I will include software programs under the
heading of machine, but I will also assume that software must be articulated into
matter actually to function as a machine.

5 In computer science, an inference engine is a computer program that derives answers
from a knowledge base; it is based on pattern recognition and can be qualified as
data driven because the rules that are applied to infer answers depend on the
connections between the data.

6 On the genealogy of Deleuze's quest for the virtual see Smith and Protevi (2011).

7 A virtual machine achieves hardware virtualisation by means of a software implementation of a machine, executing programs like a physical machine; it allows
different operating systems to run entirely seperately on the same hardware, sim-
ulating different machines on the same platform.

8 On applications for diabetes or heart disease see Brustein (2012). Although such
function creep, especially in the case of health data, is prohibited by law we should
not be surprised if such inferences will be legitimated via explicit unambiguous
consent packaged with insurance contracts that offer benefits for those who allow
closer monitoring of their healthcare-related behaviours.

9 On the impact of the ICT infrastructure of the script and the printing press on the
brain and the mind, see Wolf (2008).

10 Cf Stiegler (2012: 3).

11 If it is true that rational decision-making depends on the emotional fitness that
allows us to make choices and to act with intention (see eg Damasio 2000), then
computational systems may not be capable of rational decision-making – unless
guided by human intention. I leave aside the discussion of whether synthetic
emotions will resolve this problem, but see Velasquez (1998).

12 See Hildebrandt (2011b).

13 See http://www.no-free-lunch.org/ for an overview of 'no free lunch theorems'. See
also Giraud-Carrier and Provost (2005).

14 Although the capability approaches of Sen (1999) and Nussbaum (2011) do not
directly connect with notions such as 'data protection by design', it may be
important to elaborate this connection. In both cases human rights protection
may impose imperfect duties on states and other actors to provide effective means
of empowerment, without engaging in paternalism.

15 Žižek actually refers to the French philosopher Lacan, whose theory is not equivalent with those of Luhmann and Parsons, who developed the notion of double contingency. Nevertheless, Žižek's phrase aptly describes the experience of the double contingency that is at stake in this chapter.

16 In computer science, a primitive is a basic building block, 'with which to model a domain of knowledge or discourse' (Gruber et al 2009: 1963).

17 *Pace* Luhmann (1995), a social system will reproduce the contingency at the level of the system, because it must interact with other systems that can reject, misunderstand, contest or renegotiate whatever a system does or communicates, cf Vanderstraeten (2007). It is important to note that the founding fathers of the concept of autopoiesis – on which Luhmann built his systems theory – reject the idea that social systems achieve the kind of autonomy that is characteristic of individual human beings. See eg Maturana and Varela (1998: 198).

18 The term 'digital unconscious' was coined by Derick de Kerchove, Director of the McLuhan Program in Culture and Technology from 1983 until 2008. See http://www.mcluhanstudies.com/index.php?option=com_content&view=article&id=485:from-freud-to-digital-unconsciuos&catid=78&Itemid=472 (assessed 30 October 2012). On subliminal influences, see Hildebrandt (2011a, 2011c).

19 This is Andy Clark's (2003) idea of the extended mind 'inside-out'. Instead of machines being part of our minds, we become part of theirs. My aim is to make sure that we do not become merely an instrument for the information-driven cognition of these computing systems (tongue in cheek one could say I am requiring them to respect the Kantian moral imperative).

20 See Berners-Lee (2003).

21 Cognitive psychology challenges common sense intuitions about the accuracy of our memory, see eg Stark, Okado and Loftus (2010) on the complex differences between activation of true and false memories.

22 A reference to Plato's critique of writing in *Phaedrus* (Plato 2006), which is all about the effects of tertiary retention on the capability for secundary retention.

23 In *Phaedrus*, King Thamus offers 'writing' as a *pharmakon* (medicine) that can extend one's memory. The king refuses, suggesting that writing will generate forgetfulness, being a poison instead of a medicine. The notion of the *pharmakon* that can be medicine or poison has been elaborated within French philosophy, eg by Derrida (1983), Stengers (2010) and Stiegler (2012).

24 In digital security a buffer overflow is one of the most basic and prevailing vulnerabilities of computing systems. See eg Leeuw and Bergstra (2007: 639).

25 On HMI as interaction and interfacing, see Jacko (2012).

26 Draft GDPR art 20(4), available at http://ec.europa.eu/justice/data-protection/document/review2012/com_2012_11_en.pdf (accessed 30 October 2012).

27 Ibid, art 23(1).

References

Amoore, L. (2011) 'Data Derivatives On the Emergence of a Security Risk Calculus for Our Times', *Theory, Culture & Society*, 28(6): 24–43.

Anderson, C. (2008) 'The End of Theory: The data deluge makes the scientific method obsolete', *Wired Magazine*, 16(7).

Andrejevic, M. (2002) 'The Work of Being Watched: Interactive media and the exploitation of self-disclosure', *Critical Studies in Media Communication*, 19(2): 230–48.

Berners-Lee, T. (2003) 'Re: New issue – meaning of URIs in RDF documents', W3C Public Mailing List Archives, 16 July 2003, available at http://lists.w3.org/Archives/Public/www-tag/2003Jul/0158.html (accessed 30 October 2012).

Brustein, J. (2012) 'Coming Next: Doctors prescribing apps to patients, *New York Times*, 19 August 2012.

Carroll, L. (1999) *The Annotated Alice: The definitive edition* (introduction and notes M. Gardner, ed.) New York and London: W. W. Norton & Company.

Clark, A. (2003) *Natural-Born Cyborgs. Minds, technologies, and the future of human Intelligence*, Oxford: Oxford University Press.

Damasio, A. R. (2000) *The Feeling of What Happens: Body and emotion in the making of consciousness*, New York: Harcourt.

Deleuze, G. (1992) 'Postscript on the Societies of Control', in *October*, MIT Press, 59: 3–7.

Deleuze, G. (1994) *Difference and Repetition*, New York: Columbia University Press.

Derrida, J. (1983) *Dissemination*, Chicago: University Of Chicago Press.

Dewey, J. (1927) *The Public & its Problems*, Chicago: Swallow Press.

Elmer, G. (2003) *Profiling Machines: Mapping the personal information economy*, Cambridge, MA: MIT Press.

Esposito, E. (2011) *The Future of Futures: The time of money in financing and society*, Cheltenham: Edward Elgar.

Foucault, M. (1995) *Discipline & Punish: the Birth of the Prison*, 2nd Edition, Vintage.

Geisler, D. M. (1985) 'Modern Interpretation Theory and Competitive Forensics: Understanding hermeneutic text', *National Forensic Journal*, III (Spring): 71–79.

Gigerenzer, G. (1991) 'How to Make Cognitive Illusions Disappear: Beyond "heuristics and biases"', in Stroebe, W. Hewstone, M. (eds) *European Review of Social Psychology*, Chichester: Wiley.

Giraud-Carrier, C. and Provost, F (2005) 'Toward a Justification of Meta-learning: is the no Free Lunch Theorem a show-shopper?', in *Proceedings of the TCML Workshop on Meta-Learning*, Bonn, 9–16.

Gruber, T., Liu, L., and Tamer, M. (eds) (2009) 'Ontology', *Encyclopedia of Database Systems*, Berlin and Heidelberg: Springer.

Hildebrandt, M. (2009) 'Who is Profiling Who? Invisible visibility', in Gutwirth, S., Poullet, Y. and de Hert, P. (eds) *Reinventing Data Protection?*, Dordrecht: Springer: 239–52.

Hildebrandt, M. (2011a) 'Autonomic and Autonomous "Thinking": Preconditions for criminal accountability', in Hildebrandt, M. Rouvroy, A. (eds) *Law, Human Agency and Autonomic Computing. The philosophy of law meets the philosophy of technology*, Abingdon: Routledge: 141–60.

Hildebrandt, M. (2011b) 'The Meaning and Mining of Legal Texts', in Berry, D. M. (ed.) *Understanding Digital Humanities: The computational turn and new technology*, London: Palgrave Macmillan: 145–60.

Hildebrandt, M. (2011c) 'Legal Protection by Design: Objections and refutations', in *legisprudence*, 5(2): 223–48.

Hildebrandt, M. (2012) The Dawn of a Critical Transparency Right for the Profiling Era, in *Digital Enlightenment Yearbook 2012*, Amsterdam: IOS Press, 41–56.

Hildebrandt, M., and Gutwirth, S. (2007) '(Re)presentation, pTA Citizens' Juries and the Jury Trial', *Utrecht Law Review*, 3(1), available at http://www.utrechtlawreview.org/index.php/ulr/issue/view/5 (accessed 30 October 2012).

Hildebrandt, M., Koops, B. J. and de Vries, E. (2009) *Where Idem-Identity meets Ipse-Identity. Conceptual explorations*, Brussels, Future of Identity in the Information Society (FIDIS), available at http://www.fidis.net/resources/deliverables/profiling/#c2367 (accessed 30 October 2012).

Husserl, E. (1964) *Phenomenology of Internal Time Consciousness*, ed. Martin Heidegger, trans James S. Churchill, 1st ed, Indiana University Press.

Jacko, J. A. (ed.) (2012) *Human-Computer Interaction Handbook: Fundamentals, evolving technologies, and emerging applications*, 3rd edition, Boca Raton, FL: CRC Press.

Kallinikos, J. (2006) *The Consequences of Information. Institutional implications of technological change*, Cheltenham: Edward Elgar.

Kant, I. (1784) 'Beantwortung der Frage: Was ist Aufklarung?', *Berlinische Monatsschrift*, Dezember-Heft: 481–94.

Kranzberg, M. (1986) 'Technology and History: "Kranzbergs laws"', *Technology and Culture*, 27: 544–60.

Leeuw, K. M. M. de, and Bergstra, J. (eds) (2007) *The History of Information Security: A comprehensive handbook*, Amsterdam: Elsevier Science.

Lévy, P. (1998) *Becoming Virtual. Reality in the digital age*, New York and London: Plenum Trade.

Lévy, P. (2005) 'Sur les chemins du virtuel', available at http://hypermedia.univ-paris8.fr/pierre/virtuel/virt0.htm (accessed 30 October 2012).

Luhmann, N. (1995) *Social Systems*, Stanford: Stanford University Press.

Lyotard, J.-F. (1984) *The Postmodern Condition: A report on knowledge*, Manchester: Manchester University Press.

McStay, A. (2011) *The Mood of Information: A critique of online behavioural advertising*, New York: Continuum.

Marres, N. (2005) *No Issue, No Public. Democratic deficits after the displacement of politics*, Amsterdam: published by the author, available at http://dare.uva.nl (accessed 31 October 2012).

Marx, K., and Engels, F. (1998) *The German Ideology, including Theses on Feuerbach*, New York: Prometheus Books.

Massiello, B., and Whitten, A. (2010) 'Engineering Privacy in an Age of Information Abundance', *Intelligent Information Privacy Management*, AAAI: 119–24.

Maturana, H. R., and Varela, F. J. (1998) *The Tree of Knowledge. The biological roots of human understanding*, Boston and London: Shambhala.

Mead, G. H., and Morris, C. W. (1962) *Mind, Self, and Society from the Standpoint of a Social Behaviourist*, Chicago: University of Chicago Press.

Negroponte, N. (1996) *Being Digital*, New York: Vintage Books.

Nussbaum, M. C. (2011) *Creating Capabilities: The human development approach*, Cambridge, MA: Belknap Press of Harvard University Press.

Parsons, T. (1991) *The Social System*, 2nd edition, London: Routledge.

Parsons, T., and Shils, E. (1951) *Toward a General Theory of Action*, Cambridge, MA: Harvard University Press.

Pedreshi, D., Ruggieri, S., and Turini, F. (2008) 'Discrimination-Aware Data Mining', in *KDD '08 Proceeding of the 14th ACM SIGKDD international conference on knowledge discovery and data mining*. New York ACM Press: 560–68.

Pinedo, D. (2012) 'Niet alleen Tena belt incontinente patiënten', *NRC Next*, 10 August 2012.

Plato (2006) *Phaedrus* (translation B. Jowett), Middlesex: Echo Library.

Ricoeur, P. (1973) 'The Model of the Text: Meaningful action considered as a text', *New Literary History*, 5(1): 91–117.

Ricoeur, P. (1992) *Oneself as Another*, Chicago: University of Chicago Press.

Rouvroy, A. (2011) 'Technology, Virtuality and Utopia: Governmentality in an age of autonomic computing', in Hildebrandt, M. and Rouvroy, A. (eds) *Law, Human Agency and Autonomic Computing. The philosophy of law meets the philosophy of technology*, Abingdon: Routledge: 119–40.

Russell, S., and Norvig, P. (2009) *Artificial Intelligence: A modern approach*, 3rd edition, Englewood Cliffs, NJ: Prentice Hall.

Sculley, D., and Pasanek, B. M. (2008) 'Meaning and Mining: The impact of implicit assumptions in data mining for the humanities', *Literary and Linguistic Computing*, 23(4): 409–24.

Searls, D. (2012) *The Intention Economy: When customers take charge*, Harvard: Harvard Business Review Press.

Sen, A. (1999) *Commodities and Capabilities*, Oxford: Oxford University Press.

Smith, D., and Protevi, J. (2011) 'Gilles Deleuze', in Zalta, E. N. (ed.), *The Stanford Encyclopedia of Philosophy*, Winter 2011 <http://plato.stanford.edu/archives/win2011/entries/deleuze/>.

Stark, C. E. L., Okado, Y. and Loftus, E. F. (2010) 'Imaging the Reconstruction of True and False Memories Using Sensory Reactivation and the Misinformation Paradigms', *Learning & Memory*, 17(10): 485–88.

Stengers, I. (2010) *Cosmopolitics I*, Minneapolis: University of Minnesota Press.

Stiegler, B. (2012) 'Die Aufklärung in the Age of Philosophical Engineering', Lyon 20 April 2012, available at http://www.iri.centrepompidou.fr/wp-content/uploads/2011/02/Stiegler-The-Aufklärung-x.pdf (accessed 31 October 2012).

Swoyer, C., and Orilia, F. (2011) 'Properties', in Zalta, E. N. (ed.) *The Stanford Encyclopedia of Philosophy*, Winter 2011 <http://plato.stanford.edu/archives/fall2011/entries/properties/>.

Vanderstraeten, R. (2007) 'Parsons, Luhmann and the Theorem of Double Contingency', *Journal of Classical Sociology*, 2(1): 77–92.

Velasquez, J. D. (1998) 'Modeling Emotion-Based Decision Making', *Emotional and Intelligent: The Tangled Knot of Cognition*: 164–69.

Weiser, M. (1991) 'The Computer for the 21st Century', *Scientific American*, 265(3): 94–104.

Wikipedia contributors (2012a) 'Attribute', *Wikipedia, the free encyclopedia*, Wikimedia Foundation, Inc., available at http://en.wikipedia.org/wiki/Attribute (accessed 30 October 2012).

Wikipedia contributors (2012b) 'Property', *Wikipedia, the free encyclopedia*, Wikimedia Foundation, Inc., available at http://en.wikipedia.org/wiki/Property (accessed 30 October 2012).

Wolf, M. (2008) *Proust and the Squid: The story and science of the reading brain*, London: Icon Books.

Žižek, S. (1991) *Looking Awry: An introduction to Jacques Lacan through popular culture*, Cambridge, MA: MIT Press.

Index